SCIENCE & HISTORY

In God We Trust?

RELIGION, POLITICS, AND SOCIETY IN THE NEW MILLENNIUM

Series Editors: Michael Novak, American Enterprise Institute, and Brian C. Anderson, Manhattan Institute

For nearly five centuries, it was widely believed that moral questions could be resolved through reason. The Enlightenment once gave us answers to these perennial questions, but the answers no longer seem adequate. It has become apparent that reason alone is not enough to answer the questions that define and shape our existence. Many now believe that we have come to the edge of the Enlightenment and are stepping forth into a new era, one that may be the most religious we have experienced in 500 years. This series of books explores this new historical condition, publishing important works of scholarship in various disciplines that help us to understand the trends in thought and belief we have come from and to define the ones toward which we are heading.

Beyond Self-Interest: A Personalist Approach to Human Action, by Gregory R. Beabout, et al.

Human Nature and the Discipline of Economics: Personalist Anthropology and Economic Methodology, by Patricia Donohue-White, et al.

The Free Person and the Free Economy: A Personalist View of Market Economics, by Anthony J. Santelli Jr., et al.

Meaninglessness: The Solutions of Nietzsche, Freud, and Rorty, by M. A. Casey

Boston's Cardinal: Bernard Law, the Man and His Witness, edited by Romanus Cessario, O.P.

Don't Play Away Your Cards, Uncle Sam: The American Difference, by Olof Murelius, edited by Jana Novak

Society as a Department Store: Critical Reflections on the Liberal State, by Ryszard Legutko

In God We Trust? Faith-Based Organizations and the Quest to Solve America's Social Ills, by Lewis D. Solomon

Deconstructing Diversity: Justice, Multiculturalism, and Affirmative Action in Jesuit Higher Education, by Peter Minowitz

Relevant No More? The Catholic/Protestant Divide in American Electoral Politics, by Mark D. Brewer

On Ordered Liberty: A Treatise on the Free Society, by Samuel Gregg

In God We Trust?

*Faith-Based Organizations and the
Quest to Solve America's Social Ills*

Lewis D. Solomon

LEXINGTON BOOKS
Lanham • Boulder • New York • Oxford

LEXINGTON BOOKS

Published in the United States of America
by Lexington Books
A Member of the Rowman & Littlefield Publishing Group, Inc.
4501 Forbes Boulevard, Suite 200, Lanham, Maryland 20706

PO Box 317
Oxford
OX2 9RU, UK

British Library Cataloguing in Publication Information Available

Library of Congress Cataloging-in-Publication Data

Solomon, Lewis D.
    In God we trust? : faith-based organizations and the quest to solve America's social
ills / Lewis D. Solomon.
        p. cm. — (Religion, politics, and society in the new millennium)
    Includes bibliographical references and index.
    ISBN 0-7391-0630-9 (cloth : alk. paper)
    1. Public welfare—United States—Religious aspects. 2. Church and social
problems—United States. 3. Social service—United States—Religious aspects. 4.
Public welfare—United States—Religious aspects. 5. Church charities—Government
policy—United States. 6. Church charities—United States—Finance. 7. Federal aid
to human services—United States. 8. Federal aid to public welfare—United States. I.
Title. II. Series.

    HV95.S63 2003
    361.7'5—dc21   2003000962

Printed in the United States of America

⊖™ The paper used in this publication meets the minimum requirements of American
National Standard for Information Sciences—Permanence of Paper for Printed Library
Materials, ANSI/NISO Z39.48–1992.

For my son, Michael, and our conversations about the future.

Contents

Acknowledgments

This work had its genesis in two pieces I coauthored with Matthew J. Vlissides, Jr.: a policy report, "In God We Trust? Assessing the Potential of Faith-Based Social Services" (Progressive Policy Institute, February 2001) and an article, "Faith-Based Charities and the Quest to Solve America's Social Ills: A Legal and Policy Analysis," *Cornell Journal of Law and Public Policy* 10:2 (Spring 2001): 265-302. Mr. Vlissides and Alyssa Schindler read a complete draft of this book and gave me extensive comments that guided me in my revisions. Nell B. Taylor typed the manuscript and helped index the book. Matthew A. Mantel, Reference Librarian at the Jacob Burns Law Library of The George Washington University Law School, assisted in my research.

Chapter 1

Introduction

At the dawn of the twenty-first century, the social fabric of America is unraveling. There is an unease as to who we are and where we may be going.

Though there is a body of empirical research generally supportive of my observation, this book is not meant to settle the question. Instead, the arguments presented herein, while they generate and assess policies, are framed by an admittedly difficult question: Why do chronic social problems persist in a nation that is, by most measures, the most advanced? Economics, sociology, and political science, among other disciplines, have offered myriad theories of why this is. This book contributes to that body of literature.

The problems facing American society are not confined to one particular economic or racial group, although social pathologies do affect groups differently. For those who live outside the mainstream of society, poverty, crime, violence, drug abuse, and illegitimacy are all-too-familiar problems. Perhaps most frightening is the fact that the downward spiral seems to be getting worse instead of better.

Urban African-American communities are particularly afflicted by drug trafficking and gang violence. Crime renders vast sections of our inner cities unsafe, if not uninhabitable. Work, family, and community exist in fragmented forms. With unemployment rampant and sound education only a dream, the children of these communities find themselves unable to escape the poverty and hopelessness that plague their parents. The result is a generation of inner-city children raised on distrust, indifference, and isolation.

One might ask if the problems associated with urban communities should matter to middle-class Americans? They should and not only out of a sense of altruism. The chronic problems of the inner city cannot be ignored because they impact society as a whole in at least two ways: first, criminal activity in cities affects the suburbs (e.g., cities serve as hubs for drug trafficking), and second, the worst features of urban culture influence

American culture. Importantly, the latter poses the greater danger to American society.

The pernicious impact of the underclass has not remained contained within the inner cities, but instead its attitudes and behavior have filtered into middle-class culture as well. One need only look to popular culture, particularly among adolescents, to see why. Clothing that reveals more than it covers passes as fashion. Obscenity and vulgarity are commonplace additions to the American lexicon. Violence, misogyny, and casual sex permeate the music business, television networks, and the film industry.

Unless something is done, it would seem likely that the deterioration of the urban underclass will only continue to grow and that poor and rich alike are fated to inhabit a world benefit of virtue. As the inarticulate but destructive values of underclass males–sexual adventurousness, indifference to the future, rejection of hard work–take root in our society and spread by music, television, and film, their influence on the next white generation grows stronger.

However, it is not only the white lower class which is at risk. America's suburbs, long seen as safe havens from the corruption of the inner cities, are not invulnerable. Drug addiction and sexual promiscuity are nearly as commonplace among affluent teenagers as they are among their inner-city counterparts.

America's youth desperately search for something missing in lives devoid of meaning and purpose, often in self-destructive ways. One only has to look at the spate of school massacres, routine youth violence, and gang activity in middle-class neighborhoods to know that something is amiss. We see the alienation of materially privileged adolescents, who live in leafy, well-tended suburbs, yet who drift aimlessly into socially and self-destructive behavior.

While the effects are more visible in the inner cities than in the suburbs, both communities throughout the nation face a poverty of virtue. Material wealth cannot guarantee freedom from chronic social problems. Children suffer when wealth is substituted for parental involvement because as two-income families have become the norm, parents devote less time on child-rearing. In a culture of materialism, where everyone is trying to consume more, parents are often more focused on careers and social status than on their children's emotional needs and moral well-being. As a result, adolescents often feel disconnected from their parents, adrift in a world where they are left to make their own rules. Moreover, the dearth of parental guidance reinforces the media's influence on children.

However, the shock of watching television images of gun-toting children, spraying bullets and killing their peers, forced Americans to rethink their values and priorities. The family is once again assuming renewed importance in American society.

However, materialism and socioeconomic changes among the middle class do not explain the source of societal ills–they only explain why affluent children are vulnerable to harmful cultural influences. As it turns out, ideas have contributed greatly, though perhaps unintentionally, to the creation of an environment where moral indifference thrives.

The roots of America's social ills run deep. The 1960s "if it feels good, do it" attitude and the policies it inspired encouraged many, especially the less affluent, into sexual promiscuity and dependency, which gave rise to drug-induced escapism. Unlike wealthier members of their generation, however, the underclass could not recover from the effects of this type of lifestyle. Instead, inadequate education, high unemployment, drug addiction, and crime were its legacies. Once started on a downward path, poor Americans were unable to free themselves from its grip.

Perhaps the most insidious results of these attitudes were the growing illegitimacy rates and the collapse of the family. These concerns, particularly the successful upbringing of children, are much broader than just the problem of poverty, affecting poor and rich alike. This social malaise transcends differences of race, class, religion, and politics.

The question, of course, is how to stop the downward spiral. Material wealth may make life easier, but it does not guarantee happiness or security. In a nation of staggering wealth, a poverty of virtue exists.

The search for meaning and purpose in life begins at the bottom and works its way up. It starts with a call to moral regeneration and personal responsibility in which faith-based organizations (FBOs) can play a crucial role in curtailing the destructive behavior ruining the lives of millions of Americans, black and white, inner-city dwellers, and middle-class suburbanites. To nurture change, federal, state, and local governments, through administrative reforms and legislation, must nurture and encourage FBOs.

The goal is to create what have been described as "little platoons,"[1] comprised of private charities (including FBOs), civic associations, and neighborhood groups, that aim to improve civil society one person and one family at a time. Through their efforts, individuals can find a sense of purpose and place in the world. Most important, these organizations focus on treating the impoverished and the alienated not as numbers, but as individuals, with the added benefit of encouraging responsibility and discouraging dependency on government.

A significant number of Americans, myself included, have come to doubt the efficacy of public sector social service programs. The dismal results abound. We are rightly disenchanted with outmoded governmental efforts to solve the problems of inner-city youths and suburban teens.

Now, with the benefit of experience and research, we see more clearly the moral and spiritual dimensions of social problems. Perceiving not only their economic aspects but also their psychological, spiritual, and moral components, many want to explore new policy options and approaches. This book seeks to open a dialogue about our spiritual and moral poverty and the relationship of faith, politics, and public policy in America.

In trying to deal with America's societal ills, policymakers have long been trapped in stale paradigms. Modern liberalism has long been accepted as an article of faith that government, especially the federal government, is the engine for ameliorating social problems. Equating compassion with federal dollars spent, liberals seek even larger programs and more infusions of public money. Blaming poverty on society and various external forces, liberals assume the poor are the helpless victims of racism, an unfair socioeconomic system, and economic forces beyond their control, dooming them to failure, regardless of their own efforts. Particularly to blame, say liberals, is the economic dislocation resulting from the collapse of the urban manufacturing economy. They bemoan its replacement by low-paying service jobs, often located in the suburbs that lack affordable housing. In sum, liberals view poverty as a societal problem rather than an individual problem.

Fiscal conservatives, on the other hand, have withdrawn from offering solutions, preferring to leave the poor to their own devices. Reflexively suspicious of the public sector, they maintain that reduced government, lower taxes, and deregulation will create economic growth, and the resulting tide of prosperity will alleviate America's social ills. They see the poor as mainly responsible for their own condition and, therefore, focus on self-help, personal and parental responsibility, and the strengthening of families. For fiscal conservatives, the downtrodden are accountable for their personal probity.

Fiscal conservatives maintain that the poor have the capacity to better themselves; liberals express their doubts. Fiscal conservatives offer a "sink or swim" mentality to enforce personal responsibility; liberals seem much less enamored with this approach. Nevertheless, fiscal conservatives and liberals share a common belief that more money, either through economic growth or government transfers, is sufficient. While the focus on the economic component has its place, of course, the damage is deeper. New remedies are needed.

Although individuals operate within a socioeconomic system that constrains their choices, they are ultimately responsible for the choices they make. Publicly funded, secular welfare programs, weakened by their lack of accountability and a de-emphasis on personal responsibility, miss this important point. The new approach, explored in this book, recognizes both the limitations and the potentialities of the individual. Its conclusion rests on the belief that FBOs, in the absence of compelling reasons not to, should be given the opportunity to more vigorously tackle America's social ills.

Across the political spectrum there is growing interest in testing the proposition that FBOs could do even greater good, if government, particularly the federal government, supports an expanded role. Some of society's most stubborn social problems are those that the public sector cannot effectively handle without outside help. FBOs represent a potentially valuable, albeit controversial, resource because they open a new front in the war against America's social ills, focusing on individuals and their personal and moral shortcomings, not social and economic conditions. Thus, the need for government to partner with FBOs, especially those with an extensive inner-city presence.

President George W. Bush's faith-based initiative, one of his signature proposals, presents an opportunity to test these theories and assess their effectiveness when translated into public policy. The initiative is in keeping with Bush's philosophy of a smaller, activist federal government that facilitates the empowerment of citizens and intermediary institutions, such as religious and secular groups, rather than dominating social service efforts. As President Bush put it in his first budget speech to Congress on February 27, 2001, "Government has a role, and an important role. Yet too much government crowds out initiative and hard work, private charity and the private economy. Our new government vision says government should be active, but limited, engaged, but not overbearing."[2] Implicit in Bush's initiative is the realization that government alone can only do so much and that FBOs, community groups, and families are better at instilling virtues and maintaining the social fabric. In particular, FBOs add value based on the way they operate.

The federal government and mediating institutions should not be seen as rivals. It is a delicate balancing act to coordinate government programs with the efforts of religious and secular providers so as to create a new partnership. The challenge is whether the federal government can contribute to this partnership and help rebuild a civil society, one in which families, neighborhoods, and FBOs (among other voluntary groups) function effectively, without falling prey to the errors of the Great Society.

My sense is that the Bush faith-based initiative may be one of the most important public policy undertakings in years and may well be a major domestic legacy of his presidency. The initiative also marks the beginning of a significant shift in policy making from the traditional obsession with either the public dole or laissez-faire as instruments for social progress. Rather, it represents the beginning of a holistic attack on societal ills. Government, FBOs, and secular and community groups can work together to solve social problems. This approach represents a move from merely delivering services to attempting to change lives. In seeking to end decades of hostility to religion, the Bush initiative also offers the prospect of encouraging greater respect for religion and religious beliefs in American society.

At present, it is uncertain whether Bush will be able to deliver on his promise of "compassionate conservatism"–the political moniker meant to symbolize a caring society served by local faith-based, secular, and political institutions. It will be a great experiment to see if it is possible for the federal government, by asking FBOs to undertake more social service tasks, can strengthen civil society–to revive decaying inner cities, empower the downtrodden, mend broken families, and give meaning to suburban teens. Thus, we must ask: can the federal government encourage the growth of mediating institutions that promote virtue? At least, government should let these institutions flourish without excessive interference.

Perhaps a more vexing question to some is whether it is possible to base public policy on the concept of personal responsibility? As a presidential candidate, George W. Bush stated, "I want to usher in the responsibility era, an era when every American knows with certainty that each of us is responsible for our actions, that each of us is responsible for our family and our community, that each of us is responsible for loving a neighbor as we would like to be loved ourselves."[3]

While the sentiments behind the "responsibility era" rhetoric are consistent with the philosophy of most FBOs, these sentiments are almost certainly not shared by a significant number of people. In their view, talk of personal responsibility is no substitute for economic assistance. This raises a problem, for if Bush's initiative is to outlive his administration, policymakers and all levels of government must be convinced of the practical value of FBOs, among other mediating institutions.

Seen in this broad context, the Republican-sponsored Welfare Reform Act of 1996, signed into law by President William Jefferson (Bill) Clinton, represented only the first stage in an overhaul of America's public assistance programs. The post-1996 welfare system cannot be successful without another component. If these reforms, which limit benefits and require recipients to work, constitute the government's "stick," then FBOs, among other organizations, must be the "carrot."

In the wake of dismantling much of the traditional welfare apparatus, not surprisingly, the public and politicians of both parties are more receptive to creative policy solutions. Many would agree that non-governmental organizations provide innovative solutions to countless problems. The same could be said about FBOs, yet FBOs are shunned because of their religious component, rather than on tangible criteria, such as effectiveness. Obviously, a double standard exists. This is a mistake because to evaluate FBOs through the prism of secular versus sacred is to miss the point. Concrete expectations and not religious fervor make FBOs a viable alternative.

The public interest in FBOs is not a product of heightened religiosity, instead it derives from the public's exasperation with secular social services, whether offered by a governmental unit or a nonprofit provider. Indeed, public acceptance of some level of religious involvement in previously secular programs exists because there is a general belief that FBOs work. The question then becomes: can the federal government help FBOs flourish?

Despite the overheated rhetoric from the moral right and the secular left, a closer partnership between government and FBOs need not threaten religious freedom or our civil liberties. Some religious conservatives worry that government and the temptation of public money will corrupt religion. Secularists and non-Christian faiths worry that religion will corrupt government. The latter are concerned that the public expression of faith by energized religious groups will lead to efforts to Christianize America, religiously inspired bigotry, discrimination against non-Christians and sectarianism, and religious conflicts. As Rep. Robert Wexler (D-Florida) put it, "[Bush's] program would lead to one thing only, and that is government-sponsored proselytizing."[4] According to William Gralnick of Boca Raton, Florida, the Southeast Florida regional director of the American Jewish Committee, "The question is whether the administration understands that this action could create an environment which reinforces those people who think this is a Christian country and should be a Christian country."[5]

I write this as a person of faith, as an ordained rabbi. I do not accept the message of evangelical Christians. I do not believe that faith in Jesus is the only path to salvation. Thus, I have no interest in convincing others to accept Jesus as a personal savior.

From my perspective, however, fear that one religious group or a few groups will take over the public sector and assume the status of a state religion seems overblown. The growth of secularism in America and the multitude of religious groups, often antagonistic to each other, prevents any sort of religious cabal. No religious group has that much power. Public support of faith-based groups does not represent a step to the establishment of a theocracy.

America's Moral and Cultural Transformation

From 1965 to 1995, America faced moral and social decline, precipitated by an attack on traditional virtues. Illegitimacy, soaring divorce rates, and skyrocketing crime levels exemplified this period. Something happened to American society over these thirty or so years.

At the outset, it is important to note, however, that social change is not synonymous with social decline. Surely, the civil rights movement was a profound episode of positive social change in American history. Problems arose when the new thinking rejected in toto long-standing beliefs; failure to recognize the value of traditional virtues contributed to the decline.

A transformation in cultural and societal norms occurred from the mid-1960s to the late 1970s. Many factors, including the 1960s counterculture, misguided social policies, and technological and economic forces produced this shift. The quest for individuality, expressiveness, and pleasure-seeking came to the fore, accompanied by a demand for quick excitement. This cultural rebellion led to a defiance of traditional norms marked by the devaluation of personal responsibility, social conformity, and conventional sexual morality. Many of us chose to live for the moment. With the collapse of responsibility, came an explosion of pathologies reflective of hopelessness, especially among the underclass.

Social and intellectual elites grew skeptical of traditional virtues. America's moral reorientation was initiated by the permissive attitudes of the educated elite toward sex, marriage, and parenthood, and was centered on a rejection of middle-class sensibilities. These attitudes found their way into government policy. The media made mainstream Americans evermore ambivalent about marriage, regarding it as an outdated institution. The ethics of self-expression and the liberation from social constraints, rather than accommodating traditional virtues, replaced the ethos of self-control, deferred gratification, moderation, thrift, and acceptance of personal responsibility in the minds of influential Americans.

Elites could no longer preach the merits of virtues they themselves abandoned. They did not pride themselves on their hard work, sobriety, thrift, and personal responsibility. They became less insistent on a conventional family structure, the work ethic, and respect for the law. Support for the two-parent family eroded. The prospects offered by entry-level jobs came to be regarded as too little for any self-respecting person to bother with.

Furthermore, the rise of the consumption society in post-World War II America, with its emphasis on spending and material acquisitiveness, undermined the traditional middle-class virtues of hard work, diligence, sobriety, frugality, and sexual restraint. Boom times minimized these virtues, which previously were requisites for employment, entrepreneurship, and the creation of wealth. This new value system also led to a decline in savings, as Americans demanded instant gratification.

The well-to-do were moral trendsetters and promoters of a permissive attitude that met with acceptance from the poor because the financial rewards of government programs were built on negative virtues. However, the consequences for the underclass were far more devastating. Wealth provides a buffer against present-oriented behavior, including sexual spontaneity and permissiveness. Conversely, the poor are particularly vulnerable to the consequences of sexual improvidence and the pursuit of immediate pleasure. Thus, the failings of the underclass reflect, in part, the moral and spiritual failings of American society as a whole. The pathologies of youthful inner-city criminals mirror the tendencies of the broader culture. However, the moral failures of some rich persons do not entitle the poor to do as they please, regardless of how self-defeating their behavior may be.

Along with the transformation of elite values and attitudes, the place of females in society changed. Women were freed from their traditional roles of stay-at-home moms by a number of developments: the advent of safe and effective contraceptives; household labor-saving devices; and the rise of the service economy and the accompanying changes in the nature of work as mental labor replaced physical exertion. These brought about a profound shift in sexual behavior and family structure.

One of the principle changes in American society was the sexual revolution. The birth control pill, perhaps the single most important facilitator of this movement, marked a radical change in attitudes to sexuality. By reducing the fear of pregnancy, oral contraceptives eliminated the procreative element of sex. Women became free to decide their own reproductive future and could prevent or terminate pregnancies.

At the beginning of the twenty-first century, we are witnessing a rather complicated rise and fall of moral standards.[6] It is a mixed bag: moral standards have risen in some areas and fallen in others. Our notions about public drinking are likely more restrictive than at any time since Prohibition. Fifty years ago, people drank at lunch with abandon. Not so anymore. Our culture now stigmatizes behavior once taken for granted, such as cigarette smoking, public celebration of drug use, and anti-Semitism.

At the same time, there has been a coarsening in culture, language, and manners. Much of popular entertainment ranges from the vulgar to the obscene. We live in a highly sexualized society, one that promotes the immediate gratification of sensual longings and minimizes the consequences. There is a continuous flaunting of sexuality in movies and on television. The film industry, music business, and television networks give public standing vulgarity, violence, and hostility to others.

Popular culture radiates blatant sensuous appeals and encourages rampant sexual activity. Promiscuity on television sitcoms has a level of explicitness unthinkable thirty or forty years ago. Many are offended by the easy availability of pornography in print and on the Internet, erotic advertising, the proliferation of four-letter words in movies, the obscenity and sadism of rap music, the exhibitionism and narcissism on talk shows, and the general decline in our reticence about sexual matters. We are more tolerant of frank sexual talk and jokes in public. Ironically, we are intolerant of racial or ethnic jokes and are repulsed by any talk or conduct that could be viewed as sexual harassment.

However, the AIDS epidemic seems to have sparked a retreat to more traditional virtues. While not necessarily a complete retrenchment to pre-1960s sexual attitudes, there has been at least an emphasis on safe sexual behavior. It is perhaps telling that it took the fear of death to inspire a change in values regarding promiscuity and casual sex.

The cultural revolution also had a profound impact on the institution of marriage. Expectations about marriage changed: no longer was it sacred or lasting; instead it was transitory, easily entered into and readily dissolved. In the 1970s and 1980s people became more tolerant of divorce. As women became more independent, they demanded more of marriage and became less dependent on husbands. They would not as easily put up with "unrewarding" marriages or "flawed" husbands. At the same time, men abandoned their families and left their aging wives for ever-younger trophy wives, so-called "trade-ups." All these factors destabilized marriage and increased the prevalence of divorce. The family became brittle, while many disintegrated altogether. At the same time, the rate of unmarried cohabitation soared nearly 50 percent in the 1990s after almost doubling from 1980 to 1990.[7]

Some things have improved over the past decade. Certain social indicators are moving in the right direction. Crime rates have plummeted to the lowest levels in decades.[8] We locked up record numbers of people who might otherwise commit crimes. Crime also declined in the 1990s because of several factors: demographic (fewer young males) and social trends (crack usage declined as teens saw their parents and other siblings devoured by it); the economic boom; and innovative police tactics, such as community policing.

However, in spite of the steep drop in violent crime in the 1990s, many inner-city residents still remain fearful. Open-air drug markets and the violence they spawn still remain, as are gangs and drug disputes involving the younger generation. In short, random violence still terrorizes black neighborhoods.

The family, at least in the upper half of American society, is starting to rebuild itself. The divorce rates are dropping and teen pregnancies are down. Although the incidence of divorce remains high (more than 40 percent of new marriages end in divorce), the divorce rate (including annulments) has declined in the United States. It has drifted downward from 4.7 per thousand people in 1990 to 3.3 in 1997, reflecting, in part, a trend toward marriage at older, and presumably more mature, ages.[9] Today, people view divorce as more tragic than they did twenty-five years ago.

The teenage birthrate decreased more than 20 percent between 1991 and 1999, from a peak of 62.1 to 49.6 births for every 1,000 girls, age fifteen to nineteen, as a result of less teen sex and greater use of birth control devices.[10] However, America's teenage birthrate remains the highest in the developed world, with about 1 million babies born each year to teen mothers. About four in ten women will get pregnant at some point in their teens; moreover, about eight out of ten births to teen mothers are out-of-wedlock. Indeed, few teen mothers put their children up for adoption or marry the baby's father, so these offspring are at an immediate disadvantage. As discussed later in this chapter, there is a general consensus that teens having babies without a father-husband in the household leads to bad results for both the children and their mothers.

There are other social indicators that our culture is still cycling downward. There has been a notable surge in nonmarital childbearing over the past three decades. For millennia, it was "illegitimate" to have children outside of marriage. The age-old social stigma associated with out-of-wedlock births has been overthrown, resulting in an astonishing rise in births to unmarried mothers. The sexual revolution of the 1960s eradicated the link between sex, procreation, and marriage. Having babies without marrying the father has become commonplace and represents perhaps the single most important social problem.

This trend is more evident when out-of-wedlock birth rates are examined within various racial and ethnic categories.[11] Nearly 70 percent of African-American babies are born to unmarried mothers, a startlingly high figure for any one racial group. Among Hispanics, the figure is 42 percent. Out-of-wedlock births as a percentage of all births in the United States rose from 5 percent in 1960 to 33 percent in 2000, reaching 22 percent among non-Latino whites. In 1999, illegitimacy rates among white women (including Hispanics) soared to 26.7 percent, a significant increase from the 16.9 percent recorded in 1990, itself a huge increase over the 3 percent figure recorded in 1970. Many experts interpret these figures to indicate that American society has reached the "tipping point,"[12] at which out-of-wedlock births will soar. Increasingly, among all races, men, who do not (and will not) marry, sire children only to abandon them.

The rise of single motherhood took place within a sea of change in attitudes toward sexual and family issues. These shifts include the status of women in society, the value or necessity of women working outside the house, premarital sex, the ideal of sexual freedom, the unreliability and irresponsibility of men, as well as accidents of fate and choices.

We recognize the harm to society done by family fragmentation and fatherlessness. There is a consensus that illegitimacy is ruinous. The destructive impact of illegitimacy is well documented in child development, crime, and the malfunctioning of community. The presence of mother-only homes, to a large degree, determines the nature of a neighborhood and the socialization of the next generation. The best predictor of poverty is single motherhood, more than race, neighborhood, or family background. Taking into account other differences, children born out of marriage are 1.7 times more likely to be poor than those born to married parents.[13]

Single-mother families, even controlling for income, are also more often characterized as dysfunctional. This contributes to a host of social ills, including juvenile delinquency and violent crime, failing or dropping out of school, engaging in early sexual activity, giving birth out-of-wedlock, and developing drug and alcohol problems. Children born out-of-wedlock face significant disadvantages in educational achievement and personal development. They have greater problems with self-control and are often diagnosed as hyperactive. They are more likely to drop out of high school, get pregnant as teens, or abuse drugs.[14] Daughters raised by single mothers are significantly more likely to marry young, have children young, or themselves become single mothers.

In the inner city, a rising generation of preteen youngsters are the offspring of the often needy, neglected, single-parent underclass. They lack a responsible father to help to instill in them impulse control. Emotionally weak and insecure, poorly fathered males tend to pursue socially destructive behavior. These young males often act aggressively, with little self-control. They can be physically violent and are desirous of immediate gratification. They see few examples of men acting as family breadwinners. They grow up unprepared to assume the responsibilities of work and family, which perpetuates the cycle.

Daughters of single mothers are significantly more likely themselves to bear one or more children out-of-wedlock. Poorly fathered girls fall victim to poorly fathered boys who prey on the vulnerabilities of girls who hunger for a father's affection. These young women search for caring through premarital sex and babies to love them, giving rise to another generation of disadvantaged children. The problems of men and women from fatherless households will continue to increase as today's infants become teens and adults.

However, children raised in single-parent households are not inexorably bound to fail in school, turn to drugs, or commit crimes. It is true that many single parents successfully raise children, but often this is the case only in wealthy households where the choice was made from the outset to raise a child alone. Child rearing involves a lot of time and money. A single-parent family is at a disadvantage. It is hard for one parent, typically a woman, to fulfill both the breadwinner and child-raising roles as well as a two-parent family can.

Other large-scale social problems have spread from black inner-city areas to pervade low-income white communities. We see increased drug use, worsening education performance, and a growing breakdown of community norms in white working-class neighborhoods. Black and white healthy males in their late teens and early twenties who are not in school drop out of the labor force. There is a growing contempt for menial jobs spreading throughout American society, as the institution of work atrophies. The decade of the 1990s saw an ominous dropout from the labor force by young men, especially black males, no longer in school. Among sixteen- to twenty-four-year-old black males not in school, the percentage not working (or not looking for work) averaged 17 percent in the 1980s. It rose to 20 percent in 1992 and stood at 23 percent by 1997. Among white males in the same age bracket, the labor force dropout rate equaled about 9 percent in 1997. However, the white male dropout rate rose 25 percent from 1990 to 1997, with white teens, ages sixteen to nineteen, recording a 33 percent increase during this same time period.[15] Those who reach age thirty with minimal education and a spotty work history will likely be confined to the margins of the economy.

In the midst of these cultural and social transformations, American society is marked by far greater diversity than ever before. There are new forms of individual and social life. We have opened American society to women and people of color. There is increased tolerance for people who differ from the norm, whether in race, religion, or sexual orientation. There is also greater sensitivity to inequities, economic and social. America is unlikely to return to the mid-twentieth-century mores of premarital chastity, low divorce, stay-at-home moms, or the closeting of homosexuals.

My Response to Two Key Questions

There are two questions of paramount importance in dealing with the social ills that plague American society. First, how are virtues formed and what can be done to change them in a positive manner and bring about a moral and spiritual renewal? Second, what is the proper role of the federal government in attempting to solve societal problems and can we devolve more power and authority to local groups, particularly nongovernmental institutions?

These questions, of course, encompass numerous smaller issues. How do we revive hope among those who view life as devoid of meaning and purpose? How can we change behavioral patterns developed over generations? In a society that no longer looks askance at single motherhood and that demands two-income families, how can we revive two key institutions: marriage and family? Can locally-based organizations reshape character and foster a return to traditional virtues? What role will FBOs play in bringing about this change and can they be successful?

At the outset, let me state my conceptual premises. To advocate virtue is to promote self-advancing and socially beneficial behavior for all Americans, whether they live in the inner cities or the suburbs. According to one academic expert, virtue means "acting with due restraint on one's impulses, due regard for the rights of others, and reasonable concern for distant consequences."[16] In short, virtue serves as a compass guiding one's everyday choices in life. Virtue encompasses behavior that also inures to the benefit of society. Though reaching a consensus on what is virtuous is fraught with difficulty, I will nonetheless try.

Nearly all of us would focus on the virtues Americans have traditionally celebrated–hard work, personal responsibility, trustworthiness, thrift, and delayed gratification. Although these are unquestioned virtues, we find it difficult to live by them in practice. It may be simplistic, moralistic, and judgmental, but I do not believe that "if it feels good, one should do it." Continuing to look to traditional Judeo-Christian morality, my criticism of socially and self-destructive behavior does not represent blaming the victim. We must address the damage one brings about by one's actions, for it is these actions that, among other outcomes, keep people mired in hopelessness and despair.

The advocacy of self-advancing and socially beneficial virtuous behavior should not, however, be construed as an attack on the poor in the name of middle-class values. Promoting the virtues of self-reliance, self-discipline, hard work, thrift, delayed gratification, law-abiding behavior, and responsibility for oneself, one's family, and one's offspring represents commonsense advice that benefits everyone.

Conversely, drug use, unwed motherhood, sexual promiscuity, and dependency are negative virtues because they harm not only the individuals involved but also society as a whole. All would agree that alcoholism and drug addiction devastate the lives of addicts and their families. In contrast to the casual acceptance of out-of-wedlock childbearing, marriage is not old-fashioned. It is the linchpin of society, the road to personal happiness, and the institution within which children are to be raised.

Because the family is the fundamental social unit, we need to encourage the formation of stable, two-parent families who create a livelihood for themselves and their offspring. This is because the family structure plays a key role in determining social outcomes. In the family, we acquire a sense of continuity with the past and a commitment to the future. Human virtues depend on the socialization of each new generation, involving the inculcation of responsibility, the need to restrain one's impulses, and concern for the consequences of one's actions. Socialization, in turn, depends on the care and resources provided by the family. It seems to me difficult, if not impossible, to revive marriage and to promote the family without the moral authority of religious faith.

Religion is perhaps the one force in American society that will help promote a cultural renewal. Although some socially and self-destructive individuals are incorrigible, faith can help solve numerous social ills. Through spiritual regeneration, when faith and hope become factors in lives, many become motivated to change their behavior. Faith helps endow life with meaning and purpose; it aids in overcoming the grip of nihilism and helplessness, offers hope for the future, and brings a new sense of self-worth.

By teaching virtues and demonstrating constructive behavior, FBOs help people actualize these virtues for themselves. Thus, FBOs can serve as indispensable allies of the public sector in helping solve social problems, changing individuals, and rebuilding families and communities. FBOs are transformative in nature as they encourage individuals to change their lives and turn them into "new" persons. FBOs provide both direction and meaning in life as well as guidelines for behavior that serve as an anchor for those who otherwise drift purposelessly through life, practicing, among other destructive acts, irresponsible sex and addiction to drugs and alcohol.

What makes FBOs unique is the spiritual and moral guidance they provide. They touch and help people on the profoundest level and offer clear sets of virtues with which one can navigate life's journey. Because FBOs focus on the person as a whole, they are often the best method for rebuilding broken lives and preventing socially and self-destructive behavior.

Changing human behavior is, however, difficult. The material is rather stubborn. "Life change is a complicated, dicey business," as Glenn Parrish of the Rising Tide Transitional Housing Program (which has its roots at Mariners Church in Irvine, California) candidly noted. He continued, "The profoundly complex nature of the problems we're trying to address leads you to include faith-based solutions. We need to address the most crucial issues our clients face: hopelessness and despair. Unless you can address the spiritual issues, you can't get in the game."[17]

Americans want to believe that people can change for the better. However, government, at whatever level, cannot (and should not) itself strive to replicate the work of FBOs by delivering the tools for moral and spiritual regeneration or facilitating a search for meaning and purpose in life by social service recipients and society at large. Public social service offices, burdened by inflexible rules, large caseloads, and devoid of any spiritual-orientation, are perhaps best at assessing individuals' eligibility for certain programs and referring them to an appropriate provider. Even if government does not directly undertake the task of moral and spiritual renewal, it can assist FBOs in their quest to promote personal responsibility and a return to traditional virtues. This leads to my second question.

What is the proper role of government at all levels–federal, state, and local–in dealing with social ills and shaping behavior?[18] It is evident that traditional welfare (and more generally, public social service) programs are not effective. However, can government now devolve operational responsibilities to religious and community organizations, those emphasizing long-standing virtues, that historically performed this task? This raises many issues, such as the funds available to these institutions, the difficulty in starting grassroots movements where hope and material resources are scarce commodities, rethinking the role that the public sector has assumed for the past seventy years, and whether it is possible to use the federal government as a catalyst to revive, facilitate, and bolster a neighborhood-oriented civic society, promoting responsibility and restraining behavior.

It may seem unusual for someone who has spent over a quarter of a century working and living in Washington, D.C. to advocate the devolution and diminution of centralized bureaucracies, often overpromising and underachieving. However, when it comes to overcoming the problems facing American society, many policy decisions and implementation strategies are best made on a local level, by the people who know what is needed to facilitate personal transformation, strengthen families, and revive neighborhoods.

I would like to see power decentralized and devolved with responsibilities pushed back to the "little platoons." Public policy ought to strengthen, not displace or overwhelm, the "little platoons" enabling them to build stronger families and neighborhoods and to overcome poverty.

FBOs and other community groups are in the best position to know what type of help is needed because these organizations deal with social problems on the front lines. They know the names and faces of the poverty-stricken, the drug-addicted, the homeless, and the hopeless.

Recognizing that government does not have a monopoly on the "public square," a civil society can and should be constructed on the local, rather than national, level. This society would rely on nonmarket, intermediary institutions that stand between the individual in his or her private life and the various levels of government. Loyalties should grow from below, not be imposed from above. To reinvigorate citizen involvement at the neighborhood level, we need to revitalize the mediating social structure–family, community and voluntary associations, and religious organizations–that give substance to our lives and provide the foundation for our moral and spiritual convictions. It is in these subdivisions of society that each of us constructs meaning and purpose for our existence. Government should, therefore, help these groups do the job for which they are ideally suited.

When it comes to solving the current societal crisis and to meeting the challenge of our weakest and most alienated members, government has responsibilities, but it need not serve as the sole provider of the services itself. Working for the "general good" through voluntary organizations, faith- and community-based, empowers individuals and gives them a greater chance to govern themselves. In short, many social problems are best understood and solved by the institutions and people closest to them.

Faith-based groups represent a key element in building a more virtuous, decentralized civil society, teaching responsible parenthood, reducing crime, and promoting lawful entrepreneurship. Houses of worship are perhaps the one American institution best suited to promoting traditional virtues and influencing personal behavior. As the most reliable institution in America's poor neighborhoods, they are often the only organization many inner-city residents trust.

Although deploring many of the policies of the federal government over the past seventy years, we cannot deny or ignore the federal government. The task is to figure out how to use federal government–both federal funds and mandates–constructively; how to connect the federal government more closely to community-based, grassroots religious and secular organizations.

Two premises ought to guide policymakers. We ought to foster virtuous behavior. At the same time, we should devolve functions to communities, nongovernmental entities, and families as a healthy corrective to massive governmental endeavors. An activist federal government can facilitate (or at least, avoid excessive interference with) the empowerment of individuals and families, using faith- and community-based groups, small, face-to-face, voluntary, less impersonal and bureaucratic, to enable people to take more control of their lives.

Although compassion does not depend on the amount of public spending directed at solving social problems, we need to join individual morality and personal responsibility with structural transformation and material aid to assist those who want to help themselves. Furthermore, additional funds would go a long way in helping FBOs, nearly all of which face nagging financial concerns, expand their social service offerings.

An Overview of the Book

Chapter 2 develops how George W. Bush, even before becoming president, recognized the transformative power of religious faith, especially its influence on behavior. In 1986, faith helped him turn from alcohol to become a business executive and a politician with a viable career. As Texas governor, he implemented reforms enabling FBOs to begin to solve social problems. Bush was concerned about the overbureaucratization of America, where trained and pedigreed social service professionals discourage local, nonprofessional caregivers from healing and renewing lives. Bush therefore sought and achieved both the deregulation for religious child care providers and the loosening of licensing and credential requirements for faith-based chemical dependency programs, so as to favor FBOs. He also helped implement the nation's first Christian prison within a state facility.

Chapter 3 sketches more than two centuries of welfare in America. Before the twentieth century, those in need turned to FBOs and other community groups that sought to instill virtues. These organizations made demands on the poor in return for assistance. Donors were required to give both money and time. As Americans became more dependent on government programs, faith- and community-based groups atrophied.

The chapter then focuses on the efforts of the New Deal of the 1930s and the Great Society of the 1960s to deal with poverty. Those who sought to deal with the nation's social problems in the 1960s botched the job. Their approach to welfare exacerbated many social problems by encouraging out-of-wedlock births, discouraging marriage and work, and creating an underclass that transmitted poverty from one generation to the next. The easy availability of government aid to a wide range of people encouraged the avoidance of finishing school, looking for work, and getting married–three keys to avoiding long-term poverty. When parents act irresponsibly, their children are likely to do the same. The United States, therefore, came to contain a sizable underclass with all sorts of dysfunctional characteristics.

The chapter then highlights the landmark 1996 Welfare Reform Act and its reaffirmation of the work ethic. Americans realized that a job improves one's self-respect and that work imposes discipline and regularity in life. The perverse economic incentives of earlier welfare programs promoted learned helplessness, subsidized sloth, and rewarded illegitimacy. These social policies facilitated a hopeless dependency into which young, unmarried mothers with their children were drawn, with disastrous results that ruined lives and neighborhoods. Policymakers therefore decided that new incentive structures were needed to encourage people to behave properly.

Since 1997, a spectacular drop has occurred in welfare rolls. Ex-welfare recipients have shown that they are not victims of circumstances, that they are not fatalistic or passive, and that many can solve their problems. With respect to the remaining hard core of welfare recipients, the chapter concludes by focusing on future public policies.

As chapter 4 demonstrates, FBOs are already there in staggering numbers doing good works for hard-core welfare recipients, the working poor, and suburban and inner-city teens. FBOs, everything from small, local congregations to national, parachurch institutions, already play an important role in delivering a wide array of social services, while attending to the spiritual needs of those they help. These organizations marshal financial and human resources and channel them to provide social services as a means of practicing their faith.

After presenting various surveys of the social service activities of FBOs (particularly local congregations), the chapter considers the historic and current role of African-American churches in general and specifically the range of services provided by one large, inner-city church in Los Angeles. To put a human face on citywide and national FBOs and their dynamic leaders, the chapter examines two types of faith-based approaches: Boston's more secular Ten-Point Coalition, led by Rev. Eugene Rivers, III, and the evangelical Prison Fellowship Ministries (PFM), a global organization founded by Chuck Colson of Watergate fame.

Chapter 5 presents the empirical evidence that FBOs can affect a moral transformation. Although scientific studies do not conclusively prove the efficacy of faith-based approaches to solving social ills, we know that "religion" can make a positive difference. Beyond anecdotal stories of successes, this chapter summarizes the empirical evidence, carefully sifting through research studies, and demonstrates that religion deters deviant behavior. The research suggests an inverse relationship between "religion" and pervasive social ills, such as substance abuse, premarital sex, and delinquency and crime. Those who are "religious" are less likely to engage in self-destructive or antisocial behavior. To develop the "faith-factor," this chapter employs studies that measure religion's impact on behavior generally. This measure of the faith-factor serves as a proxy for assessing the potential effectiveness of FBOs.

Studies also show that FBOs rehabilitate individuals. There is a positive empirical record for two religiously oriented programs aimed at changing destructive behavior. Studies show that the PFM reduces convicts' recidivism. Teen Challenge helps rehabilitate drug addicts more successfully than its secular counterparts. These studies directly assess FBOs; thus they measure the effectiveness of FBOs in dealing with social problems rather than the effects of religion on society in the abstract.

From both a preventive and a rehabilitative perspective, FBOs appear effective at dealing with chronic social problems because they combine material assistance with spiritual uplift, sparking a personal transformation. The bonds formed by FBOs facilitate behavior modification "one person at a time." Moreover, doctrinal religious differences among FBOs are irrelevant. That is why FBOs sponsored by various religious denominations achieve similar positive results in dealing with societal ills not otherwise adequately handled by existing secular programs, whether offered by nonprofit groups or the public sector.

In the 1990s, perhaps the most important development for FBOs was the enactment of the Charitable Choice provisions of the 1996 Welfare Reform Act. Charitable Choice, considered in chapter 6, mandates that states receiving federal block grant antipoverty money must allow religious organizations to bid for contracts just like any other secular organization, instead of discriminating against them because they are religiously based. If a state (or locality) wants to contract out some of its antipoverty social service efforts to nongovernmental providers, it cannot exclude FBOs because of their religious character. Thus, Charitable Choice levels the playing field and allows FBOs to compete with secular groups for a limited range of publicly funded social service contracts. Religious organizations are no longer required to sacrifice their religious identity in order to participate as providers.

Charitable Choice strives to honor the religious integrity of FBOs through various safeguards. It also seeks to protect the rights of beneficiaries. An FBO's services must be available to all and clients cannot be pressured into conversion or participation in religious activities. Additionally, federal monies cannot directly fund sectarian instruction, proselytization, or worship.

The chapter next considers the expansion of Charitable Choice during the Clinton presidency. It also examines the slow implementation of

Charitable Choice on the federal and state levels and why relatively few FBOs lined up for public sector contracts and what can be done to make the existing Charitable Choice provisions more effective.

Chapter 7 examines President Bush's efforts to clear away the obstacles to greater participation by FBOs in the delivery of social services. During the 2000 presidential campaign and throughout the early part of his administration, Bush saw "compassionate conservatism" as an ambitious agenda, not merely a meaningless slogan. Bush's faith-based initiative sought to connect personal responsibility to a larger public good, especially on behalf of the less fortunate.

The chapter approaches Bush's efforts as president analytically, rather than chronologically. The chapter first considers administrative actions that did not require congressional approval, such as deregulatory measures designed to assist FBOs compete for government contracts. Bush's initiative also focused on gaining Congress to approve additional funds for FBOs working to change lives. For Bush, "compassionate conservatism" means that the federal government should take an active role, not only as a catalyst, but also as a financing source for the work done by religious and neighborhood groups.

The chapter also examines the controversy surrounding the expansion of Charitable Choice to more programmatic areas. Apart from the constitutional objections, discussed in chapter 8, increased direct federal funding of FBOs as contract recipients raises a number of questions. Compliance with ongoing monitoring and accounting requirements may have unintended negative consequences. Wary of the strings often attached to public funds, some fear that entanglement with government will lead FBOs to water down or eliminate their faith elements. Removing the religious content of FBO programs may also diminish the effectiveness of the social service programs offered by these organizations. Another drawback is the risk that FBOs will become increasingly dependent on government funding.

Policymakers must also balance the pros and cons of direct and indirect government funding for FBOs. There are two basic options for government support: directly, via grants and subsidies, or indirectly, via the Tax Code or vouchers. The Bush proposals would expand the direct federal support of FBOs by opening more contracts to bidding by nonsecular sources, as well as enhance indirect funding mechanisms–tax deductions–to stimulate more contributions to FBOs.

If a choice must be made between the direct and indirect approaches, the chapter concludes that financing FBOs through the Tax Code is preferable to increased direct federal funding. The fear that public funding will result in a government takeover of religion serves as perhaps the greatest impediment to a more expansive role for FBOs. For that reason, direct funding of FBOs is problematic. It is therefore better to encourage taxpayers to contribute more by allowing deductions for nonitemizers and through tax credits. Direct funding also suffers from another weakness: governmental bureaucracy and political patronage.

Also, any federal policy to expand the role of FBOs must demand the same standards of effectiveness and accountability that apply to their secular counterparts. Policymakers should not assume that the faith-factor alone can make an FBO effective in meeting its social mission. Direct government support of an FBO through contracts must be performance-based and contingent on the achievement of demonstrable results. A program must have a success rate that can be quantified. The amount a group spends per person must be sensible in relation to the services offered and their outcomes.

Chapter 7 also analyzes another funding option–vouchers–one that is already permissible under Charitable Choice but that could be put to wider use. Vouchers permit government funds to be used for the sectarian purposes of FBOs by allowing an individual recipient, not the public sector, to choose a religious or a secular provider.

The funding of FBOs reopens important questions of constitutional law. Many claim that the Bush faith-based initiative will break the wall separating church and state. Chapter 8 examines these concerns.

Rather than the complete prohibition of the funding of religious organizations, the chapter supports the concept of neutrality, or equal treatment of religion, to guide our interpretation of the Establishment Clause of the U.S. Constitution. Under the neutrality theory, government policies may neither favor nor disfavor religion. By remaining neutral among all religions, government policies ought not to subordinate religion to nonreligion. Subject to certain restrictions delineated in this chapter, equal treatment opens nondiscriminatory direct aid to FBOs.

Although predicting the U.S. Supreme Court's resolution of church-state issues is fraught with difficulties, the Court has begun to move away from the secularism that previously dominated public policy and constitutional law. A more supple reading of the First Amendment will lead to a new paradigm for the role of religion in public life. Thus, the emerging equal treatment of religion by the High Court suggests a more permissive attitude toward direct public funding of FBOs. Under this view, there is no constitutional ban to direct government funding, as long as no one denomination is favored, monies do not go to religious activities, clients are given a choice of alternative providers, and they may opt out of any privately funded religious exercises. This approach will facilitate the constitutionality of more public funding of faith-based initiatives, although it remains unclear, from a constitutional perspective, whether an FBO that receives government monies may choose to hire only persons in agreement with its religious beliefs as to sexual orientation. Furthermore, the tax and voucher approaches seem almost certain to pass constitutional muster.

It seems promising that FBOs will become even bigger players in the delivery of social services and helping solve America's societal ills. We now realize that many secular bureaucratic programs, with faceless staff and impersonal routines, are insensitive and destructive. However, one major caveat to greater involvement of FBOs is the FBO itself, as examined in chapter 9.

The religious character of an FBO is what makes it uniquely suited to cope with difficult social problems. If government funding comes at the cost of stifling the encouragement of traditional virtues or if the expansion robs FBOs of their strengths (e.g., personal attention), then FBOs become victims of their own success. Thus, FBOs must be assured an independent role in the eyes of the law and the cost of participation must not be unduly burdensome. In reality, it is too early to tell if FBOs are convinced. Some FBOs are cognizant of the risks of accepting public sector money, while others, fearful of becoming wards of the welfare state, may opt not to participate.

FBOs are not a substitute for government action or a panacea for solving America's societal ills. The work of reclamation will be long and hard. No one pretends that FBOs will somehow miraculously solve all our social ills overnight. Because they likely will prove effective at dealing with seemingly intractable societal problems, because they can be funded without expanding the public bureaucracy, and because additional funding can be provided in ways that withstand constitutional scrutiny, FBOs ought to be given the chance to enlarge their vital contribution to our nation's efforts to revitalize a society that cannot look to the future of its children without a sense of fear and hopelessness.

Notes

1.   Charles Murray, *In Pursuit of Happiness and Good Government* (New York: Simon & Schuster, 1988), 260-292.

2.   "Address Before a Joint Session of the Congress on Administration Goals," February 27, 2001, *Weekly Compilation of Presidential Documents* (March 2, 2001): 351-357, at 352; Transcript of "President Bush's Message to Congress on His Budget Proposal," *New York Times*, February 28, 2001, A14.

3.   George W. Bush, *A Charge to Keep* (New York: William Morrow, 1999), 229.

4.   William E. Gibson, "Soul-Searching Over Bush's Proposal: Plan to Fund Religious Groups Spurs Enthusiasm–and Hard Questions," *Chicago Tribune*, February 9, 2001, 8.

5.   *Ibid.*

Chapter 2

George W. Bush's
Road to a New Deal for Faith

A cursory examination of the political career of George W. Bush reveals the significance of faith-based solutions to his domestic agenda. As governor of Texas, Bush implemented Charitable Choice aggressively, promoted an ambitious legislative agenda designed to free FBOs from government red tape, and lent personal support to two controversial programs: Teen Challenge International U.S.A. and the InnerChange Freedom Initiative. Now, as the principal political patron of "compassionate conservatism," the Bush Administration has sought to institute a national faith-based policy.

This chapter traces Bush's religious conversion as a prelude to understanding his policy choices. Moreover, it discusses how Marvin Olasky and Myron Magnet shaped Bush's views. Their writings present the two faces of faith and responsibility-based social policy: criticism of moral relativism coupled with a call for greater involvement of FBOs in government assistance programs. Olasky's writings espouse utilizing FBOs as a means of delivering social services. Magnet's writings explore the harm done to the poor by America's moral decline. In sum, this chapter identifies the intellectual strands of the new social policy and describes how Bush put them into practice while Texas governor.

George W. Bush's Personal Road to Faith

As he made clear during the 2000 presidential campaign, George W. Bush credited religion with changing his life for the better. He personally witnessed the transforming power of faith. Until his fortieth birthday, he drank to excess. However, like many baby-boomers he turned to faith as an antidote. Bush's personal struggle with alcohol instilled in him the belief that "when a person changes his heart, it changes his behavior."[1]

George W. Bush, the son of an Episcopalian father and a Presbyterian mother, grew up in Midland, Texas. His father moved there from Connecticut to drill for oil. The older Bushes joined the First Presbyterian Church in Midland, where his father taught Sunday school and subsequently served as a church deacon and elder. When the family moved to Houston, they joined an Episcopal church where George W. Bush served as an altar boy.

After finishing college and working in Houston, Bush, still a bachelor, moved back to Midland. Although it is widely known that Bush did not live like an altar boy, he did spend Sunday mornings teaching religious school at his boyhood Presbyterian church. When he married Laura Welch in 1977, he joined her Methodist church in Midland and both remain Methodists.

Living in Dallas while Bush was a part owner and managing partner of the Texas Rangers baseball team, they became members of the Highland Park United Methodist Church, a large affluent congregation, traditional in ritual. Beginning in 1994, as Texas governor, the Bushes attended the Tarrytown United Methodist Church in Austin. However, beyond the litany of formal religious affiliations, Bush's faith did not affect his behavior. Indeed, into his thirties, George W. Bush was having problems with alcohol, his marriage, and his job.

In the fall of 1985, when the Texas economy was going belly-up, five of Bush's friends flew to California to be trained by a national group called the Community Bible Study.[2] When they got back to Midland, they set out to establish a study program of their own. Bush was one of the initial ten contacted and quickly joined.

The group soon grew to 200, meeting every Tuesday after work at a local Presbyterian church. The large gathering broke up into groups of about ten with someone leading a close textual reading of the Bible. This reading typically focused on a biblical problem and then led to a more intimate discussion about personal problems, such as whether members had been too involved with making money. The format included personal testimonies, in this case seeing the truths of the Bible lived out in the lives of leaders and class members.

At first, Bush was the clown of his group. When his group leader asked, "What is a prophet?" Bush flippantly replied, "It's when revenue exceeds expenses." He then added, "No one's ever seen that around here since Elijah."[3] This was a particularly biting comment when many businesses in Midland were in free fall. Indeed, before merging with a larger firm, Bush's oil development company was, at that time, on the verge of collapse.

Gradually, however, Laura and others in his group noticed a change. "He became much less sarcastic, much more patient," someone in Bush's core group remembered. "You could tell that by the end this was a changed man."[4]

The Bush family counts among its closest friends the Rev. Billy Graham (one of the nation's foremost evangelists) and his wife, Ruth. Bush credited Graham with providing the impetus for his spiritual awakening. The summer before he turned forty, Bush encountered Graham, who vacationed with the Bushes nearly every year in Kennebunkport, Maine. Graham pulled Bush aside for a walk on the beach. "Are you right with God?"[5] Graham asked. Bush said that he was not but thought he should be.

"I asked him a lot of questions about God and Jesus Christ–the skeptic's questions," Bush remembered. "Billy Graham's presence is such that he can melt a skeptic." Although Graham planted the seed, Bush did not immediately declare himself "born again." Bush noted, "When you are dealing with a skeptic, it takes a while for the message to sink in."[6] Bush returned home with an autographed copy of one of Graham's books and the resolve to stop drinking and turn his life around.

Bush and several friends in Midland who turned forty in 1986 decided to go with their wives to Colorado Springs in May to celebrate. After waking up with a bad hangover, he declared he would stop drinking. He then abruptly quit drinking–cold turkey. According to Bush, "A person with a changed heart is less likely to be addicted to drugs and alcohol.... I've had some personal experience with this....The main reason I quit [drinking] was because I accepted Jesus Christ into my life."[7]

Abstinence from alcohol for Bush also had a practical side. It was also about meeting personal goals, and becoming more effective and productive. "It made me much more disciplined, more focused,"[8] Bush recalled.

Marvin Olasky: Bush's First Intellectual Guru

In 1993, when Bush was thinking about running for governor, he sought the advice of Karl Rove, a self-educated University of Utah dropout, who became Bush's closest political advisor. During the 2000 presidential campaign, Rove served as campaign strategist and, subsequently, as a senior advisor to the President with purview over the offices of political affairs and public liaison.

Rove would serve as Bush's link to writers who sought to fashion a policy approach that repudiated the modern welfare state but did not turn its back on America's social ills, especially the nation's poor. Bush began reading their books and meeting with them even before his 1994 race for governor.

Marvin Olasky played a role in leading Bush from personal faith in 1986 to: policy proposals as a gubernational candidate; policy changes and legislative proposals as governor; policy pronouncements as a presidential campaigner; and now implementator as President.[9] In 1993, Bush and Rove met with Olasky, a University of Texas journalism professor, who started at Yale the year (1968) Bush left.

Olasky had gone on his own personal pilgrimage. Born Jewish, he was bar mitzvahed at thirteen, but turned to atheism by fourteen. He later became a Marxist and joined the Communist Party U.S.A., traveling across the former Soviet Union in his early twenties. By twenty-six he was a baptized Christian and a vocal proponent of pushing evangelical Christianity into the public sector.

Olasky's work was inspired by studying nineteenth-century private charities and how they differed from the twentieth-century public welfare system and its soul-sapping entitlements. In a foreword to an Olasky book, Bush would write that Olasky was "compassionate conservatism's leading thinker."[10]

Olasky published *The Tragedy of American Compassion*[11] in 1992. Olasky's thesis proclaimed the public welfare model to be morally bankrupt. The impersonal welfare system, according to Olasky, placed far too little emphasis on moral and spiritual development. He saw the welfare state as stingy with love, time, care, and hope. It did nothing to cure spiritual poverty–the poverty of the soul. He therefore called for a return to pre-twentieth-century social service delivery, what he referred to as the "Early American Model of Compassion." This model, which eschew any kind of charity that resulted in dependency, encouraged voluntary participation by the needy in private FBOs. Rather than simply distributing financial handouts, Olasky credited these nineteenth-century institutions with providing material help and spiritual, character-shaping sustenance.

Olasky addressed three questions: first, how were private charities organized; second, what made them effective; and third, what, in comparison, made later government programs ineffective. The first question is taken up in chapter 3, though it is important to note that organization, according to Olasky, accounted for much of their success.

Beyond organization, private charities were effective because they treated the behavioral problems that often led to or were the result of poverty. Their approach entailed personal involvement by volunteers, armed with Bibles and imbued with a missionary's zeal. Volunteers were motivated by (and in turn, sought to instill) religious belief. They sought to make a difference in one life over several years by educating and befriending the less fortunate. They did this by practicing what in modern terms would be described as "tough love," in contrast to what Olasky regarded as large-scale, impersonal, soulless modern welfare bureaucracies, rendered useless by their lack of emphasis on personal responsibility. Charities sought to relieve distress and change the lives of the poor, to distinguish between the deserving and the undeserving, and to relieve the personal failings that led to poverty and degradation. Assistance was conditioned on an individual's willingness to assume responsibility for himself or herself. Thus, private charities combined an optimist's belief in the individual's capacity to change for the better with the realist's knowledge that improvement only comes to those who seek it.

With these precepts firmly in mind, volunteer-benefactors provided religious-transformative assistance, in a humane manner, by encouraging responsibility and building self-esteem. They opened their own homes to deserted women and orphaned children and offered employment to men who had lost hope and most human contact. In these ways, they changed lives on a personal level.

Olasky asserted that the religious charities of the nineteenth century were more effective than public welfare programs because they made demands on those who sought assistance and those who offered it. Beneficiaries had to take responsibility for their own lives. Benefactors had to expend both time and money. These FBOs helped the poor, Olasky maintained, far more effectively than any government program could.

According to Olasky, government welfare programs represent false compassion. They are doomed to failure because they focus exclusively on the material needs of the poor with little regard for fostering personal development. Many of the poor require spiritual nurturing to motivate behavioral change. Concluding that government programs lack the personal dimension of religious charities and, thus, are powerless to change the behavior of the poor, Olasky wrote: "[I]n the end, not much will be accomplished without a spiritual revival that transforms the everyday advice people give and receive, and the way we lead our lives."[12]

Following the nineteenth-century model, Olasky offered his vision of an ideal America where private groups and concerned citizens felt it their duty to educate and befriend the less fortunate and serve as the main safety net for the poor. He urged the replacement of a paper-pushing, food-dispensing, warehousing, faceless government welfare bureaucracy because it is incapable of treating people as humans made in God's image. He proposed putting welfare programs entirely in the hands of FBOs. These groups would save the poor for God as well as feed, clothe, and house them.

Olasky maintained that as a matter of public policy value-based efforts could tackle fundamental social problems, such as drug use, violence, and family breakdown, more effectively. Olasky would have the chance to present his argument to Bush.

In their 1993 meeting, according to Olasky, Bush "asked questions that went to the heart of issues involving children born out of wedlock and men dying slowly from drug abuse on the streets."[13] Bush was clearly concerned about the plight of the American underclass–those living outside the mainstream. He began to understand that government welfare programs were cruelly disabling. The collapse of responsibility these programs engendered helped fuel an explosion of crime, drug abuse, and out-of-wedlock births, pathologies characteristic of a hopeless, urban underclass. Olasky's ideals offered Bush an alternative policy blueprint that would be tested in Texas before becoming a major issue in the 2000 Presidential campaign and a hallmark of the Bush Presidency.

Teen Challenge and the Rehabilitation of Drug Addicts

As Texas governor, Bush would again call on Olasky because of the controversy surrounding the San Antonio chapter of Teen Challenge International U.S.A. (Teen Challenge). Before we pick up this thread, some background on Teen Challenge is helpful.

Teen Challenge is a Christian drug-rehabilitation program. It serves as a ministry for people who have life-controlling problems and are without the necessary resources and opportunities to live productively. Founded in 1960 by Rev. David Wilkerson, an Assemblies of God minister, the original Teen Challenge Center was located in the Williamsburg section of Brooklyn, New York. Teen Challenge now operates worldwide, with more than 150 centers in the United States.[14] These centers provide, among other functions, school presentations, counseling, and weekly support group meetings.

Wilkerson first arrived in New York to work in a pioneering program dealing with street gangs in the late 1950s.[15] Once he developed a rapport with these young people, he saw that they needed help in coping with a variety of problems, including addiction and prostitution. On an even more basic level, he believed that these young men and women needed something positive to fill the void in their lives.

For Wilkerson that something was (and remains) devotion to Jesus. He believed that this, and this alone, formed the basis for the development of both a healthy personality and a satisfying life. A life devoted to Jesus begins with conversion (an emotional experience resulting in a personal relationship with Jesus), dedication to Christian principles, and an orientation to spiritual rather than material concerns.

After spending several years in East Harlem, Wilkerson judged drug addiction to be the greatest challenge facing people of that community.

With addicts comprising the vast majority of the young people coming to him, he felt that what was needed was a reality that was more powerful, more attractive, and more rewarding than the heroin needle. He concluded that only religious conversion was powerful enough to overcome drug addiction. By changing a person's heart and thought processes, you could change his or her behavior.

Beginning in 1964, the first Teen Challenge center began the transition to an induction and detoxification facility. The group also established a training center on a 200 acre farm in pastoral Rehrersburg, Pennsylvania–far from urban temptations.

Teen Challenge grew rapidly. Prizing independence, the program did not accept government money or assistance. Referrals and financial contributions came through a vast network of individuals, churches, and other religious organizations. Today, there is a Teen Challenge induction center in most large cities in the United States, as well as in Canada, Australia, Europe, Latin America, Asia, Africa, and the Caribbean.

According to the Teen Challenge philosophy, individuals using drugs cannot be helped until they reach the stage of desperation–"rock bottom." Each must admit to having a problem, accept personal responsibility for his or her downfall, and actively seek help.[16] The Teen Challenge induction centers are crisis units, accepting people off the streets for immediate help twenty-four hours a day. If an individual wishes to enter the residential program, he or she proceeds to an intake interview to determine whether or not the person is suited for the program. Teen Challenge accepts anyone (except someone who is "mentally ill") who has used drugs and indicates a willingness to abide by the organization's rules and practices.

As it evolved, the program was divided into three phases: first, induction, focusing on drug detoxification and rehabilitation; second, training; and third, reentry. The initial phase occurs at an induction center. This phase involves "cold turkey" drug detoxification with staff members remaining with new entrants to give them emotional support, hot baths, and rubdowns to make them as comfortable as possible.

A new entrant remains in residence at an induction center for three to six months. During the initial phase, a participant is encouraged to make a commitment and surrender to Jesus, as the cure for addiction.[17] To help make this decision, he or she spends time in daily prayer, Bible reading, and chapel services. These activities are designed to create a feeling of self-worth in an atmosphere of love, support, and warmth. However, firm discipline is also important. One of the key components of the rehabilitation phase centers on a participant's adherence to a system of rules and activities designed to build self-discipline and a sense of personal responsibility. The goal is to distance one from his or her past drug habits.

This initial period strives to instill discipline, develop Christian character, and help a resident gain insight about oneself and one's problems. Dependence on a personal commitment to Jesus as the solution for all one's problems continues to occupy a central position during the rehabilitation phase.

The training phase, lasting six to nine months, begins at a training center (or camp), usually in a rural area. Residents participate in Bible study and the fundamentals of Christian living, and take classes in secular subjects, such as English grammar and literature. In addition to routine chores at a center, such as housekeeping and kitchen duties, work in the rural training center is often of an agricultural nature. Farm chores provide residents with a sense of responsibility as well as good work habits. These attitudes help them learn to accept authority and rules, and also teach the importance of helping others. Ministers and teachers assist the residents with adjustment and other difficulties. Vocational skill training is also available.

At a training center, the residents live together, typically four to a room. The evolving camaraderie and spirit of community influence each participant's attitude and character.

Besides the supportive, orderly community and the emphasis on spiritual growth and development, the program uses other interventions. The most important is work therapy, offering the opportunity for concrete results in the form of physical output, which the individual can view as accomplishments. Work has a direct bearing on the program goal of helping each participant become a productive member of society.[18] In addition to teaching productive work habits, these programs generate income for the camp as a by-product.

The final phase of the program consists of reentry. During this period, a resident prepares for a drug-free, Christian life outside of Teen Challenge. The program strives to help participants develop their autonomy so that they will not substitute a new dependence on Teen Challenge for the old drug dependency. Because employment opportunities outside the program or the ministry are often limited for individuals with criminal records, inadequate education, or a history of drug use, most graduates study for the ministry or other work in churches and Teen Challenge centers. Many are motivated to answer the call to help others.

Teen Challenge employs a large staff. The leadership consists of ministers, missionary workers, church officials, and their spouses. Recovering addicts and others committed to the program's beliefs and methodology fill administrative positions, serve as directors of residences, counselors, Bible teachers, field representatives, and office workers. Teen Challenge does not employ secular psychologists, psychiatrists, or social workers. In its view, such services are not required because a drug user's rehabilitation comes from God's healing power, not the intervention of a human agency.

Bush and Teen Challenge

Bush had not called Olasky for two years, until mid-1995–more than six months after being elected governor of Texas. In June 1995, Rev. James Heurich, who was running the San Antonio chapter of Teen Challenge, was battling the Texas Commission on Alcohol and Drug Abuse (the Commission), which was trying to shut the center down.

In 1995, state regulators sought to close the San Antonio-based Teen Challenge of South Texas induction center because it did not meet the strict requirements for a drug treatment program. Besides noncompliance with a variety of the Commission's minor health and safety standards, such as having a torn carpet on the floor, putting minutes of a board meeting in the wrong file, and the failure to follow a directive for keeping files on clients, the principal complaint centered on the use of unlicenced drug counselors. The Commission's rules required that drug treatment facilities hire only credentialed chemical dependence counselors, trained in conventional anti-addiction techniques. Teen Challenge did not. It ran (and continues to run) its drug rehabilitation program with "homegrown" leaders, meaning ex-addicts who successfully completed the program and transformed their lives through a conversion to Christianity.

Teen Challenge's success rates in curing substance abusers, as analyzed in chapter 5, failed to sway John D. Cooke, the Commission's Assistant Deputy Director of the Program Compliance Division. "Outcomes and outputs are not an issue for us," Cook stated, taking a hard-nosed position. "If they want to call it treatment, then state law says they must be licensed."[19]

Refusing to bow to state licensing rules, Heurich fought to preserve Teen Challenge in San Antonio. Supporters of the organization staged a rally in 95-degree heat at the Alamo, the Texas symbol of defiance. Olasky, as advocate and journalist, showed up at the public rally.

In the end, Heurich remained in business, mainly because of the timely intervention of then Governor Bush. What caught Bush's attention was "how ridiculous it seemed" for a state agency to shut down a drug program that "was successfully fighting addiction."[20]

Bush's office stepped in and helped work out an agreement that allowed Teen Challenge to operate, while he looked for more permanent ways to promote the active involvement of people of faith in meeting social problems. Embracing the broad outline of Olasky's vision, Bush looked to

Olasky for guidance. The confrontation over Teen Challenge would be the starting point for implementing Olasky's vision across Texas.[21]

Bush's Implementation of a State-Level Strategy
to Promote the Involvement of FBOs
in Meeting Social Problems

After Bush reined in the Texas Commission on Alcohol and Drug Abuse, in May 1996 he established a task force, composed of state officials, clergy, and representatives from faith-based social service agencies with a mandate to cut state red tape hindering charities. Beyond the Teen Challenge problem and the need for new licensing procedures that would permit religious groups to operate free from the stranglehold of state bureaucratic procedures, Bush charged the Task Force "to make sure that there is an environment in Texas that fosters efforts by faith-based and other service organizations to meet the needs of our Texans who are in crisis." He stated, "There are many loving and caring Texans who want to help others...but to be successful, they need an environment that's free of government red tape and roadblocks. The state must ensure basic health and safety standards, but it must not be so process-oriented that we stifle programs of goodwill." He was convinced that local FBOs and service groups "can help assure that every Texan who needs child care can find it; where every Texan who needs a job or wants a job can find one; and every Texan can find the training necessary to free that person from dependency upon government."[22] Bush wanted the task force to recommend ways FBOs could work with the public sector "to help people in need without violating the important principle of separation of church and state, compromising the religious nature of their mission, or being shackled by government intrusion."[23]

In its December 1996 report,[24] the Task Force recommended the creation of alternative methods of accrediting faith-based social service provider. Specifically, it recommended allowing religious groups to be accredited by nongovernmental organizations whose standards met or exceeded state minimum licensing requirements.[25] The report also noted that the state should not "crowd out" the potential contributions of religious providers by "excessive" contracting regulations.[26]

To better enable faith-based chemical dependency programs to operate in Texas, the Task Force further recommended exempting from state regulation all religious chemical and alcohol rehabilitation centers offering nonmedical treatment, such as counseling and prayer.[27] It also encouraged more spiritually based programs in state prisons.[28]

As a funding mechanism, the Task Force expressed a preference for vouchers that would allow beneficiaries to choose from a range of religious and secular providers. Vouchers would increase the autonomy and dignity of recipients, stimulate competition and efficiency among providers, simplify monitoring, and provide a better match between a client's preferences and the services sought. A voucher program would, the report noted, help avoid constitutional questions regarding the separation of church and state. It would also protect the religious liberties of all parties by allowing beneficiaries to choose a provider they were comfortable with and by ensuring that FBOs could offer social service programs without having to change or water down their religious character.[29]

In a December 1996 executive order and through legislation enacted in 1997, Bush facilitated the efforts of state agencies working with FBOs. Bush made Texas the first state to sanction the redirection of public funds to faith-based programs. The executive order prohibited state agencies from snubbing or secularizing religious charities as contract grantees. He ordered Texas executive branch agencies to "take all necessary steps to implement" the Charitable Choice provisions of the 1996 Welfare Reform Act and to preserve participating faith-based organizations' "unique ecclesiastical nature."[30] As we will see in chapter 6, Charitable Choice, enacted as part of the 1996 Welfare Reform Act, permits religious groups to compete for federally funded state (or local) antipoverty social service contracts while protecting their religious character. In signing this executive order, Bush concluded that government does not have a monopoly on compassion. He asked, "Who better to help those who need help than people of faith who are following a religious imperative to love their neighbors, feed the poor, and help the needy?"[31]

Largely as a result of Bush's support, Texas became one of the few states to comply fully with Charitable Choice. As governor, Bush worked to open competition for social service contracts to FBOs more aggressively than any other state chief executive. As a result of Bush's initiative, the Texas Workforce Commission and the Texas Department of Human Services, together responsible for implementing welfare reforms in Texas, entered into numerous financial and nonfinancial contracts with religious-based social service providers for job counseling and training programs and child care, among the myriad of services needed by those trying to make the transition from welfare to work.[32]

Following the Task Force's recommendations, Bush then sponsored an array of bills intended to encourage religious organizations to provide social and welfare-related services, with a minimum of government oversight. For instance, in response to the Teen Challenge problem, he sought to make it easier for FBOs to offer drug treatment programs, outside the intrusive glare of the state. He also proposed allowing social service providers to be accredited by private bodies instead of state licensing agencies. In offering his legislative package, Bush noted, "These bills will empower private charities and churches and synagogues to take a more active role in solving some of our society's toughest problems." He continued, "I take strong exception with defenders of the status quo who say that this is just a government attempt to dump welfare caseloads on churches and synagogues."[33]

These proposals, enacted in June 1997, ensured that FBOs could provide social services in their way. One Texas statute, implementing the Task Force's recommmentation, exempts religious chemical dependency treatment programs that rely on faith to cure addiction from state licensure and regulations imposed on their secular counterparts, provided no medical services or treatment to minors is rendered.[34] This type of program must be conducted by a religious organization and be exclusively religious or spiritual in nature. Religious chemical dependency treatment program counselors in Texas may skip the hundreds of hours of training required of their state-licensed peers. Furthermore, the Texas Commission on Alcohol and Drug Abuse cannot prohibit these programs from using the terms "counseling," "treatment," or "rehabilitation." The act explicitly provides that it "is not intended to aid religion" and that the "exemption of faith-based chemical dependency treatment programs from licensure and regulation is not an endorsement or sponsorship by the state of the religious character, expression, beliefs, doctrines, or practices of the treatment programs."[35]

Child and youth care facilities, most of them church-based, could opt out-of-state licensing and choose to be accredited by state-approved private organizations, with standards equal to or exceeding those of the state.[36] Pursuant to a sunset provision contained in this 1997 statute, in the spring of 2001 Texas legislators let expire the provision exempting religious child care providers from state licensing. In part, the Texas legislature declined to renew the provisions because of allegations of child abuse at a Texas church home for problem teens.[37]

In June 1997, the Texas legislature also endorsed a resolution favoring prison ministries.[38] To combat the shortcomings of the existing penal system, the resolution sought to allot a greater role to "faith-based correctional programs, facilities, and initiatives" in the rehabilitation of criminal offenders. To this end, it encouraged "more use of faith-based programming in public prisons and jails and treating such programs on the same basis as nonreligious programs," "the operation of private, faith-based correctional facilities for willing inmates who are nearing release," and "one-on-one faith-based programs" as an alternative to incarceration or as part of postincarceration aftercare.

InnerChange and the Quest to Reduce Recidivision

When Chuck Colson, the founder of Prison Fellowship Ministries (considered in chapter 4) approached Texas prison officials with a proposal to operate a faith-based prerelease program in a state prison, they agreed at Bush's urging, even before passage of the legislative resolution.[39] Bush helped persuade state prison officials in March 1997 to embrace the InnerChange Freedom Initiative (InnerChange), Colson's brainchild, at Jester II (now the Carol S. Vance) Prison Unit in Sugar Land, just outside Houston.

InnerChange is a joint effort of Prison Fellowship Ministries, Houston area churches, and the Texas Department of Criminal Justice. Modeled after the APAC Prison in Sao Jose dos Campos, Brazil,[40] it is a Christian immersion program operated twenty-four hours a day. It seeks to cure prisoners by identifying sin as the root of their past problems and by encouraging prisoners to convert.

The State of Texas allowed InnerChange to set up a Christian prison, the nation's first, within, and in partnership with, a state facility.[41] Privately funded, voluntary, and open to anyone of any religion, its regimen makes Christian conversion and character training, with the aim of preventing prisoners from returning to a life of crime, its explicit goal. The program accomplishes this through eighteen months of intensive religious indoctrination in biblical teachings and proper Christian behavior. Inmates, who exhibit the ability to read at a sixth-grade level and a willingness to commit themselves to the religious curriculum (among other criteria), enroll in the seven-days-a-week regime designed to set them right and give them a new foundation before their return to society. The core idea is that lawbreakers can change if they embrace ethics and morality drawn from a fundamentalist Christian understanding of the Bible. This approach is anchored in biblical teachings that underscore the importance of taking personal responsibility for one's life, the value of work, the care for persons and property, and redemption through Christ.

Once in the program, the inmates move to a separate unit, a prison-within-the-prison, eating and bunking with fellow InnerChange participants. The state provides the prison facilities and guards. Supported by private donations, InnerChange pays the program's costs. InnerChange's professional staff and volunteer teachers and counselors operate the program.

The program entry point is eighteen months prior to an inmate's release. While in prison, inmates are paired with a Christian role model from the outside world. This volunteer mentor, mostly middle-aged, middle class, and white, visits a protege weekly in prison and offers one-on-one attention and advice on the transition to freedom. Mentors also pledge to be involved in an aftercare program.

The first phase, twelve months in length, provides training in life skills, such as anger management, family and marriage counseling, and intense instruction on the foundational principles of Christianity. The program consists of Bible study and memorization, prayer, commitment to Christian living, and inmates operating as a community with their own leadership team that meets daily to help resolve conflicts among participants.

There are no perks for those who volunteer for the program. Instead, inmates face a Bible boot-camp program, sixteen-hour workdays, limited television and recreation, and heavy study schedules. During the first phase, an inmate's day starts at 5:30 A.M., and ends at 10:30 P.M., and is structured around four core program areas: education, work, support groups, and mentoring. This is done in an evangelical manner designed to change hearts and, ultimately, behavior.

The second phase, lasting six months, focuses on the living application of the principles learned in the first stage. Program participants spend much of the day at off-site work programs where they may be building homes for Habitat for Humanity, cleaning parks, or engaging in other community service. They return in the evenings for more InnerChange classes and mentoring. As they head into their final month in the program, they begin a transition toward life beyond the prison. They are assured help in finding a job, a home, and a church on release.

InnerChange also includes, as a third phase, an additional six months of aftercare and follow-up once an inmate returns home. Aftercare offers support and encouragement throughout the struggles faced on release. Ex-prisoners continue to be mentored by volunteers affiliated with local churches.

InnerChange was just the right tonic for James Peterson, who was nearing the end of an eight-year sentence for embezzlement. All his life, Peterson recalled, he took the easy way out and quit–whether college, jobs, or marriage–when things got tough. After enlisting in InnerChange, he wrote a letter to his former boss asking for forgiveness and pledged to repay him. Peterson says, "He came to visit me in prison, and we reconciled our relationship to the glory of God."[42]

Myron Magnet: Another Bush Intellectual Guru

Karl Rove gave Bush, *The Dream and the Nightmare*,[43] a book by Myron Magnet of the Manhattan Institute, that helped crystallize Bush's thinking about culture and its impact on America's chronic social problems and the urban underclass. Bush read the book in 1998 while preparing to run for a second term as Texas governor and cites it as the most influential book he ever read, aside from the Bible.[44]

Magnet, the son of a physician and a 1950s housewife, grew up in Fall River, Massachusetts. After teaching English literature at Columbia University and receiving his Ph.D., he followed his interest in political theory to *Fortune* magazine. He specialized in urban problems and in the late 1980s wrote a series of articles on poverty and social policy that evolved into *The Dream and The Nightmare*.

Magnet's book is a scathing indictment of the attitudes of the 1960s and its unfortunate legacy to the poor–leading to their destruction. Magnet essentially blames the counterculture and its values for creating an entrenched, permanent underclass.

The new ethos, which emphasized personal liberation over the traditional virtues of family and work, affected all strata of American society but had a catastrophic impact on society's have-nots. For the "haves," this transformation of values was damaging. The "haves" may pay a price for experimenting with sexual liberation, drugs, and temporarily dropping out. However, the "haves" generally possess the financial and inner resources to survive in the new culture. For the "have-nots," who do not have these resources and thus have far less margin for error, it was devastating. Thus, the "have-nots" paid a disproportionately high price in ruined lives. From this historical lesson, Magnet argued that ideas, values, and culture have profound consequences for the urban underclass because they are most vulnerable to the effects of moral relativism.

The culture of the white elite, who sought bliss through self-gratification, nonaccountability, and a rejection of the work ethic, fomented attitudes and expectations that gave rise to illegitimacy, dependency, and crime. In his book, Magnet recounted the destruction of the values that traditionally helped people out of poverty.

First, disadvantage was seen by elites as resulting from exploitation, prejudice, and denied opportunities, rather than a lack of energy, character, or skill. The new culture made the urban poor unaccountable for their failures and turned them from the way of the bootstrapper. It robbed them of responsibility for their fate, and instead told them that they were victims of an unjust, racist society.

Second, the sexual revolution had a malignant impact on the family structure. A downward spiral evolved from free love to the single mother forced onto welfare. The anything-goes philosophy of the 1960s filtered down to the poor, who ceased to take responsibility for their actions–especially for having children out-of-wedlock. Underclass males proceeded heedlessly with new sexual conquests, rather than marrying the mother of one's child.

Finally, in the wake of the counterculture's generalized scorn for authority, standards, tradition, and behavioral norms, came an embrace of self-indulgence, indolence, and protest. The underclass permitted their children to imbibe the hedonism and lawlessness of the streets, rather than raising them to be law-abiding and drug-free.

In the wake of these social trends, Magnet recognized that a caste system had developed. He detailed the growth of a hard-core underclass who, generation after generation, have not broken free from poverty, despite economic booms and a host of governmental programs.

In sum, the plight of the underclass is a cultural matter. It is the product of a code of values born of the 1960s that bred hopelessness, defeatism, and a socially destructive lifestyle. According to Magnet, members of the underclass "lack the inner resources to seize their chance, and they pass on to their children a self-defeating set of values and attitudes, along with an impoverished intellectual and emotional development, that generally imprisons them in failure as well."[45]

After reading *The Dream and the Nightmare*, Bush invited Magnet to Austin for a brainstorming session with his cabinet. During the two-day visit, Magnet suggested that Bush start group homes for unwed teen mothers. In this structured environment, children could be with their mothers and both could receive outside guidance. Churches or charities would run these homes designed to provide a stable, virtue-oriented community where a mother could obtain a fresh start, and one less likely to take her down the same road. Bush responded by setting up four of these homes run by private groups, including one church-related group.

Preparing to Run for President and the Vision of "Compassionate Conservatism"

As he looked to gain the 2000 Republican presidential nomination, Bush once again turned to Olasky by making him head of his presidential campaign's policy subcommittee on religion. Magnet also served on several informal campaign policy groups in 1999 and 2000.

In early 1999, a group assembled by Stephen Goldsmith, the Bush presidential campaign's chief domestic policy advisor, met with Bush and his top aides to prepare for the upcoming presidential primary campaign. Olasky and John J. DiIulio, Jr., then a University of Pennsylvania professor, a leading researcher of faith-based social services, and a New Democrat, were there. Among the others were Robert L. Woodson, Sr., the African-American founder of the National Center for Neighborhood Enterprise (a nonprofit organization assisting local groups battling drugs, youth gangs, and teen pregnancy), and James Q. Wilson, an academic who studies character and social policy, urban problems, and crime.

The group met in a four-hour session trying to hammer out the policy of "compassionate conservatism," one of Bush's signature themes during the 2000 campaign. They discussed public policies for the poor. Bush asked what would work and what would not. However, the group did not reach a consensus. DiIulio, who regarded Olasky's vision as utopian, stated, "You're not going to solve these problems with just faith-based approaches. There's not enough money in civic society."[46] Olasky recalled that the discussion of particular FBOs engaged Bush.

In a July 22, 1999 speech, at the start of his presidential campaign, Bush sketched his kinder, gentler brand of conservatism. His vision of an ideal America had government turning to religious groups to help serve the poor.[47] In this landmark address, Bush said that the federal government should "rally the armies of compassion in our communities" by implementing various policies to promote FBOs. In addition to promoting new federal income tax incentives to encourage people to contribute more to charities and involving the "armies of compassion in some specific areas of need," Bush promised to change laws and regulations (consistent with the reforms made in Texas) hampering the cooperation of the public sector and FBOs to "allow private and religious groups to compete to provide services in every federal, state and local social program." Bush noted, "We found that government can spend money, but it can't put hope in our hearts or a sense of purpose in our lives." He continued, "This is done by churches and synagogues and mosques and charities that warm the cold of life. A quiet river of goodness and kindness that cuts through stone."

Bush straddled the views aired months earlier in Texas. Bush, refuting the idea that compassion is "soft" or "sentimental," said that charities should make demands on aid recipients. Bush noted: "At Teen Challenge...one official says, 'We have a rule: If you don't work, you don't eat.' This is demanding love–at times, a severe mercy. These institutions, at their best, treat people as moral individuals, with responsibilities and duties, not as wards or clients or dependents or numbers." Following Olasky, Bush also promised his administration would expand the "role and reach" of FBOs "without changing them or corrupting them." This was a victory for Olasky, and a nod to FBOs whose goal is to convert client-beneficiaries.

Bush also reflected the ideas of DiIulio. Bush advised that we should abandon the "destructive" idea that "if government would only get out of the way, all our problems would be solved." Bush urged looking "first to faith-based organizations, charities and community groups that have shown their ability to save and change lives,"–but be willing to admit that the challenges these groups face "are often greater than their resources." He said that "there are some things that government *should* be doing–like Medicaid for poor children. Government cannot be replaced by charities–but it can welcome them as partners, not resent them as rivals."

In this, the first major speech of his presidential campaign, Bush emphasized the "transforming power of faith." He noted the example of James Peterson, mentioned earlier in this chapter. Offered parole, Peterson turned it down, opting to stay in prison to finish the InnerChange program. As Peterson put it, "There is nothing I want more than to be back in the outside world with my daughter Lucy, [but] I realized that this was an opportunity...to become a living [witness]...for my brothers [in prison] and to the world. I want to stay in prison to complete the transformation [God] has begun in me." "Sometimes our greatest hope is *not* found in reform," Bush asserted, "It is found in redemption."

Before analyzing how the Bush administration implemented "compassionate conservatism" in chapter 7, we need to consider four building blocks: the Welfare Reform Act of 1996 (considered in chapter 3); what are FBOs (discussed in chapter 4) and are they effective in meeting social programs (examined in chapter 5); and then the Charitable Choice provisions predating the Bush presidency (analyzed in chapter 6). Let us begin with a brief survey of the evolution of welfare in America.

Notes

1.   Hanna Rosin and Terry M. Neal, "Converting Convicts to Christians," *Washington Post*, November 27, 1999, A1, A14.

2.   I have drawn on Hanna Rosin, "Applying Personal Faith to Public Policy: 'Changed Man' Advocates Church-Based Programs," *Washington Post*, July 24, 2000, A1; Hanna Rosin, "George W. Bush: The Record in Texas, Putting Faith In a Social Service Role, Church-Based Providers Freed From Many Rules," *Washington Post*, May 5, 2000, A1; Hanna Rosin, "The Seeds of a Philosophy: Dislike for 'Elite' Began at Yale," *Washington Post*, July 23, 2000, A1; Laurie Goodstein, "The 2000 Campaign: Seeking Counsel: Matters

of Faith: Bush Uses Religion as Personal and Political Guide," *New York Times*, October 22, 2000, Section 1, 19; Laurie Goodstein, "The 2000 Campaign: The Philosophy: Conservative Church Leaders Find a Pillar in Bush," *New York Times,* January 23, 2000, Section 1, 16.

3. Rosin, "Applying Personal Faith," A7.
4. *Ibid.*
5. *Ibid.*
6. Fred Barnes, "The Gospel According to George W. Bush," *The Weekly Standard* 4:26 (March 22, 1999): 20-23, at 21.
7. Joan Didion, "God's Country," *New York Review of Books*, November 2, 2000, 68-76, at 72. Bill Minutaglio, *First Son: George W. Bush and the Bush Family Dynasty* (New York: Times Book, 1999), 209-210, 280, portrays the scenario of Bush quitting drinking.
8. Rosin, "Applying Personal Faith," A7.
9. I have drawn on David Grann, "Where W. Got Compassion," *New York Times Magazine*, September 12, 1999, 62-65.
10. Governor George W. Bush, "Foreword" to Marvin Olasky, *Compassionate Conservatism: What It Is, What It Does, and How It Can Transform America* (New York: The Free Press, 2000), xii.
11. Marvin Olasky, *The Tragedy of American Compassion* (Washington, D.C.: Regnery Gateway, 1992).
12. *Ibid.*, 230.
13. Didion, "God's Country," 72.
14. I have drawn on Teen Challenge's website www.teenchallenge.com and John Muffler, John G. Langrod, and David Larson, "'There Is a Balm in Gilead': Religion and Substance Abuse Treatment,'" in *Substance Abuse: A Comprehensive Textbook*, 2d ed., eds. Joyce H. Lowinson, Pedro Ruiz, and Robert B. Millman (Baltimore: Williams & Wilkins, 1992), 588-590.
15. David Wilkerson with John and Elizabeth Sherrill, *The Cross and the Switchblade* (New York: Jove Books, 1993).
16. Don Wilkerson, *The Cross Is Still Mightier Than The Switchblade* (Shippensburg, Pa.: Treasure House, 1996), 56, 58, 60.
17. *Ibid.*, 61, 80.
18. *Ibid.*, 104-105.
19. Marvin Olasky, "Addicted to Bureaucracy," *Wall Street Journal*, August 15, 1995, A16.
20. George W. Bush, *A Charge To Keep* (New York: William Morrow, 1999), 213.
21. Grann, "Where W. Got Compassion," 64.
22. Peggy Fikac, "Bush Tells Task Force To Cut Red Tape Hindering Charities," *Dallas Morning News*, June 12, 1996, 34A.
23. Bush, *A Charge To Keep*, 214.
24. Governor's Advisory Task Force on Faith-Based Community Service Groups, *Faith in Action...A New Vision for Church-State Cooperation in Texas* (December 1996).
25. *Ibid.*, 8-14.
26. *Ibid.*, 10.
27. *Ibid.*, 16-20.
28. *Ibid.*, 20-23.
29. *Ibid.*, 5-6.
30. Executive Order, The State of Texas, Executive Department, Office of the Governor, GWB 96-10, December 17, 1996.
31. Kelley Shannon, "Bush Wants To Remove Barriers For Charities," *Austin American-Statesman*, December 18, 1996, B9.

32. R. G. Ratcliffe, "Christianity at Center of Texas Faith-Based Aid," *Houston Chronicle*, February 4, 2001, 1.

33. Bill Minutaglio, "Churches' Role in Social Services Debated," *Dallas Morning News*, April 6, 1997, 39A.

34. Texas Health and Safety Code §464.052.

35. Texas Health and Safety Code §464.059.

36. Texas Human Resources Code §§42.001, 42.101, 42.102. A number of other states have enacted provisions allowing child care centers run by religious groups to operate without state licenses. Pam Belluck, "Many States Ceding Regulations to Church Groups," *New York Times*, July 27, 2001, A1.

37. Hanna Rosin, "Faith-Based Youth Homes' 'Lesson'; Texas Backs Away From Unregulated Programs After Abuse Charges," *Washington Post*, June 21, 2001, A3; John Gibeaut, "'Welcome To Hell,'" *ABA Journal* 87:8 (August 2001): 44-51; Pamela Colloff, "Remember the Christian Alamo," *Texas Monthly* 29:12 (December 2001): 93-97, 163-170.

38. Texas Senate Concurrent Resolution, SCR 44, 1997.

39. Bush, *A Charge to Keep*, 215.

40. APAC (Association for the Protection and Assistance of the Condemned) Case Study, Sao Jose dos Campos, Brasil, n.d. available at www.restorativejustice.org/APAC/APAC_Humanita.h.

41. I have drawn on Angus Creighton, APAC (Association for the Protection and Assistance of the Condemned) Case Study, Texas, September 1998 available from www.restorativejustice.org/APAC/APAC_Texas.h; InnerChange Freedom Initiative website, www.ifiprison.org; Richard Vara, "Doing Time for God: Christian Prison Unit Seeks Spiritual Transformation of Inmates," *The Houston Chronicle*, May 17, 1997, Religion Section, 1; Gustav Niebuhr, "Using Religion to Reform Criminals: Texas Tries Immersion In Faith to Put Inmates on Right Path," *New York Times*, January 18, 1998, Section 1, 16; Hanna Rosin and Terry M. Neal, "Converting Convicts to Christians," *Washington Post*, November 27, 1999, A1; Jim VandeHei, "Some Texas Prisoners Get Religion–16 Hours A Day, 7 Days A Week," *Wall Street Journal*, January 26, 2001, A1; Samantha M. Shapiro, "At Evangelical Jails, Jesus Saves and Texas Pays the Bills," *Forward*, September 6, 2002, 1, 8.

42. William R. Mattox, Jr., "Prison Program Uses Faith To Transform Lives," *USA Today*, March 15, 1999, 17A. See also Rena Pederson, "Can God Change Prisoners?" *Dallas Morning News*, April 19, 1998, 2J.

43. Myron Magnet, *The Dream and The Nightmare: The Sixties' Legacy To The Underclass* (New York: William Morrow, 1993).

44. Ken Ringle, "The Hard Heart of Poverty: Bush's 'Compassionate Conservative' Guru Sees Culture as Culprit," *Washington Post*, April 3, 2001, C1. For background on Magnet and his ideas I have drawn on the Ringle article and Tevi Troy, *Intellectuals and the American Presidency: Philosophers, Jesters, or Technicians?* (Lanham, Md.: Rowman & Littlefield, 2002), 188-189.

45. *Ibid.*, C8.

46. Alison Mitchell, "Bush Draws Campaign Theme From More Than 'The Heart,'" *New York Times*, June 12, 2000, A1, A22.

47. Governor George W. Bush, Speech, "The Duty of Hope," Indianapolis, Indiana, July 22, 1999. The quotes in the following paragraphs are from this speech.

Chapter 3

The Transformation of America's Social Safety Net

Towns, counties, and states throughout American history made efforts to address poverty, but only the twentieth century witnessed the creation of expansive federal welfare programs. Make no mistake, welfare of some kind existed in America before the Social Security Act of 1935 and was a subject of debate then as it is now.

However, the New Deal and, subsequently, the Great Society marked the zenith of the American welfare state. During this time, Americans accepted government's moral obligation to provide at least temporary assistance to its less fortunate citizens. This burden on government–the price of "social justice"–was taken up by presidents of both parties. But with time, moral obligation evolved into something new. Child support and unemployment assistance, no longer temporary assistance, became the front line for an expansive interpretation of government's moral *cum* legal obligation: one that stressed entitlement and welfare rights.

Beginning in the mid-1980s with the publication of Charles Murray's book, *Losing Ground*,[1] policymakers and the public came to reevaluate the wisdom of welfare as a lifetime entitlement. A palpable sense that the system was not working provided the impetus for welfare reform. Not only did the system fail to deal with poverty, the concept of welfare rights facilitated and perpetuated it, demoralizing many recipients. Welfare programs encouraged dependency and the development of a permanent underclass, wards of the state. The promise of the twentieth century–greater efficiency through federal allocation of welfare dollars–had not been realized. Murray's book altered the terms of the debate over the modern American welfare state. In the wake of this reassessment came the Welfare Reform Act of 1996. Before we go further, let us step back and briefly survey welfare over the centuries.

Welfare before the Twentieth Century

In nineteenth-century America, disparate welfare providers were incapable of excluding one another. Though there was certainly disagreement over the best way to deal with poverty, this earlier approach to welfare accepted the legitimacy of the public sector together with private and religious organizations as social service providers. Bitter divisions existed over "outdoor" (or noninstitutional or cash relief that did not require entry into a poorhouse) and "indoor" (or institutional) relief. Despite the often contentious debate between proponents of outdoor or indoor relief, no one view had the credibility or power to marginalize the other.

In Connecticut, Massachusetts, and Virginia, among other jurisdictions, the practice of subsidizing individuals living in their own residences dated back to the seventeenth century.[2] American outdoor relief programs borrowed heavily from the English system under the Poor Law of 1601, including "grants-in-aid to the unemployable and...apprenticeship for the young and work relief for able-bodied adults."[3] Although the particular methods employed to help the destitute (including tax abatements, housing the poor in private homes at public expense, and monetary grants drawn from dedicated tax revenues) varied from colony to colony, and later from state to state, programs generally adhered to four principles inherited from England: first, poor relief was a public responsibility; second, it should be managed locally; third, if possible, individuals should look to their families and not the public; and fourth, children should be apprenticed to those who would train and care for them in their homes.[4]

With population growth in the early nineteenth century, the mounting cost of outdoor relief made localities reevaluate the utility of public assistance and led to reforms predicated on indoor (or institutional) relief. Prior to the Civil War, Americans looked at the nation's exploding cities with both admiration and horror. Manhattan's Broadway served as the place for a daily parade of splendor and finery. A few blocks away in the Five Points slum, murder, prostitution, drunkenness, and disease festered, threatening, it was believed, to engulf the entire city to the horror of the Protestant elite who sought greater social control over the destitute.

To deal with poverty and juvenile delinquency, advocates of indoor relief promoted the use of institutions like poorhouses, orphanages, and workhouses. Proponents of indoor relief contended that while outdoor relief and haphazard private charity encouraged pauperism, "[i]nstitutions...seal off...individuals from the corrupting, tempting, and distracting influences of the world long enough for a kind but firm regimen to transform their behavior and reorder their personalities."[5] Thus indoor relief's appeal derived not only from its purported cost savings, but also because it promised to transform people. The "unworthy" poor would be institutionalized in workhouses, among other facilities, to control their behavior so that they would acquire the habits of labor and prepare themselves for productive, self-sufficient lives.

The justification for indoor relief coincided with a greater emphasis placed on charitable organizations. Poorhouses and other institutions that formed the backbone of indoor relief received funds both from the government and private groups. Private organizations were thought to be better suited in dealing with the "unworthy," able-bodied poor because their poverty resulted from vices like intemperance and sloth.

Nineteenth-century reformers met the challenge with a moral crusade. Ideally, these social mission pioneers imposed discipline on the poor, providing material help and spiritual sustenance that shaped and uplifted character. Charity workers saw the need for temperance, diligence, and thrift, among other virtues. Acknowledging the debilitating impact of a negative environment to life, many also worked to improve housing, employment conditions, and the public schools. However, they viewed material deprivation as only a part of the problem. Rather, they emphasized the moral and spiritual causes of poverty. Believing that self-destructive behavior lay at the root of the poor's persistent problems, reformers set out to help tenement dwellers develop the self-discipline that would lift them from poverty and turn them into productive members of society. These reformers approached the poor with "tough love," imposed moral demands, without degrading or humiliating the destitute, and sought to avoid excessive harshness or softness.

Typical of these charity pioneers was Charles Loring Brace, a Yale graduate, writer, and missionary, who seized the moral challenge of the 1850s with inextinguishable passion.[6] Brace wanted to become famous and to "do good." He found his calling among New York's destitute. Before the Civil War, New York City was in a state of urban disintegration, marked by family violence, infectious disease, unemployment, and alcoholism. Brace's hope was for a moral and spiritual renewal.

He visited the adult poor in their homes and ceaselessly talked to them about the evils of alcohol and the need to shield their daughters from prostitution. America, he taught, offered boundless opportunity for anyone willing to work; no one should despair. Yet, when he returned to his own residence, he felt hopeless and defeated.

Brace concluded that adults could not be saved. They were irredeemable. He focused on rescuing their children whom he viewed as reformable.

In 1853, Brace founded the New York Children's Aid Society (the Society) with the overarching goal of building character. After a period of trial and error, he merged material support with spiritual reform. As a short-term solution, Brace set up lodging houses for homeless orphaned or abandoned children who were either parentless or fleeing from their violent, alcoholic parents. These houses provided shelter as well as secular (reading and industrial arts) and sectarian (Bible lessons) education. To preserve the independence of the young men, who often worked as urchin Manhattan newsboys, the lodging house charged a few pennies a day for room and board.

Then, taking a longer term approach, Brace conceived his best-known program–the orphan trains–to drain Manhattan of potential delinquents. He moved orphaned, abandoned, or runaway children, mostly boys aged seven to seventeen, out of crowded Manhattan to families throughout the United States, typically on Midwestern farms. The orphan trains took the homeless and destitute children of New York's grim slums to the countryside, where they were placed with farmers (as well as artisans and merchants) for employment–redemptive labor–and a new lifesaving chance. In addition to providing an opportunity to work, a father and a mother could give them the needed personal attention and discipline.

Brace aimed not only for physical distance from slum culture but also moral distance. The children were expected to work part-time and earn their keep. Placing about 105,000 children between 1853 and the early 1930s,[7] with the bulk being placed between 1853 and 1893, the Society imposed a mandatory program of moral reform on the children. The Society intended that the youngsters be adopted by the host families and receive a Christian upbringing.

During the last three decades of the nineteenth century, public welfare continued to play a secondary role to private charity, as exemplified by Brace and the New York Children's Aid Society. At the same time, scientific charity, based on rationality, efficiency, and planning, sought to facilitate greater cooperation and coordination among the various benevolent efforts.

Arguing for the abolition of public assistance and pointing to private charitable groups as the most effective vehicles for social change, the proponents of scientific charity, at that time, generally rejected public assistance. They believed that financial help without moral and spiritual direction was an outmoded and unscientific approach to welfare. Scientific charity also introduced the idea that public assistance, even though based on the principles of indoor relief, was not charity. Charity was by definition voluntary and thus distinct from tax-funded public assistance programs. Because volunteers were not coerced into helping others and were not encumbered by the bureaucratic tangles of public programs, the exponents of scientific charity believed that charitable organizations were best suited to help the hardcore, unworthy poor who often failed to take advantage of public assistance programs.

Continuing to attribute poverty to personal defects, private charities depended on the use of volunteers to regenerate character. Charities looked to personal contact between the rich and the poor. As volunteers, charities relied on kind, concerned, successful, middle- and upper- class people, who considered the downtrodden as objects for character reformation. A volunteer made house visits to his or her clients, served as a "friend," offered sympathy and wise counsel, discerned the moral lapse responsible for the problem, and supplied the requisite spiritual guidance designed to empower the poor. They sought to spark an inner change by inculcating virtues allowing recipients to become self-reliant and succeed on their own.

Welfare in the Twentieth Century before the 1996 Welfare Reform Act

Professional social work, based on "scientific" antipoverty strategies, blossomed at the turn of the twentieth century.[8] This emphasis on professionalism in poverty work led to a concurrent displacement of volunteers. Interest in the moral and spiritual causes of poverty began to decline, as well as the attempt to distinguish between the "deserving" poor, those trying to play by the rules, and the "undeserving" poor, those whose self-destructive and antisocial behavior caused their plight, with the latter group requiring a transformation of their character. Social and economic factors, such as the devastating impact of sickness and accidents or a lack of employment, were seen as the basic causes of poverty. Focusing on these insidious social and economic problems, reformers formulated policies to remedy the structural causes of poverty, but that increasingly ignored the moral and spiritual issues posed by the self-defeating behavior of the poor. As poverty gradually came to be viewed as a structural flaw, rather than a reflection of moral weakness, states turned to provide public assistance, beginning with programs for needy widows and for women with dependent children.

Prior to the 1930s, private charities (many of them faith-based), often working with and supported by local governments, offered assistance to the needy. The charity approach continued to acknowledge the poor as accountable persons who required moral and spiritual strengthening to help them overcome the challenges they faced. However, those with resources gradually had less time to volunteer. The better-off and the disadvantaged lived further and further apart, making it more difficult for charities to attract volunteers. When the rich and the poor did not live or worship together the efforts of volunteers became less effective. In order to fill the void, charities increasingly looked to paid professional staff. However, FBOs continued to play a key role in rehabilitating the needy until the federal government created its evermore complex and expanding web of welfare programs.

The Great Depression served as the catalyst for profound change. The 1930s witnessed massive unemployment and poverty which resulted from systemic problems, not merely personal difficulties. Poverty was no longer regarded as a matter of individual weakness, but as a socioeconomic problem.

The Great Depression overwhelmed charities as well as state and local governments. Private organizations and the nonnational public sector were unable to meet the massive demands for their services as a result of the economic collapse. So many individuals had financial needs through no fault of their own. Former members of the middle class were now unemployed, destitute, and hungry.

Because the needs were nationwide in scope and the existing institutional arrangements–charities or state and local governments–could not cope with the situation, the problem required a national approach. The federal government needed to fill the void and help the poor. Persistent and widespread poverty would therefore call for a deliberate, significant national commitment. The New Deal sought to use the federal government to do the job that private institutions as well as state and local governments could not do alone.

The New Deal ratified what had already become intellectual currency, namely, social science, planning, and the notion that the wealth created by the industrial economy (and then redistributed by the federal government) constituted a more efficient approach to poverty relief than the old mishmash of local public assistance and private charities. The federal government, now imbued with an optimism like that of nineteenth-century scientific charity proponents, came to implement and bear the cost of anti-poverty programs.

The federal government filled the gap and weakened FBOs, among other community-oriented, antipoverty organizations. FBOs found themselves crowded out not only by the sheer volume of public spending, but also by the unremitting hostility of social workers who wanted to reengineer society without religion. The dominance of private charity over welfare ended. Federal aid to the states and the accompanying rules foreclosed, to a large degree, the responsibilities of both the local private and public sectors.

Federal efforts also marked a turn to professionally run, bureaucratic governmental programs, emphasizing material transfers, not moral and spiritual concerns. With millions not responsible for their economic plight, federal government programs made sense as temporary measures. However, even when jobs became available, these programs persisted.

From its modest beginning as part of the Social Security Act of 1935, Aid to Dependent Children blossomed into a key element of the American welfare landscape. In addition to providing public assistance for the blind and the needy aged who were not entitled to pensions, the 1935 Social Security Act implemented a public assistance system for destitute children from single-parent families. The federal government gave funds to the states, on a matching basis, to provide cash payments to single mothers with dependent children so that these needy minors could be cared for in their own residences. As part of this federal program for outdoor (non-institutional) relief of youngsters, the states were responsible for setting their own eligibility standards and benefit levels, within broad federal guidelines, which resulted in wide disparities in payments.

The 1950 amendments to the Social Security Act provided grants to needy mothers (or other caretaker relatives) of dependent children. In 1962, the program was renamed Aid to Families with Dependent Children (AFDC). Sparked by the continued prevalence of poverty in the United States, the 1960s witnessed an expansion of federal programs as part of President Lyndon Baines Johnson's Great Society and War on Poverty. The Great Society of the 1960s, building on its New Deal roots, was based on the notion that the federal government possessed the power to create a new socioeconomic environment, with funds dispersed through vast, "rational" bureaucracies, that would enable the poor to rise from poverty.

Poverty continued to be regarded as the result of external causes rather than personal defects. Americans became reluctant to assess the behavior of the poor in moral and spiritual terms. The 1960s brought a change in attitudes of both welfare recipients and many of the well-off. Policymakers sanitized welfare and lifted the stigma in the minds of recipients. Legislators sought to eliminate poverty by passing out dollars to bring all household income levels above the poverty line. There was a common understanding that society owed a living to the able-bodied, even if they chose not to work.

With the coming of the Great Society, social workers and poverty advocates announced that asking the poor to help themselves represented a form of blaming the victim. Those in need were seen as helpless victims of social and economic forces beyond their control, including racism, unemployment, and the maldistribution of income and wealth. The poor were viewed as passive recipients incapable of taking action on their own to whom the public sector would give financial assistance. Inner-city residents needed income transfers, not self-control, or at least that is what the prevailing wisdom maintained. From the mid-1960s until 1996, welfare policies almost exclusively aimed at meeting material needs. The welfare establishment came to see it as a moral duty to get people on (and not off) welfare.

AFDC, an open-ended entitlement program, became the largest category in the federal government's welfare system. It created and sustained the underclass by providing a steady supply of cash to single mothers. After 1965, the federal government reimbursed states, on a formula basis, at a minimum of 50 percent and a maximum of 83 percent of their respective welfare payments, inversely related to a state's per capita income.[9] AFDC supported dependent children (generally under age eighteen) who were deprived of parental support or care because their father (or mother) was absent from the home continuously, or was incapacitated, deceased, or unemployed. AFDC prohibited aid to two-parent families, unless the second parent was incapacitated or unemployed. Payments were also permitted for a child's needy caretaker relative (usually the mother), or another person in the home deemed essential to the child's well-being, or for a pregnant woman in her third trimester of pregnancy.[10] Federal law also set income and asset limits for AFDC eligibility and required that all income received by an AFDC recipient be counted against the AFDC grant, apart from income specifically excluded by definition or deduction. However, AFDC had no work requirement. AFDC thus provided mothers with a monthly cash allowance on the condition that they not work, not save, and not get married.

From 1965 to 1981, the federal government greatly expanded the entitlement concept by creating additional programs, including the establishment of Medicaid, that states were required to provide to AFDC recipients, as well as boosting welfare spending. In the late 1960s and early 1970s, federal courts converted AFDC into a program that gave recipients more secure entitlements to welfare benefits as a matter of legal right, with limits on how the states could restrict access to benefits or make invidious demands on recipients.[11] Courts did, however, place some limits on welfare entitlements, for instance, by requiring recipients to accept visits by caseworkers and participate in certain types of programs as a condition to receiving benefits. States were not required to index AFDC benefits for inflation and so many did not, thereby letting the real value of AFDC benefits decrease. However, welfare recipients also were eligible for food stamps, Medicaid, housing and child care subsidies, and school lunch benefits.

The transformation to an expansive welfare state thus involved a focus on sending monthly checks to poor, unwed mothers. An impersonal (often incompetent and insensitive) welfare bureaucracy came to replace personal contact, which was crucial to nineteenth-century relief efforts.

Although some tinkering occurred with the entitlement programs, few significant changes occurred in the workings of the programs or in their outcomes. For instance, the 1988 Family Support Act melded conservatives' demands for work requirements with liberals' desire to provide government services to prepare people for work. In addition to imposing new procedures for collecting child support payments from absent parents (generally fathers), the 1988 Act established the Job Opportunity and Basic Skills (JOBS) Program, a capped entitlement (set at, for example, $1 billion in fiscal year 1996[12]) to assure that needy families with children obtained the education and training that would, in theory, help them avoid long-term welfare dependency.[13]

JOBS required states to offer recipients educational activities, job skills training, and job readiness activities to help prepare participants for work as well as job placement.[14] AFDC recipients were obligated to participate in JOBS, but their participation did not require them to work. Furthermore, those who were ill, incapacitated, or of advanced age, those needed at home because of the illness or incapacity of another member of the household, those who were the parent or caretaker of a child under three years of age, or otherwise a member of an exempted group, were not required to participate.[15] These categories exempted about one-half of the caseload.[16] In any case, many, even if eligible, never participated because of insufficient staff.

Despite the JOBS program's stated goal to prevent long-term dependency, the broad exemptions and staffing difficulties were such that little changed. Furthermore, JOBS did not impose a work requirement or a lifetime limit on ADFC benefits. In short, it was a paper reform that failed to move recipients off welfare.

For decades, the federal government and the public at large paid little attention to the impact of entitlement programs supplying the poor with material resources. The welfare establishment seemed untroubled by dependency, a decline in diligence, or the growth in unwed motherhood, and instead pinned the blame on a decrease in the demand for blue collar jobs resulting from global economic trends. Entitlement advocates maintained that young, unskilled black males could not form stable families because of an inability to find jobs to support themselves, their wives and their children. Additionally, as more people moved away from their home towns and into cities in order to find work, the censuring role that neighborhoods had provided in the past ceased to exist. As a result, it was much easier for a man to refuse to marry a woman whom he had gotten pregnant, since he no longer had to face the wrath of his community.

The impetus behind welfare reform was not budgetary but rather the growing sense that the system was not working. Federal spending on AFDC never surpassed one-half of 1 percent of the American Gross Domestic Product, a level reached in 1972; this figure then fell to only one-fourth of 1 percent by 1996.[17] However, we failed to buy our way out of poverty. Enrollment soared to an all-time peak in 1994, covering 5 million families and nearly one-seventh (14.2 percent) of all U.S. children.[18] As many children (under age eighteen) were in poverty in 1995 (20.8 percent) as in 1965 (21.0 percent).[19] Instead of reducing poverty, the welfare system actually perpetuated it.

Gradually, more and more Americans began to understand more clearly the failure of the Great Society and the ever-expanding antipoverty effort. Although the Great Society initiatives made advances in education (notably the widely praised Head Start Program for preschoolers from low income families), over the years, the well-intended wave of publicly financed programs for the poor only contributed to the problems they were trying to solve by creating a culture of dependency, discouraging work and marriage, and contributing to the collapse of the family.

Welfare became a permanent way of life. Millions checked into the welfare state and never checked out. Mothers (and their children) who stayed on AFDC for prolonged periods became a self-perpetuating underclass. The everflowing material aid made dependency addictive. Among adults receiving AFDC benefits, work efforts dropped sharply and thrift vanished. During the 1980s and through 1995, fewer than one in ten of AFDC adult recipients worked.[20] Welfare recipients could get by without exercising virtues, such as responsibility, hard work, and thrift, that otherwise would have increased their self-reliance.

The welfare system did not set out to encourage out-of-wedlock births. Subsidizing illegitimacy, not unexpectedly, however, led to a significant rise in the number of births to unwed mothers on welfare.[21] When we allowed welfare programs to become the surrogate breadwinner, thereby making husbands expendable, the proportion of families headed by single women rose. By the mid-1990s more than one-half of AFDC children were born out of marriage; three-quarters had an able-bodied parent who lived away from home.[22]

There occurred a serious lack of role models. The rise of single-parent families posed difficulties for the socialization of many African-American children, in particular. Mothers unassisted by husbands often found it difficult to discipline any of their children.

Welfare programs (particularly AFDC) had unintended consequences that resulted in values flouting middle-class norms, forming, perhaps, the core reason for dysfunctional behavior in the inner cities. A paternalistic system of dependency came to characterize welfare arrangements based on governmental disincentives for single mothers to work and marry.

Increasingly, policymakers saw the need to deal with problems not faced during the New Deal, namely, harmful patterns of individual and parental behavior. The government could no longer be indifferent to how welfare recipients lived and raised their children.

The 1996 Welfare Reform Act

The Personal Responsibility and Work Opportunity Reconciliation Act of 1996[23] (the Welfare Reform Act) represented an unprecedented departure from political orthodoxy, and reversed six decades of federally guaranteed minimum levels of assistance, especially for children. It emerged in the wake of a "revolution" in Congress. Republicans gained control of Congress, while the first "New Democrat" president, William Jefferson (Bill) Clinton, sat in the White House. In 1994, congressional Republicans campaigned on a platform that pledged to drastically reform the welfare system. Thus, the confluence of events, both a Congress and a president willing to radically change the welfare state, was not coincidental but instead a reflection of the public's growing disappointment with the status quo. A new consensus had formed around reducing poverty, not through monetary transfers, but through the efforts of the poor themselves.

The Welfare Reform Act sought to provide limited cash assistance to needy families so that children could be cared for in their own residences (or in homes of relatives), while at the same time weaning parents off of government assistance by promoting job preparation and work.[24] At their core, the "tough" measures were meant to change behavior. Because single mothers receiving AFDC payments were deemed capable of supporting themselves and their children, they were expected to enter the labor force. A work requirement and a clear time limit for assistance lay at the heart of legislative reform. Proponents maintained that the certainty of a fixed cut-off date on benefits would promote self-sufficiency by removing welfare as a viable long-term alternative.

Work would serve as the antidote to welfare and child poverty. The able-bodied poor would be better off, economically and psychologically, in menial, low-wage jobs, than as welfare recipients. Work would not only provide income, it also would boost their sense of self-worth and hope for the future. It would impose discipline and regularity into otherwise disordered lives. The rigors of the workday would spark the development of a more structured lifestyle for the newly employed and their families. Rather than passivity, ex-welfare recipients would see that they had some degree of control over their fate. It would be unreasonable not to place some expectations on the poor to meet.

By repealing AFDC as of July 1, 1997, the Welfare Reform Act basically did the following: abolished entitlements to individual or family assistance under federal law (but entitlements still could exist under state law); reorganized federal contributions to various public assistance programs; and created one capped block grant program to the states, known as the Temporary Assistance to Needy Families (TANF). The TANF block grant program provides states with a fixed, annual monetary payment (not adjusted for inflation) by the federal government based on each state's past expenditures for certain public assistance programs, allowing states to choose the most favorable of the three historical benchmark periods.[25] With a capped block grant regardless of whether welfare rolls rise or fall, states have the incentive to cut caseloads because they could keep the unexpended funds. The TANF block grants also permit each state to design its own cash assistance program, within certain federal guidelines. (The states, in turn, could authorize counties to devise their own systems.) The result is a patchwork of various rules and programs. One basic federal statutory limit exists. A state may give TANF assistance to a family only if it includes a minor child or a pregnant woman.

Similar to AFDC, under TANF states decide how needy a family must be to receive assistance and establish their own maximum benefit levels. Unlike AFDC, TANF contains no federal rules about the treatment of earnings. Most states have raised the earnings limits above those that existed under AFDC, thereby permitting recipients to keep more of their benefits as their earnings increase. The Welfare Reform Act also gave states access to a $2 billion contingency fund that expired at the end of fiscal year 2001 for relief in the event of a recession.[26]

The federal role is basically limited to sending states money, ensuring that states report the main features of their redesigned programs, monitoring state compliance with specified performance goals, and promoting and facilitating the sharing of information and ideas among states. State and local governments became problem solvers, rather than merely implementers of federal rules. States fashioned their own programs to fit their own political, economic, and social circumstances.

Beyond changing the federal-state spending mechanism, the Welfare Reform Act conditioned federal funding assistance on a set of objective criteria–federal mandates.[27] Time limits and work requirements replaced open-ended entitlements to cash assistance, giving recipients a stronger incentive to move into the labor market. There were no longer guaranteed benefits,[28] which meant that there was no lifetime cash entitlement for any individual or family. Even if eligible for assistance, the Welfare Reform

Act placed fixed time limits in order to avoid long-term welfare dependency. There was a five-year cumulative lifetime limit (or less, at a state's option) for an adult receiving cash assistance from federal TANF funds.[29]

States may, however, exempt part of their caseload from the time limit on benefits. Recipients who receive benefits for five years can continue to receive money, so long as those eligible for the hardship or other exemptions, generally speaking, long-term, deep obstacles to work, do not exceed 20 percent of a state's caseload.[30] However, even when the federal limits were reached, states and municipalities could spend their own funds helping poor families.

The Welfare Reform Act also set work trigger time limits. The state plans must demonstrate that they require able-bodied welfare recipients to work or engage in specified work activities designed to make them employable after receiving two years of cash assistance.[31] Single-parent recipients were required to work (or engage in work activities) twenty hours per week in fiscal year 1997, increasing to thirty hours per week by fiscal years 2000-2002, with two-parent families required to work thirty-five hours per week.[32] The two-year time limit imparted some sense of urgency not only to welfare families but also to caseworkers who were forced to help clients prepare for and find work. However, the work reward policies adopted by many states enabled many recipients to remain on welfare and receive cash assistance even if they took a job.

There were exemptions from the work rule for a single custodial parent caring for a child under age six who could not find child care for one or more specified reasons and, at a state's option, for those with children under age one.[33] Unlike AFDC that provided a federal guarantee of child care to current (and former) welfare recipients who needed it to work or study, the Welfare Reform Act contained no child care guarantees (although Congress provided additional funds for child care by directly increasing the funding of the Child Care and Development Block Grant program and allowing states to use TANF funds for child care).

The Welfare Reform Act required each state to place a specific percentage of its TANF caseload in jobs or work activities, thereby forcing state (and local) agencies to assist the needy in becoming self-sufficient. States had to have work participation rates of 25 percent in 1997, which rose to 50 percent in 2002. The two-parent family rate went from 75 percent in fiscal year 1997 to 90 percent in fiscal year 1999.[34] Participation in programs to meet the challenges of harder cases, such as those involving domestic violence or substance abuse, did not count as a required work activity. Thus, individuals in these programs did not figure into a state's work participation quota.

Substantive penalties and rewards encouraged states to meet the work participation guidelines that did not exist under AFDC. The act imposed cash sanctions on states that failed to meet the escalating work requirements. A wide array of penalties were available, including a 5 percent loss in a state's block grant for the first failure to meet the work participation rate. The penalty increased by 2 percent for each consecutive failure, with a maximum reduction of 21 percent.[35] Conversely, a state that performed well could receive a bonus of up to 5 percent of its block grant.[36]

For both needy and nonneedy families, the Welfare Reform Act also sought to prevent and reduce teen pregnancies and out-of-wedlock births, as well as encourage the formation and maintenance of two-parent families.[37] In enacting the welfare reform law, members of Congress placed considerable emphasis on reducing teen pregnancies and out-of-wedlock births. Congress made changing sexual and reproductive behavior a high priority by committing hundreds of millions of dollars over five years (in addition to the TANF block grants) to reward states that reduce the number of out-of-wedlock births and abortions and to promote sexual abstinence by those who were not married.

The Welfare Reform Act, however, contained only weak illegitimacy provisions. The federal government basically pursued a hands-off strategy. As a condition to receiving assistance, single mothers under the age of eighteen were required to live with an adult relative or in an adult supervised setting.[38] If a high school dropout, they were also required to attend school once their youngest child is twelve weeks old.[39]

The Welfare Reform Act included an illegitimacy bonus of $100 million a year. From 1999 to 2002, the five states that achieved the greatest decrease in out-of-wedlock births among all women (not just teens or those on welfare), without any increase in abortions, each received $20 million annually. (If fewer than five states qualified, each would have received $25 million annually.)[40] However, the act was silent on how the states should go about reducing out-of-wedlock births and abortions. Although Congress considered imposing a family cap (i.e., denying increased cash payments to any woman who conceived or gave birth to a child while on welfare), this provision was not included in the Welfare Reform Act. Congress decided to let the states bear the burden of deciding whether to impose a family cap. About twenty states thus far have chosen to impose such a cap designed to change a potential mother's cost-benefit calculus for childbearing.

Encouraging sexual abstinence was another goal of the Welfare Reform Act. Funds were available under the act for states to establish programs to promote abstinence by unmarried persons.[41] The 1996 act guaranteed funding of $50 million annually for five years, from 1998 through 2002.

States were also required to match every four dollars of federal funds with three dollars of state funds. However, the Welfare Reform Act stipulated that the funds could only be used for programs advocating abstinence until marriage and could not be used to teach about condoms or contraceptives or give any information that might undermine the abstinence message.

The Welfare Reform Act also recognized the important role of fathers in childrearing. The act enhanced state enforcement of child support orders by emphasizing the establishment of paternity and cracking down on absent fathers.[42] This was intended to increase the perceived liability of unmarried fathers, causing them to become more responsible in their sexual behavior. Under the Welfare Reform Act, states must operate a child support program meeting federal requirement to be eligible for TANF funds. In brief, any mother who needed help in locating an absent father, establishing paternity, or setting up (or enforcing) a support obligation could apply for publicly funded services. The 1996 law thus required states to increase the percentage of fathers identified, established an integrated, automated network linking all states with information about the location and assets of absent fathers, and mandated that states implement more stringent enforcement techniques.

Usually, however, only part of the collected support is given to the mother and child. State governments typically take the rest as reimbursements for cash assistance payments made to the family. States have the option to decide how much, if any, of these child support collections will be passed through to a family. (Ending the present welfare cost recovery system would eliminate a major disincentive for fathers to pay child support and would substantially reduce child poverty.)[43] States also decide whether they treat any child support passed through to the family as income, which would in turn reduce or eliminate TANF payments.

As a result of the Welfare Reform Act, there is a new consensus that it is morally incumbent on the poor to work and seek self-sufficiency. Helping former welfare recipients retain employment may be even more difficult (but more important) than aiding them find work. Developing a system that encourages independence will cost more than the old approach because of the need to implement various structural reforms that put public funds, as many states have done, into child care, job training and placement (particularly programs directly linked to jobs in demand in a local economy),[44] and subsidies for transportation. Welfare mothers continue to remain vulnerable to child care crises. They also face difficulties in getting from inner cities to suburban jobs. States will need to continue to provide subsidies for child care and transportation to help low-income workers obtain jobs and remain employed.[45]

The Impact of Welfare Reform

Despite critics' dire prediction, there have been dramatic decreases in both welfare enrollment and child poverty. Since 1996, welfare rolls nationwide plummeted. From August 1996 to December 2001, there was a 57 percent decline in the number of welfare recipients, a decrease of nearly 7 million individuals (from 12.2 million to 5.2 million).[46] There were caseload reductions from January 1997 to June 2000 in every jurisdiction throughout the United States, ranging from a low of 10 percent in the District of Columbia to a high of 85 percent in Wyoming, followed closely by Idaho and Wisconsin.[47]

Child poverty also declined from 20.8 percent (14.6 million) of those under age eighteen in 1995 to 16.3 percent (11.7 million) in 2001. In households headed by women and in African-American families the decline in child poverty was especially sharp. The 2001 figure was the lowest child poverty rate since 1979.[48]

As more AFDC recipients went to work and fewer persons joined the rolls, caseloads and welfare bureaucracies shrank. Welfare offices turned into job centers; caseworkers become career counselors. Great hoards of people were not put on the streets. Neither did the weakening of the entitlement-based safety net subject young women and children to grave danger or great suffering, such as homelessness, child abandonment, abuse, or neglect.[49]

Five factors account for these positive trends, apart from the direct, significant impact of welfare reform, its work requirement and the lifetime benefits limits.[50] First, the economic boom and the strong job market during the second half of the 1990s played a significant part. The American economy produced work for all who wanted it, helping former welfare recipients move into the labor force.

Second, welfare recipients were not as helpless and hopeless as previously thought. They found positions in the workplace; individuals who were capable of getting jobs no longer chose welfare. This was based, in part, on an altered moral understanding that diligence and self-reliance are better than dependency. Single mothers gained work experience and the confidence to find another job if they have to.

Third, the child care market expanded to meet the increased demand. Welfare caseloads dropped, freeing up public funds. Many states subsidized child care. Single mothers also found informal child care with family and friends. The greater availability of child care (and the growth of after-school and supervised recreational programs) allowed more women to gain employment.

Fourth, former welfare recipients had (and continue to have) other sources of support, including unreported jobs and other off-the-books income, as well as funds provided by live-in boyfriends, other household members, family members, or friends. Nonworking mothers residing with (or receiving support from) others could get by, especially if they continued to receive other government benefits, such as food stamps.

Fifth, the complex federal wage subsidy, opaquely called the Earned Income Tax Credit (EITC), that only provides tax benefits for those who work, helps turn low-wage positions into jobs with a livable wage.[51] So that working families are not trapped in poverty, the EITC, a work-based wage supplement through the federal income tax system for families earning as much as $32,000 per year, provides a maximum benefit of nearly $4,000 per year to an employed mother with two children and nearly $2,400 to an employed mother with one child. It is a refundable tax credit for qualified working persons who have earned incomes below certain specified levels. Those who are eligible can use the credit to reduce their tax liabilities; they may also receive a refund from the IRS if the amount of the credit exceeds their federal income tax liabilities. Thus, the credit provides a monetary supplement to a paycheck. Furthermore, the EITC neither imposes new wage and benefit mandates on businesses nor does it require a massive administrative bureaucracy. States have also created or expanded their own EITC-like tax credits.

It seems likely that Congress will continue to increase the benefits provided by the EITC to provide a subsidy to those who are employed in jobs that do not enable them to earn enough to break out of poverty.[52] Additionally, subject to budgetary constraints, more states will enact their own tax credits and provide other wage supplements for those employed in low-paying jobs.

Where Do We Go from Here?

Millions of poor people do not need public assistance. Overall, welfare rolls have declined dramatically. However, caseload declines have been uneven. Most states have fallen far short of the progress evidenced by the leading states, such as Wisconsin. Generally caseload declines have also occurred more rapidly among whites than among African-Americans and Hispanics. The greatest decreases have been found among white recipients, those not in large cities, and among women who are not part of the underclass. In short, those who were most easily employed found jobs.

Recipients of funds provided by Temporary Assistance to Needy Families Grants are increasingly concentrated in inner cities. Eighty-nine

American urban counties contain about one-third (32.6 percent) of the total U.S. population, but had an increasing share of the national caseload, up from 47.5 percent in 1994 to 58.1 percent in 1999.[53] In 1999, ten urban counties (Los Angeles County, New York City, Cook County [Chicago], Philadelphia County, San Bernadino County, Wayne County [Detroit], San Diego County, Sacramento County, Fresno County, and Cuyahoga County [Cleveland]), with only 12.2 percent of the overall national population, had nearly one-third (32.7 percent) of the nation's welfare cases, up from 24.0 percent in 1994.[54]

The racial composition of the welfare caseload also shifted. From 1997 to 1999, for example, the portion of TANF families reporting their race as white dropped from 42 percent to 33 percent; African-American families rose from 34 percent to 46 percent. The share of Hispanic families stayed roughly the same, increasing from 18 percent to 21 percent, as did families of other races.[55] Non-Hispanic black (37.3 percent in fiscal year 1998) and Hispanic (20.1 percent in fiscal year 1998) TANF adult recipients together outnumber non-Hispanic whites (35.8 percent in fiscal year 1998) more than 3 to 2.[56]

Furthermore, there is a growing trend for children receiving TANF benefits to be living with neither parent.[57] In fiscal year 2000, 34.5 percent of welfare families lacked an adult recipient, up from 21.5 percent in fiscal year 1996.[58] Children often become child-only cases, when a mother transfers responsibility for a child to a grandparent or other relative. Mothers choose to allow their children to continue receiving assistance by placing them with a relative who is exempt from the work requirements and the time limits.

The impact of the recession that began in 2001 remains unclear. Despite the economic slowdown, most people who left welfare for employment were still working. Welfare rolls increased modestly in the downturn[59]; however, they could balloon again in a serious, long-lasting recession. Because many states opted for a strict, work-first philosophy, striving for quick placements in low-skill positions in order to cut caseloads, former welfare recipients with marginal skills and minimal job experience may be among the first let go in tough economic times. To deal with increased unemployment among the working poor, states may turn to transitional, publicly funded community service job programs that provide work experience leading to placement in permanent positions. States could also help former welfare recipients maintain their employment (or at least their employability) by upgrading their skills to improve their job prospects.

Because of their often brief and irregular job stints, former TANF recipients may not qualify for unemployment insurance benefits, typically lasting up to twenty-six weeks (but temporarily extended for up to an additional thirteen weeks for workers in states suffering severe economic distress as part of the economic stimulus package passed by Congress in 2002),[60] forcing a return to cash welfare assistance. This is because state-run unemployment insurance benefit programs are basically financed at the state level. State taxes levied on employers pay for the unemployment benefits with the federal government paying the cost of administering the unemployment insurance program. States have a wide latitude as to the tax bases they use, the tax rates, and the structure of their programs. Some generalizations, however, can be offered. Low-wage workers are often unable to qualify for unemployment benefits because eligibility is tied to previous earnings. States have diverse and complex methods of determining eligibility. In many states, an individual must have worked at least six months out of a twelve-month period, but earnings in the most recent three to six months often do not count in computing the benefits. Furthermore, an individual generally must have earned a specified minimum amount, typically only a few thousand dollars, while employed to be eligible for unemployment insurance benefits thereby cutting out many new, temporary, or part-time workers.

Moving hard-to-employ TANF recipients into the workforce remains difficult, but not impossible. Certain characteristics of recipients or their children, such as poor physical or mental health (or disability), the lack of a high school diploma, limited English language proficiency, exposure to domestic violence, or substance abuse, often make engaging in work and functioning on a day-to-day basis difficult.[61] States, therefore, need to provide work-preparation activities to meet the needs of these hard-to-employ TANF recipients. As part of an approach based on building supports for the working poor, states ought to offer effective social services to assist those facing the highest barriers to work–mental disabilities, substance abuse, domestic violence, or a lack of education. Programs to remove barriers to entering and staying into the work force include intensive mental health services and training to provide marketable job skills for those lacking formal education. Of particular interest is an attack on illiteracy which underpins many social ills, including chronic joblessness. All localities in the United States need to strive to offer quality community-based literacy (or reading improvement) programs.

Because of circumstances beyond their control, some will be incapable of self-sufficiency. Those unlikely to find or hold a job include the severely physically disabled, the chronically ill, those with severe learning problems, or those with long histories of drug and alcohol abuse. These persons will need to be exempt from workfare requirements so as to be able to continue to receive government support. States will need to separate out those who simply do not want to work, even if able (those who are shirkers), from those who are unable to work for one reason or another. The "deserving" hard-to-employ ought to be funneled into disability, not welfare, programs.

It is also unclear whether the work requirements for women will deter teen pregnancies and out-of-wedlock births and whether the enhanced enforcement of child support obligations will make males accept familial responsibilities and look after their offspring. One promising prospect is the fatherhood movement that insists males take responsibility for their children, as well as more aggressive efforts to establish paternity and enforce child support orders. Men must understand the serious consequences associated with fathering a child. Fathers need to be more than economic providers. Hopefully, cultural (and policy) changes will lead them to become more involved parents. However, it is important to realize that many fathers of children in low-income households have limited education and are unemployed (or underemployed) and thus lack the resources to provide meaningful child support.[62] States ought to be encouraged (or required) to help fathers enter the labor force and increase their earnings by providing male-oriented employment and training services. Improving male employment status and thus their marriageability may encourage marriage.

Although fewer people now consider teen sexual activity as inevitable, there is no agreement as to how to reduce the teen childbearing and nonmarital births. Significant disagreements abound, mirroring America's cultural wars, on the means to achieve these goals–premarital sexual abstinence or protection for unmarried sexually active youths. There is, therefore, a wide variation among state programs to reduce the incidence of out-of-wedlock pregnancy.[63] While some states seem reluctant to take up the challenge to lessen teen pregnancies and out-of-wedlock births, in the 1990s many embarked on substantial programmatic and funding initiatives to achieve family-oriented goals, including discouraging teen childbearing and illegitimacy.[64]

In the future, the federal government and the states will need to invest funds in pregnancy-prevention programs to sustain the welfare caseload declines. Congress may increase the bonus to the states reducing out-of-wedlock births among TANF recipients. The federal government may also help states fund demonstration programs to find effective ways to reduce teen pregnancies and illegitimacy, such as programs to promote marriage and strengthen two-parent families, abstinence and human sexuality education, and the effective use of birth control devices.

The Bush Administration's 2002 welfare reauthorization proposal included $300 million for demonstration grants to state programs promoting healthy, stable two-parent marriages and reducing out-of-wedlock births among welfare recipients and low-income persons.[65] Although the programs would be voluntary, under the Bush proposal, not enacted by Congress, state welfare plans would be required to include explicit descriptions of family formation and healthy marriage efforts, numerical performance goals and annual achievement reports. Bush proposed freeing up the requisite funds by discontinuing the financial bonuses states previously received for decreasing out-of-wedlock births.

Consideration may also be given to offering financial incentives to women, especially those receiving TANF benefits, at "high risk" of having an out-of-wedlock child, to bear children within marriage. For instance, targeted women might receive $2,000 each year for five years, conditioned on their marrying and remaining married.

It is uncertain whether policy changes, including financial incentives, will facilitate the desired behaviors. Funding of modest state programs (and their evaluation) may yield useful models of what interventions will promote marriage and what methods will facilitate the skills that make marriages succeed. The key point may not be getting couples to marry but to postpone pregnancy until after marriage. This takes us back to discouraging out-of-wedlock childbearing without increasing abortion,[66] by setting national and state goals, including reducing TANF grants to states failing to meet their targets.

It is clear that the moral remedies of the nineteenth century–diligence, sobriety, and thrift–are increasingly pertinent in the twenty-first century. We want to help the poor to take advantage of opportunities. We want to encourage virtue to help them seize these chances. In addition to society's responsibility to implement structural reforms addressing poverty's socioeconomic causes, we have come to expect more of the downtrodden themselves. The behavior of the poor is a relevant factor, one that will either help them exit from poverty or encourage them to remain mired in it. Once again, most Americans view the needy as capable of affecting their own destiny. They have the capacity to improve their situation in meaningful ways. Although the poor may be constrained by their environment and the circumstances in which they find themselves, most can still take significant and meaningful steps to improve their lot.

The policies behind the 1996 Welfare Reform Act to reduce dependency by limiting benefits and providing states with incentives to decrease caseloads contrast sharply with the pre-1996 focus on material support. We now expect females who bear a child outside of marriage to raise that child and work; furthermore, males who father a child must provide support payments. At their core, these "tough" measures are meant to change behavior; this goal makes FBOs particularly well-suited partners. As the welfare system shifts from one which merely gives money to the needy to one which teaches and seeks to inculcate those in poverty with virtue, including responsibility and self-sufficiency, FBOs will likely play an increasingly larger role, especially for hard-to-employ individuals. As President George W. Bush stated in May 2001, "The hardest problems remain, people with far fewer skills and greater barriers to work, people with complex human problems like illiteracy and addiction, abuse, and mental illness. We do not yet know what will happen to these men and women, or to their children, but we cannot sit and watch, leaving them to their own struggles and their own fate." The answer to this stage of combating poverty, Bush said, is his faith-based initiative, considered in chapter 7, that will "enlist, equip, and empower idealistic Americans in the work of compassion that only they can provide."[67]

To assist the needy (and even the working poor) overcome their situation, the nation must focus on the person as a whole, not just one's economic status. To help them deal with a high tech society that rejects the uneducated, the unskilled, and the untrained, this means creating more opportunities for education, job training, and skill upgrading to promote employment, retention, and advancement. It also means rehabilitation for substance abuse and counseling for troubled individuals. Furthermore, it rests on strengthening families and improving the life prospects for needy youth.

FBOs, because of their focus on the individual as a moral and spiritual being, rather than a number or a materialistic end, are uniquely situated to accomplish these various goals. FBOs can help facilitate the growth of healthy two-parent families by promoting marriage and responsible parenting, encouraging females to postpone childbearing until they are married, and discouraging pregnancy among young women, even within a marriage. They can also assist with preventing substance use and abuse as well as curtailing juvenile delinquency. In return for various types of assistance, FBOs can demand accountability, provide guidance, and seek to instill moral character and virtue.

Notes

1.   Charles Murray, *Losing Ground: American Social Policy 1950-1980* (New York: BasicBooks, 1984). In this book, Murray blames the welfare system for a host of social problems associated with persistent poverty.

2.   Walter I. Trattner, *From Poor Law to Welfare State: A History of Social Welfare in America*, 6th Edition (New York: The Free Press, 1999), 17.

3.   *Ibid.*,10.

4.   Michael B. Katz, *In the Shadow of the Poorhouse: A Social History of Welfare in America* (New York: BasicBooks, 1996), 14.

5.   *Ibid.*, 11.

6.   Stephen O'Connor, *Orphan Trains: The Story of Charles Loring Brace and the Children He Saved and Failed* (Boston: Houghton Mifflin, 2001); Marvin Olasky, *The Tragedy of American Compassion* (Washington, D.C.: Regnery Gateway, 1992), 32-41; Trattner, *From Poor Law to Welfare State*, 115-119; Paul Boyer, *Urban Masses and Moral Order in America, 1820-1920* (Cambridge: Harvard University Press, 1978), 94-107.

7.   O'Connor, *Orphan Trains*, 149; Olasky, *The Tragedy of American Compassion*, 37.

8.   Although differing with his conclusions and policy approaches, I have drawn on Trattner, *From Poor Law to Welfare State*, 214-385.

9.   Committee on Ways and Means, U.S. House of Representatives, *1998 Green Book: Background Material and Data on Programs Within the Jurisdiction of the Committee on Ways and Means* (Washington, D.C.: U.S. Government Printing Office, 1998), 405 (this matching formula came into existence with the creation of Medicaid in 1965).

10.   *Ibid.*, 399.

11.   Michael J. Horowitz, "Law and the Welfare State," in Peter L. Berger and Richard John Neuhaus, *To Empower People: From State to Civil Society*, ed. Michael Novak (Washington, D.C.: AEI Press, 1996); James Q. Wilson, *The Marriage Problem: How Our Culture Has Weakened Families* (New York: HarperCollins, 2002), 152-153.

12.   *1998 Green Book*, 475.

13.   *Ibid.*, 472.

14.   *Ibid.*, 473.

15.   *Ibid.*, 474.

16.   *Ibid.*, Table 7-37. Participation of AFDC-UP Adults in Jobs, By State, Average Monthly Data, Fiscal Year 1995, 487-488.

17.   C. Eugene Steuerie and Gordon Merin, "Devolution as Seen from the Budget," Number A-2 in series, Assessing New Federalism: Issues and Options for States, Urban Institute (1997), available at www.newfederalism.urban.org/html/anf_a2.h.

18.   Committee on Ways and Means, U.S. House of Representatives, *2000 Green Book: Background Material and Data on Programs Within the Jurisdiction of the Committee on Ways and Means* (Washington, D.C.: Government Printing Office, 2000), Table 7-4. Historical Trends in AFDC/TANF Enrollments, Fiscal Years 1970-1999, 353 and 376.

19.   Joseph Dalaker and Bernadette D. Proctor, U.S. Census Bureau, Current Population Reports, Series P60-210, *Poverty in the United States, 1999* (Washington, D.C.: U.S. Government Printing Office, 2000), Table B-2. Poverty Status of People by Age, Race, and Hispanic Origin: 1959 to 1999, B-7.

20.   *2000 Green Book*, 431.

21.   Wilson, *The Marriage Problem*, 147; Charles Murray, "Family Formation," in *The New World of Welfare*, eds. Rebecca M. Blank and Ron Haskins (Washington, D.C.: Brookings Institution Press, 2001), 158-159.

22.   *2000 Green Book*, 352, 438.

23.   Public Law 104-193 (1996). For an analysis of the political maneuvering behind the 1996 welfare reform legislation, see R. Kent Weaver, *Ending Welfare as We Know It* (Washington, D.C.: Brookings Institution Press, 2000), 252-328. See also, Hugo Heclo, "The Politics of Welfare Reform," in *The New World of Welfare*.

24.   42 USC § 601(a).

25.   42 USC § 603(a)(1).

26.   42 USC § 603(b).

27.   42 USC § 602(a).

28. 42 USC § 601(b).

29. 42 USC § 608(a)(7)(A).

30. 42 USC § 608(a)(7)(C).

31. 42 USC § 602(a)(1)(A)(ii). States face strict limits on the types of work activities, among other items, unsubsidized and subsidized employment, on-the-job-training, job search and job readiness assistance, community service, up to twelve months of vocational training, or providing child care services to an individual participating in a community service program, they can count toward meeting federally required work participation rates. 42 USC § 607(d).

32. 42 USC § 607(c)(1).

33. 42 USC § 607(b)(5) and (e).

34. 42 USC § 607(a).

35. 42 USC § 609(a)(3).

36. 42 USC § 603(a)(4).

37. 42 USC § 601(a).

38. 42 USC § 608(a)(5).

39. 42 USC § 608(a)(4)

40. 42 USC § 603(a)(2).

41. 42 USC § 710.

42. *2000 Green Book*, 463-536.

43. In 2002, President Bush urged allocating federal matching funds for states to increase the current state passthrough of child support payments to TANF families and providing states with financial incentives to increase the amount of collections on overdue child support payments given to families, especially families that have left welfare. The White House, *Working Toward Independence*, February 26, 2002, 27-28; Blaine Harden, "Finding Common Ground on Poor Deadbeat Dads," *New York Times*, February 3, 2002, Week in Review Section, 3. A variety of child support policy issues are analyzed by Irwin Garfinkel, "Child Support in the New World of Welfare," in *The New World of Welfare*, 449-456.

44. Judith M. Gueron and Gayle Hamilton, "The Role of Education and Training in Welfare Reform," The Brookings Institution, Policy Brief No. 20, April 2002, 6-7.

45. The Joyce Foundation, *Welfare to Work: What Have We Learned?* March 2002.

46. Robert Pear, "Federal Welfare Rolls Shrink, But Drop is Smallest Since '94," *New York Times*, May 21, 2002, A12.

47. Statement of Cynthia M. Fagnoni, Managing Director, Education, Workforce, and Income Security Issues, U.S. General Accounting Office, Hearing on Welfare Reform, Subcommittee on Human Resources, Committee on Ways and Means, House of Representatives, March 15, 2001 (GAO-01-522T), 2-3; *2000 Green Book*, Table 7-5. ADFC/TANF Families, Monthly Average by Fiscal Year, 378-380. Ron Haskins, Isabel Sawhill, Kent Weaver, "Welfare Reform: An Overview of Effects to Date," Welfare Reform & Beyond Policy Brief No. 1, The Brookings Institution, January 2001, provide a helpful summary of the positive consequences of welfare reform (welfare reform was responsible for more than half of the caseload decline, while the economy accounted for less than 20 percent).

48. Bernadette D. Proctor and Joseph Dalaker, U.S. Census Bureau, Current Population Reports, Series P60-219, *Poverty in the United States, 2001* (Washington, D.C.: U.S. Government Printing Office, 2002), Table A-2. Poverty Status of People by Age, Race and Hispanic Origin: 1959 to 2001, 26; Robert Pear, "Number of People Living in Poverty Increases in U.S.," *New York Times*, September 25, 2002, A1; Steven Pearlstein, "U.S. Poverty Rate Rises, Income Drops," *Washington Post*, September 25, 2002, A3; Tamar Lewin, "Child Well-Being Improves, U.S. Says," *New York Times*, July 19, 2001, A14; Ron

Haskins, "Effects of Welfare Reform on Family Income and Poverty," in *The New World of Welfare*, 119-126.

49. Rob Green, et al., "Welfare Reform's Effect on Welfare Caseloads," Assessing the New Federalism: An Urban Institute Program to Assess Changing Social Policies, The Urban Institute, Discussion Paper 01-04, February 2001; Pamela A. Morris, et al., "How Welfare and Work Policies Affect Children: A Synthesis of Research," Manpower Demonstration Research Corporation, March 2001; Bruce Fuller, Sharon Lynn Kagan, and Susanna Loeb, *New Lives for Poor Families? Mothers and Young Children Move through Welfare Reform*, Executive Summary and Technical Report, April 2002, available at www.teacherscollege.edu/new-lives/downloads/fullreport.pdf. For an analysis of the negative impact of welfare reform on adolescent children of recipients see Jennifer L. Brooks, Elizabeth C. Hair, and Martha J. Zaslow, "Welfare Reform's Impact on Adolescents: Early Warning Signs," Child Trends Research Brief, July 2001; Lisa A. Genetian, *How Welfare and Work Policies for Parents Affect Adolescents: A Synthesis of Research*, Manpower Demonstration Research Corp., May 2002.

50. For a summary of analytical studies, see Stephen H. Bell, "Why Are Welfare Caseloads Falling?" Assessing the New Federalism, An Urban Institute Program to Assess Changing Social Policies, The Urban Institute, Discussion Paper 01-02, March 2001. See also Douglas J. Besharov and Peter Germanis, "Welfare Reform Four Years Later," *The Public Interest* 140 (Summer 2000): 17-48; and June E. O'Neill and M. Anne Hill, "Gaining Ground? Measuring the Impact of Welfare Reform on Welfare and Work," Center for Civic Innovation at the Manhattan Institute, Civic Report No. 17, July 2001 (welfare reform was responsible for more than half of the caseload decline, while the economy accounted for less than 20 percent).

51. IRC § 32. For an analysis of the credit see V. Joseph Hotz, Charles H. Mullin, and John Karl Scholz, "The Earned Income Tax Credit and Labor Market Participation of Families on Welfare," in *The Incentives of Government Programs and the Well-Being of Families*, eds. Bruce Meyer and Greg Duncan (Joint Center for Poverty Research, 2001), available at www.jcpr.org/book/index.html and David T. Ellwood, "The Impact of the Earned Income Tax Credit and Social Policy Reforms on Work, Marriage, and Living Arrangements," *National Tax Journal* 53:4 (Part 2) (December 1, 2000): 1063-1105.

52. For an analysis of the policy options regarding the Earned Income Tax Credit see Isabel Sawhill and Adam Thomas, "A Hand Up for the Bottom Third: Toward a New Agenda for Low-Income Working Families," The Brookings Institution, May 2001 20-35.

53. Katherine Allen and Maria Kirby, "Unfinished Business: Why Cities Matter to Welfare Reform," Center on Urban & Metropolitan Policy, The Brookings Institution, July 2000, 4.

54. *Ibid.*, 6; Robert Pear, "As Welfare Rolls Shrink, Cities Shoulder Bigger Load," *New York Times*, June 6, 1999, Section 1, 22 (urban counties containing the 30 largest cities with 20 percent of the U.S. population had 39 percent of TANF recipients). See also Margy Waller and Alan Berube, "Timing Out: Long-Term Welfare Caseloads in Large Cities and Counties," Center on Urban & Metropolitan Policy, The Brookings Institution, September 2002 (survey of adult-headed welfare cases).

55. Sheila R. Zedlewski and Donald W. Alderson, "Before and After Reform: How Have Families on Welfare Changed," The Urban Institute, New Federalism, National Survey of America's Families, Series B, No. B-32, April 2001, 2; Sheila R. Zedlewski and Donald W. Alderson, "Do Families on Welfare in the Post-TANF Era Differ from their Pre-TANF Counterparts," Assessing the New Federalism: An Urban Institute Program to Assess Changing Social Policies, The Urban Institute, Discussion Paper 01-03, February 2001, 8-9.

56. *2000 Green Book*, 438-439.

57. Nina Bernstein, "Child-Only, Cases Grow In Welfare," *New York Times*, August 14, 2002, A1; Nina Bernstein, "Side Effects of Welfare Law: The No-Parent Family," *New York Times*, July 29, 2002, A1.

58. Vee Burke, "Welfare Reform: TANF Trends and Data," CRS Report for Congress, June 7, 2002, CRS-5.

59. Douglas J. Besharov, "Welfare Rolls: On the Rise Again," *Washington Post*, July 16, 2002, A17.

60. Sections 201-208 of the Job Creation and Worker Assistance Act of 2002, Public Law 107-147.

61. Zedlewski and Alderson, "Before and After Reform," 3-4; Zedlewski and Alderson, "Families," 15-21. See also Sheila Zedlewski and Pamela Loprest, "Will TANF Work for the Most Disadvantaged Families" in *The New World of Welfare*.

62. Elaine Sorensen and Chava Zibman, "Poor Dads Who Don't Pay Child Support: Deadbeats or Disadvantaged?" New Federalism: National Survival of America's Families, The Urban Institute, Series B, No. B-40, April 2001.

63. Britt Ehrhardt and Karen Spar, "Welfare Report: TANF Activities to Reduce Nonmarital Pregnancy," CRS Report for Congress, December 18, 2001.

64. Richard Wertheimer, Justin Jager, and Kristin Anderson Moore, "State Policy Initiatives for Reducing Teen and Adult Nonmarital Childbearing: Family Planning to Family Caps," New Federalism: An Urban Institute Program to Assess Changing Social Policies, The Urban Institute, Series A, No. A-43, November 2000, 4-6; Richard Wertheimer and Kristin Moore, "Childbearing by Teens: Links to Welfare Reform," New Federalism: Issues and Options for States, Assessing the New Federalism: An Urban Institute Program to Assess Changing Social Policies, The Urban Institute, Series A, No. A-24, August 1998. See also Blaine Harden, "2-Parent Families Rise After Change in Welfare Laws," *New York Times*, August 12, 2001, Section 1, 1; and Laurent Belsie, "Where Single Moms Are The Norm," *Christian Science Monitor*, December 27, 2001, 1, at 4.

65. The White House, *Working Toward Independence*, 19-21; President George W. Bush, "Remarks on the Welfare Reform," February 26, 2002, *Weekly Compilation of Presidential Documents* 38:9 (March 1, 2002): 295-299, at 297-298.

66. Isabel V. Sawhill, "The Perils of Early Motherhood," *The Public Interest* 146 (Winter 2002): 74-84; Isabel Sawhill, "Welfare Reform and the Marriage Movement," October 2001, available at www.brook.edu/dybdocroot/wrb/wip/200100.pdf. See generally Wade F. Horn and Isabel V. Sawhill, "Father, Marriage, and Welfare Reform," in *The New World of Welfare*.

67. President George W. Bush, Commencement Address at the University of Notre Dame, May 20, 2001, *Weekly Compilation of Presidential Documents* 37:21, Week Ending Friday, May 28, 2001, 779-783.

Chapter 4

Armies of Compassion:
What Are Faith-Based Organizations
and What Do They Do?

To better understand the contribution FBOs make to the public welfare, an attempt must be made to define their essential attributes, functions, and philosophy. This is an admittedly difficult task. FBOs defy facile characterization.

FBOs are often portrayed as small, parochial groups. While this may be an accurate description of a significant number of FBOs, it is incomplete. As a practical matter, religious affiliation is less of a distinguishing feature than one might assume. An FBO can be a Catholic, Protestant, Jewish, or Islamic organization. It may be found in the inner city or in the suburbs. An FBO often has a distinct ethnic identity, typically either African-American or Caucasian. It also may provide a wide array of social services, including housing, economic development assistance, teen recreational programs, and soup kitchens, depending on the needs of the surrounding community. FBOs serve people in need not only by providing social services but also by transforming lives. FBOs attend to the spiritual needs of those they help.

FBOs can also join together to create a more influential organization. These collaborations can be citywide or regional, and frequently comprise transdenominational or interfaith groups. In this type of FBO, clergy from different denominations or religions join together to provide services that would normally be beyond the scope of any one congregation. An FBO may also encompass national (and global) groups under religious auspices, including faith-based para-church organizations, as well as national denominations and their social service arms.

This chapter provides an overview of FBOs and the social services they provide. However, it is important to remember that these organizations have a very human character, and thus are very different from their secular counterparts when it comes to the provision of social services. To this end, this chapter also focuses on two faith-based groups and their dynamic leaders: Rev. Eugene F. Rivers, III of Boston's Ten-Point Coalition and Chuck Colson of Prison Fellowship Ministries (PFM), a global organization.

Local Congregations as Social Service Providers

The more than 350,000 congregations in the United States, affiliated with more than 200 religions and denominations, do more than tend to a community's religious needs. By providing aid through a broad range of social services and other charitable work, these houses of worship are a big social service player. The primary beneficiaries of these good works are families and youths who are not members of the congregations that serve them.

One cannot appreciate the significant role local worship groups play in the delivery of social services without examining empirical studies. These surveys generate two basic findings. First, the overwhelming majority of congregations provide at least one type of social service. Second, the types of social service offered are extremely varied, though most congregations provide a set of core programs.

It is now the norm for congregations to be involved in social service activities. However, the percentage of local houses of worship that provide at least one type of social service cannot be determined with precision. Although the 1998 National Congregations Study of 1,236 houses of worship reported that only 57 percent participated in or supported some type of social service projects within the prior twelve months,[1] the consensus is that 85 percent to over 90 percent fall into this category. This figure demonstrates the massive scope of voluntary activity by congregations throughout the United States.

In a study (the Six-City Study) of 111 congregations housed in historic properties in six metropolitan areas (Chicago, Indianapolis, Mobile, New York, Philadelphia, and the San Francisco area), 92.8 percent of those surveyed provided at least one social service.[2] A 1992 national survey of 727 congregations found that nearly 92 percent (91.7 percent) offered at least one program in human services and welfare.[3] Health and education programs were provided by, respectively, 90 percent and 53 percent of the congregations.[4] A more recent national survey of 14,301 local faith communities, the largest survey of its kind ever conducted in the United States, indicated that over 85 percent of congregations provided social services from preschools, health clinics, and tutoring programs, to food pantries and literacy classes.[5]

Members and strangers approach local houses of worship as a last resort. More than two out of three congregations, in excess of 200,000 worship groups, sponsor or support a thrift shop. To provide basic human needs in emergency situations, congregations typically offer crisis care. They provide cash and various services, such as food, clothing, and shelter, for individuals and families in emergency situations. More than eight out of ten congregations operate or support programs providing food to the needy.[6]

Citywide and regional studies produce similar results. A study of 1,044 Philadelphia congregations found that 87 percent sponsored at least one community program serving children, youth, elderly, the homeless, or the needy.[7] A study conducted in 1997 of 266 congregations in Washington, D.C., and its surrounding suburbs reported that almost 95 percent provided at least one social service, while more than 75 percent offered short-term emergency services and 50 percent, some type of family service, such as child care.[8] An earlier (1988-1989) study of 128 major white and black congregations in Greensboro, North Carolina, showed that 84 percent offered at least one in-house social service program, with 85 percent having counseling services.[9]

The absolute number and types of social services provided by congregations are far greater than what the one-to-one ratio (congregations to social programs), assumed above, suggests. On average, research indicates that congregations are more likely involved in more than one social service program. The Six-City Study placed the figure at over four programs per congregation, and a survey of 401 Philadelphia congregations (the 401 Study) reported 2.5 programs per congregation.[10] Additionally, the Six-City Study and the 401 Study may in fact underrepresent the true total because both limited each congregation's response to only five programs. Many houses of worship provide eight or ten different services.

In terms of breadth, the Six-City Study determined that a wide array of some forty-nine social programs were offered by more than 25 percent of the houses of worship surveyed.[11] These programs varied greatly in terms of targeted beneficiaries, and included programs for children, teens, and adults, as well as food services and distribution. The most frequently offered programs include: food pantries (60.36 percent), music performances (56.76 percent), clothing (53.15 percent), holiday celebrations (53.15 percent), community fairs (51.35 percent), choral groups (51.35 percent), international relief (51.35 percent), recreational programs for teens (45.95 percent), hospital visitation (44.01 percent), visitation of the sick (43.24 percent), recreational programs for children (42.44 percent), soup kitchens (41.44 percent), and tutoring (40.54 percent).

In addition, this study showed that congregations offered unique programs that were not widely reproduced. Houses of worship in particular cities were likely to offer different programs from those in other cities based on community needs. Thus, regional differences impact on at least some of the programs offered by local worship groups.

Based on the survey data, it is evident that local congregations typically address the immediate physical needs of individuals and families for food, clothing, and shelter, rather than fund projects or programs requiring sustained involvement to meet longer term goals, such as the transformation of character. Because of limited financial and human resources, many local houses of worship are less likely to provide ongoing or professional services, such as substance abuse treatment or job training. For example, in the 1997 study of congregations in Washington, D.C., and its suburbs, fewer than 5 percent of all the responding congregations offered vocational or job training, mental health services, medical or legal services, foster care, or child welfare services.[12] However, indicative of future trends, the 401 Study revealed a number of long-term efforts, including antiviolence programs for gang members (25.7 percent), prison ministries (21.4 percent), programs for prisoners' families (10.7 percent), and police-clergy programs (11.2 percent). Day care was provided by more than one-fifth of the houses of worship surveyed, with 11.2 percent providing (or hosting) nursery schools. Job training programs for the homeless or extremely poor people were supplied by 11 percent and vocational training by 8 percent of those surveyed. Over 15 percent of the Philadelphia congregations offered job counseling and placement, as well as adult literacy training for the wider community.[13] In particular, megachurches throughout the United States are expanding their reach into housing, drug treatment, counseling for battered women, and rehabilitation for ex-inmates.

In addition to houses of worship, social services are provided by local, independent FBOs that are not under the auspices of any one congregation or church. These FBOs often offer long-term rehabilitative programs, such as helping the poor with substance abuse problems and providing counseling for especially troubled individuals and families.

For example, the Bowery Mission, founded in 1879, was purchased in 1895 by the New York-based Christian Herald Association, a magazine publisher and global relief organization with a long-standing tradition of spreading the Gospel and practicing what was preached in the pages of its publication. Under the leadership of its current president, Edward Morgan, the Christian Herald Association has expanded its provision of social services. It started several new ventures including forming a secular arm, the Transitional Center, a drug-rehabilitation program for men, that is discussed in chapter 7. After renovating its run-down homeless shelter in the Bowery in Manhattan, the association could boast a totally privately supported, robustly religious shelter and discipleship residency program consisting of a daily regimen of work, personal counseling, seminars, education, and recreation. The Bowery Mission's food van travels throughout Manhattan distributing food and blankets. In extreme weather, the mission's chapel is converted into an emergency shelter.[14]

Church ministries sometimes serve as incubators for these local, independent FBOs, providing facilities and volunteers, as well as some funding to get an organization off the ground. Subsequently, however, some church-sponsored FBOs grow to the point where church funds can no longer support them. This may lead to a decision to incorporate, apply for federal tax-exempt status, and seek foundation (and other donor) funding for continued expansion.

The Historic and Current Roles of African-American Churches

Historically, the African-American church emerged as a holistic institution, one where a variety of nonreligious functions–social, economic, and political activities–were pursued. The black church was more than a place of worship. It is also served as a focal point for the African-American community.[15]

In addition to its role as a community spiritual center, the church functioned as a multifunctional organization, developing community institutions for African-Americans. It sponsored numerous social endeavors that strengthened and empowered the African-American community and assisted its members. It also served as the institution in which blacks took care of their own in the midst of generations of discrimination. Finally, it helped strengthen the social, educational, and economic fabric of the community it ministered to, combining a tradition of self-help with a social mission.

Black churches organized schools and provided a wide range of social services. In the nineteenth century, these churches formed mutual aid societies, burial associations, and fraternal organizations. These church-based groups helped, in turn, organize secular businesses. More than a century ago, African-American banks, insurance companies, and other businesses were created through church activities and sponsorship.

Today, African-American churches constitute the most reliable institutions in the inner cities. The only institution left in many inner-city communities is the church, and increasingly the mosque. Rather than fleeing to the suburbs, many African-American houses of worship chose to remain. These congregations, operating where material resources are scarce, comprise the only institution with credibility in many urban neighborhoods.

The black church historically had a unique and powerful community outreach tradition. From the small Cookman United Methodist Church in North Philadelphia to the gigantic First African Methodist Episcopal Church in South Central Los Angeles, African-American congregations have worked to serve and save the inner city. Most urban black churches run or participate in a variety of community outreach activities from food banks and shelters for the homeless, to substance abuse programs and day care facilities. For example, a 1993-1994 survey of 150 black churches in Atlanta indicated that 87 percent were engaged in some type of community outreach program beyond providing religious services.[16] A 1988 nationwide study of 1,862 houses of worship concluded that predominantly black congregations were more likely than their white counterparts to be involved in activities directed at underprivileged sectors of their communities.[17]

For many years, the Cookman United Methodist Church in Philadelphia has run an after-school nutrition program, a weekly community dinner, and an informal counseling program. These programs enable the congregation to help many low-income families and welfare recipients. In 1998, Cookman began receiving public sector funding for its welfare-to-work program, called Transitional Journey, discussed in detail in chapter 7. The program, designed to be holistic and relationship-based, offered life-skills training, interview preparation, people skills, and confidence building for the hardest-to-employ welfare recipients, who continue to face, as we have seen in chapter 3, multiple barriers in gaining employment and remaining employed.[18]

Transcending the traditional sponsorship of social service activities, such as soup kitchens and food pantries, some African-American churches are becoming prime engines of community economic renewal. The trend, at least among large churches, is toward a more entrepreneurial perspective. This involves not only operating job training centers but also constructing low-income housing and encouraging the formation of businesses that will produce jobs for inner-city residents.[19]

Seeing the church as more than just worship behind stained-glass windows, African-American churches frequently take economic development into their own hands, serving as catalysts. In the words of Kirbyjon H. Caldwell, pastor of Windsor Village United Methodist Church in Houston, church-based economic development initiatives represent a way of "taking the sanctuary to the streets."[20]

Rooted in a philosophy of economic self-help, African-American churches have drawn on the financial support of their congregants and the public sector to foster business opportunities designed to enhance the communities they serve. African-American megachurches not only have social capital, the ties that bind those of faith together in service to one another, but also the financial capital to begin to meet the needs in their communities. There has been an expansion of community-building creativity on the part of black churches during the past several decades.

Beginning in the 1970s, some large African-American congregations started to focus on developing affordable housing. For example, Second Baptist Church, the oldest African-American Baptist congregation in Los Angeles, became a real estate developer to meet the needs of congregants and residents who live near downtown.[21] It built two senior citizen apartment complexes on adjacent church properties and established temporary shelters nearby. The church subsequently created the Canaan Housing Corp. (Canaan) to focus on constructing affordable housing. Canaan allied with other nonprofit organizations to renovate two skidrow hotels and build two multifamily developments in the church's immediate neighborhood.

The First African Methodist Episcopal Church (FAME) in Los Angeles exemplifies a megacongregation that has taken on the problems of substance abuse, homelessness, and unemployment in its community. Founded in 1872, it is the oldest African-American congregation in Los Angeles, with a membership of some 20,000 people. According to its dynamic senior minister, Dr. Cecil L. Murray, "Word must become flesh"[22] through outreach ministries.

In serving the low- and moderate-income residents of South Central Los Angeles and striving to take care of a community's needs, FAME secured funds from the public sector and private businesses (as well as from its members), hired paid staff (mostly from the neighborhood), and recruited hundreds of volunteers. Most of those who benefit from the church's social ministry are not members of the congregation.

FAME thus typifies the increasing need for churches to shift from commodity-based (food, clothing, shelter), stop-gap, mercy ministries to more holistic, permanent change ministries, based on an enlarged and deepened understanding of their spiritual mission. Devoting resources to comprehensive community assistance programs, FAME has done this by integrating social services, such as housing, economic development, and employment, under its congregational auspices.

Fulfilling a traditional social service role, as a congregation, FAME offers premarital, job stress, family, and crisis counseling, provides referrals to mental health care professionals, and offers free tutoring and computer training. Its monthly feeding program provides groceries to hundreds of families.

FAME has improved the social, educational, physical, and economic lives of those in its community through the creation of numerous affiliated corporations.[23] Several examples illustrate FAME's use of affiliated, nonprofit entities.

The FAME Assistance Corp. meets a broad range of social needs through food and shelter programs, relief programs, and more than twenty youth programs. The Cecil L. Murray Education Center runs a private elementary and middle school offering parents an alternative to public schools.

The FAME Health Corp. has two arms. First, the FAME Operation in AIDS Prevention and Education Corp. provides teens with educational programs on AIDS/HIV prevention. Second, it administers the African-American Tobacco Coalition of Los Angeles County, consisting of over thirty-five community-based organizations. Its Tobacco Youth Program offers education and training on the hazards of tobacco use.

To promote that development of affordable housing, a task undertaken by many large African-American congregations beginning in the 1970s and 1980s, FAME sponsors, through two affiliated corporations, several housing projects. The FAME Housing Corp., its housing development arm, built housing units for low- and moderate-income individuals and families. It also operates a day care center and provides after-school tutoring at an on-premises library. The FAME Good Shepherd Housing Development Corp. manages federally subsidized housing units for physically disabled individuals.

Typifying the approach of many large African-American churches, community economic development evolved from FAME's social ministry. Shortly after the 1992 riots in Los Angeles, FAME swung into action. As an economic lifeline for a devastated community, the church created another affiliated organization, FAME Renaissance, to fund community services and a multitude of business and economic development programs.[24] FAME Renaissance strives to improve the economic livelihood of the South Central Los Angeles area FAME serves. In addition to operating a multimedia, manufacturing, and service business incubator and training center, Renaissance's Business Resource Center has become a vital source of funding for local small firms by providing loans (and technical assistance) to new and existing businesses that do not qualify for bank credit. Its microloan program also provides short-term loans to minority-owned businesses.

Sensing the need for equity investors to back small business ventures, FAME started a venture capital arm–an equity investment fund–for community businesses. It also offers an Entrepreneurial Training Program to promote self-sufficiency and job creation by equipping new and existing entrepreneurs in the low- and moderate-income areas of South Central Los Angeles with the knowledge, skill, and insight needed to manage a successful business.

FAME Renaissance also seeks to meet a variety of other community needs. For example, the FAME Immediate Needs Transportation Program serves tens of thousands of seniors, students, and physically disabled persons each month, providing subsidized taxi services and bus tokens to those with an immediate transportation need not met by other modes of transportation. This program also provides employment and entrepreneurial opportunities in the taxi industry. Additionally, the FAME Job Creation and Employment Program offers full-time, part-time, summer, and holiday positions for teens and some adults.

FAME even set up a for-profit subsidiary, FAME Personnel Service, to place skilled employees in permanent and temporary jobs throughout the greater Los Angeles area. Originally, FAME did not charge for this employment service. When the church realized that venture could make a profit, it established a for-profit employment agency to match job-seekers with employers.

Today, throughout the United States black clergy and church volunteers continue to monitor, mentor, and minister to the needs of inner-city children and teens, striving to help those youngsters avoid violence, achieve literacy, and obtain jobs. Increasingly, African-American churches, at least those with the financial and human resources to do so, are energizing communities through economic empowerment, thereby keeping individuals off drugs and out of jail. "People need faith but they also need jobs, housing, and money to start businesses," Rev. Mark Whitlock, executive director of FAME Renaissance stated. He continued, "The church has a role to play in strengthening the economic fiber of our communities."[25]

As the activities of FAME illustrate, black churches often occupy a strategic position to stimulate economic development. Many mega-churches located in poor urban areas are channeling their wealth (and their access to capital) into massive redevelopment projects. The African-American church is the one institution in inner-city communities able to secure significant amounts of credit to help create new businesses. These enterprises enrich the neighborhood by providing jobs and much needed services. Black-owned enterprises also help create financially viable and stable communities. As once empty storefronts become thriving businesses, the value of neighboring homes increase. At its best, the cycle of inner-city poverty is reversed, providing a foundation for economic, personal, and social empowerment.

Local and Regional Partnerships of
Congregations and Other FBOs

Local congregations and clergy from different religious and denominations often join together to provide social services beyond the scope of any one institution. Clergy reach across denominational lines to pool resources, tap others' strengths, and form interdenominational FBOs.

Congregations also collaborate with other organizations to provide social and community services. Institutions involved in these collaborative relationships include other congregations, other faith-based groups, government agencies, and secular community organizations. The benefits of collaboration include the sharing of space and financial resources as well as gaining access to increased staff and supplies.

Research studies back up these observations. For example, nearly one-third (29.9 percent) of the 401 Philadelphia congregations surveyed indicated that they collaborated with other FBOs to develop and deliver community service programs; more than one-third (33.2 percent) reported collaborating with secular organizations to deliver a service or run a program.[26] In a 1992 national survey, among the nine out of ten congregations that reported programs in human services and health, nearly half (47 percent) reported running programs both within their congregation and in affiliation with other programs.[27]

On both a neighborhood and a citywide level, FBOs today face an enormous challenge. It is difficult to reach and retain teens, especially males involved in at-risk activities, such as violence, crime, and substance use. To attract teens off the streets and into their programs, FBOs need to engage in grassroots gang-intervention programs, particularly through collaborative endeavors. This work is often done late at night, on the streets, and ad hoc.

Among the most successful in meeting this challenge is Rev. Eugene F. Rivers, III, an African-American minister. Rivers heads the Azusa Christian Community, a tiny Pentecostal church with about thirty members located in an impoverished corner of the Dorchester section, one of the poorest neighborhoods of Boston.[28] He typifies the new breed of inner-city ministers: well educated and able to switch seamlessly from street talk, to the academic style of program evaluators, and to pulpit-style exhortation.

His father, a black Muslim, left his mother, a black Pentecostal, when Rivers was three. At the age of twelve, Rivers was forcibly inducted ("drafted") into "the life," North Philadelphia's gang culture. The boys from the Somersville gang began bouncing his head inside a toilet. He had a choice: join the gain or get beaten up everyday for the rest of his short life. Rivers joined.

Fortunately, at age sixteen, Rivers was drawn out of that life and into the culture of Rev. Benjamin Smith, the spiritual leader of the inner-city Philadelphia Deliverance Evangelical Church, and ultimately to Harvard. Rivers undertook his intellectual quest largely because of a thirst for literacy resulting from his conversion experience.

Along the way, Rivers fathered a child out-of-wedlock. He carved three identities for himself, collecting welfare checks in New Haven, New York, and Philadelphia.

In the mid-1980s, Rivers left Harvard without a degree. Shortly thereafter, Rivers, together with about a dozen members of a Harvard black Pentecostal group, moved to Dorchester to live their faith as an intentional community, sharing their resources and working with the poor. Rivers set an example by relocating to the inner city so as to build relationships within the community. He soon began to compete with drug dealers and pimps for the souls of the inner city residents, particularly teens.

Shortly after moving to the Dorchester section, Rivers befriended a young drug dealer, Selvin Brown, who would come to trust him. In one conversation, Rivers asked Brown why he thought drug dealers were more successful than the church at reaching youth in the streets. Brown replied, "When Johnny goes past my corner on the way to school, I'm there, you're not. When he comes home from school, I'm there, you're not. When he goes to the corner store for a loaf of bread, I'm there, you're not. When he leaves to take it home, I'm there, you're not. I win, you lose."[29]

In targeting high-risk youth, Rivers realized that the church needed to establish a presence on the street, get to know young people, and build relationships with and gain their trust. Brown, the drug dealer, offered to help the Azusa Christian Community on how to do outreach to young people. He told Rivers, "I deal in drugs because there was no adult in my life to tell me that what I was doing was wrong; I don't have a father figure who functions as a sign of love, authority, and discipleship."[30] Members of the community began to cultivate a relationship with this drug dealer, who in turn introduced them to other players involved with drugs. He showed them what was happening "on the street."

Although small in numbers, members of the Azusa congregation, having a vested interest in the welfare of their community, understood the church's commitment to place caring adults in the lives of neighborhood youth. Rivers and his Azusa community became an increasingly constant presence on the troubled streets of Dorchester, trying to rescue at-risk youth.

The Azusa program was such a success that, in 1991, shots were fired into Rivers' residence in one of the most violent sections of Dorchester. These shots brought home to Rivers the dangers of conducting a one-man campaign against youth violence. Seeing the lives of his wife and children in jeopardy caused a shift in his attitude, and he became more open to the possibility of forming alliances with other ministers and those in the law enforcement community.

Rivers once again sat down with Selvin Brown, the drug dealer, and developed a list of ten things–the Ten-Point concept–that churches needed to do to save kids. Basically, the plan involved churches commissioning street missionaries to go into the streets, homes, schools, and the courts to serve as advocates for youngsters, in cooperation with the police and probation officers. Churches would also organize cluster operations to sponsor adopt-a-gang programs to organize and evangelize youth in gangs. Inner-city churches would also serve as open-door centers for at risk youth.[31] By making teens on the streets extensions of congregations, these activities made local faith-based groups more effective in rebuilding neighborhoods.

Prior to 1992, the activities of most African-American clergy in Boston rarely involved a street-oriented presence to address the ever-mounting teen violence within their communities. Although Rivers had established a strong outreach to gang members and other youth on the troubled streets of Dorchester, his criticisms of other clergy left him isolated.

A tragic event spurred the collaborative efforts of Boston's African-American clergy and the formation of the Ten-Point Coalition, an interdenominational group of black clergy focusing on a wide range of youth and community problems. In May 1992, Rivers attended a funeral at the Morning Star Baptist Church in a tough, poverty-stricken Boston neighborhood, for a twenty-year-old man who had been shot in the head while standing near a window.

During the funeral service, a gang chased a young man into the church. Gunfire blazed inside and outside the sanctuary. Youths, wearing black hoods, chased the man around the church, beating and stabbing him in front of the mourners. The shoot-out and the multiple stabbing threw the service into chaos.

The brazenness of this attack within a church, the bringing of violence and the flashing of guns and knives ignited a fire of anger, forcing Boston's black clergy to take action. They realized they could no longer ignore the situation on the street. Rivers recalled:

> We looked at the bullet holes in the sanctuary and we realized that we had to step up our involvement. We were dealing with a generation of young people who were alienated not just from the church but from all the institutions of the black community. We knew that if we didn't come out of our sanctuaries, roll up our sleeves and start dealing with these kids in a real way, we as a community were going to be overwhelmed.[32]

Rivers and others decided that black churches were not doing enough to save the endangered children of the black community. A group of ministers formed the Ten-Point Coalition (the Coalition), in an effort to respond to Boston's record homicide rate in the early 1990s and to counter the myriad of problems faced by black and Latino youth, especially those at risk for violence, drug abuse, and other destructive behaviors. The Coalition, a network of forty-three ministers, mostly from small black churches, was led by Reverends Jeffrey Brown of Union Baptist Church in Cambridge, Ray Hammond of Bethel AME Church, and Rivers.

As a call to churches to address the violence occurring in their communities, the Coalition drew up "A 10-Point Plan to Mobilize the Churches." In a major step toward meaningful collaboration, the Coalition inaugurated a number of initiatives, ranging from neighborhood patrols to offering safe havens. Ministers and lay people took their churches into the streets and engaged the youngsters. Some youths needed little more than a safe place to play. Others needed to be diverted from violent crime into alternative programs. For those in between, the Coalition sought to deal with other issues: fatherlessness, child abuse, substance abuse, teen pregnancy, and chronic joblessness.

Building on the admonitions of Selvin Brown and Rivers' own activities, the Coalition focused its attention on street patrols. On weekend nights and weekday afternoons, clergy and lay persons hung out on street corners and in parks. Relationship building emerged as a key part of the patrol strategy. Initially, very few neighborhood people talked to them until the patrols became a constant presence. In entering into a dialogue with street youth and drug dealers, the street patrol members did not preach. They asked how churches and church leaders could be of service to youth. They offered counseling, job and educational opportunities, and alternatives to life on the streets. To shame the police into action, members of the Coalition held vigils in front of crack houses. They worked house by house, block by block.

Rivers realized that churches had to cooperate with government if either were to be effective. The Coalition thus sought to build partnerships with public sector institutions committed to the revitalization of neighborhoods. Individuals from the faith community, law enforcement, and probation and social service agencies began to put the needs of children before ego and turf issues and, in a coordinated manner, to reach out to teens on the street. Local police and probation officials started working hand in hand with the clergy in anti-gang policing, juvenile probation monitoring, and crime prevention. They developed several strategic partnerships to remove the racial overtones previously typifying law enforcement in Boston.

The Coalition began by acknowledging the Boston Police Department's progress in an awards ceremony, the "People's Tribunal," initiated in 1992 to publicly honor "good" police officers. The clergy also began serving as bridge-builders and mediators between low-income communities and law enforcement officials. Staff and volunteers from Rivers' church, Azusa, became a quasi-formal presence at the Dorchester District Court. One of its youth workers became an advocate for teen offenders, helping find alternatives to incarceration. Also, at the Azusa parish house first time offenders on probation began to attend an innovative, ongoing twelve-week Fatherhood Program, led by an Azusa youth worker, a probation officer, and a court psychologist. As it developed, the program came to focus on the issue of responsible fatherhood. It challenged fathers to play an active, nurturing role in their children's lives.

These positive, collaborative steps culminated in Operation Cease-Fire, beginning in May 1996. In addition to fully institutionalized interagency collaboration among Boston's various crime-fighting agencies (police; probation; Department of Youth Services; street workers; agents from the U.S. Drug Enforcement Administration; and the Bureau of Alcohol, Tobacco, and Firearms), key community members, primarily from the Coalition, were involved. These groups worked together to identify gangs and gang members responsible for violence around Boston. Through their combined efforts, police and inner-city clergy targeted hardened criminals, mainly gang members involved in narcotics-related turf battles, for removal from the streets. In exchange for guarantees that police officials would respect the civil rights of the community and work with its leaders, the local clergy used their moral authority to help neutralize a small, but influential, group of hardcore criminals. As a result, they gave the police in Boston's "worst" neighborhoods a new "legitimacy," thereby reducing gang-related youth violence.

Then in the spring of 1998, the Bloods and Crips Initiative was established to mobilize lay and pastoral workers to intervene and prevent youth involvement in gang activity. Clergy and members of Boston police, probation, school police, Department of Youth Services, street and youth workers, and the Massachusetts Bay Transit Authority Police began to meet and share information regarding developments "on the street." Agency and clergy representatives participated in the initiative's activities, focusing on the targeted youth through school presentations, home visits to youths suspected of gang involvement, a strong presence in "hanging out" areas during popular times, and regular street patrols. The initiative's collaborative approach strives to notify youths of alternative options to gangs and to bring them in contact with various resources designed to meet their needs in a constructive manner.

Through the efforts of his congregation and interdenominational Coalition (and its collaboration with public sector institutions) Rivers sought to put responsible adults into lives of youngsters to monitor them, with the aim of helping at-risk children avoid violence, achieve literacy, and ultimately, gain employment. Clergy and lay persons involved in the Coalition mentor kids who never knew their fathers; they try to wrestle black male teens from drug dealers.

Rivers learned to work with others and temper his evangelical bent. Early in his ministry, Rivers "pushed religion harder on the kids, but found that it intimidated–and turned off–many of them. So now he keeps preaching to a minimum."[33]

Rivers has watched the fruits of his efforts for nearly two decades. By providing unconditional love, serenity, and security for children surrounded by violence, chaos, and poverty, while at the same time demanding mutual respect and civility, Rivers, and other Azusa members, have become a surrogate parent, a "father figure," to young men and women in the community. Selvin Brown was for a time the most powerful person in Rivers' neighborhood. Before his death, Brown told Rivers: "You literally have to take my place. I worked very hard to corrupt these children."[34]

National and Global Faith-Based Organizations

There are two types of national (and global) FBOs: first, organizations under religious auspices; and second, paradenominational organizations not officially affiliated with any religion or denomination. The religious-affiliated organizations, national religious networks with chapters throughout the United States, have become a major force in providing social services locally. A central headquarters coordinates and monitors the activities of the various local branches and sets the boundaries within which they operate. The national headquarters typically represents all the local chapters.

There are numerous examples of such national FBOs. With agencies throughout the United States, Catholic Charities USA and Lutheran Children and Families Services in America are an integral part of America's social service delivery system. They are illustrative of national FBOs that continue to maintain an affiliation with their respective, originating religious bodies. Although they receive some financial support from a founding religious group (whether directly from an area-wide headquarters or through local congregational fund-raising), many of these national organizations are now significantly funded by the public sector.

They typically employ secular social workers as the service providers and managers.

Begun in 1910, Catholic Charities, an umbrella organization, has become one of the nation's largest nonpublic social service organizations. Through a network of more than 1,400 local agencies and institutions, it serves nearly 10 million people annually, offering emergency and social services.[35] In many states and cities, an arm of Catholic Charities is the most important provider of social services–secular or religious. When it contracts with government agencies to deliver social services, it is scrupulously secular in dealing with its clients. The organization delivers a wide scope of assistance to a diverse population, including orphans, the elderly, inner-city blacks, and the latest group of refugees.

Local agencies of Catholic Charities provide a vast array of services in two broad categories. First, these local agencies offer emergency services, including food assistance programs (soup kitchens, food banks, and pantries), temporary shelter for children and families, battered women and senior citizens, and clothing and utility payment assistance. Second, the social service arm offers child and adult day care, respite care, employment and transportation services, educational and family programs (including Head Start as well as drug and alcohol awareness), counseling, refugee resettlement, housing (helping families and individuals keep or obtain permanent housing), and health-related services.

There are also national (and even global) paradenominational organizations, based on religious principles, with strong theological concepts underpinning their mission statements. However, they are not affiliated with any religion or denomination.

One of the largest paradenominational organizations is the Prison Fellowship Ministries, the world's largest prison ministry. It aims to reform convicts and prevent recidivism by converting nonbelievers to evangelical Christianity.[36] The program was founded by Charles W. (Chuck) Colson, after he served a prison term in the Maxwell Federal Prison Camp in Alabama.

Colson began his journey to Christian faith while special counsel in President Richard M. Nixon's inner circle.[37] At the suggestion of an old friend, Raytheon President Tom Phillips, Colson read C.S. Lewis' *Mere Christianity* in the summer of 1973, at the start of the meltdown of the Nixon presidency over Watergate. The book sent Colson's lawyerlike mind into a tailspin, leading, within a few weeks, to committing his life to Jesus. In September 1973, Colson joined a weekly prayer group.

Subsequently, in June 1974, Colson pleaded guilty to the obstruction of justice, resulting in his incarceration. His time in prison sparked another conversion, this one on crime. "The system wasn't doing anything to restore or rehabilitate them," Colson recalled. "It was just warehousing them."[38]

At Maxwell, Colson helped organize a prayer group. He saw firsthand the impact of faith as a tool to reform bitter and despairing men. "Therapy teaches people how to manage their problems," Colson explained, "[b]ut Christian conversion transforms the human will."[39] He sensed a call to embark on an unglamourous mission—prison ministry—on his release.

In 1976, Colson founded PFM, basing its prison programs on two theological ideas. First, crime represents an offense against both individuals and God, whose image the perpetrators bear. Thus, the criminal justice system must pay greater attention to victims and communities hurt by crime.

Second, punishment should be regenerative, making people what they never were. It should turn criminals into citizens. Although chronic, remorseless, violent offenders must be warehoused, most inmates do not fall into that category. Many of them, with God's help, Colson believed, could change. He had an idea: give inmates an intensive exposure to Christian teaching and fellowship, initially outside of prison.

Soon after his release, Colson persuaded the director of the Federal Bureau of Prisons to furlough federal inmates to attend discipleship seminars. They would get two weeks of Bible training in a fraternity-like setting, at a Washington, D.C., row house. However, most wardens balked at the off-site program. Within one year, PFM was working almost exclusively inside prisons.

Today, its vast ministry offers privately funded programs in most of the U.S.'s 2,000 federal and state prisons, annually serving more than 200,000 inmates. It relies on church-based volunteers, as many as 50,000 each year, drawn from nearly all Christian denominations. It has broadened into a family of ministries striving to address various aspects of crime, by ministering to prisoners, ex-prisoners, victims, and their families.

PFM tries to help inmates cope with the stress of incarceration and to prepare them for release through religious instruction. It organizes three-day seminars laying out the basics of Christian doctrine and living. Bible studies, revival meetings, and worship services are included in the mix. It promises salvation: by accepting Jesus one can liberate oneself from a life of degradation.

It also produces America's most widely circulated prison newspaper, *Inside Journal*, featuring interviews with sports figures and ex-prisoners, news and advice, as well as a Gospel presentation. Its InnerChange Freedom Initiative, a prerelease program, discussed in chapter 2, started in Texas and now expanded to Kansas, Iowa, and Minnesota, helps inmates transition to the outside world by ministering to them before and after release.

Through its Network For Life (the Network), it helps ex-offenders get their lives together. As an after-prison program, the Network emphasizes service to the community, providing an accountability structure as well as spiritual, emotional, and material support.

PFM also offers a variety of programs for inmates' families and crime victims. Through its Angel Tree Program, church volunteers buy Christmas gifts and deliver them to upwards of 600,000 prisoners' children, on behalf of incarcerated parents. Its Evergreen Youth Ministries provide holiday visits, mentoring, summer camps, and after-school programs to the children and families of prisoners and recent parolees. It also runs Sycamore Tree, bringing crime victims to prisons to meet inmates, though not usually the criminals who victimized them.

Although FBOs are not easily defined, in terms of the services offered or their organization, no one model has shown itself to be superior or inferior to any other. Some are pervasively sectarian, such as the PFM, in that they proselytize, making religious worship or instruction a precondition to receiving aid. Others are secular in approach, such as Catholic Charities. Of the sectarian organizations, some do not want to compromise their evangelical mission by accepting any direct government funding. Others, such as Cookman United Methodist Church and the Bowery Mission take government funds, segregate public sector monies from their evangelical mission, and sometimes establish separate social service arms. The diversity among FBOs is in fact their strength because FBOs adapt to the needs of their communities. As long as FBOs succeed at providing effective assistance, how they operate is less of a concern. Whether or not FBOs are effective is next taken up.

Notes

1.   Mark Chaves, "Religious Congregations and Welfare Reform: Who Will Take Advantage of 'Charitable Choice'?" *American Sociological Review* 64:6 (December 1999): 836-846, at 838; Mark Chaves, "Congregations' Social Service Activities," The Urban Institute, Charting Civil Society, Center on Nonprofits and Philanthropy, Number 6 (December 1999), 2.

2.   Ram A. Cnaan, *Social and Community Involvement of Religious Congregations Housed in Historic Religious Properties: Findings from a Six-City Study*, Final Report to Partners for Sacred Places (May 1998), 10.

3.   Virginia A. Hodgkinson and Murray S. Weitzman, *From Belief to Commitment: The Community Service Activities and Finances of Religious Congregations in the United States*, 1993 Edition (Washington, D.C.: Independent Sector, 1992), 2, 105.

4.   Independent Sector, *America's Religious Congregations: Measuring Their Contribution to Society*, November 2000, 6-7.

5.   Hartford Institute for Religion Research, *Faith Communities Today: A Report on Religion in the United States Today*, March 2001, 46-48.

6.   *Ibid.*

7.   Ram A. Cnaan and Stephen C. Boddie, "Black Church Outreach: Comparing How Black and Other Congregations Serve Their Needy Neighbors," University of Pennsylvania, Center for Research on Religion and Urban Civil Society, *CRRUCS Report 2001-1*, 10. See also Ram A. Cnaan, "Keeping Faith in the City: How 401 Urban Religious Congregations Service Their Neediest Neighbors," University of Pennsylvania, Center for Research on Religion and Urban Civil Society, *CRRUCS Report 2000-1*, 15 (91 percent of 401 Philadelphia congregations surveyed sponsored at least one social service program).

8.   Tobi Jennifer Printz, "Faith-Based Service Providers in the Nation's Capitol: Can They Do More?" The Urban Institute, Charting Civil Society, Center on Nonprofits and Philanthropy, Number 2 (April 1998), 1-3. In another statewide survey, three out of four respondents in New Jersey indicated offering some type of emergency assistance. Carol J. DeVita, Tobi Jennifer Printz Platnick, and Eric C. Twombly, "Report to The Human Services Faith-Based Organization Task Force: Findings from The Survey of Community Services of Faith-Based Organizations in New Jersey," Center for Nonprofits and Philanthropy, The Urban Institute, April 1999, 4.

9.   Robert C. Wineberg, "A Community Study of the Ways Religious Congregations Support Individuals and the Local Human Services Network," *The Journal of Applied Social Sciences* 15:1 (Fall/Winter 1990-1991): 51-74, at 58.

10.   Cnaan, "Keeping Faith in the City," 15; Cnaan, *Social and Community Involvement of Religious Congregations*, 10. The Greensboro survey of 128 major congregations reported providing approximately 5 services per congregation from their premises. Wineberg, "A Community Study," 58.

11.   Cnaan, *Social and Community Involvement of Religious Congregations*, 13.

12.   Printz, "Faith-Based Service Providers," 1-2.

13.   Cnaan, "Keeping Faith in the City," 17.

14.   Susan Adams, "Corporate Communion," *Forbes* 165:8 (April 3, 2000): 82-84; Testimony of Edward Morgan, President, Christian Herald Association, United States Senate, Committee on the Judiciary, Hearing on Faith-Based Solutions: What Are the Legal Issues? 107th Congress, 1st Session, June 6, 2001; and the Bowery Mission's website, www.bowery.org.

15.   C. Eric Lincoln and Lawrence H. Mamiya, *The Black Church in the African American Experience* (Durham: Duke University Press, 1990).

16.   Naomi Ward, et al., "Black Churches in Atlanta Reach Out to the Community," *National Journal of Sociology* 8:1/2 (Summer/Winter 1994): 49-74, at 61. See also Cleopatra Howard Caldwell, Angela Dungee Greene, and Andrew Billingsley, "The Black Church as a Family Support System," *National Journal of Sociology* 6:1 (Summer 1992): 21-40 (a survey of 634 northern black churches showed 7 out of 10 provided at least 1 family support program); and Stephen B. Thomas, et al., "The Characteristics of Northern Black Churches with Community Health Outreach Programs," *American Journal of Public Health* 84:4 (April 1994): 575-579. Surveying programs offered by black churches directed at adolescent nonmembers, mostly from low-income homes, Roger H. Rubin, Andrew Billingsley, and Cleopatra Howard Caldwell, "The Role of the Black Church in Working with Black Adolescents," *Adolescence* 29:114 (Summer 1994): 251-267, note the lack of health-related substance-abuse, AIDS support, youth at risk, and parenting/sexuality

programs. See generally, John J. DiIulio, Jr., "Living Faith: The Black Church Outreach Tradition," Manhattan Institute, The Jeremiah Project, Report 98-3.

17. Mark Chaves and Lynn M. Higgins, "Comparing the Community Involvement of Black and White Congregations," *Journal for the Scientific Study of Religion* 31:4 (December 1992): 425-440, at 433-435, 438.

18. Jill Witmer Sinha, *Cookman United Methodist Church and Transitional Journey: A Case Study in Charitable Choice* (Washington, D.C.: The Center For Public Justice, 2000), 4-6.

19. Tomika De Priest and Joyce Jones, "Economic Deliverance Thru the Church," *Black Enterprise* 28:7 (February 1997): 195-202; Susan Anderson, "Saving Grace: African American Churches Are Revitalizing Neglected Neighborhoods in Ways More Than Spiritual," *Los Angeles Times*, December 24, 2000, Part M, 1; Glenn C. Loury and Linda Datcher Loury, "Not by Bread Alone: The Role of the African-American Church in Inner-City Development," *The Brookings Review* 15:1 (Winter 1997): 10-13; Krystal Miller, "More Black Churches Go Into Business," *Wall Street Journal*, January 27, 1993, B1.

20. Anderson, "Saving Grace."

21. Linda J. Wong, "L.A. Churches: Natural-Born Leaders of Community Revitalization," *Los Angeles Times*, October 19, 1997, Part M, 1.

22. Teresa Watanabe, "Religious Groups, Such as L.A.'s First AME Church, Are Stepping In To Provide Houses and Apartments For the Poor In California, Which Is Beset By a Crisis of Affordable Housing," *Los Angeles Times*, September 23, 2000, B2.

23. Ram A. Cnaan with Robert J. Wineburg and Stephanie C. Boddie, *The Newer Deal: Social Work and Religion in Partnership* (New York: Columbia University Press, 1999), 29-30; and First African Methodist Episcopal Church website, www.First_AME_Church.org.

24. Marla Dickerson, "Full Faith and Credit: Some Churches Get Entrepreneurial in Bid to Aid Communities," *Los Angeles Times*, October 9, 1998, Part C, 1.

25. *Ibid.*

26. Cnaan, "Keeping Faith in the City," 19.

27. Hodgkinson and Weitzman, *From Belief To Commitment*, 2, 25, 30.

28. I have drawn on Joe Klein, "In God They Trust: Washington Faces a New Challenge: Should It Let The Churches Take Over The Inner Cities?" *The New Yorker*, June 16, 1997, 40-48; Jenny Berrien, Omar McRoberts, and Christopher Winship, "Religion and the Boston Miracle: The Effect of Black Ministry on Youth Violence," in *Who Will Provide?* eds. Mary Jo Bane, Brent Coffin, and Ronald Thiemann (Boulder: Westview, 2000), 272-274; Christopher Winship and Jenny Berrien, "Boston Cops and Black Churches," *The Public Interest*, Number 136 (Summer 1999): 52-68; Statement of Rev. Jeffrey L. Brown, "Bringing Worlds Together," United States Senate, Committee on the Judiciary, Hearing on What Works: The Efforts of Private Individuals, Community Organizations, and Religious Groups To Prevent Juvenile Crime, 105th Congress, 1st Session, March 19, 1997, 37-39.

29. John D. DiIulio, Jr., "The Lord's Work: The Church and the 'Civil Society Sector,'" *The Brookings Review* 15:4 (Fall 1997): 27-31, at 28; John Leland with Claudia Kalb, "Savior of the Streets," *Newsweek* 131:22, June 1, 1998, 20.

30. *America*, "Addressing Youth Crime: An Interview with Eugene F. Rivers," 183:9 (September 30, 2000): 21-23, at 22.

31. *Ibid.*

32. Bob Herbert, "In America: Out of the Sanctuary," *New York Times*, September 28, 1997, Section 4, 15. See also Robert A. Jordan, "Clergy's Anger Can Bring Hope," *Boston Globe*, May 16, 1992, 13.

33. Leland, "Savior of the Streets," 25.

34. Herbert, "Out of the Sanctuary."

35. Joe Loconte, *The Anxious Samaritan: Charitable Choice and the Mission of Catholic Charities* (Washington, D.C.: The Center for Public Justice, 2000), 10-11; the website of Catholic Charities USA, www.catholiccharitiesusa.org; Dorothy M. Brown and Elizabeth McKeown, *The Poor Belong to Us: Catholic Charities and American Welfare* (Cambridge: Harvard University Press, 1997).

36. I have drawn on Joe Loconte, "Ex-Con: The Remarkable Second Career of Chuck Colson," *The Weekly Standard* 4:39, June 28, 1999, 21-26; *Standing at a Threshold*, Prison Fellowship Ministries Annual Report 1998-1999; and its website, www.prisonfellowship.org.

37. Charles W. Colson, *Born Again* (Old Tappen, N.J.: Chosen Books, 1976), 108-135, 146-151.

38. Loconte, "Ex-Con," 22.

39. *Ibid.*

Chapter 5

Are Faith-Based Organizations Effective?

Empirical research points to an inverse relationship between "religion" and pervasive social ills, for example, crime, delinquency, and substance abuse, such that high degrees of religiosity tend to reduce such problems. Even so, the "faith-factor" thesis remains a subject of debate, one which is hamstrung by a poor understanding of how religion influences behavior. This "how" gap makes confirmation of the faith-factor thesis impossible. To bridge the gap, and thus lend credence to the faith-factor thesis, this chapter assesses how religion affects behavior.

In summarizing the empirical evidence, this chapter demonstrates that religion deters some deviant behaviors although the impact is not as strong as some might predict. The empirical record is more positive for faith-based programs aimed at rehabilitation.

With the exception of the empirical analyses of the PFM and Teen Challenge (and an impressionist analysis of the Ten-Point Coalition), this chapter employs studies that measure religion's impact on behavior generally, rather than examining FBOs directly. This measure of the faith-factor serves as a proxy for assessing the potential effectiveness of religion as utilized by FBOs.

In itself, a statistical relationship linking religion and socially undesirable behavior is not dispositive; the observed correlation must be the product of religion (the independent variable) acting upon behavior (the dependent variable) and not the product of other independent or mediating factors. Thus, knowing the direction of "causation" is critical to either illuminating or debunking the faith-factor thesis.

The causation question asks whether religion is a predictor of socially beneficial behavior or only tangentially linked to it. However, aside from knowing the direction of causation, two reasons exist for understanding the faith-factor's relative significance. First, without a mechanism explaining how much religion prevents crime, delinquency, substance abuse, or teen premarital sex, the faith-factor thesis remains vulnerable to competing theories that account for a substantial part of the relationship with other proximate mediating factors, such as peer, parental, or nonreligious institutional factors. Second, from a public policy standpoint, policymakers need to know how to use religion in order to foster effective programs nationwide. At present, legislators (like the public) have only a vague notion that faith-based programs succeed where government has failed.

The theory developed in this chapter attempts to define a faith-factor mechanism that reconciles inconsistent empirical findings, and in so doing answers three questions: (1) Is religion a deterrent against pervasive social problems? (2) Are FBOs particularly effective in the most troubled communities? (3) Why is religion apparently more effective at rehabilitation than preventing deviant behavior?

Toward a "Faith-Factor" Theory

Developing a theory that reconciles data from many sources is difficult because of the methodological differences found in empirical studies. Two examples are differences in research quality (e.g., controls for race and gender) and the number of factors used to measure religiosity. However, mathematical precision is not an issue. My proposed theory, rather than attempting to prove anything beyond a reasonable doubt, offers a degree of clarity that informs the faith-factor debate. It shows that religion can have a predictable effect on some but not all forms of deviant behavior.

In this framework, FBOs serve two principal functions: "deterrence" and "rehabilitation." Deterrence refers to religion's positive role in shaping and enforcing normative behavior to prevent deviancy. Four mechanisms or "protective factors" explain how: (1) religion helps to strengthen family solidarity; (2) religious organizations provide viable parental support systems (e.g., parenting classes and pastoral family counseling); (3) religious doctrines set boundaries; and (4) religious organizations provide young people with a coping resource outside the family.[1]

Rehabilitation strives to "reform" substance abusers or convicts. For those who are incarcerated, this means preventing recidivism. As developed in chapters 2 and 4, prison ministries use activities such as Bible study and seminars to achieve this goal. These activities, by helping inmates cope with the psychological trauma of prison life, transform behavior during incarceration and after release.

Critics of the faith-factor thesis argue that religion serves as a significant predictor for only a few types of deviancy and that other proximate, mediating factors are far better predictors for most others. According to this view, predominant among secular-oriented researchers, religion is an insignificant predictor for most forms of deviancy when nonreligious factors are accounted for. In other words, family and friends are better placed than religion to create an environment nonconducive to deviant behavior. Favorable analyses of the faith-factor thesis reject the assertion that religion is a limited predictor of delinquency and argue that studies supporting such a conclusion contain "soft variables" (e.g., self-reported data rather than data derived from observable behavior), are of poor quality (e.g., lack of clarity, weak controls), or fail to address the "cumulative" effect of religion on the probability that a religious person will engage in any deviant behavior. However, these analyses do recognize that, at least empirically, certain types of deviant behavior are not consistently affected by religion.

Interestingly, both views focus on methodology, including the sample surveyed, whether it is too small or not representative, and the manner in which religiosity or deviancy are defined. These determinations are used to substantiate claims that the faith-factor is either mostly significant or mostly spurious. Nevertheless, assuming that their respective arguments are correct and that the effects of religion have been grossly overstated or understated, why claim that religion is either a predictor of every form of deviancy or none at all? These extremes reject a middle ground into which religion probably falls. Because the data do not support an all or nothing conclusion perhaps these conflicting results are not the product of inexact measurement, but are a reflection of reality. This suggests that religion and deviancy are not monolithic concepts and that the actual causal mechanism governing the faith-factor is best viewed as flexible.

Flexibility is incorporated into the proposed faith-factor theory by disaggregating religion into two separate (though not mutually exclusive) "identities." The first identity is termed "structural," in that it relates to the organizational aspect of religion rather than theology. The second identity is termed "evangelical" and focuses on the spiritual, psychological, and emotional impacts of religion (e.g., salvation and forgiveness). These identities are linked to the two functional categories–deterrence and rehabilitation. Although the evangelical identity is a more important part of rehabilitation, both identities are a necessary part of deterrence when the secular community offers little positive reinforcement.

Recognizing that FBOs need both identities in varying amounts to accomplish deterrence and rehabilitation offers greater accuracy than what is found in conventional analysis. Indeed, the proposed faith-factor theory predicts that inconsistencies will be found in the empirical record. It holds that it is easier to rehabilitate convicts because they live in a structured environment; however, rehabilitation is more difficult in a community devoid of secular controls. The reason for this is that prison ministries can focus attention on their evangelical identity, whereas faith-based programs aimed at deterrence must provide both structural and evangelical identities in the most troubled communities. As we will see, the success of the PFM at reducing recidivism, in contrast to the highly fragmented and inconsistent results associated with deterrence, supports this conclusion.

In short, the significance of faith-based solutions depends on the environment in which they operate and the number of functions undertaken. Because the most troubled communities lack the capacity to promote normative behavior, religion's evangelical identity will likewise not be significant unless FBOs go to extraordinary lengths to compensate for the lack of secular structure. By contrast, in a structured environment, such as in a prison, the faith-factor will have greater significance because it need only focus on its evangelical identity in order to function properly.

Deterrence through Faith?

"Deviancy" is a generic term for harmful behaviors, most of which are well represented in troubled communities. Crime, juvenile delinquency, substance abuse, and teen premarital sex are distinct problems with separate characteristics. FBOs are likewise varied in their use of religion, when religion is defined as "encompassing the spectrum of groups and activities whose focus extends beyond the material reality of everyday life, i.e., to a spiritual reality."[2] FBOs do not provide services according to one model but rather field programs that have a religious orientation also meeting the temporal needs of the community. These programs include conflict mediation, drug treatment, and after-school activities.

Faith-factor studies reflect this diversity. No single research model dominated studies of religion's affect on behavior. In empirical studies, deviancy includes anything from teen pregnancy to crimes against people and property. Let us begin by examining studies focusing on the following three issues: substance abuse, teen sex, and crime and delinquency.

Substance Use and Abuse

Studies point to a negative association between religion and substance use or abuse. According to one research report, "These findings hold regardless of the population under study (i.e., children, adolescents, and adults), or whether the research was conducted prospectively or retrospectively.... The greater a person's religious involvement, the less likely he or she will initiate alcohol or drug use or have problems with these substances if they are used...."[3]

Literature reviews report that religion is consistently associated with a decrease in adolescent substance abuse.[4] Studies show a "persistent tendency" for an inverse relationship between religion and substance abuse by middle school youth and high school adolescents. The relationship is "rather modest," however, and is higher for marijuana than alcohol use.[5]

Two large surveys reach the conclusion that religion has a statistically significant impact on the use of illicit drugs and alcohol. One national sample of over 17,000 high school seniors conducted in 1982 by the Survey Research Center at the University of Michigan showed that religiosity (that is, attendance at religious services and the importance of religion in one's life) had a moderate impact on alcohol and marijuana use. Adolescents who were actively religious tended to use less alcohol and marijuana than adolescents uninvolved in religious activities. Involvement in any religious group, whether or not it specifically taught against use, decreased the level of substance use and abuse.[6]

A series of studies have drawn on questionnaires completed in the 1970s by over 3,000 Midwestern adolescents in grades seven through twelve together with numerous follow-up interviews. These studies used a twofold measure of religiosity: first, religiousness (how religious a person are you?), and second, the importance of church activities in which you participate (or would like to participate). The studies also considered personal attitudes to alcohol and marijuana use. The researchers found that religious youths were significantly less likely to use marijuana or alcohol than their nonreligious peers.[7]

Using the same database, a subsequent study concluded that the religiosity effects on drug use are statistically significant and inverse, with slightly weaker effects for adolescent use of alcohol. The impact of religiosity was stable across drug types (soft and hard drugs).[8]

Another study using this survey data and focusing on the impact of religiosity on adolescent frequency of use, found its strongest negative impact on hard liquor and beer, and its weakest (almost nonexistent) impact on wine. The effects of religiosity on the use of beer and hard liquor were largely identical.[9]

More recently, researchers used data from a nationwide survey of 676 predominantly white Christian adolescents between the ages of fifteen and nineteen.[10] The subjects were assessed for substance use and abuse with the level of religiosity developed through responses to seven questions: 1) how important are religious (or spiritual) beliefs in your daily life; 2) how often do you attend religious services; 3) when you have problems in your life how often do you seek spiritual comfort; 4) when you have decisions to make in your daily life, how often do you ask yourself what God would want you to do; 5) have you been "born again," that is, had a turning point in your life when you committed yourself to Jesus; 6) do you encourage people to believe in Jesus as savior; 7) is the Bible the actual Word of God, to be taken literally word for word?

In this study, the researchers found that three dimensions of religiosity (personal devotion, personal conservatism, and institutional conservatism) were inversely associated with alcohol consumption. Personal devotion and institutional (but not personal) conservatism were inversely associated with substance dependence or abuse.

In addition to these findings, racial differences are noteworthy. Researchers analyzed data from a national survey of high school seniors, conducted by the University of Michigan's Institute for Social Research.[11] The sample consisted of 11,728 students, self-identified as black or white, with blacks comprising less than 16 percent of the sample. Predictably, this study indicated that religion did provide some protection from drug use by adolescents; however, religiosity in terms of affiliation, attendance, and importance had less of an impact on the drug use by black adolescents. While white teenagers who had no religious affiliation were more at risk for substance abuse, religious affiliation did not affect the drug use of African-American students. In the black community, low participation in formal religious services was not an indicator of drug use. Rather, it was the importance of religion to the individual that determined the likelihood of substance abuse, such that those who did not deem religion important were the most likely to use illicit substances. The researchers concluded that while the church in the black community may have been an integral part of the lives of its members, it had a relatively modest impact on drug use among black teens. The impact of the church, in terms of varied and multiple roles played in their daily lives, social, psychological, and political, may have overshadowed its role as an instrument of social control, at least with respect to drug use.

More recently, other researchers report that among African-American youth living in poverty areas in three large cities, those who attended church at least once a week were half as likely to use illicit drugs as comparable nonreligious youth who never attended church.[12] Furthermore, analysis of data from the National Youth Survey, a national probability sample of 1,505 persons aged eleven to seventeen in 1977, arrived at two significant findings. First, religious (in terms of frequency of attending religious services) low-income urban teenagers are much less likely to use illicit drugs than comparable nonreligious teens living in the same high-poverty neighborhoods. Second, highly religious youth living in poor urban neighborhoods are somewhat less likely to use illicit drugs (7 percent less likely to use marijuana and 2 percent less likely to use hard drugs) than nonreligious youth living in middle-class suburban neighborhoods.[13]

Premarital Sex

A negative correlation exists between religious involvement and premarital sex. One literature review concludes that "those who are religious are less likely to engage in premarital sex....In fact, approximately 97 percent of those studies reviewed reported significant correlations between increased religious involvement and lower likelihood of promiscuous sexual behavior...."[14]

Studies show that religiosity in teenagers reduces the likelihood of premarital sex. Data generated by the huge National Search Institute Survey showed that after age, religion has the strongest negative effect on such behavior.[15] Other researchers have also found support for linking religiosity to adolescent sexual behavior, with increased religious participation associated with decreasing premarital sexual permissiveness.[16] In fact, some experts estimate that religiousness may decrease the likelihood of premarital intercourse by as much as 50 percent.[17]

Not all researchers arrive at the conclusion that religious socialization, as tied to participation in some type of congregation, encourages adolescents not to engage in health-compromising behavior choices. Using data from a survey of 869 urban middle school students between the ages of eleven and fifteen, one study found that young adolescents who reported being very religious (in terms of frequency of attendance) were nearly as likely as their less religious peers to engage in sexual activity, based on an evaluation of both prior sexual history and future intentions.[18] Yet, this study and its conclusions constitute a distinct minority view among experts.

Some studies of black adolescents also failed to find a significant impact of religiousness on sexual behavior.[19] However, other researchers have concluded that the frequency of church attendance and the perception of the sexual permissiveness of close friends were significantly related to the premarital sexual attitudes of African-American adolescent females, suggesting a more important influence of black religious institutions on permissiveness than previously assumed.[20]

Stepping back from this brief overview, most researchers report a consistent finding that, among adolescents, religious commitment is negatively associated with at-risk behavior, such as alcohol use, drug use, and premarital sex.[21] Beyond these empirical observations, the question remains "Why?" Briefly looking at two theories–social control and social learning–may help.[22] Religion may operate as a social control mechanism by reinforcing moral virtues related to abstinence from alcohol and illicit drug use as well as premarital sex. Religious beliefs constrain undesirable behavior in youths. In situations where alternatives have advantages and disadvantages, religious beliefs (and accompanying proscriptions) may serve as guidelines for personal decision making in ambiguous and difficult matters.

The social learning theory focuses on the reinforcement or punishment of certain behaviors by one's social groups. Behavior patterns are mainly derived from one's peers, and thus, peer and reference group identification reinforce socialization attitudes. Religious organizations fall into this class, and involve voluntary, sustained interaction with reasonably clear criteria for group participation and membership. Religious groups also often impact other human interactions (such as the choice of friends), further strengthening the role of the religious organization as a reference group for adolescents. Through clear guidelines as to what constitutes acceptable behavior, religion can thus have a great impact on personal choices. For instance, religious involvement may be an important protective factor decreasing the chance that one will choose friends who use alcohol and illegal drugs. Involvement in a religious organization may also provide a network of support and friendship that insulates adolescents from opportunities to use illicit drugs. Religiously oriented adolescents generally develop a group of friends who do not use illegal drugs and who are not tolerant of drug use because it is deemed inappropriate, harmful, or evil.

Commitment to a religious organization and its goals may further provide meaning and purpose in life, making, for example, drug use less attractive. The belief system of a religious group may also reinforce personal beliefs against drug use.

Delinquency and Crime

The impact of religion on criminal behavior (acts against people and property) has been the subject of intense empirical investigation. At the outset, it is fair to say that the empirical studies generally indicate an inverse relationship between religiosity and various forms of delinquency and crime, including crimes against persons and property. One study states that the inhibitory impact of religiosity on deviant behavior is "consistent enough to be formulated into an empirical generalization: *Religiosity is inversely related to delinquent behavior.*"[23] Furthermore, recent literature review concludes, "There is growing evidence that religious commitment and involvement helps protect youth from delinquent behavior and deviant behavior....There is mounting evidence that religious involvement may lower the risks of a broad range of delinquent behaviors, including both minor and serious forms of criminal behavior. There is also evidence that religious involvement has a cumulative effect throughout adolescence and thus may significantly lessen the risk of later adult criminality."[24]

A "systematic review" of the studies on religion and juvenile delinquency between 1985 and 1997 provides a quantitative assessment of the empirical literature.[25] Explicit criteria were used to choose the studies. The first step was to identify 362 articles appearing in peer reviewed journals in the fields of criminology, sociology, and psychology that made some mention of religion, spirituality, delinquency, and deviant behavior. Of these, forty contained an analysis of the impact of religion on juvenile delinquency. The authors then analyzed the forty studies (which varied in terms of methodological rigor) and assessed the overall evidence.

Over eighty percent of the studies reviewed found that measures of religiosity had a beneficial impact on delinquency. In other words, the higher the religiosity score the lower the likelihood of delinquency. Religiosity consisted of six categories: attendance; religious salience (i.e., the importance of God in one's own life); denominational affiliation; prayer (active and/or a meaningful part of one's spiritual life); independent Bible study; and participation in various religious activities inside and outside of church, synagogue, or mosque setting. Only one study reported a positive relationship, with the remainder of the studies—a distinct minority—yielding inconclusive results. Of the nine studies using the most comprehensive measures of religiosity, with three taking into account all six dimensions, five using five variables, and one examining four different dimensions, all found that religion decreased delinquency. Similarly, the thirteen studies that assessed the reliability of their religious measures all found that religion related to lower levels of juvenile delinquency.

In sum, this systematic review showed that religiosity reduced delinquency with the pattern becoming stronger as the methodological rigor of the study was enhanced. In contrast, of the studies generating mixed findings regarding the impact of religiosity on delinquency, not one used multiple indicators or administered reliability tests.

An earlier literature review reached a similar conclusion, namely, higher levels of religiosity were associated with a lower likelihood of delinquency. In this review of sixty-five published studies (fifty-nine of which used students as subjects), only ten failed to report a significant negative association between some measure of religiosity and some indicator of rule breaking.[26]

Again, some researchers question the significance of the observed religiosity-delinquency relationship. Viewing the religiosity-delinquency relationship as spurious, they see religiosity as irrelevant to delinquency. For example, according to the arousal theory, adolescents who become delinquents are neurologically predisposed to criminality.[27] These observers maintain that an underaroused nervous system, highly influenced by genetic factors, causes youth to be prone to seek intense stimulation from their environment through various activities, such as delinquency. Those who are easily bored are thus less likely to voluntarily attend religious services which they find uninteresting because they fail to satisfy their arousal need.

Most experts, however, see an inverse relationship between religiosity and various forms of deviance, delinquency, and crime. One study used data generated from interviews conducted in 1975 of over 1,000 teenagers.[28] Attendance at services and importance of religion were used to measure religiosity. Delinquency was measured by whether the interviewees had done any of twelve items during the past year. The authors broadly concluded that there was a negative association between religion and delinquency that is not confined to certain offenses (or to certain social contexts) and that was not readily accounted for by the types of controls that seemed reasonable to introduce. In other words, religion exerted a strong negative impact on all offenses.

Other researchers report a more nuanced impact of religion on criminal activity. A well-known study of adults, using 1980 data from seventy-five American metropolitan areas outside of New England, compared church membership rates with six classes of crime: murder, rape, assault, burglary, larceny, and robbery. Adult church membership had a significant inhibitory effect on four of these classes, assault, burglary, larceny, and robbery. Yet there was no correlation with murder or rape, impulsive crimes generally undeterred by religion.[29]

Another study, using information collected from 3,000 adolescents during the 1970s (mentioned earlier in the chapter), found that the deterrent impact of religion increased as offense seriousness decreased.[30] The largest differences in the predicted probability between the strongly and weakly religious (based on how religious you are and how important are church activities in which you participate or would like to participate) was observed for the least serious offenses, namely, vandalism and minor theft (as well as for marijuana and alcohol use). Much smaller differences were observed for more serious offenses, including motor vehicle theft, assault, weapon use, and major theft.

If we accept the general thesis that religion deters crime and delinquency, we can then focus on when and in what context. To help answer these questions, researchers have investigated the impact of family and peers as well as the social context.

The Impact of Family and Peers

The waters become far muddier once other variables besides religiosity are introduced into the analytical mix. Even if they view the religiosity-delinquency relationship as substantively meaningful, some researchers maintain that the relationship between religiosity and adolescent deviance becomes insignificant after controlling for family relationships and peer influences. For adolescents, religion may be so entangled with other law-abiding influences, such as parental and peer influence, that its direct contribution may be redundant. It can, therefore, be difficult to measure the impact of religion on deviant behavior. For example, a study of 724 public high school students in Oklahoma and Arkansas found that social bonding (e.g., family) and social control (e.g., peers) factors mediated the impact of religiosity on deviancy.[31]

Supporters of the faith-factor view many of these multivariable studies as taking too narrow a measurement of religiosity. Multiple item indicators are rare in the literature, and there is a pronounced reliance on church attendance to serve as an adequate proxy for religiosity. Because religiosity is multifaceted, some researchers maintain that it needs to be represented by using multiple-item indicators in order to better demonstrate its impact.

Other experts conclude that the effect of religion is neither spurious nor weakened by the presence of other variables. One study analyzed data from a national survey conducted in 1977 of 1,725 youths between the ages of eleven and seventeen.[32] Religiosity was defined in multifaceted terms: 1) frequency of attending religious services; 2) the importance of religion in one's life; 3) time spent on community-based religious activities during weekends; and 4) the importance of involvement in community-based religious activities. The authors concluded that the negative effects of religiosity on delinquency remain significant and "quite robust" even after controlling for all the independent, intervening variables as well as sociodemographic factors. This suggests that there is indeed a strong correlation between religiosity and the deterrence of delinquent behavior.

In contrast to this study bolstering the faith-factor, other studies using multivariables and multiple measures of religiosity point to a different conclusion. Examining data from 600 interviews in 1974 with well educated, relatively affluent students from twenty-one Atlanta, Georgia, high schools, researchers found that within a multivariate context, religion's contribution as an independent variable was not statistically significant.[33] Three measures of religion were used, namely, church attendance, religious affiliation, and religious salience (or importance). Although religious youths were less likely to be delinquent than the non-religious, the authors concluded that the source of this tendency was in the types of families and friends that religious young people had. They saw religion as but one of a larger set of influences encouraging law-abiding behavior. Furthermore, these researchers asserted that the relationship of religiosity to delinquency was so closely tied to family and peers that it had little influence statistically independent of these other predictive variables.

Subsequently, researchers analyzed data, obtained in 1991, from 263 questionnaires completed by students attending a public high school located in a middle- to upper-middle class suburb of a large Midwestern city.[34] The study defined religiosity in terms of: religious activity (attending services and social events at church); religious salience (importance of religion in daily life); and hellfire beliefs and fears. The authors noted that delinquent involvement was negatively influenced by personal religiosity and the religiosity of one's friends (one's religious network). The most religious respondents were less involved in delinquency as were those who had a majority of close religious friends. However, the authors observed that the general religiosity and peer religiosity effects on delinquency were muted after controlling for secular bonds (family, school, or peers). In searching for an explanation of the impact of a community of religious believers, the authors suggested that the threats of sanction and risk of embarrassment were more visible and viable through such a moral community.

Other studies using large data sets analyzed the impact of multiple variables on substance abuse, sexual behavior, and delinquency reached mixed results. One such study used data from the National Longitudinal Study of Adolescent Health, a national study of 12,118 adolescents in grades seven through twelve. This analysis showed that children with "religious identities" (defined as one who "pray[s] frequently, view[s] self as religious, affiliate[s] with a religion") were less likely to abuse alcohol or marijuana. A higher level of importance ascribed to religion and prayer was also associated with a "somewhat later age of sexual debut...." To complicate things, two competing variables, "parent-family connectedness" and "school connectedness," more effectively inhibited alcohol and marijuana use than religious identity.[35]

A Search Institute study of over 34,000 adolescents between 1989 and 1994 measured religiosity using three criteria: (1) time spent per week attending services, groups or programs at a church or synagogue; (2) frequency of attending religious services; and (3) the self-reported importance of religion. Religiosity inhibited alcohol and illegal drug use as well as premarital sexual intercourse. Religiosity, particularly church attendance and importance of religion in one's life, had an inhibitory impact on violence. Yet the statistical significance of religiosity as an explanatory factor for violence was weaker than three background variables, namely, educational ability, educational aspiration, and gender. However, the authors concluded that religion "is as strong (or as weak) as any of the background variables that are more frequently cited as determinants of attitudes and behavior [for example, binge drinking, driving while intoxicated, sexual intercourse]....It deserves attention as an important explanatory variable in these areas." They also indicated that for most adolescents, religious socialization is linked to participation in some type of a congregation. A common thread running across houses of worship, they noted, includes "socialization pressure to avoid health-compromising behavioral choices....These messages are essentially constant across religious communities in the United States, regardless of theological perspective...."[36]

The Impact of the Social Context

Possible explanations for the disparate findings and the welter of confusing and contradictory conclusions emanating from empirical studies include erroneous interpretation of the data and competing theories that derogate the importance of religion or fully mediate its affect on deviancy. Of particular interest, however, is the religious ecology thesis and its explanation for the inconsistent empirical findings. The religious ecology theory posits that social context plays an important role in the deterrent power of religion. This theory came out of an analysis of three different sets of self-reported data from juvenile samples. The authors found that the social context of the community exerts an important effect on the religiosity-delinquency relationship.[37] They theorized that religion has its greatest inhibitory impact in moral communities where a substantial portion of the population are church members and where religious influences permeate the culture and the social interactions of individuals.

Thus, where only a minority are religious, as measured by church membership rates, religion may have no power to deter delinquency even among religiously observant youth. Conversely, where the majority are religious, the power to deter such behavior is greater. The social context ratifies individual religiosity, leading to an acceptance of religion as a valid basis for action and a connection between belief and behavior.

Thus, where organized religion is relatively strong (as measured by church membership rates) and where religious beliefs and concerns permeate the community, the religious ecology theory posits that church-going and believing individuals are far less likely to engage in delinquent behavior (e.g., theft) than their nonreligious peers. When most of the people in the community are religious, then religious norms are salient and will work better to deter delinquent behavior. Within a significantly religious social climate and a religiously dense, moral community, an individual's faith generates the power to constrain delinquent behavior.

In nonreligious areas, an individual's personal beliefs are not salient and religious youths are as likely as others to commit delinquent acts. In these communities, the religious variable fails to distinguish between the likelihood of youth delinquent activity and places religion's capacity to deter deviant behavior in doubt. Thus, if a local community is highly secular, the impact of individual religiousness will be muffled and will not influence delinquency.

Other theorists, taking a diametrically opposite approach, assert that even if religious indifference is manifest in a local community and religious persons are very isolated, the religious impacts will appear, provided that these individuals belong to an organized group of believers.[38] In other words, through social integration, religious beliefs deter delinquent acts when supported by the social bonds among individuals.

In contrast to the religious ecology theory, these theorists judge the impact of religion to be most powerful in those communities where the general culture is more secular. Under this theory, religiosity can act as a greater deterrent to deviant behavior in communities where there is little social integration, where religious values do not dominate, and where the community has very few structural controls.

It is useful to take a moment to develop a little more fully the concept of social disorganization.[39] In communities where there are few formal and informal controls, there is a reduced incentive to conform to moral standards, and thus high rates of crime and delinquency are more likely. Members of these communities withdraw from neighborhood life, and consequently from any formal or informal social control processes. As a result, the community is unable to regulate itself through these processes. Additionally, a decline in a neighborhood's organizational life, deteriorating business conditions, and dramatic changes in population composition can lead to social disorganization.

When secular moral guidelines are unavailable, in flux, or have lost their authority, the importance of religious proscriptions may be enhanced–at least for those who are religiously active. Where the secular community fosters little sense of community attachment or general social bonding, persons involved in local religious groups may intensify their commitment to compensate for the lack of social support from the larger community. Religious organizations, in this context, provide the social controls that are absent in the general community, through strict adherence to religious precepts and proscriptions. As a result of the social ties developed in these organizations, individuals will be more likely to adopt and follow moral guidelines in order to remain a member of the religious group and to distinguish themselves from the rest of the community.

In short, individual religiosity may have its greatest impact on behavior where conditions of secular disorganization prevail, where the proportion of people who are nonreligious is the greatest, and where the larger environment lacks mechanisms normally curtailing deviance and producing general conformity. Conversely, individual religiosity may be least effective in highly integrated and organized communities. Religious beliefs are seen as redundant in such communities, given other sources of moral authority and social control. As a result, the affect of religion on delinquency is much weaker.

It is not necessary to serve as a referee between these two competing theories. Suffice it to say that both use social context as a reference point. Religious ecology theorists focus on a larger community, i.e., a city or a town. Critics of the religious ecology theory focus on a much smaller community consisting of a church (or a group of churches), even in the midst of a larger, socially disorganized neighborhood or city.

Disregarding the social context of the broader community, several studies give credence to the deterrent impact of religion. One study concluded that religion can deter hedonistic deviance (e.g., drug use, heavy alcohol consumption, and promiscuous sexuality) in communities where religion is weak in terms of overall church attendance. This study, using 1971 data from nearly 900 high school students in the Pacific Northwest, revealed a moderately strong inverse relationship between religion (in terms of church attendance and belief in supernatural sanctions) and the use of marijuana and alcohol.[40] Even when not sustained by the social majority, religion may warn youth in a convincing manner that they will be hurt by indulging in drugs, excessive alcohol, or uncontrolled sex.

Structural deficiencies and the socioeconomic disadvantages of inner-city communities lead many youths living in these urban areas into criminal and other deviant activities. However, in the face of structural adversity, a significant proportion of black youths develop through adolescence without serious behavioral problems. What then protects disadvantaged youth, so-called "resilient youth," from negative community influences?

Several studies have examined the impact of religiosity on delinquency in the inner city. These surveys show that the structural identity of religion is less important to a community that has a strong secular structure. With such a secular structure, religious organizations can focus on their evangelical identity. As a result, the evangelical identity easily takes root and is mediated through peer and family relationships. However, troubled neighborhoods frequently lack secular structure and thus the effectiveness of the evangelical message lessens unless the members of a neighborhood become extraordinarily religious and thereby create a greater degree of structure, for example, African-American churches in the inner city.

One small study compared sixty African-American males in 1989, between the ages of twenty and thirty-five, who had a history of incarceration with those who had never been incarcerated.[41] The authors noted that those not in prison had more friends who attended churches from ages ten to eighteen; they also participated actively in church activities themselves, attending worship services and Sunday school more often throughout their childhood up to age twenty-one. Those not in prison were likely to report a belief in working hard to support themselves and were more likely to report being "born again."

In addition to the small sample size, some caveats come with this study. The participants were not randomly selected. There may have been a pre-selection bias because both groups consisted of volunteers who were not paid. Also, it is not clear whether the family's failure to encourage church attendance indicated dysfunctionality or a lack of concern for family members.

Using data from 1979-1980 National Bureau of Economic Research-Mathematica Survey of Inner-City Black Youth and 1979-1981 National Longitudinal Surveys of young men (black and white), another researcher sought to determine which black youths are more likely to escape from the pathological environment of the inner city, particularly disordered neighborhoods. He determined that church attendance, rather than religious attitudes, affected behavior and provided a good predictor of who escapes. The role of the church as a social institution underpinned the author's conclusion.

Churchgoing led to substantial differences in the behavior of youths and their chances to escape inner-city poverty. It increased the amount of time youths spent on productive activity, increased school attendance, and acted as a deterrent to socially deviant activity. The higher the level of one's religious involvement, the lower the level of crime. Churchgoing influenced or reinforced decisions to engage in activities with a potential future reward without affecting one's immediate labor market position, in terms of wage rates or annual income.[42]

Two recent studies also analyzed data from the National Youth Survey, focusing on interviews of 2,358 inner-city black male youths from poverty areas in Boston, Philadelphia, and Chicago conducted in 1979-1980. Church attendance (the frequency of attending religious services) had a significantly inverse and independent impact among disadvantaged youths on nondrug-related crimes (a 39 percent reduction), drug use (a 46 percent reduction), and drug dealing (a 57 percent reduction). Religious salience (the perceived importance of religion in one's life), however, was not significantly linked to reductions in juvenile delinquency.[43]

In attempting to answer why churchgoing makes such a difference, the authors suggest that black youths who frequently attend religious services are bonded to an institution of informal social control (the church) and that nonreligious youth are not. Sanctions derived from religion guide the behavioral patterns of religious youth, by helping to internalize and strengthen traditional beliefs and by nurturing relationships among their peers and others within the church. These youths are exposed to more "definitions" favoring conformity instead of deviance. These attachments reduce their chances of making delinquent friends and engaging in various types of deviance often associated with inner-city poverty areas.

Another study by these researchers, using data from the same National Youth Survey, found that the harmful affects of a "high disorder" neighborhood on serious crime (felony, assault, robbery, felony theft, sale of illegal drugs), but not minor crime (minor assault and minor theft), were not as great as when black youth frequently attended church or other religious services.[44] Disorder in a neighborhood connoted both a lack of social order (peace, safety, and observance of the law) and social control (acts that maintain order). Social disorder, as evidenced by higher crime rates and substance abuse problems, created a sense of danger on the streets and likely discouraged social ties among neighbors. Family dissolution and female-headed households may also contribute to a weakening of informal controls because there are fewer adult caretakers in the community to maintain surveillance over potentially wayward members.

This study indicated a negative relationship between religious involvement and serious crime. Religious involvement connoted the participation of an individual in a religious group and his integration into a social network that provided social and emotional support. The higher one's religious involvement, the lower the risk that he will commit a serious crime.

The constraining affect of religious involvement on serious crime among black youth was more pronounced in neighborhoods with "higher" levels on disorder than in "low disorder" neighborhoods. For those reporting high levels of religious involvement, the average level of self-reported serious crime among those living in high "bad" (high disorder) neighborhoods tended to be lower than that of their counterparts living in "good" or "better" (lower disorder) neighborhoods. The authors observed that an individual's religious involvement may weaken the detrimental impact of neighborhood disorder on youth behavior by mediating, in part, the adverse consequences. Those who are highly involved religiously, at least in terms of church attendance, but living in a high disorder neighborhood may live in small, more moral communities than those living in lower disorder neighborhoods.

These studies demonstrate that a church in a "bad" or socially disorganized neighborhood can compensate for its social context through its own structural and evangelical identities. The church can thereby impose consequences for deviant behavior that are absent in the larger community, such that youths who more frequently attend religious services will be less likely to engage in these activities. This is achieved on two levels: first, condemning certain behaviors acts as an external control on these behaviors; and second, the internalization of the moral virtues advocated by the church which in turn creates a personal abhorrence for such behavior.

Religion and FBOs can thus perform a social control function. Religious institutions and traditions maintain social order by discouraging deviance, delinquency, and self-destructive behavior. Religion opposes antisocial values, advances constructive behaviors, urges forgiveness and reconciliation, and strives to mediate and defuse conflict. It guides behavior by a system of norms and virtues favoring personal restraint and responsibility. Religion, through its institutions and group worship services, provides faith, hope, and a sense of connectedness to give meaning and purpose to those in need, thus also serving a social learning function. As one literature review concludes, religious involvement helps "adolescents learn 'prosocial behavior' that emphasizes concern for others' welfare. Such prosocial skills may give adolescents a greater sense of empathy toward others, which makes them less likely to commit acts that harm others."[45]

If little secular structure exists in a disordered community for transmitting normative beliefs and virtue, such as strong families and effective schools, it is less likely that religion's evangelical message will have a significant impact on deviancy unless FBOs build those institutions from scratch–a difficult task indeed. However, once an FBO successfully builds a viable institution, it can serve as an effective agency of local social control in protecting youth from the potentially detrimental impact of neighborhood disorder.

The Impact of the Ten-Point Coalition

As discussed in chapter 4, some FBOs take the structure of a group of ministers forming a coalition, such as the Ten-Point Coalition (the Coalition). According to one impressionist study, the Coalition did not play a direct, significant role in reducing youth violence in Boston.[46] The core of the Coalition consisted of three ministers who could not devote full-time attention to the reduction of youth violence. Furthermore, the diminution in youth crime occurred in the context of a broad-based move to community policing in Boston. Also, new cooperative relationships between the Boston police and probation departments, including new policies and practices, led to more effective procedures for dealing with youth violence. However, the authors concluded, "First, and most important, we want to establish that despite [these] observations, the Ten-Point Coalition has been critical to the reduction of youth violence in Boston."[47]

The key contribution of the Coalition centered not in its programs for at-risk youth, but rather in changing the way Boston's inner-city community and the police (as well as other elements of the criminal justice system) related to each other. The community frequently had conflicting goals: the desire for safe streets versus a reluctance to see its young men jailed. The police, therefore, were forced to make difficult decisions that members of the community deemed unjust. The Coalition served as an intermediary between the two sides and changed the relationship between the Boston police and inner-city communities from open antagonism to partnership in two respects.

First, it created an umbrella of legitimacy for the police to work under by supporting police activities the Coalition deemed beneficial to the community and criticizing those activities that were not. If the police adopted certain policies, such as focusing on truly problematic youth, dealing with these youth in a "fair and just" way, and acting in cooperation with the community through the three core ministers, then the Coalition provided public support and legitimacy for the police efforts. Conversely, if it regarded certain police efforts as not constructive or going beyond what the community would tolerate, for instance, if the police used indiscriminate and abusive methods in dealing with teens, then the Coalition stood ready to subject the police to explicit public criticism in the media. By providing informal oversight of police actions and an umbrella of legitimacy for police work, the group of ministers legitimized the entire criminal justice system.

Second, the Coalition increased police effectiveness by providing remote surveillance capacity in troubled neighborhoods. Ministers involved in the Coalition helped identify youths who were "out of control" or were the most likely to get involved in violence and, thus, posed the greatest threat to the community. They singled out particularly dangerous teens to the police and indicated the need for arrests. Because most of these youths had outstanding arrest warrants, they were arrested even if an actual crime did not precipitate a minister's call.

Because of the Coalition's involvement in the criminal justice process, the community was more likely to regard the differential treatment of individual teens as legitimate. The police still had to make tough decisions, but these choices were typically viewed by the community as "fair and just." Targeting youths who were the "true" problems insured that police focused on the "right" teens, thereby enhancing police legitimacy.

The Coalition's moral authority rested on two types of public trust: first, the black community's trust in the independence and integrity of the clergy; and second, the public sector's recognition of the centrality of religious institutions to concerned inner-city residents. These clergy, as African-American church leaders well known for their extensive work with inner-city youth, occupied a unique structural position that gave them the opportunity to serve as intermediaries. Their status as clergy allowed the three core ministers to reconcile divergent interests. They could not only critique structures of power, such as the police or even the entire criminal justice system, but they could also demand moral accountability from the neighborhoods they represented, holding young people responsible for their own behavior, and presenting clear and viable opportunities for personal transformation and renewal.

Rehabilitation and Renewal:
PFM and Recidivism

The empirical record for recidivism and survival (the period of time until recidivism occurs) for those in PFM is less muddled than the findings in deviancy research. Moreover, prison studies directly assess a specific FBO; thus, they measure the value of religion as utilized by an FBO rather that the effects of religion on society in the abstract. There are, however, far fewer studies that focus on the impact of religion in a prison environment and confirmation of its success awaits further research.

As developed in chapter 4, PFM strives to help inmates cope with the stress of incarceration and to prepare them for release through religious instruction. It organizes seminars and Bible study groups and distributes newspapers, among other activities. Moreover, its InnerChange Freedom Initiative (a prerelease program discussed in chapter 2) assists the inmate's transition to the outside world by ministering to them before and after release.

One study focused on the Prison Fellowship's Nationwide Discipleship Seminar program.[48] Between November 1975 and November 1986, PFM conducted fifty-nine Discipleship Seminars in Washington, D.C. (It no longer operates this type of program, working instead within prisons.) At each seminar, fifteen federal inmates from federal correctional institutions throughout the United States were furloughed to the Washington, D.C., area to participate in an intensive two-week ministry program. These seminars aimed at supporting and deepening their Christian faith, fostering religious commitment and fellowship, integrating them with a wider support network in the community at large, and preparing them to provide, as volunteer prison ministers, Christian fellowship and support for their fellow inmates within their respective prisons. Inmates volunteered to participate and were selected for the program upon the recommendation of their prison chaplains and based on their leadership qualities and religious commitment. The seminars included, among other features, devotional sharing, worship experiences, small group discussions, individual prayer time, Bible study, and leadership training workshops.

The study compared recidivism data over an eight- to fourteen-year follow-up period for the 180 seminar participants, in the first twenty-one Discipleship Seminars conducted between November 1975 and November 1979, with data drawn from a matched control group of 185 federal inmates. The control group was selected from a group of 2,289 federal inmates, representing a 50 percent random sample of all prisoners receiving prison sentences of more than a year who were released during the first six months of 1978.

The study showed that the seminar group had a significantly lower rate of recidivism than the control group. Recidivism was defined as any new arrest (including parole violations) following release from prison during the duration of the study period–ranging from eight to fourteen years. The researchers found that the PFM group maintained a higher crime-free survival rate for a longer period of time than the control group. The seminars were effective with inmates at low risk for recidivism (but not with high-risk subjects), white males, and especially with females.

The researchers admitted that they did not know if the control group met the selection criteria for the PFM group or were equally self-motivated. However, the likelihood of false positive errors (i.e., ex-convicts are prone to rearrest on suspicion) and false negative errors (i.e., those who return to criminal behavior may not be arrested) was likely equivalent for both groups in the study. Although the FBI Records of Arrest (RAP sheets) may not always record all arrests, there was no reason to question the equivalence of validity between the two groups.

Focusing on the efficacy of the current PFM program, another study examined 402 adult, male inmates in 1992 from four New York State prisons, three medium-security prisons, and one maximum security facility.[49] Given the problems of data collection, the authors candidly admitted that the sample was not random, nor did it represent inmates in general or New York State inmates in particular. The authors selected these four prisons because the data on the PFM participation in these four prisons for 1992 was "far superior" to other New York State prisons offering PFM programs. PFM staff members and prison volunteers at these four prisons were more strongly committed to data collection than staff members at other New York State prisons.

The PFM group of inmates participated in at least one of three PFM activities: a weekly Bible study program, three-day in prison seminars designed to deepen a person's life of faith and fellowship, or two- or three-day life plan seminars seeking to help inmates prepare for their release. These inmates evidenced varying degrees of involvement in these programs. Some participated at least once in three activities, while others participated several times in only one activity.

A control group of 201 former inmates most closely matching the PFM inmates on seven variables (age, race, religious denomination, country of residence, military discharge, minimum sentence, and initial security classification) comprised the non-PFM matched group. Each member of the non-PFM group was assigned a non-PFM match.

The study found that while participation in fellowship programs had no appreciable affect on behavior while in prison, recidivism and survival rates were far better among highly active members. The PFM and non-PFM groups were very similar with regard to the violation of prison rules and the seriousness of any institutional infractions, such as assault or attempted escape. In fact, during the one-year period preceding release from prison, more PFM inmates than non-PFM inmates (36 percent vs. 31 percent) committed institutional infractions. No significant differences existed among the low, medium, and high PFM participation groups with respect to committing institutional infractions. PFM participants, who attended ten or more Bible studies during the one-year period, were as likely to commit infractions as those who participated to a lesser degree, but were slightly less likely than their non-PFM counterparts to commit any institutional infractions.

There was no significant difference between PFM inmates and non-PFM inmates regarding the seriousness of any institutional infractions. High PFM participants were slightly less likely than their non-PFM matches to commit serious institutional infractions, but, surprisingly, they were significantly more likely to do so than low or medium Prison Fellowship participants.

The perceived failure to affect behavior while incarcerated may be due to uncertainties over causation. The data used in the New York study did not specify whether problem behavior occurred before or after participation in a PFM activity. Thus, it may be that problem behavior brought on by mental and psychological distress led inmates to seek religious counseling. Another possible explanation is that even highly religious inmates view certain behaviors as acceptable while incarcerated that they would condemn in the outside world. This is because in prison, survival and protection become paramount, trumping even religious values.

The study also measured recidivism, defined as any arrest of a former inmate during a relatively short time frame, a one-year postrelease period. No significant difference existed between the PFM and non-PFM groups (37 percent vs. 36 percent) regarding recidivism. However, greater participation in Prison Fellowship activities led to a significant decrease in the likelihood of arrest during the one-year follow-up period.

The finding that limited involvement in a Prison Fellowship program was not related to low recidivism, as opposed to active involvement, suggests that religion is not a quick cure but a more long-term remedy. Many of the beneficial effects of religion can only be obtained by in-depth participation, and limited commitment to religious programs may be insufficient to change the antisocial attitudes and behaviors of inmates.

The researchers also examined the relationship between postrelease behavior and inmates' risk levels, based on each inmate's previous record of violence, adult convictions, and prison disciplinary record. These factors bear on the risk of recidivism. Among those both in the PFM group and those in the control group, inmates at a higher risk of repeat offenses had higher recidivism rates and shorter arrest-free survival times. Although there is less empirical data from which to draw a conclusion, participation in the PFM program helps lower recidivism among active, but low-risk participants who are not prone to repeat offenses.

Although religious instruction may not be an effective course of therapy with hardened criminals, the finding that religion helps those on the fringe is in keeping with some of the theories behind rehabilitation. Particularly, the notion that the act of incarceration is psychologically traumatizing and that lessening its shock reduces the risk that the trauma suffered in prison will spill over into life after prison. Reduced recidivism may be a by-product of religious commitment. The PFM program holds the promise of decreasing recidivism rates for inmates who become committed to the Christian faith.

Although the authors cautiously concluded that "our findings at least suggest that religious programs have the potential to affect former inmates' behavior after release,"[50] several caveats must be noted. First, the demographics of the study are noteworthy. Hispanics were overpresented in this study, comprising nearly 40 percent of both the PFM inmates and non-PFM inmates. Whites, consisting of slightly more than 12 percent of the PFM and non-PFM inmates, were underpresented. Second, only a small number (22 of 201 inmates or 11 percent) were in the high participation Prison Fellowship category. Third, the one-year follow-up period is not optimal for determining the influence of religious programs on recidivism over time. Several more years of observation would better capture the recidivism rate.

Another study analyzed data from Lieber Correctional Institution, a medium-security facility for men in South Carolina.[51] The researchers divided 1,792 convicts released from incarceration in the facility from 1996 to 1999, excluding certain offenders, into three groups. The first group, numbering 1,171, had no religious involvement during the study period. The second group of 345 were involved in religious programs not offered by PFM. The third group consisted of 276 people who were involved with PFM during their incarceration at the facility, either attending an ongoing, weekly Bible study session or an in-prison two- or three-day seminar held several times a year. The three groups did not differ markedly with respect to major demographics (such as marital status, race, age, years of education) or criminal history (number of prior convictions) variables. The study indicated that the (PFM) group had the lowest percentage of recidivism (42 percent) (based on rearrest from the date of release until November 2000), followed by those who had no religious participation (51 percent) and those who participated in other religious programs (55 percent). Even controlling for the risk of recidivism and demographics, those in the PFM program were about one-third less likely to be re-arrested than those who had no religious involvement or those members of the non-PFM group.

Again, this study comes with several caveats. Only a small proportion of the offenders in the study were released from incarceration for a period of thirty-six months or more. Because many were released toward the end of the data collection period, the study may lack a sufficient time period to get an accurate picture of recidivism. Also, re-arrests after release occurring outside of South Carolina were not included in the study. However, the likelihood of re-arrest outside South Carolina may be roughly similar for all three groups.

It is also necessary to assist ex-inmates with a successful reintegration into society. One preliminary evaluation of the aftercare Transition of Prisoners Program (TOPP) in Detroit, a project of PFM and twenty-four churches in Detroit, showed that participation by ex-offenders in TOPP significantly reduced their risk of recidivism and their actual rate of recidivism.[52]

Religion and the Rehabilitation of Prisoners

Religion can be more effective when administered in prisons than when attempted as a deterrent in the worst neighborhoods. This is because an inmate is generally in an environment that is more conducive to promoting normative behavior than the communities from which he or she came, especially those from inner-city areas. Removed from these dysfunctional environments and given adequate structure, an inmate is free to focus on moral and spiritual growth and, in so doing, not only mitigates the incarceration process but also uses the time to develop a sound moral and spiritual foundation.

Although the data do not indicate that programs offered by PFM make inmates into model citizens while incarcerated, the long-term impact (as shown by the lower recidivism rates) may be more profound because it means that there is a slow process of moral and spiritual growth that translates into an ability to live without crime. In essence, this view rediscovers the value of the old penitentiary: it is a place that gives wayward people a chance at renewal and transformation. Thus, the structure imposed in prisons allows religion to focus on its spiritual identity. As opposed to the problems experienced by communities without secular structure, prison ministries operate in an environment with an abundance of structure and need not dwell on providing what the secular authorities have failed to do. In the worst communities, religious groups must do both. They are successful only if they go to tremendous lengths to make up the lack of secular structure.

Rehabilitation and Renewal:
Teen Challenge and the Treatment of Substance Abuse

Empirical studies demonstrate the positive results achieved by Teen Challenge, a Christian drug rehabilitation program. As discussed in chapter 2, Teen Challenge follows a religious model of addiction treatment, focusing on an eight-month or longer stay in an out-of-town residential facility.

The most in-depth study to date compared a group of graduates of the Teen Challenge program and a sample of the clients of the publicly funded Short-Term Inpatient (STI) drug treatment programs, the latter using the disease model of addiction and requiring thirty- to sixty-day hospital stays.[53] Teen Challenge graduates were surveyed out of a nationwide group of adult males from its three largest residential programs in Pennsylvania,

Missouri, and California. All three of these programs had uniform curriculum, rules, and general program structure. The three groups graduated in October 1993, April 1994, and October 1994, providing groups twelve, eighteen, and twenty-four months posttreatment. Fifty-nine of the Teen Challenge survey participants were also interviewed, mainly in October 1995.

Although detractors often claim that FBOs pick and thus obtain "better" clients, the study indicated that the members of the Teen Challenge group were involved in fewer productive pretreatment programs, used a greater range of illegal drugs, and were more severely addicted.[54] Before the program, 86 percent of the Teen Challenge respondents used drugs other than alcohol at least weekly, while 47 percent of the STI group used nonalcoholic drugs that often.[55] The Teen Challenge group came from a more disadvantaged population and many had few or no productive relationships.[56]

The results of this study show, in comparison with one popular secular drug treatment program, that Teen Challenge was in many ways more effective. In particular, Teen Challenge helped its members gain new social skills, so that on leaving the program the Teen Challenge graduate (in comparison to an STI graduate) was productively employed at a much higher rate with a dramatically lower chance of returning for further treatment.

There were differences in the two groups' respective employment rates. Teen Challenge graduates were employed at a far higher rate than their STI counterparts. Forty-one percent of STI clients were employed full-time after treatment compared with 90 percent of the Teen Challenge sample.[57] However, eighteen of the fifty-nine worked or volunteered at Teen Challenge (or a similar program), full- or part-time.[58] As noted in chapter 2, Teen Challenge relies on former beneficiaries to run its programs.

Teen Challenge graduates were also less likely to need further treatment and more likely to be free from addictive substances. Thirty-one percent of the STI sample returned to treatment in the six months prior to the survey interview, while none of the Teen Challenge graduates returned during this same period.[59] The study also found that 86 percent of the Teen Challenge graduates interviewed were abstaining from drug use. This figure is better than the 74 percent abstinence rate for the STI graduates.[60] In short, the study showed that in comparison to their STI counterparts, most Teen Challenge graduates led normal lives, held down full-time jobs, and very rarely needed to return to treatment or attend frequent meetings of twelve-step programs.

This in-depth study corroborated a mid-1990s survey of a random sample of fifty Teen Challenge of Chattanooga, Tennessee, graduates from a twelve-year period (1979 to 1991), that obtained twenty-five responses. The Chattanooga survey found that most of the graduates of this small survey group were employed with some level of stability and financial independence, evidenced little need for additional drug treatment, mostly abstained from drug use, and were free from trouble with the police. Seventy-two percent were currently employed, with 76 percent indicating the financial ability to support themselves. Of those who were employed, 94 percent earned enough to support themselves. Eighty-eight percent of the respondents were not involved in additional drug treatment programs after Teen Challenge. While 25 percent reported current drug use, none indicated heavy use (at least once a day), one-third used drugs one or two times a week and two-thirds used drugs at least once a month. Finally, 76 percent of the respondents were free of the judicial system, in that they had no charges pending and were not on probation, on parole, or in jail. In short, the changes in behavior and lifestyle, the author concluded, were significant and long lasting.[61]

An earlier study reported similar results. This study drew on a seven-year follow-up survey conducted in 1975. It surveyed 186 applicants who entered the Teen Challenge program in 1968, with 90 percent of the program entrants coming through the Brooklyn, New York Induction Center. There was a striking drop in heroin use for training center graduates: nearly a 85 percent reduction in use. The decline (77 percent) was even remarkable for those admitted to the training center, but who subsequently dropped out and failed to graduate.[62] The researcher who conducted the follow-up survey stated, "...[I]t appears reasonable to conclude that involvement with Teen Challenge is associated with dramatic changes in behavior for a substantial number of heroin users."[63]

Other significant, positive behavioral shifts occurred. The figures were equally impressive with respect to posttreatment criminal activity and treatment subsequent to participation in the Teen Challenge program. The incidence of obtaining money through illegal sources declined the longer a member remained in the program: 20 percent for Induction Center dropouts, 3.9 percent for Training Center dropouts, and 1.6 percent for Training Center graduates. Also, graduates were as much as 59 percent less likely than other groups (Induction Center and Training Center dropouts) to have been involved in treatment programs after Teen Challenge.[64]

What accounts for the success of the Teen Challenge rehabilitation program? Three elements stand out, namely, character building, a sense of community with fellow students and staff, and the "Jesus-factor" or the high level of religious belief.[65]

The Teen Challenge model focuses on character development. Each ex-addict, as he or she goes through the program, becomes responsible for building character and developing positive virtues as well as deciding to overcome a destructive habit. He or she is an active (rather than passive) agent in the recovery process. This model creates an empowering sense of purpose for each student. Through job training activities and their work assignments, the graduates contribute to the program.[66]

Each Teen Challenge student experiences a profound sense of community not only with his or her fellow students but also with the "cure" made real to them through caring and committed live-in staff, most of whom are graduates of the program.[67] As a key part of the residential experience, a student must learn how to participate in community life and form close social relationships. Because of the trust and cooperation fostered with other students and the staff, these relational skills impart the ability to develop healthy and productive relationships with others after graduation. They also provide the skills needed to find and use a network of contacts to further sound social relationships. Thus, Teen Challenge is effective, in part, because it dispels an addict's loneliness and emptiness by building productive social skills and equipping students to utilize those skills upon graduation. Participation in the program has a positive impact on students. They learn to trust, so that they continue to build and maintain positive relationships.

The staff plays an important role in the program's success. Students sense the dedication and commitment that the ex-addict staff members feel about their work. One graduate spoke of the "determination of the staff. It takes a lot of patience, a lot of time, a lot of courage and sacrifice to work there."[68] The staff live in the residential treatment centers and become like family to the students. Respondents described the staff as "available, caring, loving people willing to put forth the effort to help others....No one else wanted to reach down to me."[69]

A tight social network develops. Obligations are owed and met, trust is nurtured, and sanctions against "bad" behavior are enforced. Healthy and positive relationships are built not only with one's fellow students, but also with the staff.

Teen Challenge fills the spiritual void in addicts' lives through religion, the Jesus-factor. In the in-depth study by Aaron Bicknese, respondents credited Jesus as the primary factor in overcoming their previous feelings of emptiness and loneliness, stressing that the relationship with Jesus made Teen Challenge work. As one respondent put it: "It was an attempt to satisfy an area in my life that couldn't be satisfied until that emptiness was filled with Christ."[70] A commitment to Jesus provided Teen Challenge graduates with the moral and spiritual willpower needed to overcome a wide range of serious addictions.

Faith is also relevant to the successful reentry of Teen Challenge graduates into society. First, faith imparts a positive meaning and purpose to their lives. Second, that faith occurs in a healthy social setting. The Jesus-factor continues to give alums the power to overcome the loneliness and nothingness that previously filled their lives. Third, ex-addicts feel empowered by having Jesus take control of all their addictive behaviors, rather than relying on a program of regular, maintenance meetings for the remainder of their lives.

What Can FBOs Hope to Accomplish?

Based on the empirical evidence, we can begin to answer three questions posed in this chapter's introduction: first, does religion deter deviant behavior; second, are FBOs effective at translating this into social renewal; and third, why is religion a better rehabilitator than a deterrent?

We begin first with religion's affect on deviant behavior. Despite the often contradictory evidence, the proposed faith-factor theory spells out the conditions under which religion can lessen deviant behavior and explains the necessary requisites. For religion to be a successful promoter of normative behavior or a deterrent of deviant behavior, there must be structure. This structural identity can be secular or religious, but in either case it is a vital mechanism for social control. If such a structure exists, then it is possible for religion to have a positive role in preventing deviant behavior.

Moving next to the effectiveness of FBOs, we see that effectiveness depends on two factors: a structured environment and competent organizations. The latter condition, a basic assumption in this analysis, is crucial. It is too easy to overlook the fact that an FBO providing social services must meet the temporal needs of its clients while remaining faithful to its spiritual mission. While the faith-factor is most powerful in communities that have secular structure, FBOs are most needed in inner-city neighborhoods lacking any structure. To be effective, FBOs must first set up their own structures and then use these institutional arrangements to promote their moral and spiritual message. In both cases, FBOs must be competently run in order to achieve these goals.

Finally, we must ask: why religion functions better to rehabilitate than to deter? The answer is that a prison or residential drug treatment environment is a far better vehicle for instilling normative virtue, especially for low-risk prisoners. Indeed, the structure of these environments is preferable to highly dysfunctional inner-city neighborhoods. FBOs can therefore concentrate on the evangelical mission of building moral character and virtue, making rehabilitation much easier.

Drug treatment programs do, however, face a difficult problem because of the high dropout rate. The study conducted in 1975 reported that over 70 out of 186 Teen Challenge applicants surveyed dropped out of the program during the first phase (the Induction Center),[71] in line with the current estimates indicating that 25 to 30 percent drop out during the program's first four-month phase.[72] Participants in the early study disliked the "cold turkey" aspect of the program. Many of the Induction Center dropouts did not like giving up all drugs (including cigarettes) at once or the lack of any medication. Participants must also accept the religious nature of the program and those who cannot find it difficult to remain. A number of Induction Center dropouts pointed to an "excess of religion" as a reason for leaving the program.[73]

Despite the high dropout rate, even those who did not complete the program benefit, as seen by the drop in heroin use, the decline in obtaining money through illegal sources, and the reduced involvement in subsequent treatment programs. What seems to be a low graduation rate (18.3 percent of the 366 persons admitted to the program in the 1976 study) compares favorably with the 14 percent who completed residential drug treatment programs funded by the National Institute on Drug Abuse, the Veterans Administration, and the Bureau of Prisons during the same period.[74]

Even nonresidential programs may produce positive results. FBOs in which personal development is a primary goal may evidence reductions in distress and enhanced well-being over time. One study analyzed 150 members of a nondenominational Christian Fellowship, emphasizing personal transformation and interpersonal development.[75] Personal testimony by members whose former lives were marked by despair and drug use showed that after coming to the fellowship, their lives changed dramatically. The researchers observed that the transformation was facilitated by an organizational culture focused on the following: the ideal of personal development in Jesus' image; extensive and intensive ongoing experiences of prayer-based sharing, guidance, and support in one-on-one relationships, small group interactions, and large group and congregational contexts; the gut-level experience of God's love, forgiveness, support, and caring; and meaningful roles and opportunities for contributions to the congregation and its activities. Empirical research from multiple data sources indicated dramatic personal changes over time in members. The extent of positive change was related to fellowship involvement, spiritual support, and a God-focused world view. Adult members, many of whom had a history of drug abuse and antisocial behaviors, were encouraged to "come to Jesus" through the fellowship and reported dramatic personal transformations. Considering themselves to be reborn spiritually, the members abstained from drug or alcohol use and went on to live productive lives.

FBOs that wish to act as a deterrent to deviant behavior face an intractable problem in many inner-city neighborhoods: the lack of secular structure. Without it, FBOs must create their own structure at enormous cost. In short, many FBOs lack the financial and human resources to build structures for transmitting normative virtue. Thus, FBOs are not as effective as they theoretically could be. The Charitable Choice provisions of the 1996 Welfare Reform Act and the initiatives of the Bush administration, discussed respectively in chapters 6 and 7, sought to open additional funds to FBOs subject, however, to the constitutional limitations analyzed in chapter 8.

Notes

1.   Kenneth I. Maton and Elizabeth A. Wells, "Religion as a Community Resource for Well-Being: Prevention, Healing, and Empowerment Pathways," *Journal of Social Issues* 51:2 (Summer 1995): 177-193, 179-180.

2.   *Ibid.*, 178.

3.   Byron R. Johnson, *Objective Hope Assessing the Effectiveness of Faith-Based Organizations: A Review of the Literature* (Philadelphia: Center for Research on Religion and Urban Civil Society, 2002), 12.

4.   Richard L. Gorsuch, "Religious Aspects of Substance Abuse and Recovery," *Journal of Social Issues* 51:2 (Summer 1995): 65-83; and Peter L. Benson, Michael J. Donahue, and Joseph A. Erickson, "Adolescence and Religion: A Review of the Literature From 1970 to 1986," in *Research in the Social Scientific Study of Religion: A Research Annual*, volume 1, 1989, eds. Monty L. Lynn and David O. Moberg (Greenwich, Conn.: JAI Press, 1989), 171. See also Jennifer Booth and John E. Martin, "Spiritual and Religious Factors in Substance Use, Dependence, and Recovery," in *Handbook of Religion and Mental Health*, ed. Harold G. Koenig (San Diego: Academic Press, 1998), 176-177. However, other researchers concluded, based on a 1983 survey of 13,878 junior and senior high school students in Colorado Springs, that the inverse relationship between religion and substance use was "weak" and that it did not appear "to be one of the more valuable predictors of this behavior." Barbara R. Lorch and Robert E. Hughes, "Religion and Substance Use," *Journal of Religion and Health* 24:3 (Fall 1985): 197-208, at 206.

5.   Peter L. Benson, "Religion and Substance Abuse," in *Religion and Mental Health*, ed. John F. Schumaker (New York: Oxford University Press, 1992), 212-216.

6.   Acheampong Yaw Amoateng and Stephen J. Bahr, "Religion, Family, and Adolescent Drug Use," *Sociological Perspectives* 29:1 (January 1986): 53-76. Analysis of the 1998 National Household Survey on Drug Abuse showed that teens who did not consider religious beliefs important were more than three times likelier to use marijuana and binge drink and seven times likelier to use other illicit drugs than teens who strongly believed that religion was important. The National Center on Addiction and Substance

Abuse at Columbia University, *So Help Me God: Substance Abuse, Religion, and Spirituality*, November 2001, 2, 9-10. Steven R. Burkett and Mervin White, "Hellfire and Delinquency: Another Look," *Journal for the Scientific Study of Religion* 13:4 (December 1974): 455-462 (from a survey conducted in 1971), while asserting that the effects of adolescent religiosity vary by the type of offense, concluded that more powerful effects were observed for the use of marijuana and alcohol. They saw a moderately strong, but a very definite, inverse relationship between religious participation (church attendance) and substance use.

7.   John K. Cochran and Ronald L. Akers, "Beyond Hellfire: An Exploration of the Variable Effects of Religiosity on Adolescent Marijuana and Alcohol Use," *Journal of Research in Crime and Delinquency* 26:3 (August 1989): 198-225. Robert H. Coombs, David K. Wellisch, and Fawzy I. Fawzy, "Drinking Patterns and Problems Among Female Children and Adolescents: A Comparison of Abstainers, Past Users, and Current Users," *American Journal of Drugs and Alcohol Abuse* 11:3&4 (September/December 1985): 315-348, at 341, concluded, "Attendance at church, synagogue, and other related activities (reported by both parent and child) also significantly differentiates alcohol users from nonusers."

8.   John K. Cochran, "The Effects of Religiosity on Adolescent Self-Reported Frequency of Drug and Alcohol Use," *The Journal of Drug Issues* 22:1 (Winter 1991): 91-104. In "Religion and Drug Use Among Adolescents: A Social Support Conceptualization and Interpretation," *Deviant Behavior: An Interdisciplinary Journal* 12:3 (July-September 1991): 259-276 (a study of more than 800 white male high school subjects in Seattle), David Brownfield and Ann Marie Sorenson concluded that religious affiliation seemed to appreciably reduce or limit drug use as both church attendance and religiosity yielded a negative association with drug use.

9.   John K. Cochran, "The Variable Effects of Religiosity and Denomination on Adolescent Self-Reported Alcohol Use by Beverage Type," *Journal of Drug Issues* 23:3 (Summer 1993): 479-491. See also Norma Haston Turner, et al., "Tri-Ethnic Alcohol Use and Religion, Family, and Gender," *Journal of Religion and Health* 33:4 (Winter 1994): 341-352, at 347 (ninth graders who rarely attended church were more likely to drink two or more times a week and drink hard liquor than students who attended church more frequently).

10.   Lisa Miller, Mark Davies, and Steven Greenwald, "Religiosity and Substance Use and Abuse Among Adolescents in the National Comorbidity Survey," *Journal of American Academy of Child and Adolescent Psychiatry* 39:9 (September 2000): 1190-1197.

11.   Cheryl H. Amey, Stan L. Albrecht, and Michael K. Miller, "Racial Differences in Adolescent Drug Use: The Impact of Religion," *Substance Use & Misuse* 31:10 (August, 1996): 1311-1332.

12.   Byron R. Johnson, et al. "Escaping From the Crime of Inner Cities: Church Attendance and Religious Salience Among Disadvantaged Youth," *Justice Quarterly* 17:2 (June 2000): 377-391, at 386. Grace M. Barnes, Michael P. Farrell, and Sarbani Banerjec, "Family Influences on Alcohol Abuse and Other Problem Behaviors Among Black and White Adolescents in a General Population Sample," *Journal of Research on Adolescence*, 4:2 (1994): 183-201, concluded, based on a representative sample of 699 black and white adolescents, that there is evidence that religion is a "protective" factor against alcohol abuse for black adolescents.

13.   Byron R. Johnson, *A Better Kind of High: How Religious Commitment Reduces Drug Use Among Poor Urban Teens*, Center for Research on Religion and Urban Civil Society, University of Pennsylvania, Report 2000-2.

14.   Johnson, *Objective Hope*, 12.

15. Michael J. Donahue and Peter L. Benson, "Religion and the Well-Being of Adolescents," *Journal of Social Issues* 51:2 (Summer 1995): 145-160, at 153 and 155.

16. Arland Thornton and Donald Camburn, "Religious Participation and Adolescent Sexual Behavior and Attitudes," *Journal of Marriage and the Family* 51:3 (August 1989): 641-653. See also Erika Pluhar, et al., "Understanding the Relationship Between Religion and the Sexual Attitudes and Behaviors of College Students," *Journal of Sex Education and Therapy* 23:4 (Winter 1998): 288-296.

17. Bernard Spilka, Ralph W. Hood, Jr., and Richard L. Gorsuch, *The Psychology of Religion: An Empirical Approach* (Englewood Cliffs, N.J.: Prentice-Hall, 1985), 260-261.

18. Joseph Donnelly, et al., "Sexuality Attitudes and Behaviors of Self-Described Very Religious Urban Students in Middle School," *Psychological Reports* 85:2 (October 1999): 607-610. See also Terence P. Thornberry, Carolyn A. Smith, and Gregory J. Howard, "Risk Factors for Teenage Fatherhood," *Journal of Marriage and the Family* 59:3 (August 1997): 505-522 (religious participation was not a significant factor in a survey of 615 urban seventh and eighth grade students).

19. Benson, Donahue, and Erickson, "Adolescence and Religion," 170. See also Leo E. Hendricks, Diane P. Robinson-Brown, and Lawrence E. Gary, "Religiosity and Unmarried Black Adolescent Fatherhood," *Adolescence* 19:73 (Summer 1984): 417-424; Julian Roebuck and Marsha G. McGee, "Attitudes Toward Premarital Sex and Sexual Behavior Among Black High School Girls," *Journal of Sex Research* 13:2 (May 1977): 104-114.

20. Shirley Vining Brown, "Premarital Sexual Permissiveness Among Black Adolescent Females," *Social Psychology Quarterly* 48:4 (December 1985): 381-387.

21. See, e.g., William Sims Bainbridge, "Crime, Delinquency, and Religion," in *Religion and Mental Health*, 201-202 (a survey of 1,465 college students showed that individual religiousness was significantly negatively correlated with the use of drugs and alcohol as well as premarital sex).

22. Stephen J. Bahr and Ricky D. Hawks, "Religious Organizations," in *Handbook on Drug Abuse Prevention: A Comprehensive Strategy to Prevent the Abuse of Alcohol and Other Drugs*, eds. Robert H. Coombs and Douglas M. Ziedonis (Boston: Allyn and Bacon, 1995), 164-166.

23. Cochran and Akers, "Beyond Hellfire," at 221. See also T. David Evans, et al., "Religion and Crime Reexamined: The Impact of Religion, Secular Controls, and Social Ecology on Adult Criminality," *Criminology* 33:2 (May 1995): 195-221; Douglas M. Sloane and Raymond H. Potvin, "Religion and Delinquency: Cutting Through the Maze," *Social Forces* 65:1 (September 1986): 87-105.

24. Johnson, *Objective Hope*, 12-13.

25. Byron R. Johnson, et al., "A Systematic Review of the Religiosity and Delinquency Literature," *Journal of Contemporary Criminal Justice* 16:1 (February 2000): 32-52.

26. Charles R. Tittle and Michael R. Welch, "Religiosity and Deviance: Toward a Contingency Theory of Constraining Effects," *Social Forces* 61:3 (March 1983): 653-682, at 654.

27. Lee Ellis, "Religiosity and Criminality From the Perspective of Arousal Theory," *Journal of Research in Crime and Delinquency* 24:3 (August 1987): 215-232.

28. Sloane and Potvin, "Religion and Delinquency," 92.

29. William Sims Bainbridge, "The Religious Ecology of Deviance," *American Sociological Review* 54:2 (April 1989): 288-295.

30. John K. Cochran, "The Effect of Religiosity on Secular and Ascetic Deviance: An Exploration of the Burkett and White Anti-Asceticism Hypothesis," *Sociological Focus* 21:4 (October 1988): 293-306; and John K. Cochran, "Another Look at Delinquency and

Religiosity," *Sociological Spectrum* 9:2 (Spring 1989): 147-162. See also Burkett and White, "Hellfire and Delinquency."

31. Brent B. Benda and Robert Flynn Corwyn, "Religion and Delinquency: The Relationship After Considering Family and Peer Influences," *Journal for the Scientific Study of Religion* 36:1 (March 1997): 81-92.

32. Byron R. Johnson, et al., "Does Adolescent Religious Commitment Matter? An Examination of the Effects of Religiosity on Delinquency," *Journal of Research in Crime and Delinquency* 38:1 (February 2001): 22-44.

33. Kirk W. Elifson, David M. Petersen, and C. Kirk Hadaway, "Religiosity and Delinquency: A Contextual Analysis," *Criminology* 21:4 (November 1983): 505-527.

34. T. David Evans, et al., "Religion, Social Bonds, and Delinquency," *Deviant Behavior* 17:1 (January-March 1996): 43-70.

35. Michael Resnick, et al."Protecting Adolescents from Harm: Findings from the National Longitudinal Study on Adolescent Health," *Journal of the American Medical Association* 278:10 (September 10, 1997): 823-832, at 825, 830.

36. Donahue and Benson, "Religion and the Well-Being of Adolescents," 155-156.

37. Rodney Stark, Lori Kent, and Daniel P. Doyle, "Religion and Delinquency: The Ecology of a 'Lost' Relationship," *Journal of Research in Crime and Delinquency* 19:1 (January 1982): 4-24. See also Rodney Stark, "Religion as Context: Hellfire and Delinquency One More Time," *Sociology of Religion* 57:2 (Summer 1996): 163-173.

38. Tittle and Welch, "Religiosity and Deviance."

39. Robert J. Bursik, Jr., "Social Disorganization and Theories of Crime and Delinquency: Problems and Prospects," *Criminology* 26:4 (November 1988): 519-551, provides a helpful overview of the social disorganization literature.

40. Steven and White, "Hellfire and Delinquency."

41. Naida M. Parson and James K. Kikawa, "Incarceration and Nonincarceration of African-American Men Raised in Black Christian Churches," *The Journal of Psychology* 125:2 (March 1991): 163-173.

42. Richard B. Freeman, "Who Escapes? The Relation of Churchgoing and Other Background Factors to the Socioeconomic Performance of Black Male Youths from Inner-City Tracts," in *The Black Youth Employment Crisis*, eds. Richard B. Freeman and Harry J. Holzer (Chicago: University of Chicago Press, 1986).

43. Johnson, et al., "Escaping from the Crime of Inner Cities."

44. Byron R. Johnson et al., "The 'Invisible Institution' and Black Youth Crime: The Church as an Agency of Local Social Control," *Journal of Youth and Adolescence* 29:4 (August 2000): 479-489; and Byron R. Johnson, *The Role of African-American Churches in Reducing Crime Among Black Youth*, University of Pennsylvania, Center for Research on Religion and Urban Civil Society, CRRUCS Report 2001-2. Sung Joon Jang and Byron R. Johnson, "Neighborhood Disorder, Individual Religiosity, and Adolescent Use of Illicit Drugs: A Test of Multilevel Hypothesis," *Criminology* 39:1 (February 2001): 109-144, found that religiosity (frequency of attending religious services and importance of religion in one's life) buffered the effect of neighborhood disorder on illicit drug use.

45. Johnson, *Objective Hope*, 13

46. Jenny Berrien, Omar Roberts, and Christopher Winship, "Religion and the Boston Miracle: The Effect of Black Ministry on Youth Violence," in *Who Will Provide?* eds. Mary Jo Bane, Brent Coffin, and Ronald Thiemann (Boulder: Westview Press, 2000); Christopher Winship and Jenny Berrien, "Boston Cops and Black Churches," *The Public Interest* 136 (Summer 1999): 52-68; Jenny Berrien and Christopher Winship, "Lessons Learned from Boston's Police–Community Collaboration," *Federal Probation* 63:2 (December 1999): 25-32.

47. Jenny Berrien and Christopher Winship, "Should We Have Faith in the Churches? The Ten-Point Coalition's Effect on Boston's Youth Violence," (July 1999), 3 (unpublished manuscript).

48. Mark C. Young, et al., "Long-Term Recidivism Among Federal Inmates Trained as Volunteer Prison Ministers," *Journal of Offender Rehabilitation* 22:1/2 (1995): 97-118. See also Tom O'Connor, "The Impact of Religious Programming on Recidivism, the Community and Prisons," *The IARCA Journal on Community Corrections* 6:6 (June 1995): 13-19, at 13-14.

49. Byron R. Johnson, David B. Larson, and Timothy Pitts, "Religious Programs, Institutional Adjustment, and Recidivism Among Former Inmates in Prison Fellowship Programs," *Justice Quarterly* 14:1 (March 1997): 145-166. See also O'Connor, "The Impact of Religious Programming," 14-16. Byron R. Johnson, "Assessing the Impact of Religious Programs and Prison Industry on Recidivism: An Exploratory Study," *Texas Journal of Corrections* 28:1 (February 2002): 7-11, compared the recidivism rates for two Brazilian prisons, including a faith-based facility run by local church volunteers.

50. Johnson, Larson, and Pitts, "Religious Programs," 162.

51. Thomas P. O'Connor, et al., "Prison Fellowship Recidivism Study: Lieber Prison in South Carolina," Preliminary Report, November 2000 (unpublished manuscript).

52. Thomas O'Connor, Patricia Ryan, and Crystal Parikh, "A Model Program for Churches and Ex-Offender Reintegration," *Journal of Offender Rehabilitation* 28:1/2 (1998): 107-126; Tom O'Connor, Crystal Parikh, and Angela Frusciante, "From Prison to the Free World: An Evaluation of an Aftercare Program in Detroit, Michigan," September 1995 (unpublished manuscript).

53. Aaron Todd Bicknese, *The Teen Challenge Drug Treatment Program in Comparative Perspective*, Ph.D. dissertation, Northwestern University, June 1999.

54. *Ibid.*, 29-33, 106-109.

55. *Ibid.*, 30.

56. *Ibid.*, 153.

57. *Ibid.*, 172.

58. *Ibid.*, 188.

59. *Ibid.*, 156.

60. *Ibid.*, 118.

61. Roger D. Thompson, "Teen Challenge of Chattanooga, Tn., Survey of Alumni," (n.d.), 7, 9-12.

62. National Institute for Drug Abuse, Services Research Report, *An Evaluation of the Teen Challenge Treatment Program* (Washington, D.C.: Government Printing Office, 1977), 10. See also John Muffler, John G. Langrod, and David Larson, "'There Is a Balm in Gilead': Religion and Substance Abuse Treatment," in *Substance Abuse: A Comprehensive Textbook*, 2d Edition, eds. and Joyce H. Lowinson, Pedro Ruiz, Robert Millman (Baltimore: Williams & Wilkins, 1992), 590-591.

63. Catherine B. Hess, *Research Summation: H.E.W. Study on Teen Challenge Training Center Rehrersburg, PA* (Rehrersburg, Pa.: Teen Challenge, n.d.), 22. See also Catherine B. Hess, "A Seven-Year Follow-Up Study of 186 Males in a Religious Therapeutic Community Indicates by Personal Interview and Urinalysis That 70% Are Drug Free, 57% Never Used an Illegal Drug Following Graduation From the Program," in National Drug Abuse Conference, Inc., *Critical Concerns in the Field of Drug Abuse* (New York: Marcel Dekker, 1976).

64. National Institute for Drug Abuse, *An Evaluation*, 10-11.

65. I have drawn on Andrew Kenney's review of the study by Dr. Aaron T. Bicknese, "Teen Challenge's Proven Answer to the Drug Program," available at www.teenchallenge. com/tcreview.h.

66. Bicknese, *Teen Challenge*, 192-196.

67. *Ibid.*, 196-203.

68. *Ibid.*, 211.

69. *Ibid.*, 197.

70. *Ibid.*, 179.

71. National Institute of Drug Abuse, *An Evaluation*, 10.

72. Laurie Goodstein, "Church-Based Projects Lack Data on Results," *New York Times*, April 24, 2001, A12 (quoting Rev. John D. Castellani, President of Teen Challenge International U.S.A.).

73. National Institute of Drug Abuse, *An Evaluation*, 8.

74. *Ibid.*, 4, 9.

75. Kenneth I. Maton and Julian Rappaport, "Empowerment in a Religious Setting: A Multivariate Investigation," *Prevention in Human Services* 3:2/3 (Winter 1983/Spring 1984): 37-72.

Chapter 6

Charitable Choice: Its Genesis, Expansion, and Implementation Prior to the Bush Presidency

Charitable Choice was added to the 1996 Welfare Reform Act to ensure that FBOs were not barred from applying for federally funded social service anti-poverty contracts because of their religious character. Subsequently, Congress extended the concept to federal community development block grants and drug treatment programs.

Building on the writings of Olasky and Magnet, discussed in chapter 2, Charitable Choice reflects the view that government welfare programs have failed and need to be supplemented by a system of private, specifically religious, charity. Charitable Choice strives to create a level playing field between faith-based and secular providers in the competition for public social service contracts. If a state (or a local government) chooses to involve any independent (nonpublic) sector provider in the delivery of certain federally funded programs, it cannot exclude providers merely because of their religious character. No longer need FBOs set up separate, secular social service arms. Charitable Choice thus seeks to reduce the governmental bias against religious nonprofits and strengthen the delivery of social services. In addition to involving FBOs in antipoverty efforts and now, with its expansion, to a broader range of social services, while protecting these organizations' religious character, Charitable Choice allows FBOs to carry on their work in the way they do best: serving the "public good" as an alternative to public and private, secular providers, while not losing their religious identity and integrity. Although FBOs may not use federal money for proselytizing, neither are they required to hide the religious character of their facilities or their organization.

Charitable Choice allows religious groups to demonstrate that they can effectively deliver the services promised, respect clients' civil liberties, and account for public funds. In short, Charitable Choice invites all levels of government to seek new partners. It is now clear to public officials that the ground rules for governmental-FBO cooperation have changed.

Charitable Choice: Its Genesis

Charitable Choice was the brainchild of John D. Ashcroft, a former U.S. senator, now U.S. Attorney General.[1] He was both the author and the key Senate sponsor of the Charitable Choice provisions of the 1996 Welfare Reform Act.

Ashcroft, an evangelical Christian and Yale graduate, had a vision: let churches and other religious groups do the public sector's work when it comes to social services. Use FBOs to reclaim both lives and the lethal streets of America's cities.

Ashcroft's views were no doubt formed by his upbringing. He is the devout son and grandson of Assembly of God clergymen, a Pentecostal denomination with strict moral tenets: no drinking, smoking, gambling, dancing, premarital sex, but plenty of missionary work and gospel singing. His late father was the president of a sectarian college and a leading figure in Springfield, Missouri, the Ozark city often referred to as "the Rome, the Jerusalem" of the Assembly of God denomination.

In his book chronicling his relationship with his father, Ashcroft related how religion permeated his life. While in school in Springfield, Ashcroft remembered getting up every morning hearing "the magisterial wake-up call" of his father's prayers. "Dad's prayers were not the quiet, whispered entreaties of a timid Sunday school teacher," Ashcroft wrote. Of his father's daily prayers, Ashcroft continued, "My father prayed as if his family's life and vitality were even then being debated on high as he bowed low."[2]

The strict tenets of his faith continue to guide him to this day. He has infused religion into every aspect of his life. Ashcroft begins every day with Bible study and prayer with his staff.[3] On the evening before his swearing in as a senator, he was blessed by the laying on of hands; his head was anointed with oil in Old Testament fashion.[4] It was this religious motivation that led Ashcroft to draft the Charitable Choice provisions, out of a belief that religious organizations are the best social service providers.

In the mid-1990s, Ashcroft led a crusade to open the federal treasury to FBOs in order to fund the kind of social welfare work traditionally handled by government. In contrast to bureaucrats who look "at people by criteria, by type," for Ashcroft, "religious people are concerned with the whole individual, with his whole life–even his eternal life. That's how you build self-esteem."[5] Violent gangs, public sector failures, and the demand for welfare reform gave Ashcroft his opening.

In March 1995, the House of Representatives passed a bill, H.R. 4, its version of welfare reform, then entitled the "Personal Responsibility Act." It contained no provisions for the administration of federal block grant funds by nongovernmental groups. In June 1995, the Senate Finance Committee reported out an amended version of H.R. 4. It included two sentences providing that religious organizations participating in the proposed block grant welfare program were to retain their independence from federal, state, and local governments and that these organizations could not deny aid to needy families with children "on the basis of religion, a religious belief, or refusal to participate in a religious practice."[6]

When the Senate began considering the House version of welfare reform in August 1995, the then Senate Majority Leader Robert Dole (R-Kansas) included Charitable Choice provisions in his comprehensive amendment to the House bill. At the urging of Ashcroft, Dole introduced the Senate Republican leadership's alternative to the House-passed H.R. 4 just before Congress' August recess. The section on the provision of aid by religious organizations was enlarged to deal with services provided by "charitable, religious, or private organizations."[7] The revised and expanded provision further indicated that states had the option to administer and provide services or benefits either through contracts with religious organizations or by means of certificates, vouchers, or other forms of disbursement redeemable by these organizations.[8]

A similar set of provisions initially appeared in Ashcroft's own welfare reform proposal, a package of five bills presented to the Senate in May 1995 as the proposed Communities Involved in Caring Act (CIVIC).[9] The Charitable Choice provisions also appeared as part of Ashcroft's proposed Individual Accountability Act of 1995.[10] This latter bill provided explicit authority for states to contract with nongovernmental organizations, including private and religious charitable groups, to help solve the welfare dilemma. Under this proposal, the states would be able to use their federal block grant funds either by contracting with these organizations directly or by giving beneficiaries certificates so that they could choose which programs to join. When he offered CIVIC for Senate consideration, Ashcroft stated that the Charitable Choice provisions sought to ensure that the disbursement of federal funds to religious social service providers would not "require radical changes in their beliefs, their structure, their facilities, their program, or their organization – changes that would rob these programs of the very characteristics and attitudes that make them successful."[11]

The Charitable Choice provisions came into existence in a somewhat haphazard manner. In early 1995, Carl Esbeck, then a professor at the University of Missouri-Columbia Law School, drafted legislation providing for federal guidelines enabling all faith-based providers, even those delivering religious messages as part of their social service programs, to compete for public sector contracts. Esbeck passed the draft to a former student who was working for Ashcroft. Ashcroft liked Esbeck's draft and, after several revisions, included it in the legislation he introduced in the Senate.[12]

Ashcroft acknowledged that Marvin Olasky's book, *The Tragedy of American Compassion*, previously considered in chapter 2, helped provide the intellectual inspiration for Charitable Choice. Olasky, a chief proponent of the notion of a private system of "effective compassion," was among those Ashcroft consulted as he fashioned the Charitable Choice language. Ashcroft wanted to do something different in the welfare field, something embodying the principles of "caring and love."

In August 1995, the Charitable Choice provisions initially received little notice. Opponents, including the Americans United for Separation of Church and State, the Baptist Joint Committee, the American Jewish Congress, and the American Civil Liberties Union, kicked off a campaign to delete the language from the measure. Some senators voiced concerns about the constitutionality of the Ashcroft provision.

During the debate over the welfare reform bill in September 1995, these concerns led then Senator William Cohen (R-Maine) to sponsor a successful two-part amendment. The first (and noncontroversial) half of the amendment merely provided that programs funded by Charitable Choice must be "implemented consistent with the Establishment Clause of the United States Constitution."[13]

The second half of the Cohen amendment, also adopted by the Senate, was more substantive and controversial. Under the original Dole Amendments, a provision explicitly barred federal and state governments from requiring an FBO to form a separate, nonprofit corporation to receive and administer federally funded assistance under the welfare reform measure.[14] In other words, this language imposed a federal mandate on the states.

The Cohen amendment eliminated this provision. It left Charitable Choice silent as to whether states could require pervasively sectarian FBOs to set up or spin off a separate, secular nonprofit entity to receive a government contract (or grant) and administer an antipoverty program. By giving the states this flexibility, a state could require an FBO to set up a secular nonprofit entity.

During the debate, Cohen stated that, in his opinion, it was unconstitutional for the public sector to fund welfare programs run by pervasively sectarian organizations. In Cohen's judgment, the Dole bill did "too little to restrain religious organizations from using federal funds to promote a religious message."[15] Cohen argued that the amendment was necessary to give states flexibility in administering their welfare programs and to shield them from lawsuits on Establishment Clause grounds. He also voiced his concern that unless states were allowed to require such separation, they would be open to suit under the "pervasively sectarian" standard of separationist jurisprudence.

The two-part Cohen amendment passed the Senate by a 59 to 41 margin.[16] After both the House of Representatives and the Senate approved welfare reform bills, the legislation went to a Conference Committee where negotiations occurred behind the scenes.

By November 1995, only a few issues remained unresolved by the Conference Committee. One contentious issue centered on Charitable Choice, and the battle over the provision reached an impasse. Then House Speaker Newt Gingrich (R-Georgia) intervened and forced a compromise between opponents of Charitable Choice and Senator Ashcroft.

The Conference Committee compromise brought about five changes to Charitable Choice. First, as originally introduced by Senator Dole, the Charitable Choice provisions contained language that it would be effective "[n]otwithstanding any other provisions of law."[17] This preemption language would allow a federal statute to override any conflicting state law, including state statutes and constitutions explicitly prohibiting government funding of religious groups.

The Conference Committee changed the language to read: "Nothing in this section shall be construed to preempt any provision of a State constitution or State statute that prohibits or restricts the expenditure of State funds in or by religious organizations."[18] This revised language deals with the expenditure of state funds; however, the welfare reform block grant funds are federal monies and must be administered according to federal standards–the principles of Charitable Choice. If a state commingles state and federal funds in a contract (or grant) program, then all the funds must be administered in accordance with Charitable Choice. States, however, have the option to separate their own funds from federal money, then exempt the separate, state funds from the Charitable Choice provisions. In other words, states may administer these separate, nonfederal funds in accordance with their own more restrictive provisions.

Second, Charitable Choice originally stated that no funds provided directly to FBOs could be expended for sectarian worship or instruction.[19] The Conference Committee added the word "proselytization,"[20] thereby clarifying what types of activities could not be funded by taxpayer dollars.

Third, the conference agreement revised the Senate language on employment discrimination by religious organizations. The original Charitable Choice language provided, in general terms, that the provision would not "modify or affect the provisions of any other Federal law or regulation that relates to discrimination on the basis of employment." A further exception allowed an FBO to require employees rendering services to follow its religious tenets and teachings, including adhering to its rules prohibiting the use of drugs or alcohol.[21] The Conference Committee included language stating that the exemption provided under Section 702 of the Civil Rights Act of 1964 would not be affected by the participation in or the receipt of funds from certain federally funded programs.[22]

Fourth, the section allowing a beneficiary to request that a state (or a locality) provide an alternative secular provider[23] was modified to include a requirement that the alternative provider be accessible to an objecting beneficiary and that the assistance be provided within a reasonable time.[24] Beneficiaries would not, however, receive notice of this right.

Finally, an FBO wishing to sue a state for a violation of the nondiscriminatory provisions of Charitable Choice could seek only injunctive relief rather than money damages.[25] Beneficiaries whose rights are violated under Charitable Choice also obtained this same cause of action.[26]

With the completion of the conference process, both houses of Congress enacted the welfare reform legislation in December 1995.[27] However, President Clinton vetoed the bill in January 1996.[28]

For a few months in early 1996, it looked as if welfare reform were dead. However, Congress continued its negotiations, deals were cut, and election year pressure was applied. The summer of 1996 saw new life breathed into welfare reform, and the bill started moving again.

In July 1996, a few senators enforced the Byrd Rule, named after Senator Robert Byrd (D-West Virginia). This rule is a Senate requirement that extraneous legislation cannot be included in certain budgetary bills. Citing the Byrd Rule, the Senate Parliamentarian concluded that Charitable Choice was an extraneous provision and stripped it from the welfare reform bill.

However, it is possible to waive the Byrd Rule if at least sixty senators vote to reincorporate an extraneous provision into a bill. On July 23, 1996, minutes after President Clinton announced he would sign the bill and moments before the Senate voted on the bill, Senator Ashcroft filed a motion to vote on waiving the Byrd Rule.

The debate on the Byrd Rule waiver was brief, lasting under five minutes. Ashcroft emphasized the need to use the services of nongovernmental charitable organizations to deliver welfare services. He noted that "America's faith-based charities and non-governmental organizations, from the Salvation Army to the Boys and Girls Clubs of the United States [that contract with governments], have been very successful in moving people from welfare dependency to the independence of work and the dignity of self-reliance."[29] The Senate approved Ashcroft's Byrd Rule waiver by a vote of 67 to 32.[30]

President Clinton signed the welfare reform bill in August 1996.[31] After his reelection, the Clinton administration included modifications to

Charitable Choice in a technical corrections bill presented to Congress. In seeking to change the term "religious organizations" to "religiously affiliated organizations that are not pervasively sectarian,"[32] President Clinton sought to narrow the category of FBOs eligible to receive governmental funds, directly or by means of vouchers. This part of the technical corrections proposal was not adopted. Thus, FBOs, even if pervasively sectarian, can compete for government contracts or receive vouchers from beneficiaries, subject to the limitations contained in the Charitable Choice provisions.

Charitable Choice: As Adopted in 1996

As developed in chapter 3, the 1996 Welfare Reform Act (the Welfare Reform Act) provides for a system of federal block grants to states that may then be used to provide cash payments and various services to the poor. The Charitable Choice provisions permit states either to contract with FBOs, among other nonpublic sector organizations, to administer and provide welfare-related social services funded by the federal Temporary Assistance to Needy Families (TANF) block grants or to provide beneficiaries with vouchers redeemable by these organizations.[33]

The Charitable Choice provisions of the Welfare Reform Act begin with a statement of purpose:

> The purpose of this section is to allow States to contract with religious organizations, or to allow religious organizations to accept certificates, vouchers, or other forms of disbursement under any [block grant] program [to provide welfare-related services]...on the same basis as any other nongovernmental provider without impairing the religious character of such organizations, and without diminishing the religious freedom of beneficiaries of assistance funded under such program.[34]

The Welfare Reform Act then provides that neither the federal government nor any state receiving federal block grant welfare funds may "discriminate" against any organization providing (or applying to provide assistance) under the Charitable Choice provisions because of its "religious character." Thus, religious organizations are eligible as contractors to provide assistance or accept vouchers "so long as the programs are implemented consistent with the Establishment Clause of the United States Constitution."[35]

The details of the ban on discrimination against religious social service providers are fleshed out through two provisions.[36] First, any religious organization with an antipoverty contract or one that accepts vouchers "shall retain its independence from Federal, State, and local governments, including such organization's control over the definition, development, practice, and expression of its religious beliefs." And second, neither the federal government nor a state can require a religious organization to alter its form of internal governance or remove religious art, icons, scripture, or other symbols in order to qualify for federal block grants, whether directly funded by contracts or through vouchers provided to beneficiaries.

The Charitable Choice provisions of the 1996 law thus protect the religious integrity of FBOs that participate in antipoverty programs. They retain their authority over their mission and governing board, and can deliver federally funded services in rooms filled with religious symbols. Additionally, the states must contract with FBOs, including religious congregations, on the same basis as any other private organization to provide federally funded welfare services or face charges of illegal discrimination.

The Welfare Reform Act then provides two further protections for FBOs. First, participating FBOs are exempt from the employment discrimination requirements contained in Section 702 of the Civil Rights Act of 1964.[37] Thus, religious providers (or voucher redeemers) may discriminate on the basis of religion and use religious standards in hiring or firing employees in federally funded antipoverty programs. They can thus refuse to hire nonbelievers to run or staff these programs. Second, participating religious providers (or voucher redeemers) can shield any of their welfare service programs that are not federally funded from governmental audit by segregating the federal funds into a separate account. If the federal funds are so separated, the federal government will only audit the financial assistance provided by such funds.[38] In other words, an FBO can limit the scope of fiscal audits by keeping a separate account to receive and disburse Charitable Choice funds.

With respect to the rights of beneficiaries, the Welfare Reform Act mandates that an FBO, whether it contracts to provide services or redeem vouchers, cannot discriminate against an individual in rendering assistance on the basis of "religion, a religious belief, or refusal to actively participate in a religious practice."[39] A beneficiary may sit out any religious activity he or she finds offensive. Furthermore, the 1996 law seeks to protect beneficiaries by ensuring that they have access to alternative secular providers. A state (or a locality) must provide any beneficiary who objects to the religious character of a provider with assistance from an alternative secular provider that is accessible to the individual, within a reasonable time period after the objection.[40]

Finally, funds provided directly by contracts with FBOs to offer services and administer programs cannot be "expended for sectarian worship, instruction, or proselytization."[41] As providers, FBOs must therefore be prepared to demonstrate that public funds do not pay for religious activities.

Although the religious restriction makes it clear that the government is not taking the side of any particular faith or endorsing any FBO's religion, several "loopholes" exist. Charitable Choice is silent as to whether an FBO, as a provider, may use its own funds to attempt conversions of those receiving government-funded antipoverty social services. Seemingly, such an FBO may proselytize using privately raised funds, e.g., tax-deductible charitable contributions. These privately paid employees or volunteers would appear able to offer optional religious activities, thereby subjecting a captive audience to an FBO's religious mission.

Also, the limitation on the use of funding for proscribed purposes clearly does not apply to assistance provided in the form of vouchers. If a beneficiary brings a voucher to pay for an antipoverty social service, no restrictions exist on using the money for worship, doctrinal instruction, or evangelism, because the beneficiary chooses the provider, even if it is pervasively sectarian. In that situation, the religious group need not segregate its secular and religious activities. It is free to conduct all its activities, including efforts at conversion. In other words, FBOs can use taxpayer funds for religious purposes if they receive public assistance indirectly through vouchers.[42]

Administrative Expansion of Charitable Choice

The Charitable Choice provisions were extended by administrative action to cover the U.S. Department of Labor's Welfare-to-Work program created by the Balanced Budget Act of 1997.[43] The Consolidated Appropriations Act of 2001[44] gave grantees an additional two years from the date of award to expend Welfare-to-Work funds, thereby allowing these expenditures, which otherwise would have expired in fiscal year 2002, to continue through fiscal year 2004.

The Welfare-to-Work program sought to help states and localities meet their welfare reform objectives and find work for "hard to employ," long-term welfare recipients, and the noncustodial parents of long-term recipients' children. As part of the TANF block grants, funds administered under this new program were subject to the Charitable Choice rules. Regulations issued by the Labor Department explicitly made FBOs eligible to apply for and receive these competitive grants.[45] In fiscal years 1998 and 1999, the Department of Labor awarded six competitive Welfare-to-Work grants (out of 188), totaling about $16 million (roughly 2 percent of the total competitive funds), to FBOs. Most of the grants going to FBOs focused on providing employment services; while some concentrated on persons with limited English proficiency.[46]

Legislative Expansion of Charitable Choice Beyond the Delivery of Antipoverty Social Services

In May 1998, Senator Ashcroft introduced the proposed Charitable Choice Expansion Act of 1998.[47] The bill, which was not enacted, would have required federal, state, and local governments to consider FBOs on an equal basis with secular institutions for any federally funded program in which a public unit is authorized to use nongovernmental providers, whether through contracts or vouchers. However, four programs would have been exempt from the expanded version of Charitable Choice: Federal education programs for children in elementary and secondary schools; the Higher Education Act of 1965; the Head Start Act; and the Child Care and Development Block Grant Act of 1990 (as amended in 1996). The latter, the primary child care subsidy program operated by the federal government, however, already had provisions to include religious organizations as service providers. Although grant or contract funds could not be expended for any religious purpose or activity, including sectarian worship or instruction, parents could use certificates to pay to child care providers, including faith-based child care centers.[48]

In 1999, Senator Ashcroft introduced a similar bill, the proposed Charitable Choice Expansion Act of 1999,[49] that once again was not enacted into law. However, in three separate, subsequent legislative initiatives, the Charitable Choice formula employed in 1996 was used, with modifications, to make FBOs eligible partners in a wider array of federal programs. Thus, some of the objectives of Ashcroft's hoped-for expansion of Charitable Choice were achieved by the Human Services Authorization Act of 1998, the Children's Health Act of 2000, and the Consolidated Appropriations Act of 2001.

The first act passed in 1998, reauthorizing the Community Services Block Grant (CSBG) program, includes religious organizations as nongovernmental providers under the CSBG Program of the U.S. Department of Health and Human Services. The federally funded CSBG program allows local agencies, generally community action agencies that receive their core funding in the form of block grants, to use these flexible dollars to offer a comprehensive array of social support services and activities. The CSBG funds are primarily used to meet the employment, education, housing, energy, health and emergency needs of the poor, thereby helping them strive to gain self-sufficiency.

The Charitable Choice provisions contained in the Human Services Authorization Act basically follow those of the 1996 welfare reform law.[50] Although not giving objectors an alternate secular provider, the 1998 act requires FBOs to segregate government funds provided under the program into a separate account, a provision that was merely optional under the 1996 provisions.

On signing the bill into law, President Clinton said its implementation would be subject to the following limitation:

> The Department of Justice advises, however, that the provision that allows religiously affiliated organizations to be providers under CSBG would be unconstitutional if and to the extent it were construed to permit governmental funding of "pervasively sectarian" organizations, as that term has been defined by the courts. Accordingly, I construe the Act as forbidding the funding of pervasively sectarian organizations and as permitting Federal, State, and local governments involved in disbursing CSBG funds to take into account the structure and operations of a religious organization in determining whether such an organization is pervasively sectarian.[51]

The Children's Health Act of 2000, in reauthorizing the U.S. Substance Abuse and Mental Health Services Administration (SAMHSA) (an agency under the jurisdiction of the U.S. Department of Health and Human Services) brought, in part, performance-based measures to the federal Substance Abuse Prevention and Treatment (SAPT) block grants to states. By making federal funding for substance abuse prevention and treatment dependent on states' developing and achieving outcome and performance goals, it allows the states broad flexibility in spending federal funds.

This act contains Charitable Choice provisions applicable to the federal block grants to the states for substance abuse prevention and treatment programs as well as to state-administered substance abuse programs. States electing to use nongovernmental organizations to administer and provide substance abuse services through contracts must consider religious organizations on the same footing as other groups when soliciting providers for these services, without discrimination on the basis of any organization's religious nature.[52]

FBOs retain their exemption under Section 702 of the Civil Rights Act of 1964 for their employment practices and, pursuant to a new provision, may require their employees providing services in substance abuse programs to adhere to their respective rules forbidding the use of drugs or alcohol.[53] For the further protection of beneficiaries, the 2000 act specifically mandates that the government must ensure that they receive notice of their rights to an alternative, accessible secular provider.[54] The act also requires religious organizations to segregate federal funds into a separate account, so that only these funds are audited.[55] Finally, the Charitable Choice provisions apply to any state funds contributed to the federally funded substance abuse program, unless the state opts to segregate its funds from federal funds.[56]

On signing the bill into law, President Clinton reiterated the constitutional concerns about Charitable Choice he had expressed in 1998 regarding the Human Service Authorization Act, as well as the limitation he previously imposed in implementing that law:

> This bill includes a provision making clear that religious organizations may qualify for SAMHSA's substance abuse prevention and treatment grants on the same basis as other nonprofit organizations. The Department of Justice advises, however, that this provision would be unconstitutional to the extent that it were construed to permit governmental funding of organizations that do not or cannot separate their religious activities from their substance abuse treatment and prevention activities that are supported by SAMHSA aid. Accordingly, I construe the Act as forbidding the funding of such organizations and as permitting Federal, State, and local governments involved in disbursing SAMHSA funds to take into account the structure and operations of a religious organization in determining whether such an organization is constitutionally and statutorily eligible to receive funding.[57]

The Consolidated Appropriations Act of 2001, in part, the appropriations law funding SAMHSA, adds Charitable Choice language to both the discretionary substance abuse grant programs administered by SAMHSA and the SAPT funds for state substance abuse programs. This act contains several notable provisions with regard to Charitable Choice.

The employment practices section includes, in addition to the usual exemption of employment practices under Section 702 of the Civil Rights Act of 1964, a provision stating: "Nothing in this section shall be construed to modify or affect the provisions of any other Federal or State law or regulation that relates to discrimination in employment...."[58]

This Act's section on nondiscrimination against religious organizations requires conformity with the U.S. Constitution's Establishment and Free Exercise Clauses.[59] The section barring discrimination against beneficiaries excludes the phrase "or refuse to participate in a religious practice." Although FBOs cannot discriminate against a program beneficiary (or a prospective program beneficiary) on the basis of religion or religious belief, the absence of this language marks an interesting development in that FBOs may apparently discriminate against beneficiaries who refuse to participate in religious activities. The Act also imposes the burden of referring a beneficiary to an alternate provider on the sectarian provider whose religious character the beneficiary deems objectionable, not on the public funding entity.[60] Mandatory notice provisions and the segregation of federal funds are provided.[61]

A special provision allows the personnel of a faith-based provider to be exempted from state (or local) education and training requirements provided their education and training are "substantially equivalent" to that of the secular providers' personnel. In enacting this provision, Congress found that "establishing unduly rigid or uniform educational qualifications for counselors and other personnel in drug treatment programs may undermine the effectiveness of such programs; and...such educational requirements for counselors and other personnel may hinder or prevent the provision of needed drug treatment services...." Thus, in determining whether the personnel of a provider that has a record of successful drug treatment for the preceding three years have satisfied state or local requirements for education and training, a state or local government cannot discriminate against the education and training provided to such personnel by an FBO, provided such education and training includes "basic content substantially equivalent to the content provided by nonreligious organizations that the State or local government would credit for purposes of determining whether the relevant requirements have been satisfied."[62]

On signing this measure, President Clinton reiterated the same constitutional limitation on the implementation of the Charitable Choice provisions he had expressed in 1998 and earlier in 2000:

> This bill includes a provision making clear that religious organizations may qualify for substance abuse prevention and treatment grants from the Substance Abuse and Mental Health Services Administration (SAMHSA) on the same basis as other nonprofit organizations. The Department of Justice advises, however, that this provision would be unconstitutional to the extent that it were construed to permit governmental funding of organizations that do not or cannot separate their religious activities from their substance abuse treatment and prevention activities that are supported by SAMHSA aid. Accordingly, I construe the bill as forbidding the funding of such organizations and as permitting Federal, State, and local governments involved in disbursing SAMHSA funds to take into account the structure and operations of a religious organization in determining whether such an organization is constitutionally and statutorily eligible to receive funding.[63]

Federal and State Implementation of Charitable Choice

Despite the federal legislation concerning Charitable Choice, the implementation rests in the hands of federal bureaucrats and state and local governments. It is for all levels of government to seek new partners for the specified social service programs, including religious organizations. One thing is clear, however: the ground rules for religious participation in social service programs have changed.

The goal of Charitable Choice is to increase the amount of public funds for social services provided by FBOs. Unfortunately, prior to 2001 the federal government and the states were slow to comply with the mandate of Charitable Choice allowing FBOs to bid on certain social service contracts.

As we have seen, the Clinton administration barred "pervasively sectarian" groups from receiving various federally funded contracts. Furthermore, Charitable Choice was not vigorously implemented by federal agencies prior to the Bush administration.

An August 2001 report, *The Unlevel Playing Field*, prepared by the White House Office of Faith-Based and Community Initiatives, found "widespread bias against faith- and community-based organizations in Federal social service programs" and that "many Federal policies and practices...go well beyond sensible constitutional restrictions and what the courts have required, sharply restricting the equal opportunity for faith-based charities to seek and receive Federal support to serve their communities."[64] This report noted "an overriding perception by Federal officials that close collaboration with religious organizations is legally suspect."[65]

Although many programs audited by five cabinet departments are covered by various Charitable Choice laws, prior to the Bush administration, the report detailed the existence of a federal administrative bias against religious organizations. The report concluded that with the exception of the Welfare-to-Work grants program operated by the Department of Labor, the Charitable Choice provisions were "essentially ignored by Federal administrators,"[66] who did little or nothing "to help or require state and local governments to comply with the...rules for involving faith-based providers."[67] Following the intent of Charitable Choice, the report noted that the Labor Department informed FBOs of their eligibility for funding, facilitated their applications, ensured that they were able to fulfill grant requirements, and provided effective assistance. However, the Labor Department neither elaborated on the Charitable Choice requirements in the Welfare-to-Work grants nor undertook a thorough review of how the new provisions should "affect grant standards or the Department's interpretation of constitutional requirements."[68]

The other three programs covered by Charitable Choice, namely, the funding for substance abuse services, TANF block grants, and the CSBGs, are administered by the Department of Health and Human Services (HHS). The 2001 White House report noted that HHS "has done very little to apply the rules to its own grant making or to ensure that the State and local governments that received covered funds adjusted their own procurement rules to comply with the congressional directives."[69] Although HHS regularly provides information and advice regarding the expenditure of formula grants, the report stated:

> it has supplied virtually no guidance at all to States about the landmark Charitable Choice requirements. Some attention was paid to Charitable Choice as an element of welfare reform through a few conferences and in other minimal ways. However, the only specific guidance given on this significant topic was a single-paragraph reply to an e-mail query from one State. When States submitted their welfare reform plans they were not asked how they would comply with Charitable Choice and States are not asked now whether they have created the required level playing field for faith-based providers, when they annually spend their billions of Federal dollars to contract for services from nongovernmental organizations.
>
> After Charitable Choice was added to the CSBG formula grant program, HHS issued some guidance to States about the new rules, but the guidance left out key provisions, such as the affirmation of the right of religious organizations to take religion into account in their employment decisions and the prohibition on the use of Government funds for inherently religious practices such as worship and proselytization. Although HHS does monitor State compliance with CSBG requirements, it has not evaluated implementation of Charitable Choice. In the absence of clear HHS guidance, misleading information about the requirements has been disseminated by special interest groups. Only within the last few weeks [in the summer of 2001] has HHS, with the assistance of the HHS Center, started to provide specific guidance on the implications of Charitable Choice for CSBG formula grant recipients.[70]

Similar to the experience on the federal level, prior to 2001, most states ignored the Charitable Choice laws. For instance, state TANF plans need not have provided Charitable Choice information. In a study, released in October 2000, of all fifty states, the District of Columbia, Guam, Puerto Rico, and the Virgin Islands,[71] thirty-seven states received a failing grade, indicating that the Charitable Choice initiative had gotten off to a slower start than proponents expected. These "deficient" states failed to restructure their social service procedures and contracts in accordance with Charitable Choice guidelines. A number of these jurisdictions failed to become more flexible in working with FBOs to provide social services or change their discriminatory or overly restrictive policies that hindered or excluded participation by faith-based groups. Some even maintained policies and practices that directly violated the Charitable Choice provisions. A few believed that the mandatory guidelines were optional. These states thus acted contrary to the Congressional mandate prohibiting discrimination against religious providers if specified social service programs were open to independent (nonpublic sector) organizations. The implementation of Charitable Choice was also hampered by ignorance of the provisions by state officials and a preference for traditional (i.e., public sector) social service providers.

Only twelve states in this study were given a passing grade. Not unexpectedly, an A+ went to Texas for aggressively promoting Charitable Choice, including the initiation of a task force, rewriting procurement rules, and redesigning the contracting process and spending programs to provide maximum openness to FBOs. A's were given to Indiana, Ohio, and Wisconsin; B's to Arizona, Illinois, Pennsylvania, and Virginia; and C's to Arkansas, California, Michigan, and North Carolina.

In addition to Texas, the greatest efforts at Charitable Choice compliance came from Indiana, Ohio, and Wisconsin. These three states took substantial steps to educate local government officials about the new rules and facilitate collaborations with the faith community in accordance with Charitable Choice. The efforts of Indiana, in particular, under the leadership of Democratic Governor Frank O'Bannon are enlightening.

In November 1999, Indiana's Family and Social Service Administration announced the establishment of FaithWorks Indiana (FWI), housed withing the state's Family and Social Services Administration, to develop partnerships among government agencies, organizations, businesses, and individuals supporting faith-based assistance programs across the state.[72] FWI's primary goal is to increase the participation of religious organizations in Indiana social service programs. To achieve this end, FWI adopted several measures to make the Indiana procurement system more accessible to religious providers. In early February 2000, FWI began holding informal meetings throughout the state to promote faith-based social services. After purchasing a state mailing list of nearly 10,000 FBOs, it invited these groups to attend workshops in different geographical regions throughout Indiana to explain the process of applying for public money for social service programs. More than 1,000 representatives of faith communities attended these informational sessions. FWI hired an accounting and consulting firm to answer questions about the government contracting process–everything from how to apply for grants to how funds could be used. Within six months, seventy-five FBOs had applied for government contracts. Of these, forty-three received grants, totaling $3,422,000. The majority of the applicants and recipients came from urban African-American churches.[73]

However, FWI did not stop with these meetings, but also implemented a number of other initiatives. These included a practice handbook and a technical assistance package for FBOs designed to help them bid on and manage government contracts for social service programs. It also established a toll-free number and a website to provide continuing assistance for FBOs. Additionally, FWI surveyed FBOs on the types of services being provided in order to refine its training sessions. FWI also provided workshops on allowable practices under Charitable Choice, how to write proposals for funds, financial and case management, and proper records maintenance. Finally, FWI held several open houses to provide technical assistance to religious organizations.

FaithWorks also sought to avoid constitutional challenges to the program by establishing an advocacy group. This group, including members from the American Civil Liberties Union, focuses on sensitive questions, such as how to deal with Establishment Clause problems, and how to avoid the misuse of government funds. This group also seeks to protect the rights of the beneficiaries by informing them of their options when participating in social service programs. Posters with the message "You Have a Choice" hang in the Indiana Department of Human Services offices and must also be displayed by participating FBOs. FWI has also conducted surveys of clients to make sure that they understand their rights to receive services from an alternative secular provider or to opt out of the religious programs offered by their current provider. These initiatives strive to solve problems before they start by ensuring that every beneficiary knows that he or she does not have to receive services from a religious organization.

Improving State Implementation of Charitable Choice

States which have been the most successful in implementing Charitable Choice recognize that it is necessary to remove administrative barriers against FBOs. Hopefully, the example of states such as Texas and Indiana will encourage other states to adopt a more proactive strategy regarding Charitable Choice. In addition to state TANF plans providing Charitable Choice information, as seems to be occurring,[74] states must take the initiative on four other fronts.

First, states ought to establish liaisons to the religious community who can provide assistance for FBOs that wish to participate in public socialservice programs covered by Charitable Choice. Regional, county, or city liaisons would also be extremely valuable. These public liaisons need to broker new collaborations between state social service departments and FBOs. For instance, Texas designated a faith-based liaison in each of its Department of Human Services' regions.[75]

Second, states must sponsor statewide or regional conferences on the new role Charitable Choice offers FBOs in delivering social services and not merely rely on publicizing Charitable Choice to religious organizations. States must reach out to religious groups not traditionally part of the social services system by initiating meetings, including advertisements (and other promotional materials) targeted at the local faith community, and inviting to these meetings congregations and other FBOs interested in providing social services. These meetings can then instruct FBOs on how to bid for government contracts for social services, particularly on the arcane contracting rules. In short, states must realize that first-time FBOs need more "hands-on" help than do more experienced providers.

The public sector needs to encourage established social service contractors–intermediary entities–to subcontract with FBOs. A governmental unit could write one large contract with an organization having the technical expertise and experience to manage a program and administer funds. Smaller FBOs that could never secure or administer a large contract on their own could then partner with the experienced intermediary organization and receive a manageable amount of funding to support their work.[76] To facilitate subcontracting, states may need to make subcontracting a "best practice" officials look for in reviewing the proposals of competing providers.

States can also assist FBOs through creative, nonmonetary collaborations. For example, a governmental unit could provide religious groups with the use of vehicles, office equipment or space, or even staff. These collaborations, not necessarily involving formal contracts, could take the form of memorandums of understanding that incorporate Charitable Choice language and guidelines.

Third, states need to educate their own officials and staff members about Charitable Choice and hold them accountable for compliance with Charitable Choice in their contracting policies and procedures. In many jurisdictions, the process of submitting proposals and bidding on social service contracts remains mired in "red tape." After assessing current procurement processes, public officials need to remove procurement requirements and other practices that shut out FBOs. They should also make sure to include FBOs in the loop to receive requests for proposals and provide FBOs with training on how to write proposals.

In addition to modifying requests for proposals to make them more accessible and user-friendly to FBOs without previous government contracting experience, bureaucrats must incorporate Charitable Choice language and guidelines into their contracts and memorandums of understanding. As an example, because FBOs receiving federally funded sector contracts to provide certain social services under Charitable Choice are allowed to select employees on the basis of religion, these contracts need to strike any language prohibiting a religious provider from discriminating on the basis of religion in its hiring practices. The major problem uncovered in a 2001-2002 survey of 389 faith-based contractors receiving federal funds regulated by Charitable Choice concerned the fact that Charitable Choice language and guidelines was not inserted in their contract documents.[77]

One early study of Charitable Choice implementation in nine states, completed in the summer of 1999, demonstrated that collaboration between the public sector and FBOs is a realistic goal and that Charitable Choice can stimulate a variety of new partnerships. This pioneering study revealed 125 new (postwelfare reform) collaborations, more than half of which (57 percent, or 71 to be exact) were with FBOs not traditionally involved in providing social services.[78] The increase in the number of nontraditional FBOs collaborating with the public sector may have resulted from the enactment (and implementation) of the Charitable Choice provisions creating a more level playing field, more services being contracted out, or more FBOs entering the competitive process. Whatever the reason, the inclusion of new players broadened the traditional social services network. These new participants expanded their realm of activities beyond food pantries and temporary emergency assistance to include mentoring and job training programs focusing on moving welfare recipients to gainful employment, fatherhood classes, domestic violence prevention, GED instruction, and after-school tutoring. The growing diversity of social services encompassed programs for children and youths.[79]

Finally, states should consider implementing systems that provide each recipient with a voucher for a specific social service. He or she can redeem the voucher and receive that service from an appropriate provider. As discussed in chapters 7 and 8, this approach offers many benefits, including helping to eliminate nearly all of the constitutional questions that might arise under Charitable Choice.

Hopefully, the states and localities will move toward greater compliance with Charitable Choice. For the time being, however, this compliance is impeded by, among other factors, public sector labor unions fearful of job losses as well as by public officials who believe that the inclusion of FBOs in social service programs may be struck down as unconstitutional.

FBOs and Charitable Choice

Preliminary research indicated that FBOs did not rush to take advantage of the federal government's new stance toward sectarian social service providers. As a result, the 1996 welfare reform law did not result in a huge shift of public funds to FBOs. Exact figures are unknown because states and local governments are not required to report Charitable Choice expenditures to the federal government. However, the expansion of

Charitable Choice in 2000 to include drug treatment programs should result in greater involvement by FBOs. More recent studies indicated a rise, described as an "exponential increase," in financial contracting by government entities with FBOs.[80]

There are three reasons why FBOs have not taken advantage of Charitable Choice and entered into contracts with governmental units. First, many groups simply do not have the personnel to undertake new projects. FBOs are typically small, church-affiliated organizations staffed almost entirely by volunteers. They lack the staff necessary to apply for government funds and manage performance-based contracts. They are not run by professional managers with ready access to lawyers, who can take advantage of an obscure provision in the 1996 Welfare Reform Act and subsequent enactments. Many FBOs also face limited financial capabilities, especially the start-up funds to administer contracts. They encounter difficulties in covering their ongoing expenses while awaiting reimbursement from the government. Limited technological and management systems make it difficult for many FBOs to handle performance-based contracts.

Second, aside from limited financial and administrative capacities, many FBOs were simply not aware of the initiative and would presumably participate if informed. Two years after the enactment of the welfare reform legislation, the 1998 National Congregations Study found that only 24 percent of more than 1,200 congregations surveyed were even aware of the Charitable Choice provisions.[81]

The long-term significance of this poor name recognition is questionable. With time and the attention given to faith-based initiatives by the Bush Administration, discussed in chapter 7, FBOs will develop a basic understanding of what Charitable Choice has to offer. Thus, ignorance of Charitable Choice does not constitute a structural impediment to its future expansion.

Third, the most problematic impediment to greater participation is the reluctance of religious organizations to contract with the government. Ultimately, FBOs need to feel comfortable when accepting government funds if we wish to encourage their participation. Some FBOs will remain suspicious of any entanglement with the public sector because they fear strings will be attached to government money. Others believe that their religious mission (or the theology that drives their commitment) is essential and they do not, in any way, want to water it down in return for public funds. Still others fear the bureaucratic "red tape."[82] They also are reluctant or unprepared to submit to the guidelines required to become government contractors that they fear will be too cumbersome. They see their real work is on the microlevel, not in keeping records or following administrative details.

An example of this problem is the Faith Teaching Church of Deliverance in Indianapolis. For Bishop Shedrick Madison and his wife Brenda, taking in children from problem families was nothing new. However, in the summer of 1999, the Madisons received a $24,100 Indiana state government contract to pay for a number of their summer activities for children, including video games, boxing, basketball, and Bible studies.

Although the state money was naturally welcomed, Mrs. Madison expressed disappointment that it took so long to receive payment. "To me, it's a lot of red tape," she said. "You got to report all these things, keep files. They want attendance records, they want assessment of kids, they want the kids' Social Security numbers." She added: "I talk to other churches who want to do grants like we got, and when I describe it, they say, 'I don't want to get involved with all that.'"[83]

Despite their reservations, many FBOs, especially local congregations, are interested in receiving contracts to provide publicly funded social services. Data from the 1998 National Congregations Study, drawn from a series of hour-long interviews with the spiritual leaders of 1,236 religious congregations, found that while 15 percent of the congregations studied had standing policies against accepting government funds, 36 percent would consider applying for government support.[84] Research conducted in Philadelphia during 1998 and 1999 found that 8.2 percent of 401 congregations surveyed were familiar with Charitable Choice and 2.5 percent reported holding discussions about taking advantage of newly open programs. As of February 2000, one Philadelphia congregation, not included in the initial sample of 401 houses of worship, had received a government contract under Charitable Choice. Although these percentages seem small, 62.1 percent of the congregations surveyed in Philadelphia answered "yes" when asked: "If not actively involved with Charitable Choice, would your congregation consider applying for government funds under the provisions of Charitable Choice?"[85]

Assuming the expanded implementation of Charitable Choice by governmental units, the 1998 National Congregations Study found that funding will likely go mainly to African-American churches and liberal white congregations.[86] Black churches were seen as up to five times more likely than other congregations to seek public support for their social service activities for two reasons. First, the need for these types of programs is the most pronounced in the inner-city neighborhoods many of these churches serve. Second, these churches feel that they have been excluded from government funding in the past, even though they are often the best suited to implement social service programs in view of their desire and their skills.

Forty-one percent of Protestant congregations that described themselves as liberal or moderate were also interested. These congregations are accustomed to working with government to help the needy. Some already had independent (basically secular) affiliates to carry out their social service endeavors. Only 28 percent of those congregations describing themselves as theologically and politically conservative said they were interested in applying for government funds to support their social service efforts.[87]

However, the 1999 study of Charitable Choice implementation in nine states found that conservative and evangelistic FBOs were involved in Charitable Choice contracting. Of the forty-five post-1996 Welfare Reform Act financial collaborations between the public sector and FBOs that had previously never cooperated in a formal capacity with government, twenty involved FBOs labeling themselves as evangelical, an "unexpected and significant" finding.[88]

Many concerned about Charitable Choice focus not only on the rights of FBOs but also those of clients. An example of the preservation of the rights of beneficiaries can be found at Campbell Chapel A.M.E. Zion Church. One of the first religious organizations to receive money in Indiana, Campbell Chapel was awarded a $127,500 contract, conditioned on meeting certain performance requirements.

The church offers a program to help clients become self-sufficient, although few clients are church members. The services offered include classes for high school equivalency (GED) diplomas and computer training courses, as well as job placement assistance. The church displays posters which say the "pledge to the Bible," but it does not pressure the students to become involved in the congregation. Additionally, the program is not headed by a minister, but by a social worker who is a church member.

The church does not discriminate against clients of other faiths. One such beneficiary was Ali Banane, a Muslim from Morocco. With the help of Campbell Chapel, Mr. Banane was able to obtain his GED and find a job as well as improve his computer skills. Although he was invited to attend Sunday worship services, Mr. Banane never felt pressured to do so. "I told them I can't because I am a Muslim," he said. "They don't want you to do something you don't want to do."[89] Banane even referred three other Muslims there for classes.

Besides anecdotal evidence, the 1999 nine-state study revealed that religious groups, in accepting government funds, were not "selling their souls." The FBOs reported that they enjoyed the trust of their government partners and that they were upfront about their religious identity. The study uncovered "almost no examples" of FBOs that felt that collaboration with government squelched their religious expression.[90] In a subsequent study conducted in 2001-2002 of 389 faith-based contractors under four federal social welfare programs regulated by Charitable Choice, less than 6 percent agreed with the commonly expressed fear that accepting government contracts threatened to undermine an organization's faith-based character.[91]

Furthermore, the 1999 study also concluded that FBOs respected their clients' civil rights. Out of approximately 3,000 clients participating in social service programs offered by FBOs holding government contracts, the study's author heard of only two complaints.[92] In both cases, the beneficiaries felt they had been subtly pressured to attend the church that provided a job training program. Both beneficiaries went to their caseworker with their concerns and received permission to opt out of the faith-based program and enroll in a similar program offered by a secular provider. The study uncovered no example of a beneficiary unable to exercise his or her right to receive services from an alternative secular provider. Even in rural areas, the study found that beneficiaries were able to exercise their right to obtain services from a secular provider. Also, in the 2001-2002 study, the faith-based contractors surveyed placed considerable emphasis on protecting beneficiaries' civil rights through three explicit strategies, namely, reassuring beneficiaries that services do not depend on religion, clarifying that religious activities are optional, and notifying beneficiaries of their right to select an alternative provider.[93]

Public-Private Partnerships

FBOs have much to offer in helping rebuild a virtue-based civil society. They cannot, however, alone turn the tide. The public and private sectors must work together. However, will FBOs, secular nonprofits, for-profit businesses, and government join forces to combat poverty and instill virtue, while competing in a constructive way? What will be the rules of engagement in these cooperative endeavors?

We may see the formation of more strategic alliances or partnerships between the public sector and FBOs (as well as secular groups). Working together and cutting across racial, denominational, and other divides, these public-private partnerships may play an important role in alleviating America's social ills.

Although FBOs and the public sector could compete in supplying social services, they can work together, allowing each to play a distinct, but complementary, role. For instance, FBOs could work with individuals and families enrolled in public programs, such as job training, providing one part of a larger package. However, we need to devise effective ways for the two sectors to work together.

Public-private social service provider partnerships may flourish, modeled on the example of the Front Porch Alliance (the Alliance) created in 1997 by Stephen Goldsmith, then mayor of Indianapolis.[94] The Alliance, a local government clearinghouse for church and community groups, perhaps best exemplifies an effort by a city government to assist congregations and neighborhood groups trying to improve distressed communities and provide services to those most at risk. The Alliance, a model public-private partnership from Goldsmith's second term as mayor of Indianapolis, acted as a liaison, a "civic switchboard," from September 1997 to December 1999, between congregations–mostly urban African-American churches–and the local government, connecting needs with resources.

This initiative redefined the role of FBOs by making them a critical part of the city's social services system. The Alliance made government a facilitator or an intermediary. It provided faith-based groups with public resources and transformed the city's role into that of a coordinator, "spotlighting" the work of neighborhood, nonprofit organizations. As a public-private partnership, the Alliance tapped into the legitimacy and virtue-shaping power of FBOs, while leaving government with a supervisory role.

The program sought to involve FBOs and other community groups in solving the problems of crime, juvenile delinquency, and teen pregnancy. A staff of nine, with an annual budget of $800,000, spent time reaching out to small, inner-city churches and neighborhood groups, explaining how the city could help their efforts. Encouraging and enhancing the work of faith- and community-based groups, the Alliance offered access to city government, a way for congregations to receive assistance from the public sector as they tried to help the poorest in their neighborhoods. It placed municipal resources behind FBOs and community-based groups to build social capital, clearing away governmental obstacles and helping these organizations turn abandoned parking lots and crack alleys into parks and playgrounds. To facilitate linkages, the Alliance offered FBOs and neighborhood groups modest grants to provide, among other activities, after-school care, job training, and family outreach efforts. Other times, the city helped an FBO or a neighborhood group obtain federal or foundation funds for a project.

One of the Alliance's favorite projects, illustrating the cooperative effort between the public and private sectors to enhance a neighborhood, was a small community garden. By eliminating an alley drug dealers used to escape whenever the police approached, the garden stopped their loitering. To solve the problem, Alliance staffers forged ties between a church-run community center that sought the city's help and a number of local businesses. City work crews jackhammered the alley to dust. A youth ministry helped build the garden. In short, the Alliance helped a virtue-shaping organization improve its neighborhood.

Charitable Choice is a work in progress. Prior to 2001, it was uncertain exactly how these provisions would be implemented by federal, state, and local governments. Much work remained to be done. The Bush administration sought to meet the challenge.

One thing is clear, however. FBOs and their role in helping those in need can no longer be ignored by the public sector. The Charitable Choice provisions enacted during the Clinton administration ensure that FBOs will play an important role in attempting to alleviate the problems that have plagued America's poverty-stricken and disadvantaged.

Notes

1. I have drawn on Howard Fineman, "The Gospel of St. John," *Newsweek* 131:22 (June 1, 1998): 29; and David Johnston, "The 43rd President: The Choice: Man in the News; John David Ashcroft," *New York Times*, December 23, 2000, A1.

2. John D. Ashcroft with Gary Thomas, *Lessons From a Father to His Son* (Nashville: Thomas Nelson, 1998), 7.

3. Dan Eggen, "Ashcroft's Faith Plays Visible Role at Justice," *Washington Post*, May 14, 2001, A1.

4. David Johnston and Neil A. Lewis, "Religious Right Made Big Push To Put Ashcroft in Justice Dept.," *New York Times*, January 7, 2001, Section 1, 1.

5. Fineman, "The Gospel of St. John," 29.

6. Report No. 104-96, H.R. 4, Section 407, 104th Congress, 1st Session. This language was adapted from another block grant bill sponsored by Senator Ashcroft, S. 842, Individual Accountability Act of 1995, Section 406(c)(1), 104th Congress, 1st Session.

7. Dole Amendment No. 2280 to H.R. 4, 104th Congress, 1st Session, Section 102; 141 Congressional Record S 22458, S 22467 (August 5, 1995).

8. Dole Amendment No. 2280, as further modified, Sections 102(a) and 103; 141 Congressional Record S 23274, S 23283 (August 11, 1995).

9. 141 Congressional Record, S 14113-14114 (May 23, 1995); 141 Congressional Record S 14121-14123 (May 23, 1995).

10. S. 842, Section 406, 104th Congress, 1st Session.

11. 141 Congressional Record S 14114 (May 23, 1995). See also 141 Congressional Record S 14122 (May 23, 1995).

12. Megan Twohey, "Charitable Choice Grows, But So Do Questions," *The National Journal* 32:42 (October 14, 2000): 3254-3255, at 3254.

13. Cohen Amendment No. 2586 to Dole Amendment, 141 Congressional Record S 24356 (September 8, 1995), S 24844 (September 13, 1995).

14. Dole Amendment No. 2280, Section 102(d)(2)(A); Dole Amendment No. 2280, as further modified, Section 102(d)(2)(A).

15. 141 Congressional Record S 24845 (September 13, 1995).

16. 141 Congressional Record S 24851 (September 13, 1995).

17. Dole Amendment No. 2280, Section 102(a); Dole Amendment No. 2280, as further modified, Section 102(a).

18. H.R. 4, as amended, Section 104(k).

19. Dole Amendment No. 2280, Section 103; Dole Amendment No. 2280, as further modified, Section 103.

20. H.R. 4, as amended, Section 104(j).

21. Dole Amendment No. 2280, Section 102(e); Dole Amendment No. 2280, as further modified, Section 102(e).

22. H.R. 4, as amended, Section 104(f); Report 104-430, Conference Report to Accompany H.R. 4, Personal Responsibility and Work Opportunity Act of 1995, 104th Congress, 1st Session (December 20, 1995), 361.

23. Dole Amendment No. 2280, Section 102(i); Dole Amendment No. 2280, as further modified, Section 102(i).

24. H.R. 4, as amended, Section 104(e)(1).

25. Dole Amendment No. 2280, Section 102(h); Dole Amendment No. 2280, as further modified, Section 102(h).

26. H.R. 4, as amended, Section 104(i).

27. 141 Congressional Record H 15533 (December 21, 1995); 141 Congressional Record S 19181 (December 22, 1995).

28. Message to the House of Representatives Returning Without Approval the Personal Responsibility and Work Opportunity Act of 1995, *Weekly Compilation of Presidential Documents* 32:2 (January 15, 1996): 30-32.

29. 142 Congressional Record, S 18464 (July 23, 1996).

30. *Ibid.*

31. Statement on Signing the Personal Responsibility and Work Opportunity Reconciliation Act of 1996, *Weekly Compilation of Presidential Documents* 32:34 (August 26, 1996): 1487-1489.

32. Proposed Correcting Amendments to P.L. 104-193, The Personal Responsibility and Work Opportunity Reconciliation Act of 1996, Section 104.

33. 42 USC §604a(a)(1)(A).

34. 42 USC §604a(b).

35. 42 USC §604a(c).

36. 42 USC §604a(d).

37. 42 USC §604a(f).

38. 42 USC §604a(a),(h)(2).

39. 42 USC §604a(g).

40. 42 USC §604a(e).

41. 42 USC §604a(a),(j).

42. Report 104-430, Conference Report to Accompany H.R. 4, 361.

43. Public Law 105-33, Section 5001 (42 USC §603(a)(5)), as modified by Title VIII of the Consolidated Appropriations Act for FY 2000, Public Law 106-113. For background on the Welfare-to-Work Grants Program see Committee on Ways and Means, U.S. House of Representatives, *2000 Green Book: Background Material and Data on Programs Within the Jurisdiction of Committee on Ways and Means* (Washington, D.C.: Government Printing Office, 2000), 442-443; Demetra Smith Nightingale and Kathleen Brennan, "The Welfare-to-Work Grants Program: A New Link in the Welfare Reform Chain," The Urban Institute, Assessing the New Federalism, The Urban Institute Program to Assess Changing Social Policies, Series A, No. 26, September, 1998; Demetra Smith Nightingale, John Trutko, and Burt S. Barnow, *The Status of the Welfare-to-Work (WtW) Grants Program After One Year,*

The Urban Institute, September 1999 (report prepared for U.S. Department of Labor, Employment and Training Administration); CRS Report to Congress, "Welfare Reform: Competitive Grants in the Welfare-to-Work Grant Program," Report RS20207, November 8, 2001.

44. Public Law 106-554.

45. Title 20, Code of Federal Regulations, Part 645, Subpart E, §645.500.

46. Vee Burke, *Charitable Choice and TANF*, Congressional Research Service Report, April 10, 2001, 4; The White House, *Unlevel Playing Field: Barriers to Participation by Faith-Based and Community Organizations in Federal Social Service Programs* (August 2001), 6, 19.

47. S. 2046, 105th Congress, 2nd Session, Section 3.

48. 42 USC §§9858c(c)(2)(A)(i)(II) and 9858n(2).

49. S. 1113, 106th Congress, 1st Session, Section 1.

50. 42 USC §9920.

51. Statement on Signing the Community Opportunities, Accountability, and Training and Education Services Act of 1998, *Weekly Compilation of Presidential Documents* 34:44 (November 2, 1998), 2148.

52. 42 USC §300x-65.

53. 42 USC §300x-65(d).

54. 42 USC §300x-65(e)(2).

55. 42 USC §300x-65(g)(2).

56. 42 USC §300x-65(j).

57. Statement on Signing the Children's Health Act of 2000, *Weekly Compilation of Presidential Documents* 36:42 (October 23, 2000), 2504.

58. 42 USC §290kk-1(e).

59 42 USC §290kk-1(c)(1).

60. 42 USC §290kk-1(f)(1).

61. 42 USC §290kk-1(f)(2),(g)(2).

62. 42 USC §290kk-3.

63. Statement on Signing the Consolidated Appropriations Act, FY 2001, *Weekly Compilation of Presidential Documents* 36:52 (December 21, 2000), 3172.

64. The White House, *Unlevel Playing Field*, 2, 10.

65. *Ibid.*, 10.

66. *Ibid.*, 19.

67. *Ibid.*, 2.

68. *Ibid.*

69. *Ibid.*, 19.

70. *Ibid.*, 20. See also Department of Health and Human Services, Center for Faith-Based and Community Initiatives, *Report to the White House Office for Faith-Based and Community Initiatives*, July 27, 2001, Charitable Choice Section, 3, 6. A Clinton administration report noted that in the fall of 1999, HHS convened a national conference "to help strengthen partnerships between the faith community and state and local agencies around the design and implementation of programs to promote self-sufficiency." A Report to the President from the Interagency Task Force on Nonprofits and Government, *Partnerships for a Stronger Civil Society* (December 2000), 17-18. In 1997, the Department of Housing and Urban Development (HUD) created the Center for Community and Interfaith Partnerships, the first office in a federal agency addressing the needs of faith-based and community organizations, specifically those interested in HUD programs. Acting as a clearinghouse, the center provided information about HUD programs and targeted education and outreach at nonprofits that never received grant assistance or those desirous of expanding their activities. Serving as a troubleshooter, the center assisted nonprofit groups

in navigating its bureaucratic system and responding to their inquiries and concerns. The center also sought to ensure that nonprofit groups were included in HUD initiatives, outreach and educational activities, and its program areas. *Ibid.*, 18.

71. Center for Public Justice, "Charitable Choice Compliance: A National Report Card," (October 5, 2000).

72. See generally, FaithWorks Indiana website, www.state.in.us/fssa/faithworks; Bill Theobald, "O'Bannon Announces Faith-Based Social Services Program," *Indianapolis Star*, November 24, 1999, B7.

73. Laurie Goodstein, "Churches Are Wary of Government Aid to Assist the Needy," *New York Times*, October 17, 2000, A1, A22.

74. Laurie Goodstein, "Eager States Have Been Steering Religious Charities Toward Aid," *New York Times*, July 21, 2001, A1.

75. Texas Human Resources Code §21.0061; Carolyn Barta, "Texas Tops List for Faith-Based Efforts; But State-Charity Links Are Difficult to Track," *Dallas Morning News*, February 8, 2001, 1A.

76. Amy L. Sherman, *Empowering Compassion: The Strategic Role of Intermediary Organizations in Building Capacity Among and Enhancing the Impact of Community Transformers*, 2002, available at www. hudsonfaithincommunities.org, found that intermediary organizations made enormous contributions to the scope, scale and effectiveness of grassroots FBOs, especially through mentoring and encouraging leaders and capacity building. Many of the eighteen organizations surveyed had experience in subcontracting with FBOs and 89 percent of those surveyed were willing to play the role of a publicly funded financial intermediary.

77. John C. Green and Amy L. Sherman, *Fruitful Collaborations: A Survey of Government-Funded Faith-Based Programs in 15 States*, 2002, 5, 35, available at www.hudsonfaithincommunities.org.

78. Dr. Amy L. Sherman, *The Growing Impact of Charitable Choice: A Catalogue of New Collaborations Between Government and Faith-Based Organizations in Nine States* (Washington, D.C.: The Center for Public Justice, 2000), 14. A subsequent study of contracting between government social welfare entities and FBOs in fifteen states found that $124 million in grants had been delivered to 726 FBOs and tentatively noted a continuation of the trend of increased government contracting with FBOs lacking any previous public contracting history. Amy L. Sherman, *Collaborations Catalogue: A Report on Charitable Choice Implementation in 15 States*, Hudson Institute, Executive Summary, 2002, 4.

79. *Ibid.*, 3.

80. *Ibid.*, 3, 7.

81. Mark Chaves, "Religious Congregations and Welfare Reform: Who Will Take Advantage of 'Charitable Choice'?" *American Sociological Review* 64:6 (December 1999): 836-846, at 839.

82. In a survey of 389 faith-based contractors under federal social welfare programs regulated by Charitable Choice guidelines, 29 percent indicated government reporting requirements were a "considerable" or a "great" burden. Green and Sherman, *Fruitful Collaborations*, 4, 29-30, 34.

83. Goodstein, "Churches Are Wary," A22.

84. Chaves, "Religious Congregations and Welfare Reform," 839.

85. Ram A. Cnaan, *Keeping Faith in the City: How 401 Urban Religious Congregations Serve Their Neediest Neighbors*, Center for Research on Religion and Urban Civil Society, University of Pennsylvania, CRRUCS Report 2000-1, 19-20.

86. Chaves, "Religious Congregations and Welfare Reform," 841.

87. *Ibid.*

88. Sherman, *The Growing Impact of Charitable Choice*, 14.

89. Goodstein, "Churches Are Wary," A22.

90. Testimony, Amy L. Sherman, Ph.D., Senior Fellow, Welfare Policy Center, Hudson Institute, Oversight Hearing on State and Local Implementation of Existing Charitable Choice Provisions, Subcommittee on the Constitution, Committee on the Judiciary, U.S. House of Representatives, April 24, 2001; Sherman, *The Growing Impact of Charitable Choice*, 10, 15.

91. Green and Sherman, *Fruitful Collaborations*, 4, 34.

92. Testimony, Sherman; Amy L. Sherman, "Churches as Government Partners: Navigating 'Charitable Choice'," *The Christian Century* 117:20 (July 5, 2000), 716-720, at 717; Sherman, *The Growing Impact of Charitable Choice*, 11, 15-16.

93. Green and Sherman, *Fruitful Collaborations*, 4, 41-45.

94. Stephen Goldsmith, "Having Faith in Our Neighborhoods: The Front Porch Alliance," in *What's God Got to Do With the American Experiment*, eds. E. J. Dionne, Jr. and John J. DiIulio, Jr. (Washington, D.C.: Brookings Institution, 2000); Terry Horne, "Goldsmith May Play Role in Bush's Faith-Based Plan," *Indianapolis Star*, January 8, 2001, A4; John Strauss, "Neighborhoods Make Progress in Alliance," *Indianapolis Star*, November 22, 1998, C1; David Holmstrom, "Front Porch Alliance Fosters Church-City Cooperation," *Christian Science Monitor*, May 13, 1998, 12; Lamont J. Hulse, "Empowering Neighborhoods," in *To Market, To Market: Reinventing Indianapolis*, eds. Ingrid Richie and Sheila Suess Kennedy (Lanham, Md.: University Press of America, 2001), 218-222.

Chapter 7

Implementation of President George W. Bush's New Deal for Faith

President George W. Bush's faith-based initiative contemplates a significant shift in the way the United States provides social services. It represents a departure from large, public sector or secular, social service providers toward smaller, local groups, many of them faith-based. The initiative requires considerable outreach not only to legislators but also to large corporations and foundations that have long supported big providers. The project threatens the secular domination of social services and existing political alignments. Not unexpectedly, it encountered serious Congressional opposition in the 107th Congress, forcing the White House to proceed by executive orders, new administrative rules, and revised grant procedures.

Throughout his campaign and into his presidency, Bush continued to advocate his concept of "compassionate conservatism," outlined in this chapter. Three aspects of Bush's faith-based initiative followed from this policy perspective: first, Bush's executive orders and his administration's modification of agency regulations and grant procedures; second, the push to obtain congressional approval for the expansion of Charitable Choice by opening more federally funded programs to FBOs as providers and by the increased use of tax incentives and vouchers; and finally, the efforts to increase corporate giving to FBOs.

One of the most important aspects of President Bush's faith-based initiative focused on gaining increased funding for FBOs. One aspect of this initiative was relatively uncontroversial. Bush proposed a series of tax incentives to stimulate additional giving to charitable organizations. Most noteworthy was a tax deduction for individuals who do not itemize their contributions.

However, the expansion of the Charitable Choice provisions according equal access for FBOs when they compete with other organizations for federally funded social service contracts proved much more controversial, especially the ability of FBOs to pursue discriminatory hiring policies. The administration also pushed for the expanded use of vouchers, making it easier for the federal government to provide funding for religious institutions while avoiding constitutional problems with the Establishment Clause. Despite the hurdles that any new Charitable Choice legislation faced in the 107th Congress, it remained an important issue on the president's agenda, with prospects brightened by Republican control of both houses of the 108th Congress.

George W. Bush's Vision of Compassionate Conservatism

During the 2000 Presidential campaign, barely a day went by without George W. Bush issuing a call to "rally the armies of compassion"–using FBOs and other nonprofits to deal with poverty, drug abuse, and other social problems. While he never asserted that his approach would solve all of America's social ills, as a presidential candidate Bush repeatedly expressed his strong belief that religious groups have a significant role to play. Bush tapped into the American respect for faith-based social services and the hope that spiritual approaches could succeed where secular ones had failed. More fundamentally, Bush hoped that as president he could change a political and policy culture hostile to any type of religion, except private religion.

If elected, Bush promised to use the government to support the work of the "armies of compassion." Indeed, it was one of his signature campaign issues. He saw the federal government as playing a limited, yet active role in promoting the work of FBOs, thereby restricting the scope of social services directly provided by the public sector. In Bush's view, the federal government would serve both as a catalyst and as a source of financing for the work done by FBOs.

From July 1999 through election day in November 2000, Bush's "compassionate conservatism" platform consisted of three main elements.[1] First, he emphasized the need for federal income tax incentives. He predicted that Tax Code changes would lead to an explosion of charitable giving. Second, Bush vowed to urge Congress to allow FBOs to compete for federally funded public sector contracts and grants on an equal footing with secular organizations. Third, he pledged to have federal regulators ease the rules that otherwise made it difficult for FBOs to work with government agencies. In other words, he aspired to integrate faith-based and community groups into the entire range of federally financed social service programs.

For Bush, this was more than campaign hyperbole, as evidenced by his speech on December 13, 2000, when he claimed victory in the presidential election. He stated, "Together, we will address society's deepest problems, one person at a time, by encouraging and empowering the good hearts and good works of the American people. This is the essence of compassionate conservatism, and it will be a foundation of my administration."[2]

As president, George W. Bush used the presidential bully pulpit to emphasize the role of faith in solving social problems and reversing America's cultural decay. In his January 20, 2001 Inaugural Address, he noted, "Government has great responsibilities, for public safety and public health, for civil rights and common schools. Yet compassion is the work of a nation, not just a government. And some needs and hurts are so deep they will only respond to a mentor's touch or a pastor's prayer. Church and charity, synagogue and mosque, lend our communities their humanity, and they will have an honored place in our plans and in our laws."[3]

During the second week of his presidency, Bush announced the formation of White House Office of Faith-Based and Community Initiatives. He told a group of interfaith and community service leaders: "Government has important responsibilities for public health or public order and civil rights, and government will never be replaced by charities and community groups." He continued, "Yet, when we see social needs in America, my administration will look first at faith-based programs and community groups, which have proven their power to save and change lives." Anticipating the arguments of civil libertarian critics discussed in chapter 8, Bush noted, "We will not fund the religious activities of any group, but when people of faith provide social services, we will not discriminate against them." He vigorously asserted, "As long as there are secular alternatives, faith-based charities should be able to compete for funding on an equal basis and in a manner that does not cause them to sacrifice their mission."[4]

One month later, in his Budget Address to Congress on February 27, 2001, Bush again set forth his vision and responded to criticisms. He also provided more details of his plans for "compassionate conservatism." The president stated:

> And my budget adopts a hopeful new approach to help the poor and the disadvantaged. We must encourage and support the work of charities and faith-based and community groups that offer help and love one person at a time. These groups are working in every neighborhood in America, to fight homelessness and addiction and domestic violence, to provide a hot meal or a mentor or a safe haven for our children. Government should welcome these groups to apply for funds, not discriminate against them.

Government cannot be replaced by charities or volunteers. Government should not fund religious activities. But our nation should support the good works of these good people who are helping their neighbors in need. So I propose allowing all taxpayers, whether they itemize or not, to deduct their charitable contributions. Estimates show this could encourage as much as $14 billion a year in new charitable giving, money that will save and change lives.

Our budget provides more than $700 million over the next 10 years for a Federal Compassion Fund with a focused and noble mission: to provide a mentor to the more than one million children with a parent in prison, and to support local efforts to fight illiteracy, teen pregnancy, drug addiction, and other difficult problems.[5]

In his first commencement address on May 20, 2001, at the University of Notre Dame, Bush reemphasized his program of compassionate conservatism.[6] He made an impassioned plea for his plan to reform the Great Society and increase government funding for FBOs performing social services. Expressing his belief that citizens, who all too often are bystanders, should help bear another's burden, the president noted, "Much of today's poverty has more to do with troubled lives than a troubled economy." He then stated:

And often when a life is broken, it can be restored by another caring, concerned human being. The answer for an abandoned child is not a job requirement; it is the loving presence of a mentor. The answer to addiction is not a demand for self-sufficiency; it is personal support on the hard road to recovery.

The hope we seek is found in safe havens for battered women and children, in homeless shelters, in crisis pregnancy centers, in programs that tutor and conduct job training and help young people who may happen to be on parole. All these efforts provide not just a benefit but attention and kindness, a touch of courtesy, a dose of grace.

In pointing to a future strategy for combating poverty in the United States, Bush urged, "Our society must enlist, equip and empower idealistic Americans in the works of compassion that only they can provide." "Government has an important role. [It] will never be replaced by charities," he stated. Showing no signs of backing down from his desire to expand Charitable Choice, Bush asserted, "Yet, Government must do more to take the side of charities and community healers and support their work." While declaring that FBOs should not be discriminated against on the grounds of religion when competing for government funded social service contracts, Bush continued, "Government should never fund the teaching of faith, but it should support the good works of the faithful."

However, beyond his noble and high-flying rhetoric, President Bush found it easier to implement his vision of compassionate conservation through executive orders and federal administrative agency actions rather than through legislation in the 107th Congress.

Helping FBOs through Executive Orders and Revamped Federal Administrative Rules and Procedures

Bush advisers decided to devote the second week after inauguration to promoting faith-based programs. This would fulfill a campaign promise and demonstrate the president's deep devotion to his signature initiative.

On January 29, 2001, President Bush signed two executive orders dealing with faith-based programs. In signing these executive orders, Bush, flanked by more than thirty religious leaders, including a score of Christian ministers, a Jewish leader, and a Muslim imam, noted, "It is one of the great goals of my administration to invigorate the spirit of involvement and citizenship. We will encourage faith-based and community programs without changing their mission. We will help all in their work to change hearts while keeping a commitment to pluralism."[7]

Office of Faith-Based and Community Initiatives

Through one Executive Order, Bush established the Office of Faith-Based and Community Initiatives (the OFBCI or the Office). The OFBCI functions within the Executive Office of the president as an emblem of his compassionate conservative political philosophy. OFBCI does not hand out grants. Rather, as charged by Bush, it assumed the lead responsibility within the Executive Branch "to establish policies, priorities, and objectives for the Federal Government's comprehensive effort to enlist, equip, enable, empower, and expand the work of faith-based and other community organizations to the extent permitted by law."[8]

The purpose of OFBCI is to study and promote the expansion of partnerships between government and FBOs that provide social services and strengthen their capacity to meet social needs in communities throughout the United States. It is also responsible for the development and integration of policies within the federal government that deal with faith-based groups. In addition to serving as a liaison to nonprofit groups and helping to improve existing government practices, rules, and regulations, the Office fulfills a number of other functions, including developing, leading and coordinating the administration's policy agenda affecting faith-based and other community programs and initiatives. OFBCI is responsible for expanding the role of civil society institutions and increasing their capacity by providing faith-based and community programs with better access to federal and private funding for social services. This is done through executive action, legislation, and regulatory, relief designed to remove unnecessary legislative, regulatory, and bureaucratic barriers impeding faith-based and community efforts to solve social problems. OFBCI also identifies best practices and programs. It showcases innovative and exemplary grassroots nonprofit organizations and other civic initiatives as national models that others could learn from.

The Office head was first offered to Stephen Goldsmith, a Jewish Republican, a two-term mayor of Indianapolis and domestic policy advisor to Bush's 2000 campaign. Goldsmith declined because he sought a larger office with an even broader sweep.

Instead, as the Assistant to the President for Faith-Based and Community Initiatives, reporting directly to the president, Bush tapped John J. DiIulio, Jr., a University of Pennsylvania professor. DiIulio, an expert on public administration, criminology, and social problems, had studied FBOs for years. He had written, edited, or coauthored a dozen books on public policy, including one on the role of FBOs.[9] DiIulio is a Harvard Ph.D. from a working-class ethnic neighborhood on the south side of Philadelphia, a self-described New Democrat, and a fellow at both the Manhattan Institute and The Brookings Institution. He brought to the task a commitment to the faith-based initiative and close ties to religious conservatives as well as his previous, extensive work with black ministers in urban areas. The choice of DiIulio, an academic admired by Senator Joseph I. Lieberman (D-Connecticut), seemed an excellent way to unite a divided Congress and pave the way for a smooth path through Congress for the Bush plans.

Like many others involved with the Charitable Choice initiative, DiIulio had his own story of spiritual reawakening. DiIulio, who oversaw the administration's faith-based initiative from February 20, 2001 to September 15, 2001, is a devout Roman Catholic. On Palm Sunday, 1996, while at Mass with his family, DiIulio committed himself to a deeper faith and to working with children and the poor in the inner city.[10] He experienced a personal conversion of the heart, teaching him more humility and patience.

Prior to issuing the Executive Order establishing OFBCI, the administration envisioned that the Office would deal with more than faith-based groups. It was seen as generally strengthening civil society institutions. Bush advisors wanted the new office to be called the Office of Community and Faith-Based Initiatives.[11] Before he signed on as head, DiIulio objected, saying that if that was how Bush wanted it, he could get someone else to run the Office. DiIulio wanted faith-based to be first, in recognition of the fact that expanding the efforts of FBOs was what was new and significant about the initiative. To get DiIulio on board, Bush aides gave in to DiIulio resulting in the Office of Faith-Based and Community Initiatives.

The OFBCI officially opened for business on February 20, 2001. The Office emphasized outreach and exhortation, seeking to publicize Bush's faith-based initiative and gain public and legislative support for the administration's plans. To fulfill these goals, DiIulio gave speeches and Congressional testimony to promote the initiative. Although awareness and support for providing more public help to FBOs increased, DiIulio revealed his lack of practical political experience and his distaste for Washington infighting and contentiousness. He lasted less than seven months on the job, citing for his departure health problems, the need to be with his family, and frustration in the job. Also, the OFBCI was under-staffed and underfunded. Instead of the hoped-for twenty-five staff members, DiIulio had to make due with only three staffers. He also lacked autonomy and budgetary authority as well as the power to implement his own political strategy. DiIulio, who opposed the administration's initial "quick push" legislative strategy and sparred with conservative Republi-cans over the details of the president's faith-based program, grated on the Republican leadership and White House officials.

On February 1, 2002, Bush named James Towey director of the OFBCI, with the title of Deputy Assistant to the President, a less senior rank than held by DiIulio.[12] Towey is a Democrat, a Roman Catholic, the former Florida Secretary of Health and Rehabilitative Services under Democratic Governor Lawton Chiles, and a close associate and volunteer attorney for Mother Teresa. Since 1996, Towey had headed of a nonprofit group, Aging with Dignity, that aimed at improving the quality of life for the dying by advocating hospice care.

As head of the OFBCI, Towey traveled throughout the nation to promote Bush's initiative. Under his leadership, the office organized regional conferences in the fall of 2002 and early 2003 spelling out the rights and responsibilities of religious and secular groups in competing for federal Charitable Choice funds and teaching them how to use the existing laws to win federally funded contracts and grants.[13] It also prepared a guidebook explaining how FBOs can qualify for government grants and what they can and cannot do with taxpayers' funds.[14]

Centers for Faith-Based and Community Initiatives

Simultaneously, through another January 2001 Executive Order,[15] Bush directed five cabinet agencies, namely, Justice, Education, Labor, Health and Human Services, and Housing and Urban Development, that perform the bulk of the federal government's grant-making, to create centers for faith-based and community initiatives. These centers were designed to examine the existing barriers to the participation by faith-based and other community nonprofits in the delivery of social services, including activities that "discriminate against or otherwise discourage or disadvantage" their participation in federal programs. Together with the OFBCI, these centers sought to clear away bureaucratic obstacles, promote greater cooperation, and bridge the gap between the independent sector and the five cabinet departments heavily involved in the funding of the delivery of social services.

These agency centers also sought to coordinate efforts to "eliminate regulatory, contracting, and other programmatic obstacles to the participation of faith-based and other community organizations in the provision of social services." They were instructed to report back on these regulatory barriers to the public sector working with nonprofit groups in the provision of social services and recommend how these barriers could be removed.

As charged by President Bush in January 2001, the five centers performed a number of other functions, including a comprehensive departmental effort to incorporate and coordinate faith-based and other community organizations in their respective programs and initiatives "to the greatest extent possible." They were to propose the development of innovative pilot and demonstration programs to increase the participation by faith-based and other community organizations in federal, state, and local initiatives. They were also charged to improve the dissemination of information to faith-based and other community organizations.

The centers in the Departments of Health and Human Services and Labor performed two additional functions. First, they conducted a comprehensive review of practices impacting the funding streams governed by the existing Charitable Choice laws in order to assess each department's compliance with the Charitable Choice requirements. As noted in chapter 6, the review by HHS concluded that the department had done "very little to apply the [Charitable Choice] rules to its own grant making or to ensure that the State and local governments that receive the covered funds adjust their own procurement rules to comply with the congressional directives."[16] Second, they were to promote and ensure compliance with Charitable Choice by their respective departments, as well as by state and local government partners and their contractors.

For six months in 2001, the centers, supervised by the OFBCI, quietly combed through regulations of the five cabinet-level agencies that disburse or regulate social spending. Conducting an extensive audit, each center reviewed the ways in which its agency's regulations and grant procedures had a negative impact on the federal funding of charitable social services.

The White House Report

In July 2001, each center submitted its review to the OFBCI, which, in turn, in August released a report entitled *Unlevel Playing Field*[17] (the Report), summarizing the findings of these centers. The Report, probably the Office, and the centers' biggest accomplishment in 2001, documented more than a dozen barriers to FBOs applying for or receiving funds from federal social service programs. First, the Report noted the existence of prohibitions against certain kinds of religious organizations from applying for funding. Based on the premise supported by many federal officials that "close collaboration with religious organizations is legally suspect,"[18] the Report indicated that some federal programs flat out ban applications from FBOs. The Report noted:

> But Federal officials, and State and local officials participating in Federal formula grant programs, often seem stuck in a "no-aid," strict separationist framework that permitted Federal funding only of religiously affiliated organizations offering secular services in a secularized setting, and deny equal treatment to organizations with an obvious religious character. As the Labor Department's report notes, reviewers of grant applications assume that Jefferson's "wall of separation" metaphor automatically disqualifies all but the most secularized providers, leading to Federal resistance to collaborating with religious groups, and thus the actual exclusion of faith-based organizations despite the absence of any constitutional or statutory basis. One Education Department official asserted that the Constitution flatly forbids the use of grant funds even for activities that merely have a religious component. Such restrictive attitudes beget an administrative bias against religion and religious organizations where the Constitution requires that there be none.[19]

Generally, however, the problem is more subtle with FBOs encountering an "unwelcoming environment" or a requirement that they not be "overtly religious to be eligible for funding."[20]

Second, the Report highlighted the existence of excessive regulatory restrictions on religious activities of FBOs that are prohibited neither by the U.S. Constitution nor by federal statutes.[21] For instance, the Report stated:

> HUD regulations for Community Development Block Grants, among other programs, expressly require religious organizations not only to agree to avoid giving "religious instruction or counseling" but even to affirm that they will "exert no religious influence" at all in providing the Federally funded assistance. Such exceedingly vague language chills the participation of many faith-based providers, who have no intention of conducting government-funded worship services, but who fervently believe that their social services should be informed and prompted by their religious impulse and that the lives of staff members should set a good example and influence others positively. Some faith-based organizations applying

at the local level for CDBG funds have been informed that they would qualify for the support only if they first removed references to "God" from their mission statements or stripped their walls clean of religious symbols.[22]

Third, the Report noted that some programs contain anticompetitive mandates.[23] For example, these mandates may require grant applicants to demonstrate support from government agencies or others that might also be competing for the same funds.

Fourth, FBOs, particularly small groups, the Report concluded, face an array of burdensome and cumbersome regulations and other requirements. They also encounter limited accessibility to federal grants information and complex contract and grant procedures and agreements.[24]

Fifth, the federal government was viewed as favoring large providers over smaller ones in awarding social service contracts. The Report noted "a funding gap between the government and the grassroots. Smaller groups, faith-based and secular, receive very little Federal support relative to the size and the scope of the social services they provide."[25] According to the Report, the funding gap could not be explained on the grounds that bigger providers outperform smaller ones. Washington simply does not know much about the performance of the groups it funds, the Report concluded.

Although the Report, which will be issued annually, made no recommendations, it noted, "Legislation requires some restrictions on the full participation of faith-based organizations, but many of the regulations are needlessly burdensome administrative creations. Congress's remedy to barriers to faith-based organizations...[Charitable Choice] has been almost entirely ignored by Federal administrators, who have done little to help or require State and local governments to comply with the new rules involving faith-based providers." The Report concluded, "Few Federal funding programs have undergone a thorough evaluation with an eye to ensuring that expenditures yield the planned-for positive results in the lives of people who need help."[26]

After the issuance of the Report, President Bush indicated that he appointed people in the five agencies "to end this bias, and soon." He said his faith-based office is also working with religious charities and community groups to "help them know their civil rights" and "know how to effectively apply for funds so their good works can be expanded."[27] Proposals for improvements will be made to the president by each of the five agencies. Thus, the issuance of the Report marked the beginning of an effort to devise administrative remedies to end the pervasive bias against FBOs receiving federal social service grants and attain the goal of fair and effective federal contracting for these services.

Administrative Changes

With the legislative difficulties encountered in expanding Charitable Choice and providing meaningful tax incentives for increased charitable giving in the 107th Congress, Bush placed great emphasis on administrative changes to help level the playing field to encourage the work of FBOs, particularly small ones offering one-on-one assistance. The Department of Education established the novice competitive priority and applicant procedure.[28] The Department of Labor included twenty-five grants of up to $25,000 each, as part of a grant program, from discretionary funds, totaling more than $15 million for employment training, to assist small congregations and community groups providing job training and other employment programs.[29]

Agencies revised regulations and procedures that interfered with FBOs competing for government contracts and grants. The Department of Labor modified certain solicitations for grant applications to provide equal treatment for FBOs.[30]

Emphasis was placed on the implementation of the existing Charitable Choice provisions, enacted from 1996 to 2000. For the first time since Charitable Choice was enacted in 1996, the Department of Health and Human Services issued regulations implementing Charitable Choice laws for the TANF, the SAMHSA, and the CSBG programs.[31] The Department of Education issued regulations on the eligibility of FBOs to provide supplemental services, such as extra help before and after school, to low-income children who attend schools that have not made adequate yearly progress for two years, and schools that have not improved after the initial two-year period.[32] The Department of Housing and Urban Development revised regulations that apply to programs operated out of its Office of Community Planning and Development and repealed regulations prohibiting FBOs from participating in certain programs.[33]

The rewriting of hundreds of regulations would open the flow of federal funds to FBOs by removing the barriers preventing faith-based social service providers from qualifying for contracts and grants.[34] Changes in HUD regulations cover $8 billion in grants; while the Department of Education regulations open more than $1 billion in programs to competition.[35]

The White House Office of Faith-Based and Community Initiatives continued to work with the five cabinet departments to level the playing field, eliminating barriers to governmental dealings with FBOs and allowing FBOs to compete for federal grants and contracts on the same footing as secular groups. These regulatory measures may, in the long run, be more important than new funding sources.

In December 2002, President Bush signed an Executive Order establishing new centers for faith-based and community initiatives in the Department of Agriculture and the Agency for International Development. He directed these centers to undertake an audit of existing faith-based and community efforts in their programs.[36]

Although a great deal of Bush's faith-based initiative was accomplished by administrative action and regulatory reform that avoided the media spotlight, other parts needed Congressional approval. Gaining House and Senate acquiescence proved far more difficult.

Bush's Efforts Requiring Congressional Approval

President Bush required Congressional action to implement portions of his faith-based initiative in four areas: the expansion of Charitable Choice to other government programs, through direct funding and vouchers; other initiatives designed to develop partnerships between the federal government and FBOs; increased tax incentives for charitable giving; and lifting the liability consequences of corporate in-kind contributions. Broadening the scope of Charitable Choice became as divisive as any part of the Bush domestic agenda. Democratic support was thin; religious conservatives remained wary. Although Bush persisted, the 107th Congress, however, gave the president little support for his initiative.

Expanding Charitable Choice

In outlining legislative proposals to expand Charitable Choice, Bush sought to make billions of dollars of federal spending available to FBOs by giving these organizations the same chance to vie for contracts and grants as other groups. He wanted his faith-based initiative to allow FBOs to administer social services for the poor, the addicted, or the disadvantaged. These services were previously dominated by public sector agencies or secular groups. Bush focused on a results-driven approach and maintained that religious groups had a proven record of effectiveness in working with drug addicts, the poor, and the homeless. He sought their skills, dedication, and links to the community by further opening the competition for federal dollars. He wanted to add government money to his father's "thousand points of light" strategy that looked to volunteers and charities, rather than the public sector bureaucracy, to meet community needs.

In the administration's February 2001 budget proposals, the president indicated his support for initiatives to make Charitable Choice applicable to all federal laws authorizing the public sector to use nongovernmental groups to provide social services to beneficiaries using federal funds.[37] If the 107th Congress had enacted Bush's vision, Charitable Choice would apply to all federally funded domestic assistance areas, including job training, youth intervention, corrections, community policy, family preservation, and after-school programs, thereby opening tens of billions of dollars of contracts and grants to FBOs. It would also apply across federal agencies.

Republican lawmakers were eager to go ahead with the 180-day post-inauguration action plan devised by White House strategist Karl Rove, Senior Counselor and Political Advisor to the president. This script called for the Bush initiative to move through Congress once the Bush tax cut and education proposals were off the House and Senate agendas.

In March 2001, Representatives Julius Caesar (J.C.) Watts, Jr. (R-Oklahoma), the Republican Conference Chairman, and Tony P. Hall (D-Ohio) introduced a bipartisan bill, H.R. 7, the proposed Community Solutions Act of 2001.[38] Mirroring the president's desires, the original Watts-Hall bill sought to expand the Charitable Choice provisions to eleven additional domestic program areas carried out using federal funds,[39] thereby opening tens of billions of federal funds, along with eased rules for charitable tax deductions (considered later in this chapter). Apart from constitutional and federalism concerns, discussed later in this chapter and in chapter 8, the expansion of the Charitable Choice funding concept encountered little resistance. The revised version of H.R. 7, passed by the House of Representatives in July 2001, expanded the Charitable Choice provisions to nine federally funded programmatic areas.[40]

The revised Watts-Hall bill also authorized the expenditure of up to $50 million annually for various forms of training and technical assistance to small nongovernmental organizations, as determined by the attorney general,[41] again without objection. The types of assistance to be funded would include information relating to the creation of a tax-exempt organization, grant-writing help, information and referrals to other nongovernmental organizations providing accounting, legal, tax, and program development expertise. The bill further provided that in giving this assistance, "priority shall be given to small nongovernmental organizations serving urban and rural communities."[42] The importance of educating FBOs could not be minimized. Training and technical assistance would encourage groups otherwise leery of the government contracting process to apply for funding.

The Gathering Storm of Opposition

In February and March 2001, the Bush initiative to expand Charitable Choice to additional federal programs ran into a firestorm of protests, leading DiIulio and key senators to slow the president's effort. The negative reactions of strict church-state separationists and civil libertarians, fearful that the federal government's power and purse would be used to take a massive step towards establishing a theocracy by "Christianizing" America and coercively evangelizing vulnerable individuals, was expected. They were predictably worried about the blurring of the boundary between church and state, as well as the employment discrimination practiced by some FBOs. These concerns of secularists and others, who accuse Bush of being pastor-in-chief, are examined in chapter 8.

Other opponents included credentialed experts who oppose the methods of some spiritual counselors. Government-employee unions, fearful of private sector competition, not unexpectedly weighed in against the diversion of funds from public sector bureaucracies. Economic libertarians also joined the naysayers, voicing their concerns that with public sector contracts would come government standards and excessive regulation designed to ensure accountability and quality services.[43] Economic libertarians and political conservatives also feared that Bush's faith-based initiative could expand governmental bureaucracy and swell into a vast boondoggle.

Surprisingly, however, some key religious conservatives expressed a chorus of doubts about expanding direct grant programs, initially complicating the faith-based initiative and draining the OFBCI's very limited resources.[44] Prominent Christian conservatives and Bush supporters, such as Rev. Pat Robertson, the founder of the Christian Coalition, and Rev. Jerry Falwell, who headed the now defunct Moral Majority, publicly criticized the initiative. They worried that FBOs would be corrupted by the public sector grant process and regulations. The acceptance of public funds would, in their view, lead FBOs to give up their religious activities and mission. They expressed "deep concerns" that strings would come attached to government subsidies. Perhaps most troubling was the possible funding of religious groups outside the "mainstream." For Rev. Robertson, the possibility of groups, such as the Unification Church (now called the Family Federation for World Peace and Unification U.S.A.) which operates abstinence programs in schools, the Church of Scientology, which operates drug rehabilitation and literacy programs, and the Hare Krishnas, a Hindu sect, receiving public funding created an "intolerable" and an "appalling" situation.[45] Robertson stated, "This thing could be a real Pandora's box."[46]

In the midst of these concerns and efforts to reach out to African-American pastors, in March 2001, DiIulio strained relations with the religious right by challenging white, middle class Christians to do more. He bluntly responded to the criticisms with an attack on the critics.[47] In a speech before the National Association of Evangelicals, DiIulio angered conservative, white religious leaders by stating that the president's initiative would largely be directed to inner-city black and Latino churches with "benevolent traditions and histories that make them generally more dedicated to community-servicing missions, and generally more confident about engaging public and secular partners in achieving those missions without enervating their spiritual identities or religious characters." He continued, "With all due respect, and in good fellowship, predominantly white ex-urban evangelical and national parachurches, should be careful not to presume to speak for any persons other than themselves and their own churches." Indicating that overtly evangelical social programs would be eligible for vouchers, but not direct government grants, DiIulio concluded, "The indivisibly conversion-centered program that cannot separate out and privately fund its inherently religious activities, still can receive government support, but only via individual vouchers."

Some white, Christian evangelicals were furious. Rev. Louis P. Sheldon, chair of the Traditional Values Coalition, told a top Bush aide that DiIulio should be fired. Sheldon stated, "If I had someone on my team like that, either you reel them in, straighten them up and fly right or they would not be there anymore."[48] After DiIulio antagonized religious conservatives, other Bush officials took charge of the faith-based initiative.

Marvin Olasky, a surprise critic, worried that Bush's program would lock out FBOs that are basically evangelical. He became concerned about the apparent plan to refuse to provide direct funding of overtly evangelistic programs, such as Teen Challenge. Olasky saw a bias against organizations that make religious conversion central to their mission and was more disturbed than ever about how the Bush initiative was being shaped. Fueling a charged atmosphere, Olasky stated, "That seems to me to be discriminatory and wrong. There already is so much suspicion in the evangelical community about government activity and this will only intensify it."[49] He added, offering his own interpretation of constitutional law, "If the federal government puts out the welcome mat for some religious groups and tells others to 'opt out,' it is preferring one religious belief over another. This is exactly the type of religious discrimination the First Amendment is designed to prevent."[50]

The Ensuing Calm: Building Support
for Expansion of Charitable Choice

As a result of the storm of surprisingly vehement opposition to the expansion of contracting opportunities for FBOs, in March 2001, the Bush Administration postponed sending its own bill to Congress. Aware of the criticism from all sides of the political spectrum, the White House moved slowly. The administration realized it needed to quiet some of the opposition to the initiative and secure its base.

In early March, DiIulio, who favored consensus-building, urged a go-slow approach at a meeting with Republican congressional aides in the office of Bush's then Domestic Policy Council Chair John Bridgeland. However, figuring the best chance was to pass a comprehensive bill early in the 107th Congress, House Republicans wanted to run with a far-reaching bill they had drafted. Bush's senior political advisors and House Republicans prevailed over DiIulio.

At the same time, Senator Richard John (Rick) Santorum (R-Pennsylvania), Chairman of the Senate Republican Conference and the lead Republican sponsor in the Senate of the Bush faith-based initiative, split the proposal in two. The original bipartisan Santorum-Lieberman bill included various tax incentives to encourage charitable giving, but lacked the Charitable Choice provision due to constitutional concerns of its cosponsor, Senator Lieberman, whose sentiments on faith in public life served as a hallmark of his 2000 vice presidential campaign. In declining to cosponsor the Charitable Choice expansion legislation in the spring of 2001, Lieberman, who supported the faith-based initiative in principle, stated, "I've been waiting to see where the White House is going on this, but for now, they aren't directly confronting the most difficult Constitutional problems." He continued, "I believe in this, and I approach this believing that these faith-based groups can help the government make this a better country. But there are serious questions that haven't been answered."[51]

Santorum saw the need to approach the expansion of Charitable Choice incrementally. In the spring of 2001, Santorum felt that legislative action should come after the Bush administration used the existing statutes as a "proving ground." Regarding the Charitable Choice expansion proposals, Santorum said, "My sense is we're looking within the next year for them to work out the bugs. The timing may be right then." Santorum, indicating that the White House concurred with a slower approach, stated, "My sense is the administration will continue to work on this and work through this within the agencies. They want to build a consensus."[52]

The White House remained undaunted, allowing conservative House Republicans to spearhead the faith-based initiative. However, Bush remained amenable to negotiations on the specific details of expanding Charitable Choice. The administration came to recognize more clearly the need for both public education and the mobilization of its allies. Despite the barrage of criticism and the lack of specific constituency committed to its success, support began to build from a broad spectrum.

After the flurry of objections, Christian evangelicals, a key Bush political base, began to come around. In April 2001, the Coalition for Compassion, an ad hoc group of various organizations and individuals, including the National Association of Evangelicals (representing 51 denominations with more than 30 million members) and Olasky, stated it welcomed Bush's desire to involve FBOs in meeting human needs. It offered a statement of principles for FBOs accepting public funds, basically echoing the Bush initiative and noting, "Government funds may not be used to pay for religious instruction or instructional material, but a faith-based organization that accomplishes socially beneficial purposes through a pervasively religious approach may receive funding for other expenses equivalent to what other faith-based or secular government grantees receive."[53] However, Reverends Robertson and Falwell were not among the signers.

DiIulio accepted the coalition's statement on behalf of the administration.[54] Fudging on the exact funding mechanism, he agreed with its important principle of giving pervasively sectarian groups equal standing with others to receive government moneys.

Rove began assembling a professionally run coalition to promote the Watts-Hall bill. One key objective focused on landing support from the Salvation Army. In private talks, the Salvation Army offered its support in exchange for the White House considering new administrative regulations shielding FBOs from state and local laws banning discrimination in hiring, specifically sexual orientation discrimination and the need to provide domestic partner benefits.

Going back to December 2000, soon after claiming victory in the presidential election, Bush had sought to build his support among African-American ministers for his faith-based initiative. At that time, he hosted a meeting of religious leaders at the First Baptist Church in Austin to outline his faith-based plan. Although Catholic, Islamic, and Jewish leaders were present, the largest group represented was the African-American clergy. The attendees cut across ideological lines with a significant number identified with community efforts to help the inner-city poor.[55]

After his inauguration, Bush continued to try to build a new African-American coalition of ministers seeking friendly relations with the

Republican Party, including those leading megachurches, such as Bishop Charles E. Black of the West Angeles Church of God in Christ in Los Angeles.[56] For other African-American clergy, there was a division among those who welcomed financial support to help the poor and those who suspected that Bush was trying to lessen their Democratic loyalties.

In March 2001, Bush summoned leaders of the Congress of National Black Churches, representing eight major African-American denominations and including 65,000 churches and 20 million members, to the White House for a brief meeting. Seeing the need for some institutional, mainstream backing, Bush encouraged the ministers to speak with their congregants about the power of faith-based groups to provide social services, such as drug rehabilitation. The meeting participants issued a statement saying, "We are here to declare our uncompromising support for President Bush in this endeavor...."[57]

Those who favored the expansion of Charitable Choice included many urban African-American clergy who daily confronted the needs of the poor and the leaders and clergy from Pentecostal and evangelical denominations as well as Habitat for Humanity and the United States Catholic Conference. Other supporters included the Call to Renewal, a national coalition of various wings of Christianity fighting poverty in America, with representatives from a wide spectrum of the Christian community.

This new "religious center," consisting of a broad cross section of groups, found the terms under which they supported spending public money on the poor. It favored new partnerships between nonprofits and all levels of government to create the type of civil society that may solve many of America's social problems. As Rev. Jim Wallis, head of the Call to Renewal, put it, "The real issue here is not a church-state controversy. The real issue is developing the political will to overcome poverty and to rebuild shattered lives and neighborhoods. Creating partnerships that respect the pluralism of America and that honor the First Amendment does not mean separating faith from public life."[58]

When Bush's faith-based initative stalled in Congress in May 2001, despite these coalition building efforts, Rove stepped in at Bush's request and rejuvenated the effort.[59] Rove's efforts superseded DiIulio's attempts to promote the proposal. Bush spoke with Michael S. Joyce, former head of the Bradley Foundation, about the faith-based initiative during a White House ceremony on May 10. Fearful the initiative was languishing, Bush called Rove, told him to speak with Joyce, and get it moving again. Rove then helped energize House Republican leaders.

Rove's careful planning was thrown into disarray in May when Senator James M. Jeffords (I-Vermont) quit the Republican party and control of Senate shifted to the Democrats. With the Senate's Democratic leadership having little interest in supporting Bush's initiative, the president turned to the House to take up the challenge. However, Bush miscalculated in allowing conservative Republicans to write a needlessly partisan bill.

On June 6, Bush summoned House Speaker J. Dennis Hastert (R-Illinois) to the Oval Office. In a brief, but pointed conversation, Bush told Hastert he wanted legislative action in time for his scheduled July Fourth speech to promote the initiative.

Overcoming a New Roadblock:
The House Judiciary Committee

Passage of the Watts-Hall proposal proved arduous. Many expressed the view that the expansion of Charitable Choice was dead on the Hill. Nevertheless, House supporters persevered, but a roadblock came from an unexpected source.

Throughout most of June, House Judiciary Chair F. James Sensenbrenner, Jr. (R-Wisconsin), whom the White House had failed to consult but who had jurisdiction over the nontax aspects of the bill, held up a "stop sign" to the expansion of Charitable Choice. The original version of H.R. 7 stalled in the House Judiciary Committee because of Sensenbrenner's concerns about the constitutionality of its church-state implications. Moving from the premise, as Sensenbrenner put it, that "Every member of the House took the...oath to support the Constitution,"[60] he concluded that the Charitable Choice aspects of the original Watts-Hall bill lacked sufficient safeguards to prevent the unconstitutional mixing of federal funding with religious instruction.

In early June, when Vice President Richard B. (Dick) Cheney inquired about the lack of Judiciary Committee action, Sensenbrenner relayed that there were "very serious problems."[61] He told Cheney that the administration would never achieve bipartisan support for the legislation in its original form.

After Sensenbrenner indicated to Cheney the dimensions of the constitutional problems, the White House quickly responded with a salvage operation. Attorney General John D. Ashcroft contacted Sensenbrenner and attempted to explain why the proposed measure would receive constitutional approval from the federal judiciary. Sensenbrenner was not satisfied.

With his July Fourth speech looming, Bush called Sensenbrenner and demanded that he set a date for committee action. The chairman dug in his heels. "I told him we could if the constitutional issues were ironed out by that time," Sensenbrenner recalled. "As of that point, they were not."[62]

On June 25, Bush opened another offensive on behalf of the bill in an address to the U.S. Conference of Mayors. The president sought to build support among mayors for his faith-based initiative. While acknowledging widespread congressional opposition, Bush asked the mayors to make their support known to the skeptics on Capitol Hill. The mayors gave Bush what he wanted. They endorsed his plan with a proclamation indicating that the group would work closely with the administration to assist national faith- and community-based initiatives.[63]

In a further attempt to satisfy Sensenbrenner's objections, Bush dispatched Solicitor General Theodore B. Olson. Olson indicated that the administration wanted to include vouchers as part of the plan. When Olson asserted that recent U.S. Supreme Court rulings had blessed the constitutionality of vouchers going directly to individuals, Sensenbrenner warmed to the idea.

Sensenbrenner then sought another White House meeting in the presence of White House Chief of Staff, Andrew H. Card, Jr. On June 27, the White House and Congressional Republicans– House Speaker Hastert, Representatives Richard E. (Dick) Armey (R-Texas) (House Majority Leader), Tom DeLay (R- Texas) (House Majority Whip), and J. C. Watts, Jr.–agreed on changes to the bill, thereby allowing the proposal to proceed.[64] On June 28, the nontax portions of the Watts-Hall bill passed the Judiciary Committee, despite vehement Democratic objections, putting the measure on track to meet Bush's July Fourth target.

Revising the Safeguards Built Into the Expanded Charitable Choice Provisions

While continuing the ban on the expenditure of federal grant funds to support religious activities, specifically, "sectarian worship, instruction, or proselytization,"[65] the revised version of the Watts-Hall bill put firewalls in place between an FBO's spiritual endeavors and its secular, government-funded social service activities. The amended version provided: "If the religious organization offers [sectarian instruction, worship or proselytization], it shall be voluntary for the individuals receiving services and offered separate from the program funded under this [bill]. A certificate shall be separately signed by religious organizations, and filed with the government agency that disburses the funds, certifying that the organization is aware of and will comply with this [requirement]."[66] In other words, if any part of an FBO's activities involve religious indoctrination, these activities must be set apart from the government-funded program and privately funded. However, as discussed later in this chapter, the revised House bill added a provision for vouchers which would bypass the need for an FBO to separate its voucher-funded social services and its religious activities.

For critics, the new language seemed to mean the bill discriminated against evangelical Christian groups that make religion an essential, inseparable element of their social service programs. Thus, programs such as Teen Challenge and PFM, discussed, respectively, in chapters 2 and 4, two groups repeatedly used as examples of the successes of FBOs in providing social services, would be ineligible to receive federally funded contracts and grants because religion is an integral part of their programs.

Olasky resumed his objections to the Bush faith-based initiative now embodied in the amended Watts-Hall proposal. It is so watered down, Olasky decried, "it won't do diddly" to help finance FBOs that tend to the needy.[67]

The Watts-Hall bill sought to protect both organizational and individual religious freedom. The revised bill contained the same general safeguards for protecting an FBO's autonomy as mandated in earlier Charitable Choice enactments. Funding agencies could not exclude an FBO from competing for a contract because it has a religious character or, according to the amended version, it "is religious."[68]

Additional safeguards protected an organization's character.[69] Neither the federal government nor a state or local government offering federally funded programs could require an FBO providing social services to alter either its form of internal governance or provisions in its charter documents. The original version only referred to its internal governance.[70] Furthermore, it need not "remove religious art, icons, scripture or other symbols, or to change its name because such symbols or names are of a religious character." The original version did not contain any safeguards with respect to the organization's name.[71]

Beneficiaries also remain protected. Both the original and amended opt-out provisions were basically the same with little practical difference. The revised bill removed a requirement that if a beneficiary has an objection to a religious social service program, he or she must be provided with "an alternative, including a nonreligious alternative, that is accessible to the individual."[72] Instead, the revised bill stated that a beneficiary must be provided with an alternative that is "accessible to the individual and unobjectionable to the individual on religious grounds."[73] Thus, if a beneficiary receiving social services objects to one or more religious programs, he or she must be provided a secular alternative.

As an additional protection, beneficiaries must be notified of their right to seek an alternative program.[74] Clients remaining in faith-based programs could opt out of activities they do not like. As previously noted, participation in sectarian worship, instruction, or proselytization, if it occurs, is voluntary and must be offered separately from the funded program, whether through a grant or a cooperative agreement (the latter phrase was used in place of the term "contract").

The revised proposal also contained enhanced accountability provisions. While generally subjecting FBOs to the same performance reviews and accounting aspects as other nongovernmental organizations, it mandated that FBOs create separate accounts for federal dollars, whether received in the form of grants or cooperative agreements.[75] Segregation of funds would, however, remain voluntary for FBOs receiving indirect assistance, such as vouchers. The revised version added a provision requiring an FBO to conduct a self-audit regarding compliance with its duties to segregate government funds into a separate account(s) and submit a copy of the self-audit to the appropriate governmental funding agency, together with a "plan to timely correct variances, if any, identified in the plan."[76]

With respect to compliance, the original bill allowed a civil action against the federal government "for appropriate relief."[77] The revised version limited the action against state officials, local government agencies, or a federal official (or agency) to injunctive relief.[78]

A Public Relations Disaster

As House Ways and Means Committee Chair William M. (Bill) Thomas (R-California) prepared to offer a scaled down $13.3 billion, ten year tax package, a *Washington Post* article produced a Bush public relations disaster.[79] On June 10, the *Post* reported, based on a leaked Salvation Army internal memorandum, that the organization had received a "firm commitment" from the administration to rewrite federal regulations to protect FBOs from state and local laws regarding sexual orientation discrimination and domestic partner benefits. In return, according to the *Post* article, the Salvation Army agreed to promote the administration's faith-based initiative by spending as much as $110,000 monthly on lobbying in favor of the plan.

The story provoked a thunderous reaction from inflamed Congressional Democrats and some moderate Republicans. Senate Democrats warned that the issuance of such a regulation might imperil, if not "terminally wound," the Bush initiative.

White House officials denied making any deals with the Salvation Army.[80] Disputing the document's claim that it had made a "firm commitment," the administration acknowledged that it was just considering the request and the type of regulation the Salvation Army proposed. The White House quickly cut its losses, stating that it would not issue a regulation designed to meet the Salvation Army's goal of denying federal funds to state or local governments requiring FBOs to hire homosexuals or provide them with domestic partner benefits.

The House Approves the Bush Proposal

The House Rules Committee combined into one measure the nontax portions of the revised Watts-Hall bill approved June 28 by the House Judiciary Committee and the tax breaks, discussed later in this chapter, approved July 11 by the House Ways and Means Committee. In gaining approval of the bill on July 19, House Republican leaders overcame opposition from homosexual rights groups and their allies, who asserted that the measure would allow FBOs to discriminate against homosexuals in employment. After an intense White House lobbying effort to control the damage and maintain a winning coalition, including last minute telephone calls to representatives by Vice President Cheney, the measure passed, likely costing more political capital than Bush strategists expected, by a party-line vote of 233-198, with only fifteen Democrats joining all but four Republicans in favor of the proposal.[81]

In a fierce floor debate, opponents of the bill made the antidiscrimination issue their focal point. The vote followed a one-day postponement called by the House Republican leaders after moderate Republicans said they would support a Democratic motion to recommit the measure to address a provision that would exempt FBOs from following state and local laws that bar discrimination in hiring.[82]

The bill's preservation of the right of FBOs to hire staff who support their respective religious missions provided the focus of the controversy. Two aspects of the proposal were noteworthy. First, the bill continued the long-standing exemption provided by Section 702 of the Civil Rights Act of 1964 regarding discrimination by FBOs in their employment practices. An FBO's participation in or the receipt of federal funds for the specified social service programs would not affect that exemption. Furthermore, the revised bill stated that "any provision in such programs that is inconsistent with or would diminish the exercise of an organization's autonomy recognized in section 702 or in this section shall have no effect."[83] The bill also mandated (both in its revised and original forms) that FBOs receiving directly funded assistance or providing social services indirectly paid for with vouchers must comply with a variety of nondiscrimination provisions including those in Title VI of the Civil Rights Act of 1964, prohibiting discrimination on the basis of race, color, and national origin, but not sexual orientation.[84]

Second, the crux of the controversy in the House turned on provision that would allow religious groups to ignore state and local civil rights laws, thereby achieving by legislative action what the Salvation Army had sought by regulatory means. Both the original and revised versions of H.R. 7 sought to protect an FBO's character by giving it "the right to retain its autonomy from Federal, State, and local governments, including such organization's control over the definition, development, practice, and expression of its religious beliefs."[85] Thus, if an FBO receives a social service contract funded by federal monies or a mix of federal and state (or local) funds it could ignore state (or local) laws and regulations, specifically those mandating domestic partner benefits or nondiscrimination in hiring based on sexual orientation, at least with respect to staffing that particular program.

Representatives Mark A. Foley (R-Florida) and James T. (Jim) Kolbe (R-Arizona) led an effort by House Republicans to resolve any outstanding questions about the bill's impact on state and local civil rights laws in the days prior to the House vote. Resisting rewriting the legislation, the House Republican leadership won support from moderates in exchange for a promise to work out differences in conference. The motion to recommit was defeated by a 195-234 vote with four Republicans supporting the motion and seventeen Democrats opposing it.[86]

During the July 19 debate, in a colloquy on the House floor between Watts and Representative Mark S. Kirk (R-Illinois), Watts publicly promised to "more clearly address this issue"[87] during negotiations with the Senate, once the Upper Chamber passed its own version of the legislation, but before the bill would go to final approval.

The Senate Takes Up the Bush Initiative

The next step was the Senate which rarely ignores House actions. There, however, passage was much less certain. Democrats in control the Senate expressed concern regarding the discriminatory employment policies of religious organizations. Senate Majority Leader Thomas A. (Tom) Daschle (D-South Dakota) declared H.R. 7 "dead on arrival" because of the Charitable Choice provisions. He stated, "I can't imagine that we could pass any bill that would tolerate slipping back to a level of tolerance that would be unacceptable in today's society."[88] Even before the tragic events of September 11 and ensuing anthrax scares, Daschle indicated that he did not expect the bill to come to a vote in the Senate before 2002.

Striving to gain Democratic votes to assure Senate passage, in late July, Bush telephoned Senator Lieberman, their first contact in six months, and invited him to the Oval Office to discuss the initiative. On July 26, after Watts-Hall version of the faith-based initiative had cleared the House, Bush met with Lieberman and Santorum to discuss how to get a bill through the Senate. Offering the president a clear message, Lieberman indicated the chances of the Senate passing the House version of the bill were "nil." Lieberman insisted that federal preemption of state and local anti-discrimination rules be dropped.

On August 1, boosting the proposal's prospects of becoming law, Santorum said that he would drop provisions making it easier for FBOs to avoid state and local antidiscrimination laws. "Let's remove the issue and move on," Santorum stated. "I don't want to give anybody an excuse to bring up these concerns."[89]

Not wanting to tip their hands or give away a bargaining chip, Bush advisors declined to say whether the president would accept Santorum's gesture. "President Bush is pleased that Senator Santorum and Senator Lieberman share his commitment to helping Americans in need," a Bush spokeswoman indicated. "We look forward to further discussions."[90]

After the horrific terrorist attacks of September 11, waging the war on terrorism abroad and bolstering homeland defense dominated the administration's efforts, derailing much of its domestic agenda, except for education reform and an economic stimulus package. Despite putting all nonessential legislation on hold, Bush continued to press his case. He used the presidential bully pulpit numerous times to return to his compassionate conservatism theme. Based on his passionate belief that religious groups could play a more important role in solving America's social wounds, his faith-based initiative rested atop a huge pile of unfinished domestic items.

In a November 7, 2001, letter to the Senate leadership, Bush urged that the Senate pass an "Armies of Compassion" bill before the end of the congressional session in December. He called for increased tax incentives for charitable giving and, in a significant shift, equal treatment of community and faith-based charities.[91] He realized the need to drop any explicit provision allowing religious groups that accept federal funds to discriminate against job applicants whose lifestyles they oppose. Stripping any mention of discrimination in hiring (and firing), thereby neither expanding nor diminishing existing protections, would leave unsettled the issue of state and local antidiscrimination rules. This approach would preserve the existing, but uneasy, truce between civil rights groups and FBOs, the latter wanting to retain control over their employment decisions because staff embodies an organization's mission and its values.

Senators were near a deal in late 2001. However, it bogged down at the end of the session over its cost. Lieberman and Santorum continued to work to find bipartisan agreement.

With the passage of education reform legislation in December, 2001, the White House learned a key lesson in dealings with Congress. The administration came to realize it must work with prominent Democrats from the outset if Bush wanted to succeed. Also, early and active presidential involvement and leadership was critical. As one journalist put it, "The earlier and more explicit the White House's involvement, the higher the likelihood of success."[92] Following these guidelines enabled President Bush to resurrect one of his signature domestic issues.

In early 2002, Bush revived his efforts to unleash the "armies of compassion" and promote his faith-based initiative. In his State of the Union Address on January 29, Bush called on Congress "to encourage the good work of charities and faith-based groups." He continued, "I ask you to join me on these important domestic issues in the same spirit of cooperation we have applied to our war against terrorism."[93] In announcing the appointment of James Towey as Director of the OFBCI on February 1, Bush noted that his initiative "recognizes the power of faith in healing some of our nation's wounds," declaring that, although "problems like poverty and addiction, abandonment and abuse, illiteracy and homelessness...are incredibly tough problems," "I have faith that faith will work in solving the problems." He maintained that the best way to "serve our neighborhoods in need and to serve our community and our country" is "to help change America, one heart, one soul, one conscience at a time."[94]

The Lieberman-Santorum Proposal

In February 2002, Lieberman and Santorum cobbled together a compromise, the proposed Charity Aid, Recovery, and Empowerment Act (CARE Act),[95] that set aside the expansion of Charitable Choice and focused on tax incentives to encourage charitable giving, discussed later in this chapter. Gone were Watts-Hall Charitable Choice provisions giving religious groups the opportunity to bid on contracts in more federal government programs, while making hiring and firing decisions based on their religious beliefs. However, the Lieberman-Santorum bill did not offer any explicit safeguards against religious discrimination in hiring. Rather, the proposal took a more subtle approach. Responding to the August 2001 White House report that showed a lack of fair play toward FBOs applying for government funding, discussed earlier in this chapter, it included an "equal treatment" provision.[96]

Bush welcomed the bipartisan Lieberman-Santorum funding compromise. He hailed it as a "great accomplishment," but stopped short of favoring the Senate version over the measure passed by the House in 2001.[97]

Clarifying existing law, the Lieberman-Santorum CARE proposal made it clear that a nongovernmental group seeking to be involved in the delivery of a federally funded social service program could not be denied a contract or a grant because the organization had a religious name or because it displayed religious art, icons, scripture, or symbols. The bill defined the term "social service program" as a program administered by the federal government or by state or local governments using federal funds, presumably through grants, contracts, or cooperative agreements (although this is not explicitly stated), that provide services directed at helping people in need, reducing poverty, improving the outcomes of low-income children, revitalizing low-income communities, empowering low-income families and individuals to become self-sufficient.[98] Services encompassed included the following: 1) child and adult care; 2) transportation; 3) job training and employment; 4) information, referral, and counseling; 5) food; 6) health support; 7) literacy and mentoring; 8) prevention and treatment of juvenile delinquency and substance abuse and the prevention of crime and domestic violence; 9) provision of assistance for housing under federal law.[99]

Under the equal treatment provision, an important public policy milestone, a nongovernment organization could not be required to: alter or remove art, icons, scripture, or other symbols, or to alter its name; alter or remove religious provisions in its charter documents; or alter or remove religious qualifications for membership on its governing boards.[100] Furthermore, a nongovernmental organization that had not previously been awarded a contract, grant, or cooperative agreement from an agency could not for that reason be disadvantaged in a competition to deliver services.[101]

In addition to defusing the controversy over whether the federal government would be put in the position of subsidizing employment discrimination by FBOs receiving government contracts, the CARE proposal sought to provide additional funding for the Social Services Block Grant program that states use to provide child care, child welfare, and other services to families.[102] Mirroring a noncontroversial section of the House passed Watts-Hall proposal, the bill also proposed spending $150 million to expand the technical assistance to smaller nonprofit community-based organizations, thereby assisting them to better compete for public grants and contracts.[103] The technical assistance included help in grant writing, grant management, incorporation and application for exempt status, capacity building, and identifying and using best practices for delivery assistance to persons, families, and communities in need. Eligible organizations would be limited to nonprofits, having six or fewer full-time employees engaged in the provision of social services, with an annual social services budget of less than $450,000.

The administration worked to support for the Lieberman-Santorum bill, central to Bush's compassionate conservative agenda. In April 2002, urging the Democratic-controlled Senate to pass the proposed CARE Act, President Bush, at a gathering of religious and charity leaders in the White House, stated, ...[S]ome of the greatest welfare programs in America are on street corners of inner-city America in a house of worship." "Part of the reason you're here is so we can unleash your talents and energy on the Hill. And I appreciate your willingness to be practical in Washington, because there is a piece of legislation that I hope you work on. It's an urgent time for you to act....," the president continued. "Let me put it a little more bluntly: The Federal Government should not discriminate against faith. There must be a level playing field available." He added: "We need to know that in our society, faith can move people in ways Government can't....Government can write checks, but it can't put hope in people's hearts or a sense of purpose in people's lives. That is done by people who have heard a call and who act on faith and are willing to share that faith."[104]

Prospects for Senate passage appeared bright in the spring of 2002 because its moderate terms neutralized most, but not all, of the potential opposition. Lieberman joining Santorum and Bush illustrated the proposal's broad appeal. Unable to break free from congressional gridlock, the CARE proposal failed to secure Senate approval. The bill's nontax aspect never emerged from the committee.

Back to Administrative Action

With the push to involve people of faith in solving social problems stalled in Congress, in December 2002, President Bush signed an Executive Order implementing a limited version of his faith-based initiative.[105]

The order puts religious and secular social service groups on an equal footing when competing for federal dollars. It requires agencies administering or distributing federally funded social service programs not to discriminate against religious organizations. The term "social service program" connotes a federally funded, government-administered program providing services aimed at helping people in need, including reducing poverty, improving the opportunities for low-income children, revitalizing low-income communities, empowering low-income individuals and families to become self-sufficient.

One other point is noteworthy. The FBOs receiving federal contracts to operate social service programs can receive funds even if they refuse to hire employees because of their religious beliefs (or the lack thereof). Thus, FBOs that become federal contractors can hire, promote, and fire on the basis of religious belief. The order applies to religious belief. The order applies to religious groups that receive federal contracts of $10,000 or more, but not to federal grants. However, the order does not exempt FBOs receiving federal contracts or grants from state and local antidiscrimination hiring laws.

The order continues the protection accorded beneficiaries under Charitable Choice. It bars FBOs offering federally funded social service programs from discriminating against beneficiaries (or potential beneficiaries) of their services (and in their outreach activities related to these services) on the basis of religion, religious belief, or a refusal to hold a religious belief or participate in a religious practice. Furthermore, FBOs engaged in inherently religious activities, such as worship, religious instruction, or proselytization, must offer these services separately in time or location from the programs or services supported with direct federal funds. Participation in these inherently religious activities must be voluntary for the program beneficiaries.

The order also protects FBOs competing for and participating in federally funded social service programs. They can maintain their religious identity, continue to display religious symbols, maintain religious terms in their names, select board members on a religious basis, and include religious references in mission statements and chartering documents.

In the Republican-controlled 108th Congress, President Bush seemingly hoped that his clear administrative step would produce movement on the legislative front to expand Charitable Choice and the amount of federal funds available to FBOs.

Other Bush Faith-Based Initiatives
Requiring Congressional Approval

In January and February 2001, President Bush outlined other initiatives, apart from an expansion of Charitable Choice, designed to test and develop partnerships between the federal government and FBOs (and community groups) in specific areas. These programs, designed to pilot new approaches and new areas of collaboration, encompassed a variety of fields. Three of these, namely, the Compassion Capital Fund, a mentoring program for the children of prisoners, and a broadened Twenty-first Century Community Learning Centers program, the 107th Congress funded, and a pre-release pilot program Congress supported but did not fund. Congress paid "lip service" to Bush's "second chance" maternity homes, but failed to make a separate allocation to this project. Proposals to promote responsible fatherhood were not enacted by the 107th Congress.

First, the White House proposed the creation of a Compassion Capital Fund to help ensure that the federal government would play a larger role in supporting charitable organizations.[106] This fund would provide start-up and operating capital to help qualified groups that wish to expand or emulate best practices programs. The fund would also support and promote research on best practices by charitable organizations. To fund this initiative, the administration's budget proposed spending $89 million in fiscal year 2002.

For fiscal year 2002, Congress appropriated $30 million to the Compassion Capital Fund to be used for grants to public-private partnerships helping small faith- and community-based organizations replicate or expand model social service programs. The Conference Appropriations Report stated that the "funding be used to support and promote rigorous evaluations of 'best practices' among charitable organizations so that successful models can be emulated and expanded by other entities. The conferees expect funds made available through this program to supplement and not supplant private resources and encourage the Secretary [of the Department of Health and Human Services] to require private resources to match grant funding provided to public/private partnerships."[107]

For fiscal year 2003, the administration sought $100 million to help small community-based, charitable organizations increase their capacity to deliver services by financing start-up costs.[108] As previously noted in this chapter, both the Watts-Hall and Lieberman-Santorum bills proposed spending $150 million for technical assistance to certain small nonprofit organizations. However, 107th Congress failed to enact even modest technical assistance funding.

Second, Bush desired to make competitive grants available to faith-based and community groups focusing on improving the prospects of low-income children of prisoners and probationers. The administration's budget for fiscal year 2002 proposed allocating $67 million for this initiative to assist these groups in providing a range of activities, including family-rebuilding programs.[109]

Congress responded by enacting the Promoting Safe and Stable Families Amendments Act of 2001 authorizing the Secretary of Health and Human Services to make available competitive grants for mentoring children of incarcerated parents. Included in the eligible grantees were FBOs and community-based organizations located in areas having significant numbers of children of prisoners. Congress appropriated $67 million for each of fiscal years 2002 and 2003 (and such sums as are necessary in fiscal years 2004 through 2006) to fund these grants.[110]

Third, for fiscal year 2002 Bush sought $846 million (the same amount Congress appropriated for fiscal year 2001) for more flexible before- and after-school programs for children of low income families by opening all of the funding for the Twenty-first Century Community Learning Centers program (a federal before- and after-school program) so that states could award federal funds to school districts, FBOs, and neighborhood groups, thereby empowering localities to provide more choices for these students.[111] Expanding access to high quality before- and after-school programs represented a key strategy in providing students safe, drug-free, supervised environments and additional learning time to improve achievement. Under the administration's proposal, states would conduct grant competitions to support programs that were proven to be effective and advance academic achievement goals.

As part of the No Child Left Behind Act, Congress authorized $1.25 billion for fiscal year 2002 for local grants, competitively awarded to "eligible entities" for "community learning centers." An "eligible entity" includes a wide variety of providers, such as community-based organizations and other private entities (presumably including FBOs), thereby giving parents more choices. A "community learning center" assists students, particularly those attending low-performing schools, in meeting academic standards in core academic subjects by offering them academic enrichment and other activities (including drug and violence prevention and character education programs) before- and after-school and during summer recesses.[112]

Fourth, the administration sought $5 million to launch a pilot program for federal inmates nearing release and make federal funds available on a competitive basis for faith-based prerelease programs at federal correctional facilities.[113] Congress responded by indicating its support for a multifaith-based prison prerelease pilot program, consisting of five pilot prisons.[114] There was, however, no formal appropriations language.

Fifth, Bush sought to provide the states with $33 million in earmarked federal funds in fiscal year 2002 to establish "second chance" maternity homes for unwed teen mothers and their children.[115] These community-based, adult-supervised residences, some of which would be operated by faith-based groups, would provide safe, stable, nurturing environments for teenage mothers and their children who cannot live with their families.

Congress funded $88,133,00 for runaway youth programs, including $39,739,900 for the Transitional Living Program (TLP) for all homeless youth. The Conference Appropriations Report stated:

> It is the conferees' expectation that current and future TLP grantees will continue to provide transitional living opportunities and supports to pregnant and

parenting homeless youth, as is their current practice. To further ensure that pregnant and parenting homeless youth are able to access transitional living opportunities and supports in their communities, the conferees encourage the Secretary [of the Department of Health and Human Services], acting through the network of federally-funded runaway and homeless youth training and technical assistance providers, to offer guidance to grantees and others on the programmatic modifications required to address the unique needs of pregnant and parenting youth and on the various sources of funding available for residential services to this population.[116]

In its 2003 budget, the administration came back with a proposal for $10 million in competitive grants to meet the needs of young, pregnant (or parenting) women and their children. The funds would go to community-based maternity group homes providing access to community-based coordinated services, such as childcare, education, job training, and counseling.[117] The Lieberman-Santorum bill, which Congress failed to enact, sought an appropriation of $33 million for fiscal year 2003 for community-based, adult-supervised maternity group homes for young mothers and their children. In these homes, the mothers would learn parenting skills and other skills to promote their long-term economic independence and well-being of their children.[118] Although subject to the equal treatment provisions for nongovernmental providers, these funds would not have been governed by Charitable Choice.

Sixth, Bush sought to promote responsible fatherhood. His budget included $64 million in fiscal year 2002 (with $315 million to be spent over five years) to strengthen the role of fathers in the lives of families.[119] This initiative would have provided competitive grants to faith-based and community organizations that help fathers who were unemployed or had low incomes avoid or leave cash welfare arrangements. The proposal included funds to create a new discretionary grant program for these organizations that promoted responsible fatherhood, successful parenting and stronger marriages. The initiative would also have funded projects of national significance that supported the expansion of state and local fatherhood efforts. For fiscal year 2003, the administration's budget sought $20 million in competitive grants for faith- and community-based organizations to assist noncustodial parents become more involved in their children's lives.[120] These budgetary proposals were neither enacted nor funded.

The Pros and Cons of Expanding
Charitable Choice and Involving More FBOs
in Government-Funded Social Services

One advantage of using direct government assistance centers on the ability to ensure that the recipient organizations meet basic administrative, financial and managerial standards. Although Charitable Choice prohibits the public sector from discriminating against an FBO due to its religious character, a governmental unit may apply its usual criteria to decide whether a particular organization will receive a contract or a grant. Moreover, unlike a program of voluntary contributions, the government can target financial assistance to programs and faith-based contractors or grantees that serve the most troubled communities and meet the most pressing social needs.

Direct federal funding has several drawbacks, however, apart from the constitutional aspects, considered in chapter 8. Smaller and less well-financed charities may have difficulty satisfying public sector contract and grant requirements. Applying for funds is time-consuming and requires a detailed knowledge of the proposal process. Funds are therefore likely to be channeled to the largest and most politically connected ministries, reinforcing the privileges of the dominant religious organizations in local areas that may be among the least effective of faith-based groups.

Once contracts and grants are awarded, there is also a need for accountability in order to determine which faith-based programs work. Some FBOs worry that the strings attached to funds as well as the unending paperwork required by contracts and grants would take away from their flexibility, as well as from their time with beneficiaries. "When you invite Big Brother into your life you can spend your day filling out papers," as Rev. Herbert B. Chambers, Young Memorial Church of Christ Holiness in Washington, D.C., put it. "Some of these ministers have never seen $10,000 and if they don't spend it right, Big Brother will put them in jail."[121]

Others are far more willing to live with the required paperwork. Rev. Cecil L. Murray of First A.M.E. Church in Los Angeles (considered in chapter 4) endorsed the concept of a more expansive church-state partnership, stating, "The sacred and the secular must walk hand in hand because the problem is so gigantic." For Murray, financial and program-matic accountability need not be an insurmountable imposition; rather the reporting requirements represent "a necessary evil."[122]

As noted in chapter 6, all levels of government must reevaluate their grant and contract procedures and accountability requirements. The public sector ought to strive to facilitate grant and contract applications by FBOs, especially smaller organizations. Furthermore, government should not burden FBOs with endless paperwork.

Compliance with ongoing monitoring and accounting requirements may also have other unintended consequences. For example, FBOs accepting federal funding may need to comply with government regulations that require them to deliver services in an unaccustomed manner, maintain different staffing levels, employ only staff with specified credentials, or, in the future, maintain nondiscriminatory hiring practices. Critics of the direct funding approach allege that this degree of government control could result both in the diversion of much needed resources to regulatory compliance and the erosion of a charity's spiritual, moral, and caregiving mission and its effectiveness due to the focus on securing and maintaining government contracts and grants. However, if the regulations prove onerous, the federal government could modify or throw them out. This, of course, requires the federal government to have the will to do so in order to see Charitable Choice succeed.

One problem in this regard is the likely effect of monitoring and compliance associated with the specific requirements of Charitable Choice. As developed in chapter 6, the law prohibits use of any federal funds for sectarian worship, instruction, or proselytization. It also contains a non-discrimination requirement regarding servicing beneficiaries and provides for a limited fiscal audit. As it has for other grant and contract programs, the federal government must implement procedures for segregating program accounts and enforcing compliance with the antidiscrimination provision for beneficiaries. Definitions of the terms "sectarian worship," "instruction," and "proselytization" must be clarified to help FBOs honor the letter and spirit of the Charitable Choice provisions and limit their litigation exposure. The federal government must develop a mechanism for monitoring compliance with these requirements.

Observers also expressed concern about the harm to religious groups, including the undermining of autonomy, when FBOs are too closely allied with government.[123] With government funding, there is a fear that faith-based social service programs will not be religious enough. FBOs may be pressured to eliminate, compromise, or tone down the religious content of their programs in order to get or keep contracts and grants. As Cal Thomas, a conservative columnist expressed, "What concerns me is that religious organizations might be tempted, or forced, to dilute their life-transforming message to get government subsidies, thus negating the primary reason for their success. They also risk becoming an appendage to the [political] party in power."[124]

Critics assert that eliminating or diluting their religious content and unique character may reduce the effectiveness of faith-based efforts. Their contention is that faith-based social service organizations succeed in turning lives around precisely because they instill religious convictions helping individuals find meaning and hope in their lives. Government regulation will follow, it is feared, public dollars. Strings may come attached to the money, thereby compromising the mission and independence of FBOs. By accepting government funding, religious programs designed to transform lives will become more "secularized" in the delivery of social services by changing their core religious characteristics and attempting to fit into a prescribed caregiving mold. This dilution of religious character would defeat the whole purpose of involving FBOs in the first place: their effectiveness in addressing social problems. Government-subsidized FBOs could become just another branch of the bureaucracy, more like their secular counterparts.

Chasing public funds, it is argued, may lead to a confusion of mission, causing an FBO to drift away from its real purpose, and instead focus on fulfilling the mission of funding sources. Potentially adverse consequences also include: a focus on the delivery of services, rather than results; diminished religious conviction of staff members; a reduced willingness of individuals to give their money and time. Accepting government assistance may also hinder the effectiveness of FBOs because it may diminish their ability to provide religious teaching.

Another potential drawback centers on the risk of increased dependency on government funding. Because of the necessity of lobbying and currying favor with government agencies, FBOs may become virtual wards of the public sector. They risk losing focus on their spiritual mission as well as their creative and moral energies. The availability of public grants and contracts may make political connections and lobbying skills a prime qualification for FBO leadership positions. As with other grantees and contractors, the corrupting influence of public sector funding could make FBOs vulnerable to being "captured" by the grant-making or contract process. Dependence on government funding may also result in competition among religious groups (and secular charities) for funding before bureaucrats or legislators.

These fears regarding extensive government regulation and the diminution of religious character are not without merit. There are already examples of FBOs that, in attempting to follow the secular social service model, lost their dynamism and drift away from their original priorities and mission.

The story of REACH, Inc., formed in 1986 as the community development arm of the 12th Street Missionary Baptist Church in Detroit, is a good example of the problems FBOs face in contracting with the government.[125] The organization started senior outreach programs, ran day care centers, and rehabilitated old properties. REACH operations originally depended on charitable donations from parishioners and private companies. However, in the early 1990s, it began receiving grants from the U.S. Department of Housing and Urban Development, the Small Business Administration, and the city government to expand its housing redevelopment efforts and small business training. The receipt of public money and the expansion of operations transformed REACH into a bureaucratic organization, resulting in a more impersonal and less efficient program.

REACH became less informal, less reliant on volunteers, and more dependent on professionals to staff its programs. Previously, REACH had an annual budget of $1 million. Public funding increased REACH's budget to the point where one major housing project alone had funding of $1.7 million. As a result, ministry programs focused less on "moral and spiritual matters" and more on a "commodified" version of their earlier activities, such as providing people with material goods like housing. Objective criteria and statistics replaced the informality of "human development."

However, the REACH example should not act as a deterrent for the funding of FBOs. Ultimately, it is an FBO's decision as to how much public money it accepts and how this funding will affect its core mission. FBOs thus have the power to ensure that they do not encounter the same problems as the REACH program.

There are many successful models of religious leaders who know what their religious mission requires and what their neighborhoods need. Two of those that do not encourage or require anyone to profess or accept a particular religious belief are next examined.

A good example is the Christian Herald Association's Bowery Mission (mentioned in chapter 4), an unabashedly Christian agency, led, beginning in 1993, by Edward Morgan. Since 1994, Morgan has overseen the Bowery Mission Transition Center, a separate nonprofit corporation that offers a nine-month residential program designed to get men drug-free, employed, and living on their own.

The Transition's Center's seventy-seven-bed program is entirely funded by New York City's Department of Homeless Services. The evangelical Christian Herald Association set up the Transition Center as a separate nonprofit in order to receive public funds while maintaining its independence. The Department of Homeless Services has consistently ranked the Transition Center as the most effective substance abuse program in New York City.

No religious activities are required of the Transition Center's clients. The program does not promote Christianity and there is no overt proselytizing. Bibles are provided, if requested, although they are bought with private money. Volunteers lead a weekly evening Bible class, but participation is optional.

The bonds of faith rest on an informal, relational structure. Nearly all the staffers, from social workers to cafeteria employees, are deeply religious. More than half are graduates of the program. According to Morgan, the religious sentiment is "caught, not taught."[126] Morgan noted, "The client can sense our staff really cares, because they don't report just to me. They report to a Higher Power."[127] He stated:

> The not-so-secret ingredient in this successful program is employees of faith who have reached the bottom themselves and found, as countless others have through history, that a power higher than themselves is their only hope–that the real meaning of life is reaching out to other people with unconditional love, earning their trust and seeing them triumph over adversity as well. Although they do not proselytize, they are open about their faith, and will freely share their beliefs with any client who expresses interest.[128]

Another example of an FBO that has received public funding while maintaining its religious integrity is Transitional Journey, a Charitable Choice, state-funded welfare-to-work program for women.[129] Even after three years of Charitable Choice collaboration, Rev. Donna Lawrence Jones of Cookman United Methodist Church in Philadelphia kept her "Christ-centered job development program" intact.[130] Her church received an initial contract to launch Transitional Journey in collaboration with the Community Solutions Initiative of the Pennsylvania Department of Public Welfare. The work training program was designed for hard-to-employ welfare recipients who had met with little success in other programs. Transitional Journey was awarded a $150,000 contract based on performance, rather than a simple, fixed-fee contract for services provided. The contract began in March 1998 and concluded in February, 2001. Transitional Journey was also awarded a smaller second contract that involved following up and monitoring working clients.

Describing Charitable Choice funding as a "Godsend," Rev. Jones indicated that the added funding allowed the church to accomplish more. It hired additional staff who, in turn, sought out more volunteers, focusing on those less likely to burn out. The funding also helped expand the church's program of education, life-skills, job placement, and computer literacy. One year after receiving the first contract, Cookman set up a nonprofit corporation, Neighborhood Joy Ministries, to run the Transitional Journey program.

Clients may opt out of any activity calling for them to participate in religious activities or teachings. The church advertised that it had a Christian program, but was careful during orientation and regularly throughout the program, to advise beneficiaries that religious activities were not mandatory. A notice of opt-out rights was inserted into a handbook. Bible study at the beginning of the day, group prayer times, and faith-development were optional; alternative activities were provided, such as more computer lab time. Beneficiaries in fact availed themselves of their right to opt out of religious activities.

Although the boundaries of the faith component had to be worked out, the church chose not to actively proselytize those desirous of help, believing that it was inappropriate to force religion on the needy. According to Rev. Jones, "...when Charitable Choice came our way, we did not see that it would impede what we were used to doing anyway....We do not see social service (helping the needy) as evangelism so we have never had an issue with trying to proselytize someone who needs help."[131] Rather, staff formed informal relationships with beneficiaries beyond the programmatic activities. They provided spiritual counseling one-on-one or offered to pray with (or for) beneficiaries.

Rev. Jones candidly admitted that participation in the Charitable Choice-funded program increased the level of paperwork. The church initially struggled to keep up with bureaucratic requirements imposed by the government-funded program. Its staff found the paperwork time-consuming and frustrating. "While some of the paper requirements are tedious, most are necessary such as financial records, case notes, accurate client files, and employer and family information," Rev. Jones stated. "Although it was a challenge for us in the early months, now that we've been at it for a few years it has been a tremendous blessing for follow up"[132] with the families the church has helped.

Stepping back from these two examples, it is important to remember that an FBO can decline to bid on a grant or a contract if it disagrees with the way a request for proposal defines a project. It need not apply if it does not wish to observe the various criteria accompanying a grant or a contract, such as the proscription against proselytizing or the accounting requirements.

For some FBOs, for whom religion is the key aspect of their social service activities, public funding is not an option. At the Central Union Mission in Washington, D.C., those looking for overnight shelter, a free meal, or drug counseling must participate in a religious activity, such as a worship service. The Mission, which currently receives no government funding, has no interest in receiving federal money with strings attached. "I'd love to have more funds, but my problem starts right with my mission statement," Central Union Mission's executive director, David O. Treadwell stated. "We really are in the business of making disciples. We believe that the answer for these people is Christ. So we don't know any other way to meet their needs without sharing the Gospel with them."[133]

However, at other similar programs, such as Gospel Rescue Ministries (also located in Washington, D.C.), the religious sessions are voluntary. "We can live with that," John Jackson, its executive director noted. "That doesn't water down the program. We don't want [religious activities] to be mandatory....The worst thing is to force people." Candidates for its programs are told up front the "we're going to be talking about Jesus. Non-Christians usually turn it down right away or try for a few days and leave."[134]

These examples show that FBOs need to be aware of the risks of bidding on and accepting any contract (or receiving a grant). They must make informed decisions as to whether to increase their collaboration with government and compete for public funds. Those FBOs strongly insistent on the religious component of their social service mission, as opposed to the informal, relational approach of the Transition Center and Transitional Journey, ought not rush into new partnerships without seriously weighing the pros and the cons. FBOs must be able to say "no." They need to be able to prevent the lure of public money from corrupting their genuine heartfelt efforts to provide love, hope, and one-on-one support to troubled individuals.

Additionally, every FBO that participates in a publicly funded program must be able to account for and track expenditures. Complying with "red tape" is not beneath any ministry, and FBOs receiving direct government assistance must therefore maintain sound internal systems. Financial irresponsibility cannot be tolerated. This is because any FBO that fails to maintain the utmost standards of accountability, both financial and programmatic, for a government contract or a grant places in jeopardy the ability of other FBOs to obtain direct government funds.

There is one more caveat. If an FBO accepts funds, it should not take any money for its ongoing general operating expenses or core functions. This is because a government grant or a contract that brings an influx of funds into a program may disappear with the next budgetary appropriation process.

The Voucher Alternative

Vouchers are an option already permissible under the Charitable Choice provisions of the 1996 Welfare Reform Act that could be put to greater use by the public sector. While the Bush administration placed considerable emphasis on the direct funding of FBOs through contracts and grants, vouchers for social services were also an important aspect of the president's agenda. In addition to striving to build support for the expansion of Charitable Choice, the administration turned to vouchers in its efforts to open more federally funded social service programs to FBOs.

The revised version of H.R. 7, as passed by the House of Representatives, but not enacted by the 107th Congress, sought to create an indirect assistance, or voucher, arrangement. Making more explicit the 1996 language,[135] the proposal allowed the voucherization of federal funds. Federal administrators could create a voucher option for some or all of the funds in their specified social service programs wherever "feasible and efficient." Specifically, the federal cabinet department administering a social service program covered by the proposal "may direct the disbursement of some or all of the funds, if determined...to be feasible and efficient, in the form of indirect assistance. For purposes of this section, 'indirect assistance' constitutes assistance in which an organization receiving funds through a voucher, certificate, or other form of disbursement under this section...."[136]

The rights of beneficiaries receive a degree of protection under a voucher arrangement. The amended bill prevented an FBO providing indirect assistance under a program from denying a recipient (or an applicant for admission into a program) social services "on the basis of religion, a religious belief, or a refusal to hold a religious belief."[137]

With a voucher-funded program, individuals receive certificates that authorize payment for a particular service.[138] They may redeem the voucher and receive the service at any qualifying organization, including, if so authorized, a faith-based provider. Each individual determines the organization from which he or she will accept assistance.

Currently, low-income individuals who receive vouchers may buy day care from religious institutions. When Congress enacted the Child Care and Development Act of 1990,[139] it authorized the use of vouchers that allowed parents to choose the child care provider for their children, whether sectarian or secular. Thus, the federal government acknowledged it ought to treat all qualified child care providers equally. The Child Care and Development Block Grant Amendments Act of 1996,[140] enacted as part of a comprehensive welfare-child care and nutrition reform in August 1996, marked the ratification of the principle of parental choice through vouchers on the preschool level. It would, therefore, seem a logical progression to fund vouchers to help parents pay for after-school care, among other programs.

Vouchers offer numerous advantages. Individuals, on average, are in a better position than the public sector to determine what they need. Individual decisions are less likely to be determined by political favoritism, among other irrelevant factors. Vouchers give recipients more choices and thereby promote empowerment. They encourage individuals seeking assistance to take their vouchers to the most successful programs.

By stimulating competition, vouchers motivate public and nonprofit providers to offer improved services and become more responsive to clients' needs. They force organizations to become more serious about developing programs that do what they are supposed to do. In short, vouchers create a "market" for services, thereby rewarding the most effective providers.

Programs dependent on vouchers will likely be more efficient. Assuming proper programmatic design, voucher systems approximate competitive economic conditions, namely, consumer choice and sovereignty, the demise of ineffective organizations, and the entry of new providers. Voucher combat the otherwise entrenched position of public sector bureaucracies offering social services. Thus, vouchers facilitate the better tailoring of public expenditures to the services provided.

By giving beneficiaries more freedom of choice, a voucher system places fewer limitations on FBOs. Religious charities wary of rules that come with government contracts or grants are more likely to consider voucher-funded programs. Furthermore, indirect assistance monies are not subject to restrictions regarding the use of funds for worship or proselytization.

Vouchers also minimize governmental intrusion into the activities and programs of FBOs caused by direct funding. Vouchers create a more distant relationship between church and state. The government is removed from deciding which specific FBOs will receive funds and how much money FBOs generally will receive compared to secular nonprofits generally. The interference in the life of FBOs by government bureaucrats is significantly lessened, thereby avoiding the squeezing out or molding of faith-based practices. As we will see in chapter 8, constitutional objections recede as well. With a voucher program, it is unlikely a court would find a violation of the First Amendment.

On the downside, a voucher program may evolve into a new entitlement, with an ever-ballooning budget. However, the defunding of unsuccessful programs may be easier if consumers stop selecting them. Also, a government agency must decide which organizations are eligible to receive various forms of indirect assistance. Thus, once again, as with any discretionary grant program, considerable leeway is placed in bureaucratic hands.

Voucher programs for social service programs face a hard reality. Grassroots groups generally serve clients, especially families and individuals who fall through the cracks of existing social service programs, on an as needed, "rolling" basis. Given the ad hoc, emergency nature of the services clients request, it may be difficult to structure an effective voucher program.[141]

While pushing ahead on removing regulatory obstacles to FBO efforts and expanding Charitable Choice, the administration also proposed increased tax incentives to encourage charitable giving.

Enhancing the Income Tax Incentives for Charitable Giving

President Bush outlined a legislative strategy that would change the Internal Revenue Code to provide enhanced income tax incentives for charitable donations. In 2001, he set forth his tax proposals in the President's Agenda for Tax Relief,[142] as part of his first budgetary plan,[143] and in a detailed explanation of the administration's 2001 tax relief proposals.[144]

In brief, Bush offered four tax proposals. First, he proposed creating a special charitable contribution deduction, in addition to the standard deduction, for the 80 million taxpayers (70 percent of all filers) who do not elect to claim itemized deductions under the Tax Code. Second, he also advocated allowing retirement-age individuals (over age fifty-nine and a half) to make income tax-free withdrawals from their individual retirement accounts for charitable contributions. Third, he sought to increase the cap on corporate charitable contributions from 10 percent to 15 percent of taxable income. Fourth, he also encouraged states to provide a credit (of up to 50 percent of the first $500 for individuals and $1,000 for married couples and corporations) against state income (or other) taxes for contributions to charities addressing poverty and its impact. (Obviously, a state would need to define what is an eligible charity.) As part of the tax credit system, a state would be given the flexibility to offset the costs of a charitable state tax credit by using funds otherwise available to it from the Temporary Assistance to Needy Families program.[145]

In the May 2001 negotiations over the $1.35 trillion tax legislation, the White House agreed to do without tax breaks to aid charities. The administration put a higher priority on reducing individual income tax rates and creating the new 10 percent tax bracket, assuming that charitable giving may be more responsive to after-tax income, not tax law changes. It, therefore, opted not to open the charitable contribution deduction for nonitemizers as a targeted tax cut for low- and middle-income individuals and families. The tax reduction approach left more money in the pockets of Americans, letting them allocate funds as they wish, including FBOs of their choice. However, the administration never turned its back on the tax incentives, choosing to move them separately from the big tax package.

The first three Bush tax proposals were embodied in H.R. 7,[146] the Watts-Hall bill. The Lieberman-Santorum CARE proposal[147] also addressed the tax-related provisions of the Bush faith-based initiative. Both of the House and Senate proposals would also have enhanced the charitable contribution deduction for donations of food inventory by business taxpayers, including restaurants and farmers, not just corporations.[148] A discussion of food inventory contributions is beyond the scope of this work.

Let us take up the first three Bush tax incentive proposals.[149] First, the president's proposal, as embodied in the original version of H.R. 7,[150] would have allowed taxpayers who do not itemize their deductions to deduct their charitable contributions (up to the amount of the standard deduction) in addition to their standard deduction. This break was proposed to be phased in over five years, to minimize revenue losses.

When computing taxable income, an individual taxpayer who takes a standard deduction does not receive a separate break for charitable contributions on his or her federal income tax return.[151] In contrast, a taxpayer who itemizes deductions can deduct the amount of cash and the fair market value of property contributed to a tax-exempt charity.[152] The amount of the deduction with respect to the charitable contribution of property may be reduced depending on the type of property contributed, the income of the taxpayer, and the type of charitable organization to which the property is contributed.[153]

The standard deduction provides relief to taxpayers who do not itemize their deductions but who incur expenses that are otherwise permitted as itemized deductions, such as charitable contributions and state income taxes. Taxpayers itemize their deductions, rather than claiming the standard deduction, if it is in their financial interest. Those who take the standard deduction receive a tax benefit in excess of their expenses that would otherwise be deductible. The standard deduction minimizes Internal Revenue Service (IRS) administrative burdens as well as record-keeping and paperwork by taxpayers.

The Bush administration sought to increase charitable giving by allowing the 70 percent of taxpayers who do not itemize their deductions a tax break for their charitable donations. A taxpayer who does not itemize his or her deductions receives no value from the tax deductibility of charitable contributions in excess of his or her standard deduction.

Extending the charitable contribution deduction to nonitemizers would reduce the tax price of charitable contributions by this group of taxpayers. Assuming taxpayers respond positively to the incentive provided by the deduction for charitable contributions, expanding the charitable contribution deduction to nonitemizers should increase charitable contributions. Why? People tend to give more when the price of giving is reduced.

With the 2001 economic downturn sapping the budgetary surplus and sensitivity to Democratic charges that further tax relief would endanger the Social Security and Medicare surpluses, the House Ways and Means Committee drastically scaled back the tax package. The Bush tax plan was compromised to a shell of its former self.

The revised Watts-Hall bill, as approved by the House of Representatives in July 2001, allowed a limited deduction for charitable contributions paid in cash by individual taxpayers who do not itemize their deductions. However, this aspect, designed to encourage charitable giving by nonitemizers, was for all practical purposes gutted.

The amended bill would have permitted a $25 deduction for single nonitemizers ($50 for joint filers) in 2002 and 2003, $50 for single filers ($100 for joint filers) from 2004 through 2006, $75 for single filers ($150 for joint filers) in 2007 through 2009, $100 for single filers ($200 for joint filers) beginning in 2010.[154] Because of budgetary constraints, this change reduced the cost to $6.37 billion over ten years, not the $84 billion as in the president's proposal.[155]

As a token gesture, the provision represented a parody of an incentive tax break. Democrats ridiculed it as minuscule. In the House floor debate on H.R. 7, Rep. Charles B. Rangel (D-New York), the ranking minority member on the House Ways and Means Committee, caustically noted, "[I]f you are a charity, you are in trouble.... If an individual is in the 15 percent bracket, they will be able to get [on a $25 deduction] a return up to $3.75. So much for a realistic incentive."[156]

Post-September 11, charitable generosity focused on helping the victims of the terrorist attacks. Contributions to other groups, not directly related to victim relief, declined markedly.

The Lieberman-Santorum approach emphasized the need to make it easier for more individuals to receive income tax advantages for charitable contributions to FBOs as well as the entire range of nonreligious charities. In striving to encourage Americans to contribute to charities that struggled for donations post-September 11, the Lieberman-Santorum CARE bill fixed the charitable deduction for nonitemizers at $400 for single taxpayers ($800 for joint filers). Although the charitable incentives were significantly larger and more immediate than in the House version, presumably motivating more charitable giving, these incentives would have been in effect for only two years, 2002 and 2003, to hold down the cost.[157] Senator Lieberman called the bill a "real step forward"[158] to help charities that saw their contributions dip as Americans directed their charitable dollars to groups dealing with the September 11 attacks. However, unless extended these short-term tax breaks were unlikely to impact significantly on the habits of givers.

The second Bush proposal, again contained in the original version of H.R. 7,[159] would have permitted income tax-free withdrawals made after age fifty-nine and a half from traditional or Roth individual retirement arrangements (IRAs), if the distributions were made directly to an IRS qualified charitable organization. Although not specifically spelled out by Bush, this tax break would also apply to distributions made to deferred charitable arrangements, such as a charitable remainder trust, a pooled income fund, or a charitable gift annuity.

Tax-free rollovers to charities would remove a significant barrier otherwise discouraging individuals from making contributions to their favorite charity while they are living, rather than at death. Tax-free withdrawals would simplify the process of giving for taxpayers who have more money than they need for retirement. In particular, the baby boomers have huge amounts of wealth in IRAs. As they retire, this wealth could enable them to make unprecedented, new financial resources available to faith-based groups, among other charities.

Donors do not receive charitable deductions for the IRA distributions. If an amount withdrawn from a traditional or Roth IRA is donated to a charitable organization, the rules generally relating to the income tax treatment of withdrawals apply. Furthermore, the deductibility of the charitable contribution is also subject to the normally applicable limitations on such contributions. Thus, for income tax purposes wealthy taxpayers face percentage limits on the use of the charitable deductions from their IRA distributions.

The revised Watts-Hall bill excluded from gross income otherwise taxable withdrawals from a traditional or a Roth IRA for qualified charitable distributions.[160] However, a qualified charitable distribution could only be made on or after the date the IRA owner attained age seventy and a half, not fifty-nine and a half as in the original version of H.R. 7, thereby reducing the cost over ten years from $3.73 billion to $2.75 billion.[161] The Lieberman-Santorum CARE bill allowed individuals sixty-seven and over to make tax-free distributions from their individual retirement accounts for charitable purposes.[162] These distributions could be made to IRS approved charitable organization or to a split interest entity, namely, a charitable remainder trust, a pooled income fund, or a charitable gift annuity.

The president's third proposal sought to increase the present 10 percent of taxable income limit on corporate charitable contributions[163] to 15 percent. The revised Watts-Hall bill raised the cap for deductible corporate charitable donations to 15 percent by 2010. This provision would have been phased in over nine years as follows: 11 percent in 2002 through 2007; 12 percent in 2008; 13 percent in 2009; 15 percent in 2010.[164] The total cost for this tax break would have equaled $917 million over ten years, not $1.86 billion as in the president's proposal.[165] The Lieberman-Santorum proposal increased the corporate charitable deduction to 13 percent in 2002 and then to 15 percent in 2003; thereafter, it would have reverted to 10 percent.[166]

With the shift in the Senate majority in June 2001, the package of charitable giving tax incentives faced a difficult road in the Senate, mainly because of revenue considerations. Leading Democrats continued to voice concern about the $1.35 billion cost of Economic Growth and Tax Relief Reconciliation Act of 2001. Based on the assumption that the federal government coffers could not afford more tax breaks, Senate Majority Leader Daschle vowed not to pursue additional tax cut measures in 2002, unless revenue offsets (in other words, tax increases) were found.[167]

By calling the tax proposals an "emergency measure," proponents of the Lieberman-Santorum proposal sought to deal with the federal budget crunch and avoid finding a way to pay for it. "This is declared to be an emergency in response to 9-11 and the recession and the tremendous and rising human needs in our country," Lieberman stated. "And, obviously, government cannot itself meet them all. So we are, in this bill empowering a whole range of charitable organizations, including...faith-based, to do that."[168] However, Lieberman could not convince his Democratic colleagues to handle the measure as an "emergency" with no revenue offsets (tax increases) required. In the end, Lieberman yielded and supported offsets for the charitable incentives.[169]

The tax aspects of the CARE proposal moved slowly through the Senate Finance Committee, receiving approval on June 18, 2002.[170] Unpersuaded by Senator Lieberman's reasoning, the revised version of the charitable giving bill, a bipartisan effort by Finance Committee Chairman Max Baucus (D-Montana) and the ranking minority member Charles Grassley (R-Iowa), included tax offsets. These tax offsets would, among other measures, have required corporations to disclose transactions that have the potential for tax evasion[171] and have curbed offshore relocations of corporate headquarters designed to avoid federal income taxes (so-called inversion transactions).[172]

The Finance Committee tinkered with two key aspects of the charitable contribution deduction. First, the committee raised the ceiling for cash (including checks and credit card payments) contributions by nonitemizers from House-passed version's $25 to a floor of $250 and a maximum of $500 for individual taxpayers, twice these amounts for joint return filers.[173] The new version, effective for tax years 2002 and 2003 would not have allowed couples, who took a standard deduction, to deduct the first $500 they gave to charities, but would have let them deduct the next $500 if they made a $1,000 charitable contribution. The limited charitable giving deduction for nonitemizers would have reduced revenues in these two years by an estimated $2.56 billion.[174]

Second, the Finance Committee provided an exclusion for direct distributions from traditional and Roth IRAs to qualified charities made on or after an IRA owner attained age seventy and a half. Distributions to split-interest trusts would have been eligible for the exclusion if made on or after the IRA owner attained age fifty-nine and a half.[175] These tax-free distributions from IRAs for charitable purposes would have cost the federal government $2.88 billion for ten years from 2003 to 2012.[176]

The proposed CARE Act, as amended by the Finance Committee, included a charitable deduction for contribution of food inventory by business taxpayers,[177] but omitted an increase in the tax-deductible amount corporations could donate to charity. The Committee also approved the restoration of Social Services Block Grant Funding for fiscal year 2003,[178] following the Lieberman-Santorum proposal. The Finance Committee–approved bill was placed on the Senate calendar as a substitute for the House–passed the charitable giving initiative.

Senate Minority Leader Trent Lott (R-Mississippi) refused a June 27 Democratic request by Senate Majority Whip Harry Reid (D-Nevada) to agree to consider the bill before Congress's August recess under conditions of limited debate. In declining the offer for early consideration, Lott stated that the amended bill was a "brand new amendment" with which he was unfamiliar. Lott indicated he wanted to "get in touch with Grassley and others to make sure they are familiar with this and have had a chance to look over the substitute amendment to make sure there is no problem with it."[179]

President Bush continued to urge, as he did on July 1, Congress "to get the bill on my desk that does two things: first, allows for faith-based programs to compete for taxpayers' money to change people's lives; and second, allows nonitemizers to receive a deduction on their income taxes when they give money to a charity."[180] However, despite his praise for the bill, Senate Majority Leader Daschle seemed in no hurry to bring the proposal to a Senate vote.

The proposed CARE Act fell the victim of political gridlock and the press of other business–regular spending bills, the proposed Homeland Security Department, and the war on Iraq. Senator Santorum valiantly sought, but could not secure, consent to bring up the bill for consideration under a limited time agreement. Some Democratic senators, concerned about employment discrimination by FBOs, blocked efforts to secure a unanimous consent agreement that would have provided for a limited number of amendments to the bill.[181]

The Pros and Cons of Increased
Income Tax Incentives for Charitable Giving

Proponents argue that use of tax incentives allows individuals and corporations, rather than federal, state, or local bureaucrats, to select and evaluate the work of FBOs. This would free FBOs from the need to lobby and appease legislators and government officials. In theory, this approach makes charitable organizations directly accountable to their contributors, as opposed to far-off government officials and agencies. In other words, funding is free from much of the burdensome regulation and bureaucratic interference that would otherwise accompany direct government assistance. Together with the use of vouchers, tax incentives offer the best means of preserving the independence and integrity of FBOs.

It would also be much easier to guarantee the inclusion of FBOs. The federal government need only certify the charitable status of FBOs and, thus, their eligibility. Individuals would then be able to deduct contributions made to eligible FBOs. This type of procedure has already been proven successful by the IRS. The lessened role of the government and the attendant reduction in FBO administrative costs would also result in a greater percentage of each dollar contributed being put to work by charities. FBOs would not waste funds for the needless overhead required to lobby politicians and bureaucrats, write grant or contract proposals, and attend conferences. In short, the tax mechanism protects the autonomy of charitable entities from governmental encroachment.

Although I favor the use of the tax incentive approach as a means for encouraging more charitable giving and the funding of FBOs without fostering a loss of mission, there are several drawbacks.[182] First, restoring the charitable deduction for nonitemizers (which existed prior to the Tax Reform Act of 1986) adds complexity to individual returns and may encourage cheating. Taxpayers who do not otherwise itemize their deductions would need to maintain records to substantiate the charitable deductions claimed. Record keeping and limits on availability of tax benefits are some of the key sources of complexity for individuals in the federal income tax system. The new deduction would also add at least one line to the individual tax forms filed by low- and middle-income taxpayers.

Increased administrative burdens would also be imposed on the IRS to ensure that taxpayers claim deductions for charitable contributions that are actually made. This would require the IRS to expand its audit capabilities. As noted earlier, the standard deduction simplifies record keeping for non-itemizers and enforcement by the IRS. The IRS would likely encounter administrative problems in monitoring small charitable contributions by nonitemizers.[183]

Second, restoring the charitable contribution for nonitemizers creates a double deduction (a "double-dip") problem. As a substitute for itemized deductions, the standard deduction includes a number of components, such as built-in charitable deduction. Thus, it already compensates for the inability of nonitemizers to deduct charitable contributions. Congress could avoid the doubling up problem resulting from the standard deduction and the proposed itemized deduction by allowing a deduction only in excess of a specified floor amount.[184] However, a floor, in limiting the ability of small givers to itemize charitable contributions, would further compound the complexity problem.

Third, using a deduction rather than a credit is subject to criticism on equity grounds. A deduction reduces tax liability indirectly by decreasing the amount of the income subject to taxation. A credit results in a dollar-for-dollar reduction in income tax liability equal to the amount of the credit. Compared to tax deductions, the credit approach provides taxpayers a more economically valuable incentive because it reduces taxes directly and accords a greater tax benefit for lower income taxpayers. To deal with the objection, President Bush coupled his tax deduction initiative with his charitable state tax credit proposal.

Fourth, will the increased tax breaks encourage a big jump in charitable giving by individuals and corporations? Proponents assume so and that additional charitable giving will exceed its revenue cost. According to one study, the original Bush proposal, without a floor or a threshold amount, would have stimulated an additional $14.6 billion in charitable giving in the first year, an increase of over 11 percent (more than double the cost of the provision), and more than $80 billion in additional giving over five years.[185] This study concluded that the Bush proposal would have encouraged 11.7 million tax filing units (individuals and families) to become new givers. The largest increase would likely have occurred among individuals whose incomes were less than $70,000. Those within the $20,000 to $30,000 income bracket would have increased their annual giving from $611 to $767. Even if the income tax incentives do not lead to an outpouring of new funds for FBOs, policymakers may always revisit the direct funding and/or voucher proposals.

Finally, expanded use of the income tax system may not channel financial assistance to inner-city and other charities where it is most needed. Through the tax mechanism, individuals, and corporations, rather than the government, would decide what groups receive contributions. Would the increased giving mainly go to FBOs fighting poverty and social ills? Some experts answer "yes" because giving by low-income persons tend to go to faith-based and secular programs in their communities providing shelters for the homeless, drug treatment and prevention, job training, and various youth programs.[186]

However, the stimulus to new private giving may benefit other non-profit institutions, such as suburban hospitals and educational institutions. To deal with this problem, and at least ensure that the charitable donations are used wisely, new publications and information services may emerge to examine charities and guide givers to the most effective groups. However, these groups may not necessarily be those providing the most needed social services.

Beyond new information sources, our trust in the American taxpayers to direct funds to effective charities, and discussions about where the donated funds would (and should) go, some type of special federal income tax credit may be required. This new credit could be directed at donations to charities, both religious and secular, devoted to providing a percentage of funds (perhaps 50 or 70 percent) to specific purposes, for example, preventing or alleviating poverty or providing social services for the needy.

In addition to the need to categorize charities by legislation, officials would have to write and interpret regulations implementing the statutory definitions of eligible nonprofits. The IRS (or the CFBCI or some other federal agency) would need to certify "approved" FBOs, based on "objective" standards, including, for example, performing services for the poor as well as demonstrated financial integrity, record keeping, and accountability. These approved FBOs could then be listed in an annually updated federal government registry.[187]

The difficulty, of course, is that the IRS (or other federal agency) could exclude from this "approved list," albeit subject to judicial review, organizations it did not favor for theological, ideological, or political reasons. Furthermore, limiting the new tax credit to organizations defined as "poverty fighting" would remove some of the most effective groups, such as local congregations, as potential donees.

Even if Congress redefines and narrows the definition of a qualified charity, it is uncertain whether taxpayer-donors would become more involved in social service projects. Would they take a more active role? Would they provide oversight? At present, the answers to these questions are uncertain.

Revising the Liability Consequences of In-Kind Charitable Contributions by Businesses

In January and February 2001, the Bush administration outlined a further initiative designed to limit the liability of corporations making good faith, in-kind donations to charitable organizations. Through donation of equipment, facilities, vehicles, and aircraft, corporations could enhance the ability of nonprofit groups to serve neighborhoods and families.[188]

This initiative was embodied in H.R. 7, the proposed Community Solutions Act of 2001.[189] Representatives Watts and Hall broadened the liability reform measure to include a variety of business entities, not only corporations. The bill provided blanket protection from federal and state civil liabilities for business entities relating to injury or death from the use of equipment, including mechanical, electrical, and office, donated to nonprofits.

Somewhat more limited, but still broad, exemptions from federal and state civil liabilities were proposed for business entities providing the use of facilities, motor vehicles, and aircraft to nonprofit organizations. To deal with the problem of donations of unsafe equipment, the bill contained exceptions for acts or omissions by business entities constituting gross negligence or intentional misconduct.

The revised version of H.R. 7, as passed by the House in July 2001, generally followed the original proposal deleting however, among other changes, the exemption from liability for business entities providing tours of facilities.[190]

The Lieberman-Santorum bill was silent on this point. In the end, the 107th Congress did not go along with limitations on the liability consequences of corporate in kind charitable contributions. This aspect of the Bush initiative, in conjunction with additional income tax incentives, sought to encourage corporations to be full partners in mobilizing and strengthening charities. The Administration believed even more was needed.

Jawboning Large Corporations to Increase Their Contributions to FBOs

In addition to tax and liability breaks, President Bush sought to encourage increased business donations to FBOs, particularly by large corporations.[191] In order to achieve this goal, Bush determined that the present restrictions by many business entities against contributions to organizations with the remotest connection to religion had to change.

In an opening salvo in the presidential battle against Fortune 500 corporations that refuse to contribute to religious organizations, Bush called on businesses to help alleviate poverty. In his May 2001 Notre Dame Commencement Address, the president stated, "Faith-based organizations receive only a tiny percentage of overall corporate giving. Currently, six of the ten largest corporate givers in America explicitly rule out or restrict donations to faith-based groups, regardless of their effectiveness." He continued, "The Federal Government will not discriminate against FBOs, and neither should corporate America."[192]

Bush's faith-based initiative received a boost when two new entities, Americans for Community and Faith-Centered Enterprise, a citizens' lobby, and the Foundation for Community and Faith-Centered Enterprise opened for business in 2001. Both organizations are headed by Michael S. Joyce, a long-time proponent of faith-based organizations.

At a Rose Garden ceremony on May 10, 2001, Bush asked Joyce, "Did Karl [Rove] call you yet?" Rove phoned later that day asking Joyce "to undertake a private initiative to help get this legislation through."[193] Joyce insisted on independence from the administration and that the specifics be left up to him.

These private groups touted two parts of the Bush program. The first part was the expansion of Charitable Choice, designed to put FBOs on an equal footing with secular groups in applying for federal grants. Joyce initially focused on helping House Republicans pass the Watts-Hall bill, building public support for the Bush faith-base initiative in Congress and among the public, and serving as a coordinator for the Lieberman-Santorum CARE bill. The second aspect focused on stimulating increased giving to FBOs by philanthropies and corporations, assisting FBOs in understanding federal laws and grant and contract requirements, and helping groups demonstrate the positive results of their activities.

To produce the desired outpouring of corporate contributions, what may be needed is a United Way for Faith-Based Outreach. This type of independent organization, on a national, regional, or local basis, could identify fiscally sound and effective faith-based programs, run by serious, honest people, aimed at dealing with certain types of social ills we are concerned about, such as people at risk for harmful behavior.[194]

––––––––––––

Although far from perfect, a tax-oriented funding policy may be the best scheme for federal government support of FBOs. Tax-oriented funding is, as we will see in chapter 8, is more likely to withstand constitutional scrutiny than direct aid. Unlike direct funding, tax incentives do not impose administrative burdens on FBOs or cause FBOs to run the risk of government "capture." Tax incentives do, however, have two serious drawbacks. First, they may only serve to subsidize existing charitable contributions without encouraging additional giving (although this seems unlikely). Second, they may fail to target contributions to the communities and charities most in need. Reality could, however, defy these fears. The wrong approach is to do nothing. Rather, the appropriate path is to expand direct funding and the use of vouchers as well as increase tax incentives and make adjustments as necessary.

Notes

1. Governor George W. Bush, Speech, "The Duty of Hope," Indianapolis, Indiana, July 22, 1999.

2. President-elect George W. Bush, "Remarks on End of the Race," *New York Times*, December 14, 2000, A18.

3. Inaugural Address, January 20, 2001, *Weekly Compilation of Presidential Documents* 37:4 (January 29, 2001): 210; President George W. Bush, "I Ask You To Be Citizens," *New York Times*, January 21, 2001, 12-13.

4. President George W. Bush, "Transcript of Announcement of Formation of the White House Office of Faith-Based and Community Initiatives," January 29, 2001, *Weekly Compilation of Presidential Documents* 37:5 (February 5, 2001): 232-233.

5. "Address Before a Joint Session of the Congress on Administration Goals," February 27, 2001, *Weekly Compilation of Presidential Documents* 37:9 (March 2, 2001): 351-357, at 353; "Transcript of President Bush's Message to Congress on His Budget Proposal," *New York Times*, February 28, 2001, A14.

6. President George W. Bush, Commencement Address at the University of Notre Dame, May 20, 2001, *Weekly Compilation of Presidential Documents*, 37:21 (May 25, 2001): 779-783, at 781. The quotes are from this address.

7. "Remarks Announcing the Faith-Based Initiative," January 29, 2001, *Weekly Compilation of Presidential Documents* 37:5 (February 2, 2001): 232-233; "Bush on the Creation of a White House Office Tied to Religion," *New York Times*, January 30, 2001, A18.

8. Executive Order No. 13199, Establishment of White House Office of Faith-Based and Community Initiatives (January 29, 2001), *Federal Register* 66:21 (January 31, 2001): 8499-8500.

9. *What's God Got To Do With The American Experiment?* eds. E. J. Dionne, Jr. and John J. DiIulio, Jr. (Washington, D.C.: Brookings Institution, 2000).

10. Richard Morin, "Leading With His Right," *Washington Post*, February 26, 2001, C1, C3.

11. Fred Barnes, "The Minister of Ministries," *The Weekly Standard* 6:21, February 12, 2001, 8, 10.

12. Elisabeth Bumiller, "New Leader Picked for Religion-Based Initiative," *New York Times*, February 2, 2002, A12; Elisabeth Bumiller, "White House Letter: Faith, Politics and One Eye on Heaven," *New York Times*, May 13, 2002, A12.

13. Mike Allen, "'Faith-Based' Initiative to Get Push," *Washington Post*, August 31,

2002, A1, A8.

14. White House Office of Faith-Based and Community Initiatives, *Guidance to Faith-Based and Community Organizations on Partnering with the Federal Government*, n.d.

15. Executive Order No. 13198, Agency Responsibilities with Respect to Faith-Based and Community Initiatives (January 29, 2001), *Federal Register* 66:21 (January 31, 2001): 8497. The quotes are from this Executive Order.

16. The White House, *Unlevel Playing Field: Barriers to Participation by Faith-Based and Community Organization in Federal Social Service Programs* (August 2001), 19.

17. See generally, The White House, *Unlevel Playing Field*.

18. *Ibid.*, 10.

19. *Ibid.*, 11.

20. *Ibid.*, 12.

21. *Ibid.*, 2, 13-15, 25.

22. *Ibid.*, 14.

23. *Ibid.*, 2, 23-24.

24. *Ibid.*, 2, 20-22.

25. *Ibid.*, 2. See also *Ibid.*, 8-10.

26. *Ibid.*, 2.

27. "The President's Radio Address," August 18, 2001, *Weekly Compilation of Presidential Documents* 37:34 (August 24, 2001): 1186-1187; Dana Milbank, "Bush Urges Senators To Act on Faith Bill," *Washington Post*, August 19, 2001, A4; Joyce Howard Price, "Bush Prodes Senate on Faith Initiative," *Washington Times*, August 19, 2001, A2.

28. Department of Education, Office of Chief Financial Officer, Direct Grant Programs, *Federal Register* 66:231 (November 30, 2001): 60135-60138 and Department of Education, Office of Elementary and Secondary Education, Carol M. White Physical Education Program, *Federal Register* 67:78 (April 23, 2002): 19737-19740.

29. Department of Labor, Employment and Training Administration, Grants for Small Faith-Based and Community-Based Non-Profit Organizations, *Federal Register* 67:74 (April 17, 2002): 18930-18933. Another grant program awarded $5 million to intermediary organizations to manage these grants, connect grassroots faith-based and community organizations to the U.S. workforce development system, and educate these smaller organizations in how to apply for and manage grants. *Ibid.*, 18946-18949. Grants totaling $9.9 million were awarded to states to work toward increasing the number of community- and faith-based organizations as partners in the One-Stop career centers for the unemployed or those who need training. *Ibid.*, 18938-18941. Larry Witham, "Labor Debuts Bush's Faith Plan," *Washington Times*, April 18, 2002, A11. See also Department of Labor, Office of Disability Employment Policy, Notice of Availability of Funds and Solicitation for Grant Applications for Customized Employment Grants, *Federal Register* 67:123 (June 26, 2002): 43154-43169 and Department of Labor, Office of Disability Employment Policy, Working for Freedom, Opportunity and Real Choice Through Community Employment (Work FORCE) Grant Initiative, *Federal Register* 67:140 (July 22, 2002): 47844-47860.

30. See, e.g., Department of Labor, Employment and Training Administration, Workforce Investment Act: Indian and Native American Employment and Training Programs; Solicitation for Grant Applications: Final Grantee Designation Procedures for Program, Years 2002 and 2003, *Federal Register* 67:45 (March 7, 2002): 10437-10443.

31. U.S. Department of Health & Human Services, HHS Proposes New Regulations For Fair Treatment of Religious Grantee Organizations and Their Clients, December 12, 2002; Department of Health and Human Services, Proposed Charitable Choice Regulations Applicable to States Receiving Substance Abuse Prevention and Treatment Block Grants, Projects for Assistance in Transition from Homelessness Formula Grants, and to Public and Private Providers Receiving Discretionary Grant Funding From SAMHSA for the Provision

of Substance Abuse Services Providing for Equal Treatment of SAMHSA Program Participants (December 12, 2002), *Federal Register* 67:242 (December 17, 2002): 77349-77369; Proposed Rule for Charitable Choice Provisions Applicable to Temporary Assistance for Needy Families Program (December 12, 2002), *Federal Register* 67:242 (December 17, 2002): 77361-77366; Proposed Rule for Charitable Choice Provisions Applicable to Programs Authorized Under the Community Services Block Grant Act (December 12, 2002), *Federal Register* 67:242 (December 17, 2002): 77367-77371.

32. U.S. Department of Education, President Bush Unveils New Guidance Empowering Faith-Based and Community Groups to Provide Extra Academic Help to Low-Income Students, December 12, 2002; U.S. Department of Education, Supplement Educational Services, Draft Non-Regulatory Guidance, December 12, 2002.

33. U.S. Department of Housing and Urban Development, Bush Administration Proposes To End "Regulatory Discrimination" Against Faith-Based Organizations in HUD Programs, December 12, 2002; U.S. Department of Housing and Urban Development, Proposed Rules for Participation in HUD Programs by Faith-Based Organizations; Providing for Equal Treatment of All HUD Program Participants (December 11, 2002), *Federal Register* 68:3 (January 6, 2003): 647-654.

34. See, e.g., U.S. Department of Health and Human Services, Office of Community Services, Fiscal Year 2002 Training, Technical Assistance and Capacity-Building Program: Availability of Funds and Request for Applications, Spring 2002 Announcement, *Federal Register* 67:134 (July 12, 2002): 46339-46362.

35. President George W. Bush, "Remarks at White House Conference on Faith-Based and Community Initiatives in Philadelphia, Pennsylvania," December 12, 2002, *Weekly Compilation of Presidential Documents* 38:50 (December 13, 2002): 2152-2156, at 2155.

36. Executive Order 13280, Responsibilities of the Department of Agriculture and the Agency for International Development With Respect to Faith-Based and Community Initiatives (December 12, 2002), *Federal Register* 67:241 (December 16, 2002): 77145-77146.

37. Executive Office of the President of the United States, *A Blueprint For New Beginnings: A Responsible Budget for America's Priorities* (Washington, D.C.: U.S. Government Printing Office, 2001), 57.

38. H.R. 7, 107th Congress, 1st Session.

39. H.R. 7, Title II, Section 201, as originally introduced, provided for the expansion of Charitable Choice to the following programs: 1) the prevention and treatment of juvenile delinquency and the improvement of the juvenile justice system; 2) the prevention of crime; 3) federal housing laws; 4) Title I of the Workforce Investment Act of 1998; 5) Older Americans Act of 1965; 6) Child Care Development Block Grant Act of 1990; 7) Community Development Block Grant Program established under Title I of the Housing and Community Development Act of 1974; 8) the intervention in and prevention of domestic violence; 9) hunger relief activities; 10) Job Access and Reverse Commute Grant Program; and 11) activities to assist students in obtaining recognized equivalents of secondary school diplomas and activities relating to nonschool-hours program.

40. H.R. 7, as amended, Title II, Section 201 (adding proposed 42 USC §1991(c)(4)), 107th Congress, 1st Session. The nine areas are as follows: 1) the prevention and treatment of juvenile delinquency and the improvement of the juvenile justice system; 2) the prevention of crime and assistance to crime victims and offenders' facilities; 3) the provision of assistance under federal housing statutes, including the Community Development Block Grant Program; 4) programs under certain aspects of the Workforce Investment Act of 1998 providing basic grants to states for adult and youth training and grants for special nationwide programs administered by the Department of Labor; 5) programs under the Older Americans Act of 1965; 6) the intervention in and the prevention of domestic violence, including

programs under the Child Abuse Prevention and Treatment Act and the Family Violence Prevention and Services Act; 7) hunger relief activities; 8) the Job Access and Reverse Commute grant program established under the Federal Transit Act; and 9) activities to assist students in obtaining the recognized equivalents of secondary school diplomas and activities relating to nonschool-hour programs.

41. *Ibid.*, adding proposed 42 USC §1991(o).

42. *Ibid.*, adding proposed 42 USC §1991(o)(4).

43. See, e.g., Michael Tanner, *Corrupting Charity: Why Government Should Not Fund Faith-Based Charities*, Cato Institute, Briefing Papers No. 62 (March 22, 2001), 9-10.

44. Laurie Goodstein, "Bush's Charity Plan Is Raising Concerns For Religious Right," *New York Times*, March 3, 2001, A1, A10.

45. Pat Robertson, "Mr. Bush's Faith-Based Initiative Is Flawed," *Wall Street Journal*, March 12, 2001, A22; Goodstein, "Bush's Charity Plan Is Raising Concerns for Religious Right," A10.

46. Thomas B. Edsall, "Robertson Joins Liberals in Faulting Bush's 'Faith-Based' Plan," *Washington Post*, February 22, 2001, A5.

47. John J. DiIulio, Jr., Speech, "Compassion In Truth and Action: How Sacred and Secular Places Serve Civic Purposes, and What Washington Should and Should Not Do to Help," March 7, 2001. The quotes are from this speech. For arguments in favor of aiding the efforts of black churches and inner-city communities, see John J. DiIulio, Jr., "Supporting Black Churches: Faith, Outreach, and the Inner-City Poor," in *What's God Got To Do With the American Experiment?*

48. Mike Allen and Thomas B. Edsall, "Black Religious Leaders Hear Bush's Call," *Washington Post*, March 20, 2001, A6.

49. Laurie Goodstein, "Bush Aide Tells of Plan to Aid Work By Churches," *New York Times*, March 8, 2001, A10.

50. Dana Milbank and Thomas B. Edsall, "Faith Initiative May Be Revised," *Washington Post*, March 12, 2001, A1, A5.

51. Elizabeth Becker, "Senate Delays Legislation On Aid to Church Charities," *New York Times*, May 24, 2001, A16.

52. Dana Milbank, "Senators Slow Action on 'Faith-Based' Aid," *Washington Post*, March 14, 2001, A1.

53. Statement of Coalition for Compassion, April 11, 2001.

54. Laurie Goodstein, "Battle Lines Grow on Plan to Assist Religious Groups," *New York Times*, April 12, 2001, A22.

55. Richard A. Oppel, Jr., with Gustav Niebuhr, "Bush Tells Ministers of Plan to Expand Churches' Role," *New York Times*, December 21, 2000, A29; Dana Milbank and Hamil R. Harris, "Bush, Religious Leaders Meet," *Washington Post*, December 21, 2000, A6.

56. John Leland, "Some Black Pastors See New Aid Under Bush," *New York Times*, February 2, 2001, A12.

57. Mike Allen and Thomas B. Edsall, "Black Religious Leaders Hear Bush's Call," *Washington Post*, March 20, 2001, A6.

58. Edwin Chen and Alissa J. Rubin, "Bush Gives Government Role to Faith Groups: Enlisting Their Help Against Poverty, Move Brings Praise, but Concern for Church-State Separation," *Los Angeles Times*, January 30, 2001, Part A, 1. See also Jim Wallis, "Overcoming Poverty: A New Era of Partnership," in *Welfare Reform and Faith-Based Organizations*, eds. Derek Davis and Barry Hankins (Waco: Dawson Institute of Church-State Studies, 1999); Jim Wallis, "A Seat at the Table," *Washington Post*, June 11, 1999, A37; Jim Wallis, "A Church-State Priority," *Washington Post*, January 8, 2001, A19, Jim Wallis, "Will Aid Make Churches Docile?" *New York Times*, February 3, 2001, A25.

59. Fred Barnes, "The Impresario," *The Weekly Standard,* 6:46, August 20 and 27, 2001, 22-26, at 25.

60. Jeanne Cummings and Jim VandeHei, "Faith-Based Charity Initiative Takes Worldly, Rocky Path," *Wall Street Journal,* August 16, 2001, A16.

61. *Ibid.*

62. *Ibid.*

63. Mike Allen and Serge F. Kovaleski, "Bush Argues Case for Church-Based Social Service," *Washington Post,* June 26, 2001, A2; David E. Sanger, "Bush Asks Mayors to Lobby for Faith-Based Social Aid," *New York Times,* June 26, 2001, A17.

64. Elizabeth Becker, "Changes Open Door for Bill on Charities of Churches," *Washington Post,* June 28, 2001, A17.

65. H.R. 7, as amended, Title II, Section 201 (adding 42 USC §1994a(j)).

66. *Ibid.*

67. Kim Sue Lia Perkes, "Faith-Based Bill Criticized: Bush Supporter Says Measure Leaves Out Many Religious Groups," *The Austin American-Statesman,* August 8, 2001, B1.

68. H.R. 7, as amended, Title II, Section 201 (adding proposed 42 USC §1994a (c)(1)(B)): H.R. 7, Title II, Section 201 (adding proposed 42 USC §1994a(c)(1)(B)).

69. H.R. 7, as amended, Title II, Section 201 (adding proposed 42 USC §1994a(d)(21)(A)).

70. H.R. 7, Title II, Section 201 (adding proposed 42 USC §1994a(d)(2)(A)).

71. *Ibid.,* adding proposed 42 USC §1994a(d)(2)(A).

72. *Ibid.,* adding proposed 42 USC §1994a(d)(f)(1).

73. H.R. 7, as amended, Title II, Section 201 (adding proposed 42 USC §1994a (g)(1)(A)).

74. *Ibid.,* adding proposed 42 USC §1994a(g)(2); H.R. 7, Title II, Section 201 (adding proposed 42 USC §1994a(f)(2)).

75. H.R. 7, as amended, Title II, Section 201 (adding proposed 42 USC §1994a(i)(2)); H.R. 7, Title II, Section 201 (adding proposed 42 USC §1994a(h)(2)).

76. H.R. 7, as amended Title II, Section 201 (adding proposed 42 USC §1994a(i)(3)).

77. H.R. 7, Title II, Section 201 (adding proposed 42 USC §1994a(l)).

78. H.R. 7, as amended, Title II, Section 201 (adding proposed 42 USC §1994a(n)).

79. Dana Milbank, "Charity Cites Bush Help in Fight Against Hiring Gays," *Washington Post,* July 10, 2001, A1.

80. Frank Bruni and Elizabeth Becker, "Charity Is Told It Must Abide by Antidiscrimination Laws," *New York Times,* July 11, 2001, A15; Dana Milbank, "Bush Drops Rule on Hiring of Gays," *Washington Post,* July 11, 2001, A1.

81. 147 Congressional Record H 4281 (July 19, 2001).

82. Juliet Eilperin, "Faith Initiative Hits Snag In House," *Washington Post,* July 19, 2001, A1; Alison Mitchell and Elizabeth Becker, "G.O.P. Moderates Deal New Setback to House Leaders," *New York Times,* July, 19, 2001, A1.

83. H.R. 7, as amended, Title II, Section 201 (adding proposed 42 USC §1994a(e)).

84. *Ibid.,* adding proposed 42 USC §1994a(f); H.R. 7, Title II, Section 201 (adding proposed 42 USC §1994a(e)(3)).

85. H.R. 7, as amended, Title II, Section 201 (adding proposed 42 USC §1994a(d)(1)); H.R. 7, Title II, Section 201 (adding proposed 42 USC §1994a(d)(1)).

86. 147 Congressional Record H 4280-4281 (July 19, 2001).

87. *Ibid.,* H 4274 (July 19, 2001).

88. Juliet Eilperin, "Faith-Based Initiative Wins House Approval," *Washington Post,* July 20, 2001, A1, A18; Elizabeth Becker, "House Backs Aid to Church Groups for Charity Work," *New York Times,* July 20, 2001, A1, A14.

89. Dana Milbank, "Senate Faith Initiative Backer To Drop Disputed Provisions,"

Washington Post, August 2, 2001, A2.

90. *Ibid.*

91. Text of a Letter from the president to the Senate Majority Leader and the Senate Republican Leader, November 7, 2001, *Weekly Compilation of Presidential Documents*, 37:45, November 12, 2001: 1612-1613; Elizabeth Becker, "Bush Plan Would Alter Bill to Aid Charities," *New York Times*, November 8, 2001, 17. See also Elizabeth Becker, "Bush Is Said to Scale Back His Religion-Based Initiative," *New York Times*, October 14, 2001, A14.

92. Dana Milbank, "Early, Intense Action Marks Bush's Hill Wins," *Washington Post*, December 22, 2001, A1, A6. See also Helen Dewar and Dana Milbank, "On Hill, Bush Picking His Fights With Care," *New York Times*, March 19, 2002, A4.

93. "Address Before a Joint Session of the Congress on the Sate of the Union," January 29, 2002, *Weekly Compilation of Presidential Documents* 38:5 (February 1, 2002): 133-139; Text of President Bush's State of the Union Address to Congress, *New York Times*, January 30, 2002, A22.

94. Remarks of President Bush and Jim Towey in Announcement of the New Director of the Office of Faith-Based and Community Initiatives, February 1, 2002, *Weekly Compilation of Presidential Documents* 38:5 (February 4, 2002): 164-165.

95. S. 1924, 107th Congress, 2nd Session.

96. *Ibid.*, Title III, Section 301.

97. Dana Milbank, "Bush Endorses Compromise in Senate on Aid to Charities," *Washington Post*, February 8, 2002, A4; Elisabeth Bumiller, "Accord Reached on Charity Aid Bill After Bush Gives In On Hiring," *New York Times*, February 8, 2002, A19.

98. S. 1924, Title III, Section 301(e)(2).

99. *Ibid.*, Section 301(e)(2)(A). Excluded are programs under the Elementary and Secondary Education Act of 1965 and the Higher Education Act of 1965. *Ibid.*, Section 301(e)(2)(B).

100. *Ibid.*, Section 301(a).

101. *Ibid.*, Section 301(b).

102. *Ibid.*, Section 301(b), Section 602.

103. *Ibid.*, Title V, Sections 501-505. The funds would be allocated in fiscal year 2003 as follows: $85 million to the Department of Health and Human Services (HHS), $15 million to the Corporation for National and Community Service; $35 million to the Department of Justice; $15 million to the Department of Housing and Urban Development. Also, HHS may award, all or any part of its fund, for state and local faith-based offices through grants and cooperative agreements. *Ibid.*, Section 501(b)(1).

104. Remarks on the Proposed "Charity Aid, Recovery, and Empowerment Act of 2002," April 11, 2002, *Weekly Compilation of Presidential Documents* 38:15 (April 12, 2002): 611-614; Elisabeth Bumiller, "Bush Rallies Faithful in Call for Passage of Charity Bill," *New York Times*, April 12, 2002, A20.

105. Executive Order 13279, Equal Protection of the Laws for Faith-Based and Community Organizations (December 12, 2002), *Federal Register* 67:241 (December 16, 2002): 77141-77144; Richard W. Stevenson, "Religious Groups Face Fewer Curbs In Bush Aid Plan," *New York Times*, December 13, 2002, A1.

106. *A Blueprint for New Beginnings*, 56; *Budget of the United States Government*, Fiscal Year 2002, 11.

107. Conference Report to Accompany H.R. 3061, Report 107-342, Making Appropriations for the Departments of Labor, Health and Human Services, and Education, and Related Agencies for the Fiscal Year Ending September 30, 2002, and For Other Purposes, 106. H.R. 3061 was enacted as Public Law 107-116. In October 2002, the Department of Health and Human Services awarded $24.8 million in grants from the

Compassion Capital Fund to twenty-one intermediary groups, including $500,000 to Rev. Pat Robertson's Operation Blessing International Relief and Development Corp., to provide technical assistance to faith- and community-based organizations. After training smaller groups, these intermediaries may redirect some funds to programs aimed at homelessness, hunger, rehabilitation of addicts and prisoners, welfare-to-work, and at-risk children. Four grants totaling more than $850,000 went to support research on the provision of social services by faith- and community-based organizations. U.S. Department of Health & Human Services, "HHS Awards $30 Million to Help Level Playing Field for Faith-Based and Community Institutions," October 3, 2002; Larry Witham, "HHS Issues $30 Million to Faith-Based Providers," *Washington Times*, October 4, 2002, A3; Debra E. Blum, "Making Grants on Faith," *Chronicle of Philanthropy*, December 12, 2002, 25.

108. The White House, Office of Management and Budget, *Budget of the United States Government*, Fiscal Year 2003, 141.

109. *A Blueprint for New Beginnings*, 56; *Budget*, Fiscal Year 2002, 92.

110. H.R. 2873, Title I, Subtitle B, Section 121 (amending 42 USC §629-629e), enacted as Public Law 107-133. Emilie Stoltzfus and Karen Spar, "Child Welfare: The Promoting Safe and Stable Families Program," CRS Report for Congress, January 24, 2002, provide background on the 2001 amendments.

111. *A Blueprint for New Beginnings*, 56; *Budget*, Fiscal Year 2002, 86.

112. H.R. 1 (No Child Left Behind Act of 2001), Title IV, Part B, Sections 4201-4206. H.R. 1 was enacted as Public Law 107-110. Authorized appropriations for community learning centers increase to $1.5 billion for fiscal year 2003, $1.75 billion for fiscal year 2004, $2 billion for fiscal year 2005, $2.25 billion for fiscal year 2006, and $2.5 billion for fiscal year 2007. *Ibid.*, Section 4206.

113. *A Blueprint for New Beginnings*, 56; *Budget*, Fiscal Year 2002, 135; Statement, Kathleen Hawk Sawyer, Department of Justice, Director, Federal Bureau of Prisons, House Committee on Appropriations, Subcommittee on Commerce, Justice, State and Judiciary, Hearings, Department of Commerce, Justice, and State, the Judiciary, and Related Agencies: Appropriations for FY 2002, 107th Congress, 1st Session, June 7, 2001.

114. Report to Accompany H.R. 2500, Departments of Commerce, Justice, and State, The Judiciary and Related Agencies Appropriations Bill, Fiscal Year 2002, Report 107-139, House of Representatives, 107th Congress, 1st Session, 35; Conference Report to Accompany H.R. 2500, Making Appropriations for the Departments of Commerce, Justice, and State, The Judiciary, and Related Agencies for the Fiscal Year Ending September 30, 2002, and for Other Purposes, Report 107-278, 107th Congress, 1st Session, 83. H.R. 2500 was enacted as Public Law 107-77.

115. *A Blueprint for New Beginnings*, 56; *Budget*, Fiscal Year 2002, 93.

116. Conference Report to Accompanying H.R. 3061, Report 107-342, Making Appropriations for the Departments of Labor, Health and Human Services, and Education, and Related Agencies for the Fiscal Year Ending September 30, 2002, and for Other Purposes, 105. H.R. 3061 was enacted as Public Law 107-116.

117. The White House, *Budget*, Fiscal Year 2003, 142.

118. S. 1924, Title VII, Section 701.

119. *A Blueprint for New Beginnings*, 56; 75-76; *Budget*, Fiscal Year 2002, 92. A proposal for a fatherhood grants program, including the 1996 Charitable Choice provisions (H.R. 1471, Title V, Section 501(c)), was introduced in the 107th Congress, 1st Session.

In the first session of the 106th Congress, the House approved the Count Act of 1999 (H.R. 3073), authorizing the federal government to make grants to public and private entities to promote marriage and successful parenting and help fathers and their families move from welfare to work. The bill included a provision incorporating by reference the 1996 Charitable Choice provisions. During the House debate on H.R. 3073, amendments were defeated to disallow fatherhood grants to any "pervasively sectarian" faith-based institution (145 Congressional Record H 11897-11898, H 11899-11900 November 10, 1999) and to forbid religious organizations from discriminating in their hiring on the basis of religion (*Ibid.*, H 11900-11901). The Senate failed to take action on this bill. The House also approved the proposed Child Support Distribution Act of 2000 (H.R. 4678), including Charitable Choice provisions. An amendment, among other provisions, barring entities from subjecting participants in funded programs to sectarian worship, instruction, or proselytization was rejected (146 Congressional Record H 7316, H 7318-7319 September 7, 2000). A motion to recommit H.R. 4678 with instructions to delete the section of the Charitable Choice provisions allowing participating religious organizations to discriminate in their employment practices on religious grounds was also rejected. *Ibid.*, H 7319-7321. The Senate failed to take action on H.R. 4678 and a companion bill (S. 3189).

120. The White House, *Budget*, Fiscal Year 2003, 142.

121. Elizabeth Becker, "Practical Questions Greet Bush Plan to Aid Religious Groups," *New York Times*, February 5, 2001, A11.

122. Teresa Watanabe, "Churches Divided on Role in U.S. Social Service Programs," *Los Angeles Times*, January 29, 2001, B1.

123. Many of these concerns were earlier expressed by Michael Horowitz, "Subsidies May Cost Churches Their Souls," *Wall Street Journal,* December 16, 1999, A22; Joseph Loconte, "The 7 Deadly Signs of Government Funding for Private Charities," *Policy Review* 82 (March-April 1997): 28-36; Lisa E. Oliphant, "Charitable Choice: The End of Churches As We Know Them," *Public Welfare* 58:2 (June 2000): 8-11. See also Statement of Rep. Ron Paul (R-Texas), 147 Congressional Record H 4259-4260 (July 19, 2001).

124. Laurie Goodstein, "In God We Trust. In Government We Hope for the Best," *New York Times*, Week in Review, February 4, 2001, 3.

125. Amy L. Sherman, "Cross Purposes: Will Conservative Welfare Reform Corrupt Religious Charities?" *Policy Review* 74 (Fall 1995): 58-63.

126. Susan Adams, "Corporate Communion," *Forbes* 165:8 (April 3, 2000): 82-84.

127. Joseph Loconte, "Dual Mission," *Wall Street Journal*, February 2, 2001, W15.

128. Testimony, Edward Morgan, President, Christian Herald Association, U.S. Senate, Committee on the Judiciary, Hearings, Faith-Based Solutions: What Are the Legal Issues? June 6, 2001.

129. See generally, Jill Witmer Sinha, *Cookman United Methodist Church and Transition Journey: A Case Study in Charitable Choice* (Washington, D.C.: The Center for Public Justice, 2000).

130. *Ibid.*, 18.

131. Statement, Rev. Donna Lawrence Jones, Cookman United Methodist Church, Philadelphia, Pa., "Our Experience with Charitable Choice," Subcommittee on the Constitution, Committee on the Judiciary, U.S. House of Representatives, Oversight Hearing on State and Local Implementation of Existing Charitable Choice Programs, April 24, 2001. See also Statement, Pastor Donna Jones, U.S. House of Representatives, Subcommittee on Criminal Justice, Drug Policy and Human Resources, Committee on Government Reform, Hearing on The Role of Community and Faith-Based Organizations in Providing Effective Social Services, April 26, 2001.

132. Statement, Rev. Donna Lawrence Jones, April 24, 2001.

133. Caryle Murphy, "Faith and Federal Funds," *Washington Post*, March 18, 2001, C1, C5.

134. *Ibid.*

135. 42 USC §604a(a).

136. H.R. 7, as amended Title II, Section 201 (adding proposed 42 USC §1994a(l)).

137. *Ibid.*, adding proposed 42 USC §1994a(h)(2). This provision opens the door to

discrimination against beneficiaries on the basis of religion after admission the a program; however, beneficiaries have selected the program.

138. See generally, James Q. Wilson, "Why Not Try Vouchers?" *New York Times*, April 27, 2001, A27.

139. Public Law 101-58.

140. 42 USC §§9858(c)(2)(A)(i)(II) and 9858n(2). See William J. Tobin, "Lessons about Vouchers from Federal Child Care Legislation," The Center for Public Justice, January, 1998.

141. John I. DiIulio, Jr., "Bush Keeps the Faith," *The Weekly Standard* 7:22, February 18, 2002, 30-33, at 33.

142. The President's Agenda for Tax Relief, February 8, 2001; President George W. Bush, "Remarks on Transmitting Proposed Tax Cut Plan to the Congress," February 8, 2001, *Weekly Compilation of Presidential Documents* 37:6 (February 9, 2001): 271-273.

143. A *Blueprint for New Beginnings*, 56-57.

144. Department of the Treasury, *General Explanations of the Administration's Fiscal Year 2002 Tax Relief Proposals*, April 2002, 6-9.

145. *A Blueprint for New Beginnings*, 57; *Budget*, Fiscal Year 2002, 57, 93.

146. H.R. 7, Title I, 107th Congress, 1st Session.

147. S. 1924, Title I, 107th Congress, 2nd Session.

148. For an analysis of the proposed food inventory contribution deduction, see CRS Report for Congress, "Charitable Contributions of Food Inventory: Proposals for Change under the Community Solutions Act of 2001," August 23, 2001.

149. Helpful background is provided by Staff of the Joint Committee on Taxation, Description and Analysis of Present Law and Proposals to Expand Federal Tax Incentives for Charitable Giving, JCX-13-01, March 13, 2001 and Staff of the Joint Committee on Taxation, Description of Present Law and Certain Proposals Relating To Charitable Giving and Individual Development Accounts, JCX-55-01, June 13, 2001, 2-5.

150. H.R. 7, Title I, Section 101(a) (adding proposed IRC §170(m)). In his fiscal year 2003 budget, President Bush sought a charitable deduction for nonitemizers of up to $100 for single taxpayers ($200 for joint returns) in 2002, increasing in stages to $500 for single taxpayers ($1,000 for joint returns) in 2012. The White House, *Budget*, Fiscal Year 2003, 142.

151. IRC §63(c).

152. IRC §170(a).

153. IRC §170(b) and (e).

154. H.R. 7, as amended, Title I, Section 101(a) (adding proposed IRC §170(m)).

155. Joint Committee on Taxation, Estimated Revenue Effects of a Chairman's Amendment in the Nature of a Substitute to H.R. 7, July 10, 2001, JCX-59-01; Joint Committee on Taxation, Estimated Revenue Effects of the President's Fiscal Year 2002 Budget Proposal, May 4, 2001, JCX-31-01.

156. 147 Congressional Record H 4252 (July 19, 2001). The Congressional Research Service estimated that the $25 deduction would gain charities three cents for every dollar lost by the federal government. CRS Report for Congress, Economic Analysis of the Charitable Contribution Deduction for Nonitemizers, August 31, 2001, CRS-11.

157. S. 1924, Section 101(a) (adding proposed IRC §170(m)).

158. Elisabeth Bumiller, "Accord Reached on Charity Bill After Bush Gives In on Hiring," *New York Times*, February 8, 2002, A19.

159. H.R. 7, Title I, Section 102 (adding proposed IRC §408(d)). Congress passed a provision in 1999 that would have allowed people over age seventy and a half to roll over IRA assets directly to charities and avoid being taxed on those funds (H.R. 2488 (Proposed Taxpayer Refund and Relief Act of 1999), Section 804 (amending IRC §408(d)) 106th

Congress, 1st Session. President Clinton vetoed a comprehensive tax bill in which the proposal was included. "Message to the House to Representatives Returning Without Approval the 'Taxpayer Refund and Relief Act of 1999,'" *Weekly Compilation of Presidential Documents* 35:38 (September 23, 1999): 1795-1796.

160. H.R. 7, as amended, Title I, Section 102 (adding proposed IRC §408(d)(8)).

161. Joint Committee on Taxation, Estimated Revenue Effects, July 10, 2001, and May 4, 2001.

162. S. 1924, Section 102 (adding IRC §408(d)(8)).

163. IRC §170(b)(2).

164. H.R. 7, as amended, Title I, Section 103 (adding proposed IRC §170(b)(3)).

165. Joint Committee on Taxation, Estimated Revenue Effects, July 10, 2001, and May 4, 2001.

166. S. 1924, Section 103 (adding IRC §170(b)(3)).

167. Robin Toner, "Balance of Power: The Aftermath," *New York Times*, May 25, 2001, A19.

168. Dana Milbank, "Bush Endorses Compromise In Senate on Aid to Charities," *Washington Post*, February 8, 2002, A4. The provision for emergency legislation is set forth in 2 USC §902(e).

169. Patti Mohr, "Santorum and Lieberman to Add Faith-Based Component to Charity Bill," *Tax Notes*, July 22, 2002, 494.

170. For background on the path of the proposed CARE Act through the Senate Finance Committee, see Patti Mohr, "Shelter Offsets Breathe Life Into Faith-Based Bill," *Tax Notes*, May 27, 2002, 1284-2385; Patti Mohr, "Charitable Giving Tax Cut In Flux as Sponsors Regroup," *Tax Notes*, June 10, 2002, 1559-1561; Patti Mohr, "Finance Begins Markup of Charity Bill with Tax Shelter Offsets," June 17, 2002, 1698-1700; Patti Mohr, "Finance Clears Charity Incentives With Tax Shelter, Haven Penalties," *Tax Notes*, June 24, 2002, 1847-1849.

171. Proposed Charity Aid, Recovery and Empowerment (CARE) Act of 2002, Title VI, Subtitle A – Tax Shelter Transparency Requirements, Section 601-614, 107th Congress, 2nd Session.

172. Proposed CARE Act of 2002, Title VI, Subtitle B–Tax Treatment of Inversion Transactions, Section 641, 107th Congress, 2nd Session.

173. *Ibid.*, Title I, Section 101 (redesignating IRC §170(m) as IRC §170(n) and adding new IRC §170(m)).

174. JCT Revenue Estimate (JCT-56-02) for Reversing the Expatriation of Profits Offshore Act Scheduled for June 13, 2002, Senate Finance Committee Markup.

175. Proposal CARE Act, Title I, Section 102 (amending IRC §408(d)(8)).

176. JCT Revenue Estimates (JCX-56-02).

177. Proposed CARE Act, Title I, Section 103 (amending IRC §170(e)(3)).

178. Proposed CARE Act, Title IV, Sections 401-403.

179. "Bush Pushes for Senate Charity Bill Passage After Sen. Lott Declines Democrats's UC Offer," *Tax Notes*, July 3, 2002, G-6; Elisabeth Bumiller, "Bush Backs Religious Charity and a Shaky Incumbent," *New York Times*, July 3, 2002, A12.

180. President George W. Bush, "Remarks at a Rally on Inner-City Compassion in Cleveland, Ohio," July 1, 2002, *Weekly Compilation of Presidential Documents* 38:27 (July 8, 2002): 1115-1121, at 1121.

181. Patti Mohr, "Santorum Seeks to Get Charity Bill to Senate Floor," *Tax Notes*, September 23, 2002, 1668-1669; Katherine M. Stimmel, "Santorum Unable to Secure Agreement Providing for Limited Debate of Charity Bill," *Daily Tax Reports*, September 25, 2002, G-5; Patti Mohr, "Senate Democrats Deny UC Consideration of Charity Bill," *Tax Notes*, September 30, 2002, 1809-1810; Patti Mohr, "House Prepares 'Investor Relief' Tax

Bill for Year-End Showdown," *Tax Notes*, October 14, 2002, 151-154; Bud Newman, "Senate Sponsors of Faith-Based Tax Bill Say They Are Close to Getting Bill to Floor," *Daily Tax Reports*, October 11, 2002, G-4-G-5; Katherine M. Stimmel, "Santorum Fails to Secure UC on Charity Bill, Looks to Reintroduce Legislation in 2003," *Daily Tax Reports*, November 15, 2002, G-8-G-9; Larry Witham, "Amendments Kill CARE in Senate," *Washington Times*, November 15, 2002, A10.

182. For critical analysis of the tax incentive proposals see CRS Report for Congress, "Economic Analysis of the Charitable Contribution Deduction for Non-Itemizers," August 31, 2001.

183. Statement, Donald C. Alexander, Former IRS Commissioner, Sentate Finance Committee, Hearing, Encouraging Charitable Giving, March 14, 2001 (citing Treasury Department, Statement on Tax Reform Proposal II, chapter 3 (May 30, 1985)).

184. S. 592, 107th Congress, 1st Session (the proposed Savings Opportunity and Charitable Giving Act of 2001), Section 201 would have allowed a deduction only for charitable contributions in excess of a floor of $500 for individuals and $1,000 for a married couple. The deduction would start at 50 percent of contributions over $500 (or $1,000) and increased by ten percentage points, to 60 percent in 2003, 70 percent in 2004, 80 percent in 2005, 90 percent in 2006, until it reached 100 percent in 2007. This bill included a floor because the standard deduction assumes taxpayer donations of $500 (or $1,000). Statement by Senator Rick Santorum (R-Pennsylvania), 147 Congressional Record S 2673 (March 21, 2001).

185. PriceWaterhouseCoopers, "Incentives For Non-Itemizers To Give More: An Analysis," January 2001, 4; Bureau of National Affairs, *Daily Tax Report*, "PriceWaterhouseCoopers Analyzes Effect of President's Non-Itemizer Deduction Plan," February 1, 2001, G-1. However a Congressional Budget Office study, *Effects of Allowing Nonitemizers to Deduct Charitable Contributions* (December 2002), concluded that letting taxpayers who do not itemize claim a limited deduction for charitable contributions is unlikely to increase overall giving by more than 4 percent.

186. Sara E. Meléndez and Bob Edgar, "Taxpayers, Not Taxes, Can Support Faith-Based Charities," *Christian Science Monitor*, May 15, 2001, 9.

187. Robertson, "Mr. Bush's Faith-Based Initiative Is Flawed." Former Senator Dan Coats (R-Indiana) proposed a limited annual tax credit of up to $500 for individuals (and $1,000 for married taxpayers) for contributions to charitable organizations having as their primary purpose the prevention or alleviation of poverty, specifically, those devoting at least 70 percent of their expenditures to direct antipoverty services. S. 1079 (Proposed Comprehensive Charity Reform Act), 104th Congress, 1st Session; U.S. Senator Dan Coats, *The Project for American Renewal* (n.d.), 26; Helen Dewar, "Coats Seeks to Warm GOP Image Through Poverty Tax Credit Plan," *Washington Post*, February 25, 1996, A4. See also H.R. 673, 107th Congress, 1st Session proposing to amend the IRC to provide a tax credit for charitable contributions to fight poverty. Margy Waller, "Charity Tax Credits: Federal Policy and Three Leading States," May, 2001 (unpublished manuscript) provides an analysis of existing state tax charitable credits in Arizona, Michigan, and North Carolina.

188. *Rallying The Armies of Compassion*, January 30, 2001; *A Blueprint for New Beginnings*, 57.

189. H.R. 7, Title I, Section 104.

190. H.R. 7, as amended, Title IV, Section 401.

191. Jim VandeHei, "Bush Turns to Corporations to Help Fund Faith-Based Plan," *Wall Street Journal*, May 24, 2001, A24; Fred Barnes, "In DiIulio Bush Trusts," *The Weekly Standard* 6:35, May 28, 2001, 14-15, at 15.

192. President George W. Bush, Commencement Address at the University of Notre Dame, 782.

193.   Mike Allen, "Bush Aims to Get Faith Initiative Back on Track," *Washington Post*, June 25, 2001, A1, A5.

194.   James Q. Wilson, "Religion and Public Life: Moving Private Funds to Faith-Based Social Service Providers," *Brookings Review* 17:2 (Spring 1999): 36-41; James Q. Wilson, "Human Remedies for Social Disorders," *The Public Interest* 131 (Spring 1998): 25-35; James Q. Wilson, "Religion in Public Life," in *What's God Got To Do With the American Experiment?*

Chapter 8

The Funding of
Faith-Based Organizations:
The Constitutional Dimension

The Establishment Clause and the Free Exercise Clause of the U.S. Constitution's First Amendment, ratified in 1791, provide that "Congress shall make no law respecting the establishment of religion, or prohibiting the free exercise thereof...." Over the years, courts have interpreted the Establishment Clause to prohibit governmental action that "promotes" religion. This constitutional limitation has been applied to government action that either prefers one religion over another or government action that promotes religion in general over nonreligion. The constitutional prohibition against promoting religion generally is potentially applicable to public programs that provide financial assistance to faith-based charities, including religiously neutral programs such as Charitable Choice.

There are currently two competing interpretations of the extent to which the Establishment Clause limits government action promoting religion.[1] "Separationism" disfavors any government involvement in religion, including assistance to any organization religious in character, even if provided under religiously neutral programs. On the other hand, religious neutrality or the equal treatment of religion that appears to be the successor to separationism would permit, under its most expansive interpretation, direct government assistance to FBOs as long as it is provided under a program that does not discriminate against any particular religion. Under the equal treatment view, a neutral government aid program in which religious and secular groups participate, subject to certain conditions, would be unlikely to offend the Establishment Clause.

The era of strict separation as advocated by Americans United for Separation of Church and State, the nation's preeminent group lobbying for separationism, has passed. Defenders of separationist theory are on the defensive, legally and politically.

From 1981 to the present, the United States Supreme Court has gradually transformed the Establishment Clause from a norm of separationism to one favoring the equal treatment of religion. This trend allows individuals to make their own religious choices and minimizes the impact of government action on one's options concerning religious belief and practices, while forbidding governmental endorsement and the coercive imposition of religion on any person.

The neutrality approach rejects three assumptions made by separationist theory. First, the activities of FBOs are easily severable into sacred and secular aspects. Second, religion is private, but government has a monopoly over public matters. Third, direct public assistance to faith-based social service groups represents the funding of these providers, not aid to the ultimate beneficiaries.

In any analysis of the religion clauses of the First Amendment, a degree of humility is in order. Predicting the Supreme Court's resolution of church-state issues is fraught with difficulty. Yet it is striking how closely the positions of some of the justices correspond to their own religious and educational backgrounds. Three of the four most likely proponents of the equal treatment position (Anthony M. Kennedy, Antonin Scalia, and Clarence Thomas) are practicing Catholics; two of them attended parochial schools. Scalia graduated in the top of his class at St. Francis Xavier Military Academy, a Jesuit high school in Manhattan. Thomas, who returned to Catholicism after a period of worshiping at an Episcopal church, attributes his success to the discipline imposed on him by the Irish Catholic nuns who taught him at parochial schools in Savannah in the late 1950s.

In contrast, Ruth Bader Ginsburg and Stephen G. Breyer (who is married to an Anglican) have retained the separationist instincts of secular Jews born before World War II. Ginsburg, who was director of the American Civil Liberties Union Women's Right Project in the 1970s, is an especially uncompromising separationist along with David H. Souter, an Episcopalian, and John Paul Stevens, a self-described "Protestant."

Separationist Theory and Its Evolution

From 1947 to 1981, the latter year marking the start of the presidency of Ronald Reagan, the roots of a separationist theory grew and spread. During this period, the phrase "separation of church and state" characterized the prevailing attitude toward Establishment Clause jurisprudence. Three key propositions formed the major elements of this attitude. First, religion in America should be private and unobtrusive. Separation mandated a reduction of the public celebration of sectarian religion. Following the doctrine of secular privilege, the public arena was only for secular purposes and religion should be directed to the private sphere. Second, the concept of church-state separation meant that public elementary and secondary schools, where students attended by governmental compulsion, were to be kept free from religion. Students should attend religiously-neutral–or more accurately, religiously free–public schools. Third, separationism permitted the public sector to tolerate but not assist those who chose parochial (at that time mainly Roman Catholic) schools rather than public schools. As we will see, this led to rather stringent limits on public aid to parochial schools.

Everson v. Board of Education[2] established the basic principles underlying separationism. In *Everson*, the Court considered the constitutionality of a local school board's decision, pursuant to a state statute, to subsidize the cost of public transportation to and from public and parochial schools. Justice Hugo Black, a former U.S. Senator from Alabama, an ex-Ku Klux Klan member, as well as a Southern Baptist, concerned about the Pope's power, stated:

> The "establishment of religion" clause of the First Amendment means at least this: Neither a state nor the Federal Government can set up a church. Neither can pass laws which aid one religion, aid all religions, or prefer one religion over another. Neither can force nor influence a person to go to or to remain away from church against his will or force him to profess a belief or disbelief in any religion. No person can be punished for entertaining or professing religious beliefs or disbeliefs, for church attendance or non-attendance. No tax in any amount, large or small, can be levied to support any religious activities or institutions, whatever they may be called, or whatever form they may adopt to teach or practice religion. Neither a state nor the Federal Government can, openly or secretly, participate in the affairs of any religious organizations or groups and *vice versa*. In the words of Jefferson, the clause against establishment of religion by law was intended to erect "a wall of separation between church and State."[3]

Under this view, commentators came to characterize the Establishment Clause as erecting a "wall of separation" between church and state, whereby the public sector could not fund any religious organization. However, if the organization could separate its secular and sacred functions, the government could fund its secular activities.

The broad separationist theory of *Everson* remained the dominant view of the Court until the late 1980s. Although criticized and applied inconsistently, the Court has never officially abandoned separationism and, therefore, it remains relevant today to FBOs receiving direct government assistance.

It is worth noting that although *Everson* is often cited for its exposition of the separationist theory, the Court's opinion upheld the subsidization of transportation costs for students attending parochial schools. The Supreme Court found no Establishment Clause violation because the government funds were provided under a general nondiscriminatory program available to parents of children enrolled in both public and parochial schools. The Court distinguished between financial assistance benefitting a religious institution, thereby aiding religion, and financial assistance for programs, such as transportation, that are "marked off from the religious function"[4] of parochial schools. The Court regarded the latter type of assistance as more akin to basic public services, such as police and fire protection, that could be extended to religious institutions without supporting their religious missions.

The School Prayer Cases of the early 1960s dramatically injected separationism into the American political culture. These cases applied the church-state separation doctrine to the widespread practice of school prayer, giving meaning and scope to separationism, by invalidating this common practice. In *Engel v. Vitale*,[5] the court held that the classroom use of a nondenominational prayer, composed by government authorities, violated the Establishment Clause, as it constituted public sponsorship of religion. School programs of voluntary Bible reading or the recital of the Lord's Prayer were also viewed as advancing religion.[6]

Over the years, it became clear–at least in the eyes of a majority of the justices–that government may not, without violating the Establishment Clause, advocate that students in the K-12 public school arena profess religious beliefs or observe religious practices. More recently, the Court has struck down a clergy-led, "nonsectarian" prayer for graduation ceremonies at a public middle school[7] and disallowed prayers led by students at high school football games.[8] In so holding, the Court majority reasoned that the state cannot coerce anyone to support or participate in religion or its exercise. The spectacle of students praying was deemed to send a message to nonbelievers that the school was endorsing religion.

The strict separationist position of no aid to religion grew out of Supreme Court decisions regarding public funds for religious K-12 schools. In *Lemon v. Kurtzman*,[9] the Court provided a doctrinal framework for the implementation of the separationist vision. In striking down state laws providing salary supplements to teachers of secular subjects in faith-based schools, the Court introduced a three-part test to determine whether a challenged government action is sufficiently separate from the organization's religious function. To satisfy this test, the statute in question: first, must have a secular purpose; second, must not have the principal or primary effect of advancing or inhibiting religion; and third, must not foster "excessive government entanglement with religion."[10]

The *Lemon* Court struck down the challenged statutes because it found that they fostered an excessive entanglement between church and state. In assessing the degree of entanglement, three factors were considered: first, the character and purpose of the institution benefitted; second, the nature of the aid provided; and third, the resulting relationship between the government and religious authorities.[11] In applying the first prong, the majority found that parochial schools were an integral part of the Catholic Church's religious program. The school's religious atmosphere and control indicated that sectarian teachings could be advanced in secular courses. The aid provided a subsidy for teacher salaries, and unlike textbooks, the teachers could not be monitored in advance to ensure that they would neither teach nor advance religion in the classroom. Finally, to ensure that the program did not aid religious activities or teaching, the state would need to place numerous restrictions on the schools, as well as institute a monitoring program. The character of the school and the aid provided required a complex, ongoing relationship between the government and religious authorities. These state attempts to assure the strict separation of the sacred and the secular would require continuing administrative supervision and surveillance, resulting in "excessive" state entanglement with religion.

Although recent key Establishment Clause cases have been decided without reference to the *Lemon* test, it has never been overruled. The *Lemon* test, by barring governmental programs that advance religion or even significantly involve the government with religious institutions, made separation the guiding force in church-state cases in the 1970s and 1980s. The sacred-secular distinction forms the core of the separationist line of reasoning dealing with public funds going to FBOs. Building upon the earlier *Everson* decision, *Lemon* reinforced the need for FBOs to separate their sacred and secular elements, so that the government could fund the secular part.

Separationists assumed that a neat sacred/secular dichotomy accurately described the world of faith-based providers ministering to the poor and needy. Under this view, a religious organization could obtain direct public aid for its secular services, but not for those services related to its religious practices. However, if an FBO could separate its secular and sacred functions, then direct governmental aid could flow to its secular activities. Thus, a religious hospital could receive governmental aid for its independent, secular medical functions.

However, if an FBO were pervasively sectarian and could not separate its sacred and secular aspects, the public sector could not give it direct aid under the separationist theory (except for aid that could not be converted to religious use, such as bus transportation between a student's home and school). Otherwise, the public sector would engage in the unconstitutional advancement of religion. Thus, the definition of "pervasively sectarian" assumed vital importance in the separationist theory.

In *Roemer v. Maryland Public Works Board*,[12] the Supreme Court upheld an annual grant program to qualifying private colleges (including sectarian colleges offering more than seminarian degrees) provided the institution was not "pervasively sectarian." The decision is relevant to faith-based social service organizations receiving government assistance for two reasons. First, the decision appears to indicate that the Court will be more tolerant of government aid outside the elementary or secondary school context, where students are younger and more impressionable. Second, the decision clarifies, to some degree, the "pervasively sectarian" concept. According to the Court, factors indicating that the aid recipients were not "pervasively sectarian" include: autonomy from church control, absence of religious indoctrination, academic freedom (except in religion classes), and absence of religious preference in both hiring faculty and admitting students.

The Court applied these factors to hold that the colleges in question were not pervasively sectarian. First, the colleges were autonomous because they were neither controlled by the Roman Catholic Church nor did they receive Church funds. Second, religious indoctrination was not a substantial purpose or activity, as participation in religious exercises was not required. Third, instructors were free to teach in an atmosphere of intellectual freedom. Despite prayers at the beginning of classes and the presence of religious symbols on campus, courses were taught in a manner meeting normal academic standards. Finally, religion was not taken into account in hiring faculty or admitting students.

In the years following *Lemon*, bitter struggles continued over the application of separationism to cases involving direct public assistance to religiously oriented schools. *Aguilar v. Felton*[13] illustrates the approach to the Establishment Clause in the context of K-12 schools, where the Court tends to apply separationism most strictly. The case involved a federal program of remedial education for disadvantaged students, under which public school district employees, including teachers and guidance counselors, taught remedial reading and math classes and provided guidance services at private and parochial schools. Teachers were directed to avoid involvement with religious activities, were prohibited from using religious materials, rooms were cleared of religious symbols, and were supervised by a system of unannounced visits.

In an opinion by Justice William J. Brennan, Jr., the majority held the program unconstitutional because the religious-affiliated schools were "pervasively sectarian." They reported back to their affiliated church, required attendance at religious exercises, began the school day or a class period with prayer, and granted preference to students who were members of the sponsoring denominations. Because aid was provided in a "pervasively sectarian environment," a monitoring system was necessary to avoid the program being used to inculcate religious beliefs excessively entangled the state with religion.

In a powerful dissent in *Aguilar*, Justice Sandra Day O'Connor assailed the majority's conclusion and its reasoning on two grounds.[14] First, it was hypersensitive to the possibility of religious influence in the program even though the instructors were limited to public employees, many of whom did not share the religious affiliation of their remedial pupils. Second, it was indifferent to the secular public good achieved by the program. Justice O'Connor's insistence on a case-by-case, fact-oriented adjudication, marked by a weighing of competing considerations (such as whether a program contributes to the public good) tended to undercut separationism, at least in its most strict application.

In *Agostini v. Felton*,[15] the Supreme Court reversed itself and upheld the program struck down in *Aguilar*. Collapsing the three-part *Lemon* test into two questions, the majority said that the Court would assess whether government-funded programs had first, a secular purpose and second, a primary effect that neither advances nor inhibits religion. In recasting the entanglement inquiry as one criterion relevant to determining a statute's effect, the Court set forth three primary criteria to determine an impermissible effect: first, whether the aid results in governmental indoctrination; second, whether the program defines its recipients by reference to religion; and third, whether the program creates an excessive entanglement between government and religion.[16]

The Court explained that intervening cases had undermined the basis for its conclusion in *Aguilar* for two reasons. First, the Court abandoned the presumption that public employees placed on parochial school grounds will inevitably inculcate religion or represent a symbolic union between government and religion. (This holding also undermines *Lemon*.) Therefore, there is no need to assume that pervasive monitoring is required, thereby surmounting the excessive entanglement aspect of *Lemon*. Second, the majority said it no longer presumed that all government assistance that directly aids the educational function of religious schools is invalid.

Although it did not alter prevailing Establishment Clause principles, *Agostini* signaled a change in the Supreme Court's understanding of applicable criteria, a less restrictive application of separationism, and a greater recognition that a secular purpose can exist in a religious environment. A crucial element in analyzing aid to students in religious schools is whether the aid is allocated on the basis of neutral, secular criteria, neither favoring nor disfavoring religion, and whether it is made available to religious and secular grantees on a nondiscriminatory basis.[17] If an aid program meets these criteria, it is unlikely to have the effect of advancing religion. Under the program in question, the services were available to all children meeting the eligibility requirements, no matter what their religious beliefs or where they went to school.

Separationist Theory and the
Direct Funding of FBOs

The Supreme Court applied the separationist theory to the issue of direct government funding of FBOs in *Bowen v. Kendrick.*[18] By a five to four majority, the Court upheld the constitutionality of the federal Adolescent Family Life Act (the Act). Through the Act, the federal government funded public and private sector programs that either conducted research on or provided services (such as counseling) for teenage pregnancy and premarital sexual relations.

The Act required all organizations, secular and religious, to be considered on an equal footing, expressly including FBOs to be grantees of federal funds and even requiring certain nonsectarian organizations (along with family and community volunteer groups) to take into account their involvement with sectarian organizations as a condition to receiving grants. No statutory language specifically barred the use of funds for worship, prayer, or other religious activities. Other than routine fiscal accountability to ensure that federal funds were not misappropriated, the Act contained no special financial controls.

The Court began by stating that none of its decisions had ever held that the First Amendment prevents faith-based institutions from participating in publicly funded social welfare programs. The majority applied the prevailing three-prong *Lemon* test, rooted in the then-existing sacred-secular distinction and the "pervasively sectarian" standard.

First, the majority concluded that the Act was motivated primarily, if not exclusively, by a secular purpose: eliminating or reducing the social and economic problems caused by teen sexuality and pregnancy. The parties had agreed that, on the whole, religious concerns were not the sole motivation behind the Act.

Second, the Act's primary effect did not advance or inhibit religion. The program's neutral grant requirements and its nondiscriminatory eligibility standards undercut any risk of promoting religion. The Court recognized that religious organizations had a "role to play" in addressing the social and economic problems of teenage sexuality and pregnancy and that the program successfully maintained a neutral course among religions and between religion and nonreligion. The counseling offered by religious agencies had to be done in a secular manner and the services provided did not include religious indoctrination or teaching.

Nor did the funding of these programs necessarily result in the religious organizations using monies for religious purposes, as nothing in the Act justified a presumption that the FBOs could not implement the grants in a secular manner. Thus, there was nothing inherently or specifically religious, the Court indicated, about the social services that the faith-based grantees provided to teens with premarital sexuality questions or problems. Because the Act did not favor any single religious group or religion in general, it did not have the effect of endorsing a religious view of teenage pregnancy and premarital relations, even though participation by FBOs was specifically mentioned. The majority refused to invalidate the Act on the theory that any participation of FBOs in a public sector program created a "symbolic link" between government and religion.

Furthermore, allowing religious organizations to participate as eligible grantees did not impermissibly promote religion unless a significant portion of the funds flowed to "pervasively sectarian" institutions. Although the financial assistance took the form of direct cash grants, the Establishment Clause was not violated so long as the statute did not indicate that a large proportion of the funds would go to "pervasively sectarian" organizations. The majority did not regard the faith-based teen counseling centers that received grants as any more likely to be pervasively sectarian than the higher education institutions for whom public funds had been approved, for instance, the private colleges in *Roemer*. Furthermore, in a nod to separationist theory, the religious grantees under the Act could separate their secular and sacred aspects.

Even if the beliefs of some religious organizations and the moral values urged by the Act overlapped, the legislation did not violate the Establishment Clause. As Chief Justice William H. Rehnquist wrote for the majority:

> The facially neutral projects authorized by the [Act]–including pregnancy testing, adoption counseling and referral services, prenatal aid and postnatal care, education services, residential care, child care, consumer education, etc.–are not themselves "specifically religious activities," and they are not converted into such by the fact that they are carried out by organizations with religious affiliations.[19]

Third, although the U.S. Department of Health and Human Services monitored grantees to ensure that federal money was not misappropriated, there were no requirements that the religious grantees follow any federal guidelines regarding the content of the advice given to the teenagers, nor were the grantees forced in any way to modify their programs. Because the religious grantees were presumed not "pervasively sectarian" by the majority, unlike the parochial schools in other cases, the limited federal oversight by a federal agency (including a review of grantee programs and educational materials and on-site visits to clinics or offices where grantees carried out programs) could not be deemed as the excessive entanglement of government and religion. There was, therefore, no need for the government to engage in extensive monitoring of the activities of the FBOs.

The Court distinguished between Establishment Clause challenges to an entire aid program and those to the behavior of specific grantees. Concluding that the program in question as a whole did not present an excessive risk of advancing the interests of sectarian institutions, whose efforts toward the teenagers they counseled were presumed to be secular in orientation, the Court reversed a judgment invalidating the program. It remanded the case in order to determine whether any counseling center grantee was either: "pervasively sectarian" or one that taught religious doctrine to the teens whom it counseled. This type of grant would violate the Establishment Clause by having the effect of advancing religion or giving rise to an excessive entanglement between government and religion, and the lower court was instructed to devise a remedy such that the entire program need not be invalidated.

The Application of Separationist Theory to Charitable Choice

The present (or any expansion of the carefully crafted) Charitable Choice governmental funding mechanism would likely survive challenge under the separationist theory. Let us put together the guidelines provided by *Bowen* and *Agostini* to see how separationists would regard the public funding of faith-based social service providers under Charitable Choice. *Bowen* makes it highly unlikely that the four existing Charitable Choice provisions, as summarized in chapter 6, would, on their face and in their entirety, be invalidated on the grounds that they have the primary effect of advancing religion due to the religious character of potential grantees. *Bowen* suggests that the Establishment Clause will not limit public sector funding of FBOs, at least on the face of the statute, as long as the aid is part of a larger program including nonreligious grantees. Charitable Choice, as we have seen, strives to permit FBOs to compete equally with other nongovernmental providers for federally funded social service contracts.

Beyond a constitutional challenge to the Charitable Choice provisions on their face, it is useful to go through and apply the separationist guidelines of *Agostini*. First, Charitable Choice has a secular purpose. Similarities exist between the Adolescent Family Life Act litigated in *Bowen* and Charitable Choice as both fund federal programs with a secular purpose. In *Bowen*, the Act aimed to provide counseling for teens about the dangers of premarital sex; Charitable Choice seeks to involve a wide range of nongovernmental organizations, sacred and secular, in the provision of specified social services.

In her brief concurring opinion in *Bowen*, Justice O'Connor indicated that it would be far easier to find constitutional the federal funding of programs offering faith-based soup kitchens or hospitals, in contrast to those dealing with the moral issue of teen sexuality. In Justice O'Connor's view, where the object of public assistance addresses the worldly needs of the poor and the sick, such as food, clothing, shelter, and health, a social service program including religious providers is more likely to be constitutional.[20]

Second, Charitable Choice does not have the primary effect of advancing religion. Under the current test for primary effect, as formulated in *Agostini*, we must determine whether a statute results in governmental indoctrination, defines its recipients by religion, or results in excessive government entanglement.

Under Charitable Choice, any religious indoctrination carried out by FBOs cannot be attributed to the government. Charitable Choice specifically prohibits FBOs from using federal funds for inherently religious activities, such as sectarian worship, instruction, or proselytization.[21] Although the FBOs are permitted to display religious art, icons, and scripture,[22] the federal monies support only the secular functions of the social service programs. Additionally, FBOs may maintain separate accounts under the 1996 Charitable Choice provisions[23] (or are required to do so pursuant to subsequent enactments), so that it will be easier to ascertain that federal funds do not support any religious functions. The FBOs are, therefore, allowed to maintain their religious identity, while at the same time meeting the requirements of the Establishment Clause. It is also important to note that federal law requires an independent audit of any group, sacred or secular, that receives government funds, by grant or contract, of $300,000 or more a year,[24] and that federal government rules have developed generally "reliable procedures for segregating program accounts."[25] These procedures prevent direct contract funds from going to impermissible purposes, such as proselytization.

Such an explicit bar on the use of federal funds for worship, prayer, or other inherently religious activities is not even required under *Bowen*. However, the Court noted, "Clearly, if there were such a provision in this statute, it would be easier to conclude that the statute on its face could not be said to have the primary effect of advancing religion...."[26] Justice O'Connor added in her concurring opinion that "*any* use of public funds to promote religious doctrines violates the Establishment Clause."[27] Therefore, it is clear that the Charitable Choice provisions on their face do not result in governmental indoctrination, as they exceed the requirements of *Bowen*.

However, under Charitable Choice what may FBO staff do of a religious nature? FBO staff may still discuss spiritual matters and share their faith when recipients so desire, so long as the discussion is not held during activities funded by the government. They can pray or discuss religious matters with clients after program hours.

A need exists for guidelines to delineate the requirement for secularity in government-funded social service programs together with regulations that define key terms, especially proselytization, instruction, and worship, to help FBOs honor the spirit and the letter of the law and protect them against litigation.[28] For example, religious speech and activities that are incidental and informal ("God bless you") and those that flow from an organization's general mission (e.g., posters with biblical verses) are, in my view, unobjectionable. In contrast, inherently religious speech and activities, such as prayer, devotional Bible reading, religious classes, and the dissemination of booklets laying out a plan for salvation, constitute religious instruction and are impermissible. Similarly proscribed are teachings seeking conversion to a particular faith. In short, FBO staff cannot teach religious tenets on the government clock.

Far more difficult is whether the transmission of virtues with a religious grounding, for instance, citing a biblical text on the need for personal responsibility for one's actions, constitutes religious indoctrination. Also, the line is quite imprecise between creating a warm, nurturing environment where clients feel free to discuss their spiritual questions and needs as opposed to impermissible religious instruction. If a staff social service position joins religious and nonreligious activities, thereby making clear distinctions difficult, to avoid litigation it is best for an FBO to privately fund this position.

The second criterion to determine the effect of a program is whether the program defines recipients by reference to religion. In other words, to pass constitutional muster the program must not create a financial incentive to undertake religious indoctrination.[29]

With Charitable Choice, the federally funded social service programs are available to a broad range of recipients. There are two types of recipients. Both sacred and secular groups are eligible to receive funding. Furthermore, a faith-based provider cannot discriminate against any beneficiary on the basis of religion, religious belief, or a refusal to actively participate in a religious practice.[30] As an FBO's services cannot be provided using a religious litmus test, the ultimate funding recipients are not defined by religion. Aid is offered to beneficiaries without regard to religion. To prevent litigation, an FBO ought not to make religious teaching and activities so integral a part of the social services offered that beneficiaries cannot opt out of the religious dimension without depriving themselves of a program's benefit. Because beneficiaries cannot be forced to participate in religious activities, Charitable Choice funding will not lead to the coercion of anyone to support or participate in religion or its exercise. Also, direct funding does not indicate government support and approval for religion in general or a particular religion. There is no appearance of the endorsement of religion.

Charitable Choice also includes a safeguard for the rights of recipients, whereby a beneficiary may object to the religious character of a social services provider. Given such an objection, the public sector (or the sectarian provider in the Charitable Choice version contained in the Consolidated Appropriations Act of 2001) must provide alternative services available within the same geographical area to the individual within a reasonable period of time.[31] (The alternative need not be secular unless a secular alternative is the only one acceptable to the beneficiary.)

Compliance with this requirement may, however, prove difficult. In urban areas, transportation is an important consideration. Additionally, shifting programs, e.g., going from one substance abuse program to another, may be difficult to arrange or involve starting over in a secular program. The problem may be even more acute in rural areas, where the number of programs available may be limited.

However, the teaching of *Bowen* requires detailed fact-finding as to noncompliance with the statutory requirement, not the mere assertion of hypothetical difficulties, so long as a statute is neutral on its face. Where a statute provides that no beneficiary will be forced to receive social service benefits from a faith-based provider, a challenge on the basis of governmental indoctrination is barred.

A problem may arise, however, when we look at whether Charitable Choice provides an incentive to undertake religion. It is possible that requiring beneficiaries to object to the religious nature of a provider, especially if an FBO is the sole provider awarded a contract, may send a message to those who object "that they are outsiders, not full members of the political community."[32] This problem may be avoided, however, by FBOs notifying beneficiaries of their right to obtain the services from an alternative provider before they begin a program. There is no such requirement in the Charitable Choice provisions contained in the 1996 Welfare Reform Act. However, the failure of the 1996 legislation to contain a notice provision does not constitute a fatal defect. As beneficiaries cannot be forced to participate in any religious activities, there is no explicit coercion or indoctrination.

To prevent constitutional litigation, each FBO offering government-funded social services under the Charitable Choice provisions needs to provide prospective clients with full and clear information: first, a program's religious nature and activities before they enter a program; and second, that they need not participate in any religious activities as a condition of receiving social services. Also, the disclosure requirements should be written into government contracts with FBOs for social services.

Finally, Charitable Choice does not result in excessive government entanglement, the last criterion relevant to determining a statute's effect. Entanglement analysis must consider whether government oversight of Charitable Choice entails excessive intrusion into the operations of FBOs. To avoid "excessive" entanglement, Charitable Choice limits governmental interaction with FBOs. It reduces governmental regulation of sectarian providers first by protecting the institutional autonomy of FBOs from federal, state, and local governments, including protecting an FBO's control over the definition, development, practice, and expression of its religious beliefs.[33] Second, it bars the government from requiring religious providers to change their form of internal governance.[34] Third, it limits the scope of fiscal audits.[35] Some administrative contacts will occur between government and FBOs; however, the interaction is limited to monitoring of funds so that they are not misappropriated and do not go to sectarian activities. If faith-based providers segregate federal and nonfederal funds, as the 1996 version of Charitable Choice allows them to do (or as they are required to do so under subsequent versions), then the risk of excessive entanglement is minimized. If an FBO segregates its accounts, the government may only audit the federally funded accounts, with other accounts shielded from government monitoring, at least under the Charitable Choice provisions. Conversely, despite the 1996 version of Charitable Choice allowing an FBO to separate federal funds into a separate account, some religious providers may commingle federal and nonfederal funds, necessitating a more extensive federal audit of their financial records, thereby increasing the possibility of greater, but probably less than "excessive," entanglement.

To avoid constitutional litigation by minimizing entanglement, each FBO receiving government-funded social service contracts must keep careful records of its expenditures for materials and staff activities that are clearly religious in nature. Each must use private funds to pay for any religious activity and clearly distinguish between a program's government-funded secular components and its privately funded religious components.

Finally, as previously noted, Charitable Choice bars FBOs from using public funds for sectarian worship, instruction, or proselytization. Thus, for strict separationists, a faith-based grantee cannot be pervasively sectarian. For them, the core inquiry would focus on an FBO's ability to separate its secular and sacred elements, so that direct public sector aid only flows to its secular aspects. However, the Supreme Court seems to be moving away from a prohibition on government funding of pervasively sectarian organizations.

In *Mitchell v. Helms*,[36] Justice Clarence Thomas, writing for four justices, repudiated the "pervasively sectarian" concept for four reasons. First, "its relevance in our precedents is in sharp decline." Second, "the religious nature of a recipient should not matter to the constitutional analysis, so long as the recipient adequately furthers the government's secular purpose." Third, "the inquiry into the recipient's religious views required by a focus on whether a school is pervasively sectarian is not only unnecessary but offensive." Finally, "hostility to aid to pervasively sectarian schools has a shameful pedigree that we do not hesitate to disavow."[37] However, it is important to note that Justice Thomas' opinion was only joined by a plurality of four justices. The concurring justices, although not joining in this overt repudiation, refused to accept such categorization and approved public aid to sectarian schools for secular educational purposes. Thus, for a current majority of the Court the question of whether a recipient organization is pervasively sectarian no longer is a determinative factor.

Discrimination by FBOs in Employment Practices

Religious discrimination in the employment practices of FBOs poses one of the greatest threats to Charitable Choice, from both a constitutional and a policy perspective. Charitable Choice exempts faith-based providers from the general ban on discrimination in employment practices.[38] Thus, under the current provisions, there is nothing to prevent an FBO from subjecting all employees to a "religious litmus test," whether or not employees are involved with the group's religious functions. To begin our discussion of how much autonomy an FBO, receiving public funding for its social service programs, has in implementing employment practices in an effort to fulfill its mission, consider a specific situation not involving Charitable Choice.

Alicia Pedreira was fired in 1998 by the Kentucky Baptist Homes for Children (KBHC), after it became known that she was a lesbian. Pedreira, who completed a degree in expressive therapy, was approached regarding an opening at Spring Meadows Children's Home, a branch of the KBHC. Although Pedreira was concerned because the year before KBHC "had boycotted Disney for offering benefits to gays and lesbians,"[39] Pedreira applied for the therapist position. During one of her interviews, Pedreira told Jack Cox, the clinical director of Baptist Homes, that she was a lesbian. Cox then told her it would not be a problem so long as she kept the matter to herself.

Unfortunately, although Pedreira told only a few people at work about her sexual orientation, a photo taken of Pedreira and her partner during a 1997 AIDS Walk was entered into a state fair art competition. Within a few weeks, word of the photograph circulated in the office and Pedreira was fired. The notice she received indicated that she was terminated from KBHC "because her admitted homosexual lifestyle is contrary to [KBHC's] core values." KBHC then issued a public statement with respect to her termination that "it is important that we stay true to our Christian values. Homosexuality is a lifestyle that would prohibit employment." KBHC requires all its employees to "exhibit values in their professional conduct and personal lifestyles that are consistent with the Christian mission and purpose of the institution."[40]

In response to urging from friends and family, the American Civil Liberties Union filed suit on her behalf, claiming that KBHC, which received more than three-quarters of its money from the state, had engaged in religious discrimination. Plaintiffs also argued that because KBHC received the bulk of its funding from the government, KBHC's discriminatory employment practices violated the Establishment Clause.

However, a federal judge ruled that KBHC did not violate federal or state civil rights laws when it fired Pedreira. The court held that KBHC could dismiss Pedreira based on its "behavioral code" for employees that stemmed from Baptist beliefs and that at no time were her religious freedoms violated by the code.[41]

Charitable Choice, The Civil Rights Act of 1964, and the Exemption for Religious Groups

Title VII of the Civil Rights Act of 1964 makes it unlawful for employers to discriminate with respect to hiring, discharge, compensation, terms, conditions, or privileges of employment because of an individual's race, color, religion, sex, or national origin.[42] Congress, however, enacted a special exemption from Title VII. This exemption, set forth in Section 702 of the Act, allows religious organizations to exercise religious preferences when making employment decisions.[43] Section 702 is designed to limit governmental interference with religious organizations' definition and implementation of their missions.

Without some sort of an exemption for religious organizations, the general proscription of discrimination could hinder the ability of FBOs to choose their own staff. In order to preserve their religious autonomy, the Civil Rights Act of 1964 allows religious organizations to engage in discriminatory hiring (and firing).[44]

This exemption remains unaffected by Charitable Choice and, thus, it is useful to take a look at its evolution. In 1964, the House of Representatives passed a bill containing a broad exemption excluding religious employers from the proposed Civil Rights Act.[45] The Senate substitute bill contained a more limited exemption allowing a religious organization to employ individuals of a particular religion only if they performed work connected with the organization's religious activities.[46] The Senate and House passed this substitute bill. Thus, in its original form, Section 702 allowed religious organizations to exercise religious preferences only in employment decisions affecting their religious activities.

A 1972 amendment eliminated this qualification, allowing religious preference to play a role in all of an FBO's activities, not just its religious activities. It now provides: "This subchapter shall not apply to... a religious corporation, association, educational institution, or society with respect to the employment of individuals of a particular religion to perform work connected with the carrying on by such corporation, association, educational institution, or society of its activities."[47] Thus, at least with some aspects of the employment relationship, Congress decided that the free exercise rights of an FBO outweigh the free exercise rights of an employee or prospective employee.

In 1972, some senators proposed that religious employers be removed from the jurisdiction of the U.S. Equal Employment Opportunity Commission, but the Senate rejected these proposals.[48] The subsequent Senate proposals[49] broadened the scope of the exemption to cover employees who performed nonreligious activities so as to create communities faithful to their religious principles. However, a section-by-section Congressional analysis of the statute concluded that religious employers remain "subject to the provisions of Title VII with regard to race, color, sex, or national origin."[50]

The Employment Exemption for
Religious Groups Held Constitutional

Ordinarily, FBOs can condition employment on an applicant's religion because these institutions are exempt from Title VII of Civil Rights Act of 1964. In *Corporation of the Presiding Bishop v. Amos*,[51] a unanimous Supreme Court upheld this statutory exemption, allowing the employment practices of religious organizations to favor their own adherents. The case concerned a church-sponsored Mormon recreational center and its firing of a maintenance worker who was discharged after not qualifying for a temple certificate stating that he was a member of the Mormon Church and eligible to attend its temples.

The Justices seemed to believe that the Free Exercise Clause of the First Amendment supported an exemption for at least some employment practices by religious organizations. In holding that the exemption did not violate the Establishment Clause, the Court followed the separationist model. Justice Byron R. White's analysis focused on the then-prevailing three-part *Lemon* test. The test for a secular purpose was satisfied because Congress sought to minimize governmental interference with the ability of religious organizations to define and carry out their missions. The third requirement, that a law not impermissibly entangle church and state, was met because Section 702 effectuated a more complete separation of church and state by avoiding an intrusive inquiry into religious belief.

The second requirement, often the most important consideration, focused on whether the statute in question had the primary effect of advancing or inhibiting the practice of any particular religion. Justice White stated that for a law to have such an effect, "it must be fair to say that the *government itself* has advanced religion through its own activities and influence."[52] This prong was not implicated in *Amos* because the exemption did not provide a special benefit for employees with certain religious beliefs or impose a burden on nonreligious persons. The Court held that the enactment of legislation exempting religious organizations from the provisions of Title VII, even for their secular activities, thereby allowing faith-based groups to act on their religious beliefs, did not violate the second element of the *Lemon* test.

The Court gave great deference to the creation by Congress of statutory exemptions for religious organizations based on the Free Exercise Clause. The government can therefore lift a regulation burdening the exercise of religion without providing a similar benefit to secular entities. The Court also held that the government did not violate the Establishment Clause when it refrained from imposing a burden on religion, although it imposed the same burden on the nonreligious that were similarly situated. Because the statute was neutral with respect to the benefits accorded various religions, the Court, applying a rational relationship test, held that it was not subject to strict scrutiny.

Justice Brennan, in a concurring opinion joined by Justice Thurgood Marshall, expressed concern that a categorical exemption for secular activities of FBOs would extend a preference to religious organizations.[53] He recognized that extending the exemption to cover secular activities would cause an unnecessary infringement of individual free exercise rights. However, Brennan believed that the exemption was preferable to excessive governmental entanglement in religious affairs. He reasoned that if the government attempted to distinguish between sacred and secular activities, the free exercise rights of religious organizations would be chilled.

In *Amos*, the justices recognized possible limitations on religious autonomy if FBOs could not hire (or fire) on the basis of religious beliefs and membership—even for the position of a maintenance worker. The Court seemed to acknowledge and accept the importance of religious autonomy in employment practices because it aids in the pursuit of an FBO's goals and mission, regardless of the nature of the activities involved.

Interpreting the Scope of the Employment Exemption for FBOs

Today, the key unresolved question is the scope of the employment discrimination exemption for FBOs, not its existence in general. Courts apply the Title VII exemption differently depending on whether the employment decision involves pastoral staff or other employees. Although the literal statutory language makes no distinction based on an employee's activities, courts differentiate between clergy and nonclergy.

With regard to employment decisions involving pastoral staff, courts have held that the Free Exercise Clause requires a complete exemption from Title VII's restrictions. The ministerial exception represents a judicially developed legal rule. For example, in *McClure v. Salvation Army*,[54] the Fifth Circuit upheld the district court's dismissal of a complaint by a Salvation Army minister who charged that the defendant discriminated on the basis of sex, thus violating Title VII. Because the consideration of matters involving the church-pastor relationship would plunge the state into the internal affairs of religion, that would lead to excessive entanglement, the court found that the exemption protected all aspects of this relationship, even those not based on religious doctrine. More recently, in *EEOC v. Catholic University of America*,[55] the court barred a claim that the university engaged in sex discrimination by not granting tenure to a nun in its employ. The university's motives were irrelevant once the court determined that the decision involved a pastoral appointment.

Thus, religious organizations have a free exercise right to determine the qualifications and compensation for their clergy without governmental regulation. Otherwise, the state would infringe on religious autonomy. The government cannot require FBOs to change their pastoral employment practices, without encroaching on their religious freedom protected by the Free Exercise Clause.

With respect to nonpastoral positions, the right of religious organizations to be free from governmental interference has not been viewed as sufficiently compelling to offset an individual's right to be free from employment discrimination based on race, sex, national origin, disability, or age, at least apart from religiously based beliefs and practices. For instance, in *EEOC v. Pacific Press Publishing Association*,[56] the court narrowly construed the exemption for religious organizations under Title VII. In its view, the 1972 amendment only slightly broadened the exemption, holding it did not "broadly exempt[ ] religious organizations from charges of discrimination based on nonreligious grounds." As the court explained, "Congress [has] consistently rejected proposals to allow religious employers to discriminate on grounds other than religion...."[57] Thus, for nonclergy positions, religious employers are only exempt from Title VII when making faith-based employment decisions. Religious employers remain liable under Title VII if their employment practices are based on a prohibited classification—race, gender, national origin, disability, or age. Accordingly, a state appeals court ruled against a Christian school that refused to hire women with small children for a nonpastoral position.[58] The court concluded that the employment limitations mandated by a state civil rights act did not violate the school's First Amendment rights.

Conversely, in *Little v. Wuerl*,[59] the Third Circuit read the exemption broadly, "persuaded that Congress intended the explicit exemptions to Title VII to enable religious organizations to create and maintain communities composed solely of individuals faithful to their doctrinal practices, whether or not every individual plays a direct role in the organization's 'religious activities.'"[60] The court concluded that a parochial school in discharging a teacher, Catholic or non-Catholic, who publicly engaged in conduct regarded by the school as inconsistent with its religious principles did not violate Title VII's general prohibition against religious discrimination.

Little was a Protestant teacher at a Catholic school. She sued under Title VII when the school failed to renew her contract. Little did not teach religion, but attended and participated in ceremonies and programs intended to strengthen the Catholic values of the school's students. Although Little was a tenured teacher, the annual contracts contained a clause giving the school the right to dismiss a teacher for serious public immorality, public scandal, or public rejection of the official teachings, doctrines, or laws of the Roman Catholic Church.

Little was married when hired. She then divorced and was remarried by a justice of the peace to a second husband, a baptized but nonpracticing Catholic. When Little tried to renew her contract, she was told she would not be renewed because she did not obtain an annulment prior to her second marriage.

The Third Circuit read the exemption broadly to cover nonclergy positions. It maintained that judicial attempts to forbid religious discrimination against nonministerial employees, where the position has any religious significance, is constitutionally suspect, if not forbidden. The court concluded that the exemption permitted a religious organization to discriminate in hiring and firing based on whether an employee's beliefs and conduct are consistent with her employer's religious precepts. It also reasoned that applying the general antidiscrimination provision Title VII to the school's decision would create excessive governmental entanglement with religion in violation of the last prong of the *Lemon* test because of the nature of administrative inquiries.

Courts are careful not to tread too closely on the free exercise of religious entities' beliefs. In this context, a court's role is limited to evaluating the reason offered by an FBO. The fact finder's normal latitude to infer pretext when the stated reason is implausible or absurd may not be constitutionally allowed if a religious purpose is offered.

Thus, if an employment practice is religiously based and is not a facade, courts generally give an FBO the benefit of the exemption. The court in *Little* required a showing that a defendant's employment practices were religiously based. Once it met this requirement, the employer fell under the exemption and judicial scrutiny of the employment practice in question ended. Also, if an FBO presents evidence that the challenged employment practice resulted from religious belief, then the exemption likely deprives the U.S. Equal Employment Opportunity Commission of jurisdiction to investigate further to determine whether religion was a pretext for another form of discrimination.

In a litigation context, the key question focuses on the showing an FBO must make to sustain its discriminatory practices. If an FBO must present a compelling reason, this may be difficult, but not impossible, for non-clergy social service positions.

Public Sector Funding of FBOs
Using Discriminatory Employment Practices

The constitutionality of discriminatory employment practices in government-funded programs, although specifically protected by Charitable Choice, may be called into question by the case of *Dodge v. Salvation Army*.[61] The court in *Dodge* distinguished *Bishop v. Amos* and held that a church violated the Establishment Clause by a discriminatory discharge on the basis of religion in a program funded substantially by the federal government. The *Dodge* case provides a warning with respect to the employment practices of FBOs receiving public funding.

The Salvation Army in Pascagoula, Mississippi, received public funding for a domestic violence shelter and hired Jamie Dodge as a Victims' Assistance Coordinator. The position involved contacts with victims of abuse and violence to whom the Salvation Army sought to minister. Her duties included interviewing domestic violence victims, helping them, and assisting with community education, as well as providing for shelter residents' special needs. It did not involve routine, discretionary tasks, such as clerical work, but rather required working with and counseling beneficiaries as well as serving as a representative of the Salvation Army, an evangelical Protestant group.

Dodge had indicated she was Catholic, but after about a year, the Salvation Army discovered that Dodge was a devotee of the ancient, pagan religion of Wicca. The Salvation Army fired her, maintaining that a believer in Wicca was inconsistent with her working as a counselor in a Christian organization, and also because she made unauthorized use of an office photocopy machine to reproduce cultic materials.

Dodge filed a complaint with the U.S. Equal Employment Opportunity Commission and later brought suit in federal court, claiming religious discrimination and that the Title VII exemption for religious organizations should not apply because her salary was substantially funded by a federal grant.

The district court ruled that because the Salvation Army received substantial public funds in support of Dodge's position at its Domestic Violence Center, it had no legal right to dismiss her. The court stated: "... on the facts in the present case, the effect of the government substantially, but not exclusively, funding a position such as the Victims' Assistance Coordinator and then allowing the Salvation Army to choose the person to fill or maintain the position based on religious preference clearly has the effect of advancing religion and is unconstitutional." The Salvation Army's receipt of public funds was viewed as controlling by Judge Dan M. Russell, Jr. He noted: "the benefits received by the Salvation Army were not indirect or incidental. The grants constituted direct financial support in the form of a substantial subsidy, and therefore to allow the Salvation Army to discriminate on the basis of religion, concerning the employment of the Victims' Assistance Coordinator, would violate the Establishment Clause of the First Amendment...." The court held that the Salvation Army, in dismissing Dodge, violated the second and third prongs of the *Lemon* test. First, the filling or maintaining of the government-funded position based on religious preference constituted the advancement of religion. Second, it ran the danger of excessive government entanglement with religion. The court also ruled that by virtue of accepting public money to help fund one of its programs, the Salvation Army gave up its religious autonomy. The Salvation Army settled the case with Dodge without taking an appeal.

There are several answers to the holding in *Dodge*, seemingly mandating that if an FBO receives public finds it must give up hiring only persons of a particular religious belief. Subject to certain limitations, the receipt of public funds should not force an FBO to surrender its religious autonomy. First, under a literal reading of Section 702, the source of funding does not impact on the exemption.[62]

Second, the receipt of substantial government funding by a FBO in general, or for a specific position, does not bring about a waiver of the exemption.[63] Thus, the statutory religious staff protection is available irrespective of whether an FBO receives federal funds.

Third and most importantly, only a compelling governmental interest, such as eliminating racial, ethnic, or gender discrimination, should be able to trump the exemption. Under the principle of religious autonomy, a regulation may not burden the free exercise of religion unless the government has a compelling interest in the subject matter of the regulation.[64] In reaching a decision on the scope of the exemption as applied to religious discrimination by FBOs against nonclergy employees, courts will likely balance the magnitude of the impact on the free exercise of religious belief against the existence of a compelling governmental interest justifying the burden imposed on the free exercise of religious belief. In undertaking the balancing, courts will likely strive to protect FBOs against governmental encroachment into their internal management.[65]

Generally speaking, if an FBO presents evidence of a religious reason (or reasons) for a nonclergy employment decision, most courts will likely go no further. With the exception of religiously based employment practices based on race, national origin, age,[66] disability,[67] and to a large degree, gender (including pregnant women and those with small children), where a strong public consensus exists outweighing the free exercise rights of a religious group, an FBO retains discretion as to whom it will employ in a nonclergy position to fulfill its mission. However, an FBO may engage in gender discrimination based on religious belief at least with respect to gender-based role distinctions. That leaves sexual orientation.

I personally find reprehensible and unfair employment discrimination based on sexual orientation. However, eliminating discrimination based on a sexual orientation or gender identity does not yet, in my opinion, rise to the level of a compelling state interest. Thus, an FBO may maintain its religious identity, enabling it to attract dedicated, devoted staff who seek work for an organization as a mission and a means to live out their faith. The Supreme Court's five to four decision in *Boy Scouts of America v. Dale*,[68] determining that the Scouts can ban homosexuals as scout leaders because it conforms to the group's "expressive message," reinforces this conclusion. According to the majority, forcing the Scouts to hire someone who rejects its values would turn the group into something it is not.

Sexual orientation is not mentioned in the general prohibition contained in Title VII. Although the federal government[69] and some state governments prohibit discrimination on the basis of sexual orientation for public positions, and numerous states, cities, and counties[70] bar such discrimination in the private sector, no federal statute currently bars employment discrimination in the private sector against homosexuals. The federal interest in removing employment discrimination against gays and lesbians is not clearly established, at the present time, and as such does not qualify as a compelling interest justifying this burden on the free exercise of an organization's religious beliefs. Subject to existing state and local anti-discrimination laws, if an employee's (or prospective employee's) homosexual lifestyle is in violation of an FBO's religious beliefs and practices, courts, at least for the immediate future, will likely protect an organization's religious autonomy and the free exercise of its religious beliefs–the FBO's ability to define itself and its existence as religious entity–at the expense of individual freedom of choice and autonomy, thereby foreclosing certain employment opportunities.

Yet a paradox exists. If a faith-based social service provider performs secular functions clearly separable from its religious activities and receives direct public funding for these endeavors, how can an FBO defend its practice of hiring its own religious believers to perform these secular functions? In other words, if an FBO's program or activity is secular in nature, why require a fellow believer to participate in running or operating it?

However, if an FBO can no longer define itself by hiring staff in agreement with its religious beliefs, its effectiveness as a source of help and guidance may be reduced. Worldly assistance in combating poverty and, more generally, enhancing virtue depends on an FBO's ability to maintain its spiritual identity and religious vision, to pursue religious cohesion, and to promote certain values among its employees. It may want to continue to draw on spiritual motivation and to surround its staff with those who reinforce their faith. It may seek to continue to maintain ties to believers and provide a vehicle for that group's generosity. In short, a religious litmus test for employment will advance an FBO's mission and bolster its sacred tradition.

Also, activities that appear nonreligious to the government may be vital to an organization's religious mission. From the perspective of an FBO and its staff, the group may be a ministry guided by faith to meet basic human needs and inspire virtue.

The religious belief system of an employee, even in a secular program, can make a difference. Committed to a cause, staff work for less than they could earn in the public sector or the corporate world. They approach their work as a religiously motivated calling. Thus, preserving an FBO's religious identity helps solidify the sense of community and its religious essence on which the success of a group's social service efforts may depend.

Except for clearly defined classifications, specifically, race, national origin, age, disability, and to a large degree, gender, courts will likely continue to allow FBOs to define themselves through employment practices for nonclergy in social service positions in ways consistent with their respective religious doctrines. With respect to hiring and firing, an FBO needs to be free to be what its religious-shaped belief system says it should be. Courts will likely hesitate to force an FBO to engage in actions its conscience tells it is wrong. The government's long arm ought not to reach that far into an FBO's internal affairs, inhibiting an organization's autonomy and entangling the government in religious affairs. Without the general ability to discriminate (subject to certain parameters) in hiring and firing staff, FBOs would lose the right to define their missions. However, FBOs cannot use religion as a means to discriminate on grounds of race, national origin, age, disability, and for most purposes, gender.

The Emerging Equal Treatment Concept

The competing neutrality or equal treatment view has emerged in several recent Supreme Court cases. Under this view, the Establishment Clause has the narrower purpose of forbidding the government from establishing a national church or preferring one religion over another. This view, looking to freedom for many religions, not freedom from all religion, rejects the proposition that the Establishment Clause prevents the government from assisting religion generally under neutral programs. Proponents of the equal treatment view see it as unjust and irrational to discriminate against religion and religious providers. The public sector, under this concept, cannot favor or disfavor religion.

The equal treatment view is relevant for FBOs receiving government assistance because it would allow aid to flow directly to religious institutions. The equal treatment concept allows the public sector to develop partnerships with religious groups provided it evaluates them on the basis of their nonreligious benefits. The government can provide direct assistance to an FBO that turns criminals into good citizens, even if, under an expansive interpretation, it does so by trying to save them. Conversely, the government cannot favor an FBO merely because it leads citizens to "salvation."

The equal treatment theory is based, in part, on a revised historical understanding of the Establishment Clause. In his dissenting opinion to *Wallace v. Jaffree*,[71] then Justice William H. Rehnquist directly attacked the separationist history at the heart of the *Everson* case. He argued that the original intent of the Establishment Clause was to forbid Congress from designating any church as "a national church" and from enacting laws that preferred one religious sect or denomination over another. Justice Rehnquist concluded, "As its history abundantly shows, however, nothing in the Establishment Clause requires government to be strictly neutral between religion and non-religion, nor does the Clause prohibit Congress or the States from pursuing legitimate secular ends through nondiscriminatory sectarian means."[72]

Although Rehnquist failed to persuade a majority in *Wallace* to accept his concept of nonpreferentialism, he succeeded in casting doubt on the "official" history of the Establishment Clause. His historical interpretation also provides the basis for the equal treatment of direct public aid programs that include sectarian social service providers.

Equal Treatment Gains Acceptance

The demand by student religious clubs to gather on school premises on an equal level with other student groups sparked a significant shift to the equal treatment position by the Supreme Court. In *Widmar v. Vincent*,[73] the Court, in an eight to one decision, held that a state university could not exclude a student Bible study group from access to university meeting facilities, otherwise made available generally to registered student groups, when the facilities were not used for other purposes. When a public institution creates a limited public forum open to student expression, it cannot exclude religious groups without violating their First Amendment rights of free speech and association. The university's action overstepped the requirement of content neutrality, and thus, religiously oriented student groups were entitled to access university facilities equal to that offered groups with a nonreligious character, absent a compelling state interest.

The Supreme Court reasoned that if the property is provided under a religion-neutral equal access policy, the benefit to the religious group is incidental and there is no appearance that the university is endorsing the group's religious views. An open forum at a public university does not confer the imprimatur of state approval on any group's religious beliefs or practices. Furthermore, the Establishment Clause would not be violated if the government provides a meeting space that enriches the marketplace for ideas.

Similarly, in *Lamb's Chapel v. Center Moriches Union Free School District*,[74] the Court struck down a combination of state law and school district restrictions denying a religious group access to public school premises outside school hours. The property was otherwise made available for social, civic, or recreational purposes but a bright line rule explicitly excluded religious use. The school district denied a request from Lamb's Chapel, an evangelical church in the community, to use a school auditorium in the evening to present a series of religiously oriented films and lectures on the subject of family values and child rearing, even though the district had permitted nonreligious organizations to use the facilities for similar purposes. The film series the church wanted to show was to be open to all and there was no indication that the series was a "front" for a worship service.

The Court held that the exclusion violated the church's First Amendment rights of speech and assembly, rejecting the school district's defense that the Establishment Clause compelled it to deny access to religious groups. The Court found the denial of access to be in violation of viewpoint neutrality, that is, an exclusion of a group because of its religious viewpoint. The Court ruled that there was no Establishment Clause violation because, as in *Widmar*, once a school has created a limited public forum, it must grant access to that forum on a neutral basis. Furthermore, there is no danger that the community would perceive the school district as endorsing the views of the religious group. The significance of *Lamb's Chapel* is the Court's explicit reliance on equal access in its analysis, as opposed to relying on separationism, and holding that any benefit to religion would be incidental.

In *Rosenberger v. Rector and Visitors of the University of Virginia*,[75] the Court held that the Establishment Clause did not compel a state university to bar funding for a religiously oriented student publication when such aid was provided under a program available to all bona fide student groups. The majority held that there was no violation of the Establishment Clause when a university granted access on a religion-neutral basis to a wide spectrum of student groups, including those that use the funding for sectarian activities.

A university-recognized student group published "Wide Awake: A Christian Perspective at the University of Virginia," a newspaper that ran stories on contemporary matters of interest to students from a Christian perspective–including racism, homosexuality, and eating disorders. The university provided student newspapers work space and paid the expenses of printing these publications by third-party vendors. Although the printing costs for student publications were generally paid from a fund generated by a student activity fee, the university refused to reimburse the cost of printing "Wide Awake." The refusal stemmed from a policy disqualifying the payment of printing costs for groups promoting a particular belief in or about a deity or an ultimate reality.

The Court ruled in favor of the students and directed the university to treat "Wide Awake" the same as other student publications, without regard to the newspaper's religious perspective. The majority determined that the university had created a limited public forum for student expression on a wide array of topics and that the denial of student activity funds to pay for the cost of printing "Wide Awake" represented discrimination on the basis of the newspaper's religious perspective. Whether a resource is scarce (money) or abundant (classroom meeting space), a university could not dispense its resources on a basis that was discriminatory in terms of viewpoint. Once a state creates a forum, by funding or situs, it cannot discriminate against groups on the basis of their viewpoint. The university's refusal to fund the publication therefore violated the students' free speech rights.

Funding the printing costs would not violate the Establishment Clause because religion was not singled out for favored treatment. The neutrality of the program was an important factor in Establishment Clause analysis.

Under the equal treatment line of reasoning, funding could be extended to the entire spectrum of speech–religious, antireligious, or neither. The majority focused on the fact that the financial support was distributed on a religion-neutral basis: "We have held that the guarantee of neutrality is respected, not offended, when the government, following neutral criteria and evenhanded policies, extends benefits to recipients whose ideologies and viewpoints, including religious ones, are broad and diverse."[76] Thus, the Establishment Clause was not violated when government funding, even to religious groups, benefits the marketplace for ideas. There was no real likelihood of government endorsement or coercion because the student group received an incidental benefit on a religion-neutral basis.

Justice David H. Souter dissented in *Rosenberger*,[77] joined by Justices John Paul Stevens, Ruth Bader Ginsburg, and Stephen Breyer. Regarding a direct assistance program funded by public monies, Justice Souter, following the separationist model, stated that any such program was unconstitutional if it used public monies to fund religious activities, even if the funds were distributed as part of a neutral scheme.

Moving beyond the view that nondiscrimination required by the First Amendment's Free Speech clause supplied the key to victory in *Widmar*, *Lamb's Chapel*, and *Rosenberger*, a majority of Supreme Court justices emphasized the importance of the neutrality principle in deciding Establishment Clause cases in *Mitchell v. Helms*.[78] There, the four-justice plurality opinion stated, "In distinguishing between indoctrination that is attributable to the State and indoctrination that is not, we have consistently turned to the principle of neutrality, upholding aid that is offered to a broad range of groups or persons without regard to their religion....[I]f the Government, seeking to further some legitimate secular purpose, offers aid on the same terms, without regard to religion, to all who adequately further that purpose...then it is fair to say that any aid going to a religious recipient only has the effect of furthering that secular purpose."[79] In her concurring opinion, Justice O'Connor acknowledged that "neutrality is an important reason for upholding Government-aid programs," a reason which the Supreme Court's recent cases have "emphasized...repeatedly."[80]

The Present State of Flux

The foregoing makes clear that the Establishment Clause does not prohibit FBOs from receiving direct government financial assistance. Under separationist theory, such aid is permissible if the legislation has a secular purpose and the aid itself does not promote religion. In determining the objective of an aid program, two key factors are whether the aid is provided through a religiously neutral program and whether the program excessively entangles government and religion.

By contrast, under the emerging equal treatment or neutrality theory, the government can fund a religious organization if the aid is provided through a neutral program. Neutrality forbids governmental hostility to religion. Additionally, neutrality does not require the exclusion of religion from public life, but the accommodation of religion, such that government cannot discriminate between religion and nonreligion or endorse secularism.

The Supreme Court's current approach to Establishment Clause cases is uncertain. Separationism appears to have lost force as the dominant theory but equal treatment has not yet been fully embraced as the best approach for future cases. As developed in this chapter, beginning some twenty years ago, the Supreme Court has appeared to apply the separationist doctrine less strictly or has decided cases without specific reference to the test.

Consonant with current cultural and political trends supporting a greater role for religion in the public square, I favor the equal treatment of religion model as the guiding principle of constitutional interpretation for the direct public funding of FBOs. Under this approach, courts would generally allow the direct public funding of FBOs, through grants or the awarding of contracts, provided public monies support similar programs for both religious and secular groups. It would give all social service providers, sacred or secular, an opportunity to compete for the funding of programs producing specified and accountable outcomes, if provided such programs are open to nonpublic sector grantees. In short, equal treatment is satisfied if a direct assistance program has as its object society's betterment–such as helping the poor and the needy–as long as a program offers a level playing field for all providers, religious and secular.

Equal treatment will facilitate the active role of FBOs, including pervasively sectarian organizations, in the public realm. FBOs would then become full and equal partners with secular groups in nurturing public life; secular ideology would no longer assume hegemony in the public square. By permitting the government to take positive steps to support religious groups, equal treatment protects the freedom and autonomy of all groups, sacred and secular.

Equal treatment would also allow FBOs to participate fully and equally with other groups in America's public life, without shedding or disguising their religious convictions or character. Exclusionary criteria ought not to require FBOs to engage in self-censorship and water down their religious identity as a condition for program participation.

With respect to direct governmental funding of social service programs, we ought not to advantage or disadvantage any organization because of its religious orientation or lack thereof. Equal treatment thus enables the public sector to deal with religious and secular organizations in an even-handed manner. It allows FBOs to have public benefits available to them on the same terms as secular organizations. Discrimination in eligibility to obtain government funding of activities serving the "public good," such as social services, should not exist because both sacred and secular providers promote society's betterment through the delivery of services to their beneficiaries.

When discussing the appropriate model–separationist or equal treatment–for analyzing direct funding of FBOs under Charitable Choice, a degree of realism is in order. Justice O'Connor, currently the decisive voice in Establishment Clause jurisprudence, has repeatedly stated that neutrality alone is not enough to insulate legislation from Constitutional attack. With respect to direct government funding, she has insisted that the rule is "no aid to religion." In her view, an open-ended neutrality rule would allow "the actual diversion of government aid to religious indoctrination."[81] This kind of public subsidy to promote religious doctrines or advance a religious message is inconsistent, she concluded (and a current majority of the Court probably would agree), with the Establishment Clause.

Because truly useful assistance is often religious (as we have seen in chapter 5), equal treatment allows FBOs to integrate religious concepts and themes into their social service programs. In addition to symbolic indications of an organization's religious orientations, e.g., its name, logo, the use of religious pictures or symbols in its facilities, as permitted by Charitable Choice, an FBO receiving direct public funding could offer privately funded religious exercises, such as worship services, having a proselytizing aim, provided attendance at these sacred activities is voluntary, assuming a beneficiary may realistically decline to attend, thereby avoiding coercion. Program participants must also be offered an alternative provider. Moreover, FBOs receiving direct public funding must serve all beneficiaries. Charitable Choice meets these criteria. Subject to these limited conditions, equal treatment would allow FBOs to retain the spiritual character so central to their social missions. Allowing government funds to go to FBOs in a neutral, even-handed manner, provided no public funds go for religious activities, furthermore, in my opinion, poses no realistic danger that the community (or, in litigation, a reasonable observer) would think that the government is endorsing religion.

Under my view of the equal treatment rubric, FBOs would be permitted to favor persons from their own religious tradition in hiring (and firing). It would allow a religious community to define itself by controlling who serves the organization. In order to safeguard free exercise rights, courts ought not to force an FBO to give up its religious distinctiveness as a condition for receiving public funds. Why? An organization's freedom turns on its ability to define its mission according to the dictates of its religious beliefs. However, an FBO could not use its religious beliefs, as previously discussed in this chapter, to implement discriminatory employment practices based on race, national origin, age, disability, and (to a large degree) gender.

Within the general equal treatment framework, several further limits exist. First, the Free Exercise Clause should not permit the funding of programs teaching hatred or intolerance of others, an admittedly difficult inquiry. Apart from groups teaching hatred of others, direct grant programs should not exclude nonmainstream, non-Western FBOs from participation. In broadly welcoming various religions, it is useful to keep in mind what qualifies as a "religion." The Supreme Court, in a 1965 case,[82] involving an individual's request for a draft exemption based on conscientious objector status, defined religion expansively. The Court declared that it would accept "all sincere religious beliefs which are based upon a power or being, or upon a faith, to which all else is subordinate or upon which all else is ultimately dependent."[83]

Second, a need also exists for accountability standards, including financial audits of publicly funded social service programs operated by FBOs.

Third, a governmental unit may create content criteria, neutrally applied, for a program's social service providers, secular and religious. Thus, FBOs as providers of social services must be subject to the same eligibility standards as other nongovernmental providers.

Fourth, the Establishment Clause does not appear to be offended if a general program of direct public aid affects some religious providers more than others (for instance, if some cannot separate out and obtain private funding for their inherently faith-based activities) as long as the disparate impact is unintentional. However, the public sector cannot purposefully discriminate among religious groups.

The Constitutionality of Indirect Funding Mechanisms

It is uncertain how the Supreme Court will treat direct aid programs such as Charitable Choice, addressing the temporal needs of the ultimate beneficiaries for food, clothing, shelter, and health (such as freedom from addictions), made available to an array of providers, secular and sacred. An indirect funding mechanism, such as the use of the income tax system or a voucher program, minimizes the potential for a successful constitutional challenge, even under separationist theory. The United States Supreme Court has held that a government program providing assistance to religious institutions is more likely to satisfy the Establishment Clause where the aid is provided indirectly through third parties, for instance, taxpayers, even though these funding mechanisms help FBOs promote and maintain the spiritual life of beneficiaries.

For over 200 years, religious organizations have received real property tax exemptions. In *Walz v. Tax Commission*,[84] the Court approved the exemption from taxation of real property devoted to religious use. The tax exemption survived the separationist test because of the historical evidence that governmental units since the American Revolution had granted general tax exemptions for nonprofit organizations. The exemption in question also extended to a variety of other nonprofit organizations.

The general tax exemption was found to have a secular purpose and only provided an incidental aid to religion. Drawing on the prevailing image of separation, the *Walz* Court stated: "The exemption creates only a minimal and remote involvement between church and state and far less than taxation of churches. It restricts the fiscal relationship between church and state and tends to complement and reinforce the desired separation insulating each from the other."[85] Yet, a tax exemption represents the government's election to leave a religious organization where it is found, as opposed to a tax credit or deduction, which confers a benefit similar to a direct grant to an FBO under a government contract.

In *Mueller v. Allen*,[86] the Court narrowly upheld a state income tax statute allowing a deduction on a neutral basis for tuition and other expenses incurred by parents of both K-12 public and private school students, even though virtually all of the benefits went to parents with children in parochial schools. The Supreme Court noted that the Establishment Clause objections were reduced where state aid to sectarian institutions was channeled through individual parents and became available only as a result of the private choices of numerous families to educate their school-age children privately at religious schools, rather than as the result of explicit state direction.

The majority found the law valid under the three-part *Lemon* test. The state had the secular purpose of improving the education of all young persons in the state. Thus, whether a tax incentive provision extends benefits to a broad group, i.e., all taxpaying parents, represents an important factor in determining the secular impact under an Establishment Clause inquiry.

Neither did the deduction have the primary effect of advancing the sectarian aims of parochial schools. The legislature attempted to equalize the tax burden by allowing parents, whether their children attended public or private schools, to deduct their children's educational expenses. The help was deemed to confer only the most attenuated financial benefit on religious schools. Justice Rehnquist compared this tax aid to the religiously neutral activity of government in providing a forum open to religious and nonreligious speech, previously endorsed in *Widmar v. Vincent*. The majority noted that this type of program eliminated the need for "offensive" monitoring associated with direct aid programs.[87] It concluded that government involvement in audits of deductions to ensure proper tax calculations and the disallowance of deductions for textbooks used to teach religious doctrines did not constitute an "excessive entanglement" between government and religion.

As considered in chapter 7, vouchers enable personal choice by a beneficiary to determine which social service provider receives governmental assistance. The benefit flows primarily to the beneficiaries, not the providers. The Supreme Court has held that the public sector may design programs placing benefits in the hands of individuals who have freedom of choice with respect to a provider. The chosen nongovernmental provider may be sectarian or secular. Any benefit an FBO receives results from a beneficiary's independent choice.

In *Witters v. Washington Department of Services for the Blind*,[88] a rare unanimous church-state opinion delivered by Justice Marshall, the Court upheld a state program giving physically disabled students payments to subsidize their education. The Court concluded that Washington State was free to pay an educational grant to Mr. Witters, a blind benefits claimant, who opted to use the grant at a Protestant college.

The key was the indirect nature of the aid, establishing that the program did not have a religious purpose or the effect of aiding religion. The Court found that there was a secular purpose for the program and that it did not give rise to an impermissible religious effect. The Court relied on Mr. Witter's independent choice to use public sector assistance for a religious purpose that led to public money winding up in the coffers of a religious institution.

In *Zelman v. Simmons-Harris*, the Court upheld the constitutionality of an Ohio school voucher program.[89] Writing for the majority Chief Justice Rehnquist stated: "...the Ohio program is entirely neutral with respect to religion. It provides benefits directly to a wide spectrum of individuals, defined only by financial need and residence in a particular school district.

It permits such individuals to exercise genuine choice among options public and private, secular and religious. The program is therefore a program of true choice."[90]

The Court should uphold a voucher system in the context of a Charitable Choice program. The rationale is twofold. First, the beneficiaries as independent actors, not the government, control the flow of the indirect aid to FBOs. If individuals may freely select faith-based providers, even pervasively sectarian organizations, these private decisions do not represent the governmental establishment of religion.[91] The voucher approach increases the autonomy of the ultimate beneficiaries by providing a range of choices. The public sector remains basically passive with respect to any individual's decision. As the Court noted in *Zelman*, "The incidental advance of a religious mission, or the perceived endorsement of a religious message, is reasonably attributable to the individual recipient, not to the governments, whose role ends with the disbursement of benefits."[92]

Second, the indirect nature of the assistance, channeled through numerous individual beneficiaries, reduces church-state interaction and thus the need for any public regulatory oversight. The enhanced nonentanglement provides a bulwark against successful constitutional challenge, even if faith-based providers are not restricted as to their religious activities, provided an FBO does not: engage in discrimination with respect to its clientele[93] or teach hatred or intolerance of others. Furthermore, the social service activities of a faith-based provider must remain subject to accountability standards, including a financial audit of these voucher-funded activities.

One major caveat must be noted with respect to the use of vouchers (although the extent to which *Bowen* eliminates or lessens these problems is unclear). If only nonpublic sector providers are eligible to deliver social services, and if all of these providers are faith-based, then the program will be overturned as failing to provide genuine opportunities to select secular options and thus as having a primary religious effect. In other words, neutrality must exist between faith-based and secular providers in the mix of groups eligible to receive and redeem vouchers with the recipients empowered to direct the aid to institutions of their own choosing. In short, the focus is on neutrality and private choice.

Unleashing personal religious choice allows each religion and various faith-based social service providers to compete for clients and to flourish or wither according to their own appeal. From a public finance perspective, a voucher system likely will reduce costs by creating a competitive market for services offered by various providers–public, secular, and religious.

State Constitutional Issues

Even if a program of direct or indirect aid successfully negotiates the First Amendment of the U.S. Constitution, claims may arise under state constitutional law, especially those that are stringently separationist. Some state constitutions bar the use of public funds to aid a religious institution or purpose. A few constitutions explicitly prohibit both direct and indirect assistance.[94] Thus, based on these state constitutional provisions, state legislatures may attempt to exclude faith-based social service providers from a voucher program.

Charitable Choice avoids a conflict between federal law and state constitutions. The 1996 version provides: "Nothing in this section shall be construed to preempt any provision of a State constitution or State statute that prohibits or restricts the expenditure of State funds in or by religious organizations."[95]

This provision permits the segregation of federal and state funds. If a direct assistance or voucher program uses and distributes federal funds, then the federal standard will apply. A state may decide to use only state funds and open its direct aid or voucher program to qualified social service providers, except faith-based providers. In other words, a state may choose to spend its funds according to its own rules.

If a conflict exists between either: (1) federal law (if, for instance, Charitable Choice did not contain the nonpreemption provision) or the U.S. Constitution, and (2) a state constitution, then federal law or the U.S. Constitution takes precedence and preempts a state constitutional provision. The Supremacy Clause of the U.S. Constitution (Article VI) expressly mandates: "This Constitution, and the Laws of the United States which shall be made in Pursuance thereof...shall be the supreme Law of Land; and the Judges in every State shall be bound thereby, any Thing in the Constitution or Laws of any State to the Contrary notwithstanding." Thus, a federal law such as Charitable Choice could preempt a state constitutional provision, if Congress chose to do so, which it has not.

Thus, if a social service program is federally funded or federal revenues are shared with a state, federal legislation, as enacted by Congress, may preempt state constitutional provisions. Also, the U.S. Constitution requires a state to extend eligibility to faith-based providers, even if it uses only state funds to create a direct assistance or voucher program. Excluding religious providers because of a state constitutional provision likely violates the neutrality principle of the Establishment Clause mandating nonhostility toward religion and the Free Speech Clause prohibiting viewpoint discrimination, previously discussed in this chapter.

The U.S. Constitution preempts state constitutional provisions in this context, barring a state, pursuant to its constitution, from excluding religious social service providers from a directly funded or a voucher program. The state must treat all nonpublic sector social service providers equally. By prohibiting faith-based groups from participating in a direct aid or voucher program, a state penalizes religious organizations in the market for social service providers.

If a state creates an incentive for religious social service providers to compromise or abandon their views so as to receive direct aid or vouchers, a state inhibits and interferes with religion in a hostile, nonneutral manner. Furthermore, a state's refusal to allow individuals to redeem vouchers with faith-based social services providers because of their religious character would send a message that the government disfavors religion and endorses nonreligion. The exclusion of all faith-based providers would communicate that these organizations are inferior because of their religious viewpoint.

The rigid separationist theory seems to be fading, with religious neutrality coming to predominate. The emerging equal treatment doctrine suggests a more permissive attitude to direct public sector funding of FBOs. Under this theory, if a governmental unit delegates social service activities to private sector providers, it must allow secular and sectarian organizations to compete for contracts (or receive grants) on equal terms. These nongovernmental providers must meet all relevant procurement procedures and performance standards.

A program of public funding, such as Charitable Choice, can exempt FBOs from certain regulatory burdens, such as employment practices based on religious beliefs, except for race, national origin, age, disability, and to a large degree, gender discrimination, that would frustrate or compromise their religious character. Allowing faith-based groups to define themselves as they see fit upholds their right to freely exercise their religious beliefs and fulfill their sacred missions.

Indirect programs taking the form of enhanced tax incentives for charitable giving or a voucher program, subject to certain conditions, should not run afoul of either the separationist or equal treatment theories.

Notes

1.   I have drawn on Jeffrey Rosen, "Is Nothing Secular?" *New York Times Magazine*, January 30, 2000, 40, 42-45; Jeffrey Rosen, "Why the Catholic Church Shouldn't Have To

Hire Gays," *The New Republic*, February 26, 2001, 16-17; Carl H. Esbeck, "A Constitutional Case For Government Co-operation With Faith-Based Social Service Providers," *Emory Law Journal* 46:1 (Winter 1997): 1-41; Stephen V. Monsma, *When Sacred and Secular Mix: Religious Nonprofit Organizations and Public Money* (Lanham, Md.: Rowman & Littlefield, 1996), 29-46, 147-170.

2. 330 US 1 (1947).

3. *Ibid.* at 15-16 (quoting *Reynolds v. United States*, 98 US 145, 164 (1878)). See also *Ibid.* at 33-43 (Rutledge, J., dissenting) and *Rosenberger v. Rector and Visitors of University of Virginia*, 515 US at 868-872 (1995) (Souter, J., dissenting).

4. 330 US at 18.

5. 370 US 421 (1962).

6. *School District v. Schempp*, 374 US 203 (1963).

7. *Lee v. Weisman*, 505 US 577 (1992).

8. *Santa Fe Independent School District v. Doe*, 530 US 290 (2000).

9. 403 US 602 (1971).

10. *Ibid.* at 612-613.

11. *Ibid.* at 615.

12. 426 US 736 (1976).

13. 473 US 402 (1985).

14. 473 US at 421-431 (O'Connor, J., dissenting).

15. 521 US 203 (1997). In *Mitchell v. Helms*, 530 US 1296 (2000), the Court used the approach in *Agostini* to broaden the forms of public aid that can be provided to religious schools, ruling that governments can lend computers and other instructional materials to parochial schools without violating constitutional principles.

16. 521 US at 234.

17. *Ibid.* at 231.

18. 487 US 589 (1988).

19. *Ibid.* at 613.

20. *Ibid.* at 623 (O'Connor, J., concurring).

21. 42 USC §604a(j). *In Freedom from Religion Foundation, Inc. v. McCallum*, 179 F Supp 2d 950 (W D Wis 2002) the court held that unrestricted, direct funding by the Wisconsin Department of Workforce Development of FaithWorks, a faith-based drug treatment program, violated the Establishment Clause. Relying on evidence of religious indoctrination in the program, the court concluded that the state funding amounted to government-sponsored religious coercion. The court stated that "it is not possible to separate the religious components of the FaithWorks program from its secular ones" and that "the restrictions on FaithWorks' use of the Department of Workforce Development funds are not only not failsafe but completely inadequate." The court stated that the plaintiffs did not challenge the constitutionality of Charitable Choice and thus did not address the issue.

22. 42 USC §604a(d)(2)(A).

23. 42 USC §604(h)(2).

24. 31 USC §7502. Organizations below the $300,000 threshold avoid the audit requirement but must maintain appropriate records. For federal contractor records retention see 48 Code of Federal Regulations 4, 7.

25. John J. DiIulio, Jr., "Know Us By Our Works," *Wall Street Journal*, February 14, 2001, A22.

26. 487 US at 614.

27. *Ibid.* at 623 (O'Connor, J., concurring).

28. Ronald J. Sider and Heidi Rolland Unruh, "Evangelism and Church-State Partnerships," *The Journal of Church and State* 43:2 (Spring 2001): 267-295, at 277-278.

29. 521 US at 231.

30. 42 USC §604a(g).

31. 42 USC §604a(e)(1).

32. *Santa Fe Independent School District v. Doe*, 120 S Ct 2266, 2279 (2000) (quoting *Lynch v. Donnelly*, 465 US at 688 (1984)).

33. 42 USC §604a(d)(1).

34. 42 USC §604a(d)(2)(A).

35. 42 USC §604a(h)(2).

36. 120 S Ct 2530 (2000).

37. *Ibid.* at 2551-2552.

38. 42 USC §604a(f).

39. Eyal Press, "Faith-Based Furor," *New York Times Magazine*, April 1, 2001, 62-65, at 64.

40. *Pedreira v. Kentucky Baptist Homes for Children*, 2001 US Dist LEXIS 10283, 86 Fair Employment Practice Cases (Bureau of National Affairs) 417 (W D Ky 2001).

41. *Ibid.*

42. 42 USC §2000e-2(a)(1).

43. 42 USC §2000e-1(a).

44. 42 USC §604a(f).

45. House Report No. 914, 88th Congress, 1st Session 10 (1963), 1964 U.S. Code, *Congressional & Administrative News* 2391, 2402.

46. 110 Congressional Record S 12807, 12812 (1964).

47. 42 USC §2001e-1.

48. 118 Congressional Record S 1982, 1995 (1972).

49. 118 Congressional Record S 7170 (1972).

50. 118 Congressional Record S 7167 (1972).

51. 483 US 327 (1987).

52. *Ibid.* at 337.

53. *Ibid.* at 340-346 (Brennan, J., concurring).

54. 460 F 2d 553 (5th Cir), cert. denied 409 US 896 (1972).

55. 83 F 3d 455 (D C Cir 1996). See also *Combs v. Central Texas Annual Conference of the United Methodist Church*, 173 F 3d 343 (5th Cir 1999). The ministerial exception also extends to lay employees of religious institutions whose "primary duties consist of teaching, spreading the faith, church governance, supervision of a religious order, or supervision or participation in religious ritual and worship...." *Rayburn v. General Conference of Seventh-Day Adventists*, 772 F 2d 1164, 1169 (4th Cir 1985).

56. 676 F 2d 1272 (9th Cir 1982).

57. *Ibid.* at 1277. In *EEOC v. Fremont Christian School*, 609 F Supp 344 (N D Cal 1984), aff'd 781 F 2d 1362 (9th Cir 1986) the court, in granting the plaintiff's motion for summary judgment, held that the school violated Title VII by providing men health insurance benefits not extended to women. The uncontradicted evidence established that the school's policy was to provide health insurance only to a full-time employee who was the head of the household. The school conclusively presumed this person to be the husband, thereby depriving similarly situated women of health insurance benefits. In affirming summary judgment for the EEOC, the court noted that under Section 702, as amended, religious institutions remain subject to the provisions of Title VII with regard to race, color, sex, or national origin. 781 F 2d at 1366.

58. *McLeod v. Providence Christian School*, 160 Mich App 333, 408 N W 2d 146 (1987). However, in *Dayton Christian Schools v. Ohio Civil Rights Commission*, 766 F 2d 932 (6th Cir 1985), the court held that the school might be immune from a gender discrimination suit when it told a teacher who became pregnant that she could not return to her job because school officials believed that mothers with small children should stay at home. The U.S. Supreme Court reversed and remanded, holding that the federal district court should have abstained from adjudicating the case. 477 US 619 (1986).

59. 929 F 2d 944 (3rd Cir 1991). In *Boyd v. Harding Academy of Memphis, Inc.*, 88 F 3d 410 (6th Cir 1996), the court held that the defendant could lawfully terminate an unmarried teacher after learning of her pregnancy because sex outside of marriage violated the defendant's code of conduct. The defendant, a Christian school, had given each teacher a handbook, providing: "Each teacher at Harding is expected in all actions to be a Christian example for the students...." *Ibid.* at 411.

60. 929 F 2d at 951.

61. 1989 WL 53857, 1989 US Dist LEXIS (S D Miss 1989), 48 Employment Practice Decisions (Commerce Clearing House) ¶38,619.

62. *Arriaga v. Loma Linda University*, 10 Cal App 4th 1556, 13 Cal Rptr 2d 619, 621-622 (1992).

63. *Hall v. Baptist Memorial Health Care Corp.*, 215 F 3d 618, 625 (6th Cir 2000).

64. *Sherbert v. Verner*, 374 US 398, 403, 406-409 (1963). Although the Supreme Court in *Employment Division, Department of Human Resources of Oregon v. Smith*, 494 US 872 (1990) overruled the part of *Sherbert* dealing with a valid and neutral law of general applicability proscribing an individual's religious beliefs, the freedom of an FBO to use religious criteria to select the clergy employees who will carry out its religious mission, subject to a compelling governmental interest test, seemingly remains unimpeded.

65. *EEOC v. Catholic University of America*, 83 F 3d at 461-463. This principle rests on giving churches freedom "to decide for themselves, free from state interference, matters of church government as well as those of faith and doctrine." *Kedroff v. St. Nicholas Cathedral*, 344 US 96, 116 (1952).

66. The Age Discrimination in Employment Act of 1967 prohibits discrimination in public and private employment against individuals who are at least forty years old. 29 USC §621-634. The Age Discrimination Act of 1975 prohibits discrimination on the basis of age in federally assisted programs. 42 USC §§6101-6107.

67. The Americans with Disabilities Act, enacted in 1990, prohibits disability-based disparate treatment. 42 USC §12101-12113. Section 504 of the Rehabilitation Act of 1973 prohibits discrimination under federal grants and programs for otherwise qualified, disabled persons. 29 USC §794.

68. *Boy Scouts of America v. Dale*, 530 US 640 (2000).

69. The Civil Service Reform Act of 1978 (CSRA) bans job discrimination in certain federal employment based on any nonjob-related factor. 5 USC §§7101-7703. In January 1994, the director of the federal Office of Personnel Management stated that the CSRA prohibits discrimination based on sexual orientation. Bureau of National Affairs, *Daily Labor Reports*, February 7, 1994, A-9.

70. State statutes, executive orders, and local ordinances are summarized in *Employment Discrimination Law*, 3d Edition, 2000 Cumulative Supplement (Chicago: American Bar Association, 2000), 290-293.

71. 472 U S at 91-114 (1985) (Rehnquist J., dissenting). See also *Rosenberger v. Rector and Visitors of University of Virginia*, 515 US at 852-859 (Thomas J., concurring). Douglas Laycock, "'Nonpreferential' Aid To Religion: A False Claim About Original Intent," *William and Mary Law Review* 27:5 (1986): 875-941, maintains that the founders rejected federal financial support for churches even if that support were evenhanded and non-preferential.

72. 472 US at 113.

73. 454 US 263 (1981).

74. 508 US 384 (1993). *See also Good News Club v. Milford Central School*, 121 S Ct 2093(2001), holding that a school's exclusion of a Christian children's club from meeting after hours at the school based on its religious nature was unconstitutional viewpoint discrimination.

75. 515 US 819 (1995).

76. *Ibid.* at 839.

77. *Ibid.* at 863-899 (Souter, J., dissenting).

78. 120 S Ct 2530 (2000).

79. *Ibid.* at 2541.

80. *Ibid.* at 2557 (O'Connor, J., concurring).

81. *Ibid.* at 2556-2560.

82. *United States v. Seeger*, 380 US 163 (1965).

83. *Ibid.* at 176. In *International Society for Krishna Consciousness, Inc. v. Barber*, 650 F 2d 430, 440-441 (2d Cir 1981), the Second Circuit relied explicitly on the *Seeger* test in finding Krishna Consciousness a "religion" for free exercise purposes.

84. 397 US 664 (1970).

85. *Ibid.* at 676.

86. 463 US 388 (1983).

87. *Ibid.* at 403.

88. 474 US 481 (1986). In a footnote to one decision, the U.S. Supreme Court previously indicated that educational assistance provisions, such as the G.I. Bill, did not violate the Establishment Clause even if some G.I.s choose to attend church-affiliated colleges. *Committee for Public Education v. Nyquist*, 413 US 756, 782-783 n38 (1973). In *Zobrest v. Catalina Foothills School District*, 509 US 1, 8 (1993), the Court stated that it has "consistently held that government programs that neutrally provide benefits to a broad class of citizens defined without reference to religion are not readily subject to an Establishment Clause challenge just because sectarian institutions may also receive an attenuated financial benefit."

89. 122 S Ct 2460 (2002).

90. *Ibid.* at 2473.

91. *See Siegel v. Truett-McConnell College, Inc.*, 13 F Supp 2d 1335, 1344 (N D Ga 1994), aff'd without opinion, 73 F 3d 1108 (11th Cir 1995).

92. 122 S Ct at 2467.

93. The Supreme Court has upheld the power of the Internal Revenue Service to deny tax exempt status to religious schools that discriminate on the basis of race. In *Bob Jones University v. United States*, 461 US 574 (1983), the Court stated that "the Government has a fundamental, overriding interest in eradicating religious discrimination in education" and this interest "substantially outweighs whatever burden denial of tax benefits places on petitioners' exercise of their religious beliefs." *Ibid.* at 604.

94. I have drawn on Rebecca G. Rees, "If We Recant, Would We Qualify?: Exclusion of Religious Providers from State Social Service Voucher Programs," *Washington & Lee Law Review* 56:4 (Fall 1999): 1291-1339. For a list of state constitutional provisions, see *Ibid.*, nn34-35, 1298.

95. 42 USC §604a(k).

Chapter 9

Conclusion:
Meeting the Challenge of
America's Social Pathologies:
The Long and Difficult Road Ahead

It seems clear that the road to increased involvement by FBOs in the provision of social services is not without obstacles. The Supreme Court has yet to rule on the constitutionality of federal funding for such programs. Also of great import is the constitutional determination of whether FBOs that receive government funding should be allowed to use discriminatory hiring practices. There are also many critics of Charitable Choice, FBOs, and President Bush's faith-based initiative whose fears of either a union between church and state or government control of religion must be assuaged.

What is clear, however, is that the current social service programs have failed miserably. Crime, drug abuse, illegitimacy, and poverty have become woven into the very fabric of American society. Something must be done and FBOs may well be the answer. Religious organizations can provide virtue-oriented guidance in a culture devoid of meaning. They can instill purpose in lives lacking hope. Most importantly, they may be able to change the tide of alienation and indifference that has been growing in this country.

Assuming there are no Constitutional impediments, three logistical questions must be accounted for before a broad faith-based policy can be successfully implemented. First, do FBOs want to assume a larger role? Second, how will FBOs adapt to the increased demands, particularly how will FBOs solve their new human resource needs? Finally, what effect can FBOs realistically have on human behavior?

Do FBOs Want to Meet the Challenge?

It is difficult to assess the capacity, readiness, and willingness of FBOs to become more active as social service providers. Given both the opportunity to provide expanded services and additional funds, will FBOs step forward and accept the challenge?

Some experts assume that it is unrealistic to expect local houses of worship to operate large numbers of social service programs that transform lives, such as drug abuse treatment, beyond the traditional programs catering to immediate needs, e.g., food, clothing, and shelter, simply because most do not currently run such programs and a "major redirection of mission seems unlikely for most congregations."[1] Similarly reflecting a pessimistic viewpoint, Scott Anderson of the California Council of Churches, which represents nineteen Protestant and Christian Orthodox denominations and claims 1.5 million members, stated, "Nobody asked us if we are interested or prepared to do this.... It feels like something coming from the outside and imposed on religious communities. Whether we have the capacity to run a formalized government service is a really problematic question."[2]

As discussed in chapter 4, FBOs typically are nonbureaucratic. They are flexible, innovative, and results-driven. In dealing with complex social problems, they personalize their services, adjusting care to meet each person's needs. FBOs provide emotional and psychological support, offering encouragement when one has a bad day, striving to motivate, and sometimes dealing with physical needs, such as child care or transportion to an employment opportunity. FBOs do not look at the people they serve as a statistic, but combine compassion with boundaries and structure that are intended to motivate changed behavior.

Believing that the only good FBOs are small ones, some fear that enhanced social service endeavors, however funded, may bring about bureaucratic bloat. Some smaller FBOs think that a shoestring operation is part of their key to success; if so, they may not want additional funding. Other FBOs rely so heavily on a few people that they see no way to grow bigger or deal with more personnel. Furthermore, if a local house of worship's social service ministry grows in budget and staff, some believe that the sense of ownership on the part of the congregation may decline. Also, as discussed in chapters 6 and 7, although many FBOs are strapped for financial resources, some question how they can gain access to public money, specifically through government contracts or grants, without sacrificing their principles. These FBOs, reluctant to become enmeshed in government rules and bureaucracy, are not rushing to the public sector money trough.

The importance of scale in these various dimensions cannot be dismissed as FBOs consider increasing their social service efforts. If an FBO expands both its scope and its size, it could become more unwieldy and bureaucratic.

Consider the example of the Abraham House and its rehabilitation program for ex-prisoners, run by Sister Simone Ponnet. Dozens of former prisoners have passed through Abraham House in the South Bronx, New York. Ex-convicts spend at least one year absorbing a blend of personal attention, clear rules, drug treatment, counseling, and voluntary worship. Abraham House helps ex-prisoners get on their feet, finish high school, find steady employment, and save money. Abraham House typically has eight adult residents and five youths involved in a day program.

Fearing her program would be less effective if it oversaw more ex-inmates, Sister Simone has repeatedly turned down public sector money. "If we had more than we have now, how could we know them?" she noted. "It's not a military thing. Each one is at a different stage."[3]

With success due to accessibility, caring responsiveness, and individualized attention, comes the responsibility to do more. FBOs are now presented with an unparalleled opportunity (and indeed, the obligation) to do more. Many congregations, especially those in the inner city, are committed to expand their social service programs but lack the infrastructure and the financial resources. This raises another problem. Even if more financial assistance is forthcoming, do FBOs have the competence to use the new funding to expand to meet the demand and become core providers of social assistance?

If an FBO wishes to participate and help solve societal ills, it must assess its capacity for expanded social service provision. Through a readiness assessment, an FBO can evaluate its assets and its strengths and determine the level and types of social services it can provide effectively, both now and in the foreseeable future. Obviously, not every FBO is ready or equipped to undertake the same type or level of activity.

If an FBO contemplates collaboration with the public sector to provide social services, it must weigh the costs and benefits of any compact. In some cases, Charitable Choice contracting will not be the best option. First, each FBO must ask itself what it can do effectively without compromising its religious identity, its mission, and its ministry. Some, because of their theological doctrines, cannot accept direct public funding via government grants. Others premise their efforts on sectarian worship and proselytization to such a degree that they cannot stay within the Charitable Choice guidelines that prohibit the federal funding of these activities. In short, before considering participation in direct government-funded social service programs, an FBO needs a clearly formulated and articulated mission statement, one that is faithfully pursued. A religious group must know its aims and assess whether a collaboration with the public sector will facilitate or impede its mission. It must avoid mission creep.

Second, an FBO must carefully assess whether it possesses the administrative capacity for managing even a modest government contract. Even if more financial resources become available, size limitations may hamper local congregations. One half of all American houses of worship, often operating out of storefronts and row houses, have fewer than 100 participating adult members and one quarter have less than 50.[4] Thus, many FBOs, particularly these small congregations that function as centers of spiritual activity, lack the staff, resources, and technical savvy to apply for government contracts, hack through the red tape, and deal with complex procurement rules. Given the small pool of volunteers and the lack of infrastructure to provide social services on more than an informal basis, these FBOs must carefully pinpoint what they want to do. This is especially true of urban African-American churches, the most willing and the most likely to take advantage of increased opportunities available through Charitable Choice.

Given the vast needs and concerns in communities throughout the United States, especially in the inner city, it is difficult for these small churches not to want to be all things to all people. Each FBO must, however, focus on its mission and develop a strategic plan for social service delivery to concentrate its financial and human resources.

The strategic planning process engages an FBO's leadership, staff, volunteers, and members. The planning process leverages an FBO's role in the community, provides structure, and ensures that what resources it has are brought to bear in effective social service delivery. An FBO may require more space or facilities to serve additional people or provide specialized services, such as for the hard-to-employ. FBOs need to consider whether or not they have (or can build) the organizational structure necessary to provide expanded services on a twenty-four hours, seven days a week basis. An FBO needs to set up short- and intermediate-term budgets and carefully focus on contractual payment points.

Inevitably, for some FBOs, especially smaller groups, reliance on government contracts will present cash flow problems.[5] The typical disbursement of government funds favors providers that are up and running, not organizations with large start-up costs.

The receipt of government funds will obligate an FBO to evaluate its ability to manage performance-based contracts that require the provision of specific services, with invoices submitted to the public sector as services are performed. Payments may be received months afterwards and may be available only when predetermined benchmarks are met. For instance, an FBO may receive partial payment when a welfare recipient is employed for thirty days and the remainder when he or she is employed for ninety days. Because an FBO may, therefore, lack the capital to handle a performance-based contract, particularly the funds needed to meet start-up costs, it needs to assess: (1) its cash reserves, and (2) to establish carefully constructed budgets, projecting future expenditures after receiving one or more benchmark payments. To deal with any cash flow problems, an FBO may need to obtain a bank line of credit. To ameliorate the cash crunch, an FBO may want to negotiate with government agencies to receive a greater portion of performance-based contract payments up front and provide for realistic payment points. It must also weigh the trade-offs of using volunteers or paid staff.

Charitable Choice insists that FBOs be held accountable in their use of public money. The public sector will not (and should not) assume that all FBOs are effective. FBOs, in turn, must consider how the rules regarding accountability affect their religious character and independence.

If it works with the government and accepts direct public funding, an FBO must learn to deal with the rather mundane work of tracking expenditures and documenting casework. A participating FBO must maintain good records of its disbursements and monitor the progress made by beneficiaries in achieving programmatic goals. An FBO, moreover, must understand the public sector's expectations about case management documentation and accountability. FBO staff must strictly enforce eligibility requirements, such as attendance and tardiness. A religious group must enhance its data collection, especially outcome data, and its reporting systems. In sum, FBOs need an administrative system that is at least as good as, if not better than, those used by secular organizations receiving public funds.

For many congregations, participating in Charitable Choice programs may be their first experience with a government contract for the provision of social services. FBOs inexperienced in answering requests for proposals and deficient in record keeping and reporting skills may choose to serve as subcontractors to an administratively sophisticated prime contractor, such as the Salvation Army or Goodwill Industries. These established organizations possess the requisite experience and competency in administering government contracts. They can serve as fiscal agents for smaller FBOs gaining government grants or prime contractors with smaller FBOs functioning as subcontractors.

These arrangements will allow religious social service providers to benefit from government funding channeled through an intermediary. The intermediary organization generally will require less cumbersome paperwork than a governmental agency. It will help FBOs understand the culture and policies of public sector agencies. Functioning as a subcontractor will aid an FBO in gaining the requisite "hands on" expertise. Because of the extra distance from the government afforded by subcontracting, this approach will increase the comfort level of FBOs in collaborating with the public sector. An intermediary understands and respects the religious mission of FBOs. FBOs will feel more secure about their religious character and identity. Finally, an intermediary can help several FBOs work together in a nonthreatening, noncompetitive manner.

In most inner cities, the scope of the need is too great for any one congregation. Many houses of worship will need to work together. These smaller FBOs may join together as a consortium to increase the scope of services they offer and the number of clients they can assist. By banding together, these FBOs stand a better chance of receiving and successfully implementing a government contract.

Inexperienced FBOs, whether they serve as subcontractors or organize bidding and administrative groups, ought to attend public sector sponsored technical assistance workshops. These workshops can teach a variety of skills from writing proposals to handling performance-based contracts. At some point, a religious group may also want to consider establishing a separate nonprofit entity to handle some (or all) of its social service endeavors, thereby limiting public sector oversight of an entire organization. At a minimum, a congregation must separate the records of its regular expenditures from its social service contract (or grant) expenses.

By approaching Charitable Choice contracts with as much knowledge and forethought as possible, FBOs will be much more effective. They will know what kind of contracts they are capable of performing as well as what type of relationship they want to have with the government. This will reduce the number of FBOs that are forced to drop out of these programs and make sure that those choosing to compete know what is expected of them. In the end, this means the best possible services for those in their communities.

How Will FBOs Solve Their
Human Resource Dilemmas?

If FBOs take on greater responsibilities, a second question assumes paramount importance. How will FBOs, who treat people on an individual basis, staff their expanded and often customized programs? Not only will FBOs increase in size, but they will also be called on to provide new types of services far beyond the traditional food pantries and other forms of emergency assistance. The problem is that these organizations rely on staff and volunteers who are able to interact with individuals on a one-on-one basis. They offer love and care enabling FBOs to turn lives around as no government worker could. Restoring lives requires far more than material assistance; in many instances, spiritual and moral support are also necessary. An FBO's personnel deal with an individual's whole needs, not just his or her material ones.

FBO staffers and volunteers are personally invested in the people they help. They try to live morally and they are not condescending to clients. Meeting people in their own communities, they challenge them to improve their lives, instilling a sense of personal responsibility and self-worth. They provide "tough love," hope, and spiritual guidance.

Transforming people and renewing human virtues, however, is labor-intensive and time-consuming. Personnel devote a great amount of time in forming bonds with those they counsel. It is these bonds which increase the sense of accountability and provide moral guidance to those in need. These are people who are there because they feel called to do so. Consequently, they are able to relate to their clients on a much more personal level.

A key element in forming these deep personal relationships is the proximity of an FBO's staff and volunteers to the communities they serve. Service providers ought to live around the corner from those they aid, know the culture and the people of the neighborhood, and speak their language. On call twenty-four hours a day, they generally do not go home at 5 P.M. These community-oriented staff members and volunteers have a vested interest in a neighborhood's welfare. As a leading exponent of neighborhood social entrepreneurs put it, "They have firsthand knowledge of the problems they live with, and they have a personal stake in the success of their solutions."[6]

This is especially true for the treatment of youths. Round-the-clock accessibility to teens establishes and enhances credibility. According to Rev. Eugene Rivers, III, who we met in chapter 4, "In every neighborhood in this country, it is the difference between being there and not being there that makes the critical difference."[7]

Staff and those they help share a common struggle and make demands on each other. Efforts led by reformed drug dealers or ex-criminals are especially effective in performing the task of spiritual renewal. They suffer with and walk alongside clients. Ex-addicts often make the best substance abuse counselors because they have the authority to challenge others and teach them how to get off and stay off drugs. Likewise, the most effective witnesses to gangs are former gang members.

The greater demands placed by FBO personnel, whether staff or volunteers, increase the dignity of those they help. The most downtrodden are told that they have something to offer and can be leaders, thereby improving their self-esteem. They think that they really may be made in God's image, with inherent dignity and worth. They come to see assistance as gift carrying reciprocal obligations and thus will work to implement what they have learned. They develop the outlook and the virtues of good citizens.

FBOs rely on volunteers or inadequately paid staff who devote their lives and bring their talents and their compassion to the task of human renewal. One study, undertaken between October 1, 1997, and April 1, 1998, of faith-based outreach to at-risk youth in Washington, D.C., found that volunteers formed the backbone of 101 programs for which staffing information was available. Fifty-six percent of these programs were run entirely by volunteers. Nine percent had one full-time staff person (two-thirds of whom were also full-time clergy) and 35 percent had two or more full-time staff.[8]

Furthermore, the total number of volunteers provided by a typical congregation is small. The 1998 National Congregations Study of 1,236 houses of worship showed that in 80 percent of the congregations engaged in social service activities, the number of volunteers mobilized was less than thirty, with the average mobilizing ten volunteers over the past year. The highest congregational involvement reported by this study was in traditional areas, such as food and housing, where houses of worship mobilized small numbers of volunteers to carry out well-defined tasks, particularly short-term, small-scale relief efforts, not ongoing large-scale programs.[9]

In coming years, is it realistic to expect that FBOs will find the vast numbers of new, devoted volunteers like the ones described, who offer personal commitment and skillful guidance? FBOs want to attract volunteers who believe that service to others has something to do with life's meaning and purpose. Volunteers, even if they lack professional social work training, bring to the task valuable skills and life experiences.

FBO volunteers (and staff) are willing to go to great lengths because they are motivated by high ideals. Faith-imbued individuals draw strength from their sense of mission, even if they do not press clients to find this same faith for themselves. Faith is the motivation for being involved and the impetus for caring. Those who are often the most effective see their efforts as a "calling"; they truly care about those they serve.

FBOs thus require volunteers who can provide care, advice, and support in long-term programs designed to help individuals achieve self-sufficiency and lead responsible lives, not just short-term emergency measures, such as overnight shelters and free groceries. To achieve these goals that involve a considerable expenditure of time, patience, and skillful guidance, FBOs require trained professionals who, in turn, can train others. The professional staff of FBOs offering extensive social service programs must be comfortable with achieving results through others.

As the need for volunteers mounts, FBOs will continue to seek individuals with the time and money to provide help on an ongoing basis, more than one or two days a year. However, the pool of volunteers is already engaged–teaching Sunday school, serving on committees, singing in the choir, and driving the youth group on field trips. Increasing the overall number of volunteers, moreover, will be difficult given job and family commitments. Americans are working harder and longer. With more two-income families, there are fewer homemakers, who are the traditional source of volunteers. It is unclear whether Americans will heed President Bush's call for volunteerism. In his 2002 State of the Union address, Bush called on all Americans to give, not necessarily all at once, two years or 4,000 hours of their lives to voluntary service.[10] By Executive Order,[11] he combined the existing public service volunteer programs, AmeriCorps, Senior Corps, and the Peace Corps, under a new umbrella organization, the USA Freedom Corps. In turn, the new entity created a clearinghouse for volunteer service opportunities. He sought to expand AmeriCorps, a domestic national service organization, by adding 25,000 members (from 50,000 to 75,000) and boost its budget by 50 percent. By retooling AmeriCorps to give greater authority to nonprofit groups in program design and delivery, public-minded volunteers could provide greater assistance to small faith- and community-based organizations. He also called for 100,000 new Senior Corps participants, increasing its number from 500,000 to 600,000, thereby offering older Americans more opportunities to participate in volunteer activities in their communities.[12] These proposals still await congressional action.

The shortage of volunteers and role models is particularly acute in the inner city. There has been an exodus by middle-class African-Americans from cities to suburbs. African-Americans best able to help others, especially those with strong families, have moved to the suburbs, leaving behind increasingly troubled communities. Who then is left to counsel, befriend, and encourage those who remain behind, mired in poverty and destructive behavior? Who will mentor the millions of kids who could use a responsible, caring adult's presence? Who will provide an example to the hard-to-employ who want their own chance at stability and success?

Despite these problems, after September 11, more Americans may be willing, given the right inducements, to volunteer and attempt to help solve social ills. Individuals may volunteer more if they contribute to FBOs. Tax incentives may also encourage a new pool of volunteers.

Tapping qualified seniors as volunteers to help alleviate staffing dilemmas is a promising solution. America's retirees are healthier, more prosperous, and better educated than ever before and want to be more active. Many of today's seniors do not want to retire to an old folks wasteland, sitting idly in their homes and watching television. For the more active elderly, so much free time can be depressing. Retired and semi-retired individuals, who are available during normal, workday hours and are able to provide regular, structured, face-to-face contact may, therefore, constitute a new volunteer group for FBOs.

If they expand their social service programs, FBOs will likely tap the experience, skills, talents, interest, and creativity of seniors as volunteers. These senior volunteers will mentor troubled and disadvantaged youths and serve as guides to latchkey children to prevent delinquency.

An increased reliance on seniors to meet the human resources needs of FBOs will bind the better off and the disadvantaged more closely. In bringing together the two disparate worlds of the haves and the have-nots and crossing racial lines, the two groups will come to discover each other's worth, dignity, and God-given potential. The face-to-face relationships of volunteers with the needy and the troubled will facilitate the spiritual growth in both groups.

In searching for volunteers, inner-city churches may increasingly look to black suburbanites who still remain active in their old congregations. They return every weekend for worship and fellowship. They may offer their services to improve the quality of life out of a sense of responsibility for the well-being of their former inner-city communities.

Mentoring is especially important for inner-city youths. They struggle with inadequate schools, single-parent households, the ready availability of illicit drugs, and the scarcity of sound role models. Linking older men to younger males provides role models who instill virtue by example. To succeed, mentoring must be performed consistently, week in, week out.

Local houses of worship must motivate congregants and others to go beyond merely giving money to the poor, to building friendships with them. In thinking more creatively about community outreach, the possibilities for linking an inner-city church, where the needs are vast, with one or more suburban congregations will likely be explored with greater frequency. Despite the geographical, racial, and socioeconomic gaps between the areas of need–blighted urban neighborhoods–and the areas of giving–volunteers from affluent suburbs–suburban houses of worship could provide volunteers and additional financial support for inner-city churches.

As FBOs strive to find new personnel for their expanded social service programs, they still must screen prospective volunteers to ensure that they are willing and able to stay with a program and build enduring, trusting relationships. FBOs generally ought to insist on a commitment from volunteers of at least one year, especially for those who mentor young people and economically disadvantaged families. Burnout remains, however, an ever-present danger.

FBOs must also adequately train their volunteers in listening and problem-solving skills, goal setting, and cross-cultural communication to enable them to better work with those from different backgrounds.[13] Well-trained volunteers, when supported by professional staff, perform better than FBOs that fail to direct their volunteers or simply tell their volunteers to befriend another. Volunteers need to be taught how to address individuals' and families' needs in an appropriate way, one that is legal, yet natural and noncoercive.

For volunteers to be successful in meeting the needs faced by struggling individuals, they generally require expert, professional coaching in a variety of fields, such as social work, education, psychology, ministry, and business. FBOs can use the professional expertise of outside consultants to build a cadre of well-trained, dedicated volunteers. Increasing the ability of local congregations and smaller FBOs to deliver social service programs, heavily reliant on volunteers, requires a strong infrastructure in place to train, support, and encourage volunteers, who otherwise may quit if they do not like how they are treated or if they find their tasks unrewarding. However, an FBO needs to balance the expertise of its professional staff and outside consultants with the enthusiasm of volunteers. Because of funding and personnel limitations, FBOs cannot solely rely on staff members or consultants. They will increasingly look to volunteers as the foot soldiers in the "armies of compassion."

The Ultimate Question: Can FBOs Help Solve America's Social Ills?

In the midst of societal changes over the past three or four decades, most of us value our autonomy. Americans want to determine for themselves how to construct a good and virtuous life and leave others to make their own choices, provided they do not violate others' rights or threaten society. In short, Americans shy away from judging the behavior or virtues of others.

With the loosening of behavioral boundaries, Americans have become far more ambivalent. Although many hunger for clear guidelines, we resist imposing uniform standards on others. In our discomfort with passing judgment on others, most of us strictly observe the Eleventh Commandment: Thou shall not judge.

Americans cherish tolerance and civility. Respect for diversity of views and lifestyles is deeply entrenched. In our reluctance to judge others, Americans have accepted dramatic changes, both good and bad, in society-wide norms regarding sex, reproduction, and family life. While the birth control pill and the legalization of abortion allowed women reproductive choices, which contributed to greater female employment, it also liberated men from the responsibilities of fatherhood and looking after the women they impregnated.

It is no doubt difficult to reconcile tolerance with moral instruction that clearly condemns certain kinds of behavior. Many, perhaps most, Americans are not willing to surrender their autonomy to absolute authority, obey received religious dictates, or submit to traditional sources of institutionalized faith. These Americans no longer find morality in Divine revelation or rigid moral codes. They do not want to cosset themselves by religiously mandated rules or norms that deny the fulfillment of their individual desires for a pleasurable life. For them, there is little deference to the moral authority of religious institutions.

Against this, Americans undoubtedly still perceive themselves as moral actors with responsibilities, obligations, and concerns. They want to move beyond the permissive, value-free approach that characterizes and motivates public bureaucracies and secular social service providers.

Those with this mindset realize that appeals couched in terms of autonomy, often a code word for amorality and immediate gratification, no longer suffice. They intuitively feel a reaction against the ethos of moral permissiveness. They want their children to have proper virtues and a moral order based on spiritual coherence and structure.

The older moral vision still exists (and in some parts of society is resurgent). However, we lack the convictions of nineteenth-century reformers. We do not know if the coming years will witness a moral, cultural, and spiritual revolution in the United States.[14] For many, faith is more effective than anything else, but not for everyone.

Of particular concern are elite norms. The behavior of the nonpoor, that is, the norms of a larger society, may result in a partial restoration of traditional moral virtues and better behavior among the underclass and suburban youth.

However, the competing instincts suggest not only that a delicate balance exists between permissiveness and traditional virtues but also the extent to which the public will accept religious involvement in the public square. This book, if it has done anything, has shown that FBOs do not upset this balance. In fact, FBOs restore the balance that existed prior to the 1960s without undoing the progressive gains of the recent past. The public, therefore, will tolerate FBOs not in spite of their moral component but because of it. As long as FBOs understand the boundaries imposed by the Constitution and federal legislation like Charitable Choice, there is no reason to believe that FBOs will not succeed.

Indeed, one must always return to the fact that FBOs do appear to be effective. FBOs succeed because they give individuals the faith and the hope to take the necessary steps to improve their condition. Their ethos is that each individual has the responsibility and, to a large degree, the power to chart one's own course. This is precisely what is needed to overcome the defeatism prevalent among the urban underclass, who often succumb to the view that they cannot prosper in America.

Every inner-city youth ought to be told that they are the ones who make the choices that will determine the course of their lives. Poverty is not inevitable. Education, responsible sexual behavior, particularly the avoidance of bearing children out-of-wedlock, getting (and staying) married, and a strong work ethic can lift even the most disadvantaged from the chains into which they were born. They need to be told that skilled labor is every bit as valuable as a white-collar job. Hope for the future coupled with realistic expectations and guidance can guarantee these youths escape the poverty of their parents.

Unlike their secular counterparts, FBOs are not neutral about client virtue and behavior. If someone is acting in a destructive manner, FBO personnel typically say so and require him or her to change. In a world of social disorganization and demoralization, FBOs offer structure and sound role models for those who do not know better, and for those who have not been taught better.

FBOs are transformative: they encourage people to change their lives. Even without proselytizing, FBOs can make people "better." Merely by modeling the behavior and beliefs of FBO personnel, individuals are more likely to look to God for direction in life; they are less likely to remain aimless or drift through life. Thus, of all the institutions in American society, FBOs offer perhaps the best potential for inculcating the virtues requisite for human renewal and transformation in twenty-first-century America.

However, even if adults invest time to redirect children and teens away from and out of trouble, the difficulties of effectuating a transformation of African-American culture cannot be overlooked. Black America actually has two cultures. One is self-destructive, male, violent, centered on drugs, death, misogyny, and illegitimacy. The other, religious and female, is pro-abstinence and proreligion. President George W. Bush seeks to combine a realistic view about black problems with compassion. His faith-based initiative aims to build an alliance with African-American churches.

It is not easy to strengthen the family and break the cycle of teen pregnancy and having children out-of-wedlock. There are a number of barriers to excellence and achievement. The influence of church, religion, and traditional virtues among many members of the underclass has declined. The male participation rate is relatively low in African-American churches. Women represent the overwhelming majority of church members, on the magnitude of perhaps 70 to 80 percent.

The decimation of African-American males in the American inner city cannot be ignored. The paucity of black men stems from a number of factors, including imprisonment, drug and alcohol addiction, and early mortality. The low male-to-female ratio allows those who remain to set commitment-averse terms for sexual intercourse and mating.[15]

Some blacks have difficulty accepting the virtues developed in chapter 1. Black identity is often defined in opposition to white, middle-class virtues—working hard, saving money, doing well in school, and maintaining two-parent families. Legitimate economic success may remain suspect in the African-American community. Many blacks regard success as "white."

As Prof. Henry Louis Gates, Jr., W.E.B. DuBois Professor of the Humanities at Harvard University states, "Far too many [young black kids] say that succeeding is 'white,' aspiring and dreaming are 'white,' believing that you can make it is 'white.'"[16] One sociologist concludes, "For many alienated young black people, attending school and doing well becomes negatively associated with acting white."[17]

In contemporary black urban culture, all too often the teenage girl who studies hard is mocked, while her counterpart who gets pregnant is envied. Girls may be forced to have sex to secure or maintain a relationship. Boys face teasing if they are not sexually active; males with several sexual partners attain an enhanced reputation.

By bringing moral pressure and encouraging virtuous behavior, FBOs provide leadership to encourage childbearing within marriage. By emphasizing this particular virtue, whether by advocating abstinence or the use of contraceptives, FBOs can help reorient neighborhood culture. They can also connect teens, one-by-one, to supportive peer groups.

As FBOs struggle to make virtue a part of everyday lives, what is the message of faith that these groups convey? Is it one of passivity, fatalism, and helplessness? Beyond acknowledging wrongful acts and taking full responsibility for them, black churches may fail to inculcate the need to change behavior. Elijah Anderson, an academic sociologist, maintains that fundamentalist religion may undermine efforts to reduce out-of-wedlock childbearing in inner cities. He writes:

Many women in the black underclass emerge from a fundamentalist religious orientation and hold a "pro-life" philosophy. Abortion is therefore not an option.... New life is sometimes characterized as a "heavenly gift," an infant is sacred to the young woman, and the extended family always seems to make do somehow with another baby. A birth is usually met with great praise, regardless of its circumstances, and the child is genuinely valued. Such ready social approval works against many efforts to avoid illegitimate births.[18]

Anderson continues:

However, for many such girls who have few other perceivable options, motherhood, accidental or otherwise, becomes a rite of passage to adulthood. Although an overwhelming number may not be actively trying to have babies, many are not actively trying to prevent having them. One of the reasons for this may be the strong fundamentalist religious orientation of many poor blacks, which emphasizes the role of the fate in life. If something happens, it happens; if something was meant to be, then let it be, and "God will find a way." With the dream of a mate, a girl may be indifferent to the possibility of pregnancy, even if it is not likely that pregnancy will lead to marriage. So the pregnant girl can look forward to a certain affirmation, particularly after the baby arrives–if not from the father, then from her peer group, from her family, from the Lord.[19]

There is no way to be certain, empirically, that religious social service providers are more effective at dealing with chronic societal problems than public or secular programs. Religion is not a panacea, but it can be an effective tool of public policy, particularly when coupled with public or secular social service programs. As such, it is foolish not to try to use FBOs to meet America's social ills. The quest to instill a stronger sense of personal responsibility and empower more Americans to take control of their lives is worthy of different approaches.

We need to experiment. We ought to see what works best at instilling a stronger sense of the virtues advocated in this book–the public sector, the nonprofit (sacred and secular) sector, or a problem-solving partnership of the two. The public sector may, more and more, fund and contract out to FBOs for the implementation of social service programs, while monitoring and holding these FBOs accountable. These public-private partnerships ought to be concerned about transforming lives, not merely cost effectiveness or saving money.

Let consumers choose their own social service providers because a competitive, parallel structure will challenge traditional public sector approaches and force a rethinking of their missions, strategies, and values. Perhaps, secular social service efforts will also come to encourage responsibility, self-respect, industriousness, achievement, discipline, and thrift.

For in the end, does it matter if it is a secular- or faith-based social service provider that changes an individual for the better? Isn't the real question which provider can best promote the notion that each of us is responsible for his or her success or failure. In this culture of responsibility, each of us must make the most of the opportunities offered by society, regardless of one's race or class, by developing one's talents and promoting one's personal growth.

If properly mobilized, FBOs can provide valuable strength in the "armies of compassion" envisioned by President Bush. FBOs offer us the opportunity to fight a very different (and possibly quite effective) war against America's social ills.

Notes

1. Mark Chaves, "Congregations' Social Service Activities," The Urban Institute, Center on Nonprofits and Philanthropy, No. 6 (December 1999), 4.

2. Teresa Watanabe, "Churches Divided on Role in U.S. Social Service Programs: Religious Leaders Disagree on Whether to Use Their Organizations' Assets to Run Government-Sponsored Projects, a Plan Endorsed by Bush," *Los Angeles Times*, January 29, 2001, B1.

3. Peter Slevin, "For N.Y. Felons, Nun's Home Is a Saving Grace," *Washington Post*, July 4, 2000, A1.

4. *Faith Communities Today: A Report on Religion in the United States Today*, ed. David S. Barrett and Hartford Seminary (Hartford, Conn.: The Hartford Institute for Religion Research March, 2001), 8.

5. Alexandra Starr, "A Leap of Faith That May Fail," *Business Week*, March 26, 2001, 104, 106.

6. Robert L. Woodson, Sr., *The Triumphs of Joseph: How Today's Community Healers Are Reviving Our Streets and Neighborhoods* (New York: Free Press, 1998), 92.

7. Manhattan Institute Conference, *A Look at Faith-Based Community Programs*, November 13, 1998, 126 (unpublished transcript).

8. Jeremy White and Mary de Marcellus, *Faith-Based Outreach to At-Risk Youth in Washington, D.C.*, Report 98-1, The Jeremiah Project, An Initiative of the Center for Civic Innovation, Manhattan Institute, Table 3.

9. Chaves, "Congregations' Social Service Activities," 3-4.

10. Address Before a Joint Session of the Congress on the State of the Union, January 29, 2002, *Weekly Compilation of Presidential Documents* 38:5 (February 4, 2002): 133-139, at 138; President Bush's State of the Union Address to Congress, *New York Times*, January 30, 2002, A22; Jacqueline L. Salmon, "Nonprofit Groups Cool on Call for Volunteers," *Washington Post*, February 8, 2002, A4.

11. Executive Order 13254–Establishing the USA Freedom Corps, January 29, 2002, *Federal Register* 67:22 (February 1, 2002): 4869-4871.

12. The White House, USA Freedom Corps, January 30, 2002; Dana Milbank, "Bush Seeks to Expand Ranks of Senior Corps Volunteers," *Washington Post*, April 10, 2002, A6.

13. Patrice Hudson Jonker and Douglas L. Koopman, "Volunteer Mentors in Social Welfare: Who They Are and What Happens When They Mentor," *Social Work & Christianity* 27:2 (Fall 2000): 168-187, at 181.

14. Robert William Fogel analyzes the current religious-political cycle in *The Fourth Great Awakening and The Future of Egalitarianism* (Chicago: University of Chicago Press, 2000).

15. James Q. Wilson, *The Marriage Problem: How Our Culture Has Weakened Families* (New York: HarperCollins, 2002), 49-53.

16. Henry Louis Gates, Jr., "Two Nations... Both Black," *Forbes* 150:6, September 14, 1992, 132-138, at 138.

17. Elijah Anderson, *Code of the Street: Decency, Violence, and the Moral Life of the Inner City* (New York: W.W. Norton, 1999), 93.

18. Elijah Anderson, *Streetwise: Race, Class, and Change in an Urban Community* (Chicago: University of Chicago Press, 1990),136.

19. Anderson, *Code of the Street*, 147-148.

Index

Abraham House, 269

African-American: births, out-of-wedlock, 11; Charitable Choice, and, 151-52, 270; churches, role of, 19, 77-81, 84, 177-78; culture of, 279-81; crime, deterrence, religion and, 109-12; neighborhoods, type of, 1, 4, 109-12, 119, 123-24, 275; premarital sex, deterrence, religion and, 101, 106; substance use, deterrence, religion and, 100, 110; underclass and, 2-3, 9, 18-19; Welfare Reform Act of 1996, and, 62, 63-64

Agency for International Development, Center for Faith-Based and Community Initiatives, 172

Agostini v. Felton, 231-32, 235-39

Aguilar v. Felton, 230-31

Aid to Dependent Children, 53

Aid to Families with Dependent Children, 53-54

American Civil Liberties Union, 134, 240

American Jewish Congress, 134

Americans for Community and Faith-Centered Enterprise, 212

Americans United for Separation of Church and State, 134, 235

Anderson, Elijah, 280-81

Anderson, Scott, 268

Armey, Dick, 180

Ashcroft, John: Byrd Rule and, 136; Charitable Choice and, 132-36, 140, 179; Charitable Choice Expansion Act of 1998, proposed, 140; Communities Involved in Caring Act, proposed, 133;

Individual Accountability Act of 1995, proposed, 133; religion and, 132; welfare reform and, 132-33

audits: Charitable Choice requirements, 138, 141, 148; federal rules, 235-36; scope, limited, 138, 238; Watts-Hall bill, 182

Azusa Christian Community, 82-83, 86-87

Banane, Ali, 152

Baptist Join Committee, 134

Bicknese, Aaron, 122

Black, Charles E., 178

Black, Hugo, 227

Bowen v. Kendrick, 232-34, 237, 259

Bowery Mission, 76-77, 90, 196

Boy Scouts of America v. Dale, 248

Brace, Charles Loring, 49-50

Brennan, Jr., William J., 231, 243

Breyer, Stephen, 226, 253

Bridgeland, John, 176

Brown, Jeffrey, 85

Brown, Selvin, 83-85, 87

Bush, George W.: administrative actions, 21, 161, 165-72, 188-89; armies of compassion, 162, 185, 281; Charitable Choice, legislative proposals, 21, 161-62, 172-73, 183-86; compassionate conservatism, 6, 21, 162-65, 185; corporate charitable contributions, 161, 205-6, 211-12; executive orders, 37, 165-69, 188-89; faith, and, 18, 27-29, 44; faith-based initiative, 5-6, 21-23, 165-73, 188-92, 199-200,

About the Author

Lewis D. Solomon is the Theodore Rinehart Professor of Business Law at The George Washington University Law School, where he has taught corporate and tax law for more than twenty-five years. He is a prolific writer of books and articles on a wide variety of topics, including law, business, public policy, and religion. An ordained rabbi, he is the past president of the International Federation of Rabbis. He is married to Dr. Janet Stern Solomon and the father of Michael Solomon.

Social Sciences